CONTACT, STRUCTURE, AND CHANGE

CONTACT, STRUCTURE, AND CHANGE

A Festschrift in Honor of Sarah G. Thomason

Edited by Anna M. Babel and Mark A. Sicoli

Published in the United States of America by
Michigan Publishing
Manufactured in the United States of America

DOI: http://doi.org/10.3998/mpub.11616118

ISBN 978-1-60785-607-8 (paper)
ISBN 978-1-60785-608-5 (e-book)
ISBN 978-1-60785-609-2 (open-access)

An imprint of Michigan Publishing, Maize Books serves the publishing needs of the University of Michigan community by making high-quality scholarship widely available in print and online. It represents a new model for authors seeking to share their work within and beyond the academy, offering streamlined selection, production, and distribution processes. Maize Books is intended as a complement to more formal modes of publication in a wide range of disciplinary areas.

http://www.maizebooks.org

CONTENTS

PREFACE

We are honored and delighted to contribute this preface to a Festschrift in honor of Sarah (Sally) Thomason, whom we have been fortunate to have as a colleague and friend for more than twenty years. The editors, Anna and Mark, extended the invitation because we have served as chairs of our department during many of the years in which Sally has been on our faculty. It isn't hyperbole to say that she has made our professional lives infinitely richer and our personal lives considerably more fun and interesting.

The papers in this volume are an important contribution to several fields of linguistics, including language contact, language change, and indigenous language studies, all areas in which Sally has left an indelible mark. The volume is packed with a who's who of Sally's intellectual life, filled with colleagues, former students, and even a family member. All the authors are themselves well-known experts in language contact, historical linguistics, and/or indigenous language studies, and much of their expertise was honed in conversation with Sally.

Within the area of language contact, Sally is recognized as the world's authority. She is first author of the now-classic book *Language Contact, Creolization, and Genetic Linguistics* (with Terrence Kaufman, 1988, 1991), in which she argued that language history must be studied with reference to social context. Her approach was in clear contrast to the view of historical linguists over the previous 150 years or so that nearly all language change is triggered by factors internal to the language itself. Through careful documentation of complex contact situations from around the world, the book ushered in a new era in the study of language relationships. The first section of this volume rightly focuses on questions and explorations of language contact that were made possible by Sally's ongoing thoughts about theorizing, documenting, and analyzing what happens when speakers bring multiple linguistic systems to bear on their interactions with one another.

Sally's fieldwork involving language contact situations has, over the course of more than thirty years, led to a quite distinct and highly respected expertise in the Native languages of the Northwestern United States. She is best known for her work on Salish-Pend d'Oreille (Montana Salish), a seriously endangered language spoken in northwest Montana. Originally drawn to the language through an interest in the ways in which languages in the region borrow from each other, she spends a portion of each summer working with the elders of the Confederated Salish and Kootenai Tribes. She has published an online edition of her Salish-English dictionary, the result of her many years of language documentation work. Through this and related work, Sally has become an important figure in the area of language endangerment. Her book *Endangered Languages: An Introduction* (2015) has already become a standard textbook and reference work on the topic of endangered languages and their preservation. The second half of this volume brings together work on indigenous American languages being conducted by scholars, some of them former students of Sally, who have joined her in the mission to describe endangered languages while broadening the empirical basis for the development of linguistic theory.

Readers who know Sally will appreciate our mild concern as we turn to some of the many other reasons for a Festschrift in Sally's honor because they know, as we do, that she resists being remarked on for all the ways in which she is amazing. We could have made easy (long, but easy) work of this preface by listing Sally's many accomplishments, honors, and awards, but such a list could hardly capture how profoundly Sally has influenced the field of linguistics and could only hint at how profoundly she influences those who know her as a friend, colleague, mentor, animal and nature lover, game player, and in the case of three academics, including two linguists, a family member. If there were a T-shirt created in Sally's honor, it would undoubtedly say "Sally has done it all." She is a Distinguished University Professor at the University of Michigan, former editor of the journal *Language* (and the only woman to have edited that journal in its over ninety years of publication), a fellow of the American Association for the Advancement of Science, the recipient of lifetime achievement awards from several scholarly societies, and coauthor of a book so influential that it has been cited over 10,000 times.

Sally's scholarly career is also distinguished by a commitment to stepping outside the academy and sharing her expertise with a nonlinguistic audience. The ongoing dictionary and text collection projects for Salish-Pend d'Oreille go beyond documenting this language for the purposes of theories about language; they are also being used by the Salish community for language teaching and preservation. She served as a volunteer teacher in the University of Pittsburgh's program at the State Correctional Institution and is a regular contributor to the Language Log, the preeminent voice of linguistics oriented to a nonlinguistic audience. She is regularly consulted by the news media on topics as varied as the mascot controversy at the University of Illinois to language change over the course of multigenerational space travel (obviously an exercise in imagination). She visits K-12 classrooms to excite young students about the structure, variety, and beauty of human language.

We both have numerous stories of the ways Sally provided administrative wisdom, from her perspective as a scholar, advisor, and instructor. It's the kind of wisdom you'd expect from someone who has guided our discipline, including as former president of the

Linguistic Society of America, for many years. But perhaps less obviously, it's also the kind of wisdom that, as department chairs, we regularly turned to as we figured out how to convey to higher levels of administration the role of linguistics within academia as well as within our wider society.

In addition to her stature as a top-notch academic, she is a top-notch human being. Unassuming and generous, able to be both brilliant and self-effacing at the same time, she presents her scholarly work as though she accidentally stumbled on what became field-defining discoveries and insights. This is a quality you can read about in her delightful description of how she got interested in linguistics and in the different areas of her expertise, which is available at http://linguistlist.org/studentportal/linguists/SarahThomason.cfm.

What many people have noticed if they have spent time with Sally in a meeting or talk is that she always doodles, drawing intricate images of fantastical creatures. When they first encounter Sally doodling, many people think it means she isn't paying attention to what's going on. But as we all have quickly discovered, Sally's keen concentration is facilitated by her doodles; her incisiveness, creativity, and good judgment are each embedded in every line she draws. Importantly, Sally's doodles stand as a testament to Sally herself, to all she offers in every corner of the scholarly world. They capture why it isn't an overstatement to say that Sally has done it all. We congratulate her warmly for what this Festschrift says about both her scholarly achievements and influence and her generous and creative spirit that has left such a profound mark on so many.

Robin Queen and Pam Beddor

This is the doodle Sally drew as the mascot for the 2013 Linguistic Society of America's Summer Institute in Linguistics, which we hosted at the University of Michigan. It has since become the logo for our department, an enduring means of capturing Sally's influence as well as our great appreciation of her as a colleague, teacher, and mentor.

CHAPTER 1

Deliberate Decisions and Unintended Consequences

Ratifying Nonspeakers through Code Alternation in Child-Directed Speech

Mark A. Sicoli

Among many insights on the mechanisms of contact-induced language change, Sally Thomason's work has pointed us to the importance of deliberate decision (Thomason 2001). Acknowledging the effects of deliberate decisions on multiple subsystems from phonological and grammatical constructions to code-switching patterns between languages opens the possibility of observing language change in process in documentary corpora attuned to what Erving Goffman (1981) referred to as "the interaction order" as a moral order of responses and replies. Everyday life interactions illustrate real-time decisions about language use, the actions they lead to, as well as the reactions and responses to them that accrue over time to scale up into social and linguistic change (Sicoli 2020). This paper provides a glimpse into the language and culture of the Zapotec community of Lachixío during the establishment of a pattern of code alternation where, after decades of the community resisting such culture change (Sicoli 2011), young parents began code shifting out of Zapotec to address children directly in Spanish.

Using multimodally transcribed video data recorded in Santa María Lachixío in 2008, I first establish a contrast between two *family conversation styles* of language socialization. One family speaks Zapotec, and we even see correct Zapotec language use *topicalized* into a socialization event led by an elder woman. Topicalizing language makes language use a focus of an interaction, which can be associated with the development of what Goffman (1967: 12) called an "incident" to be repaired or remediated. We see in these examples how a community may be divided on a deliberate decision affecting language use. In 2008, this style of code shifting was well in the minority. The family who made the video was in fact one of the innovators. Their choice was not without contestation from other families.

I also present transcribed data of a third encounter documented in the video corpus where representatives of the two families came together. The same elder woman who led the Zapotec language socialization sequence reacts to seeing the man speak to his daughter only in Spanish and responds by asking him if his daughter does not understand Zapotec. In his subsequent accounting for his code-switching, the young man provides us with the reasoning behind his deliberate decision. He thinks she will learn Spanish early by speaking it to her, and he believes the girl will still learn Zapotec from just being around it. This code alternation structured by participation roles is depicted as well in several video transcripts. Through attention to the grammatical form and sequence organization of the multiturn interaction between the elder woman and the young man, we then see that the elder woman, while making clear that she hears correctly what the man is saying, never publicly acknowledges his position, which would be the culturally appropriate way of showing agreement. When it was time to acknowledge his position, she rather changes the subject, which reads as contestation in a culture where overt disagreement is rare (Sicoli 2020).

1. Family Conversation Styles, Speaker Ratification, and Language Shift[1]

Contemporary methods of language documentation that produce video corpora of everyday life interactions provide for rich exemplification of a language akin to a text collection. But because the recordings are of actual social encounters that mattered in the ethical life of the participants, such corpora also provide data to document and build theory on how languages change through uses that include the moral stances people take in the practice of interpreting each other's behavior. It is common to hear in the language endangerment literature that a community *decided* to speak one language or another, or to give up one language so, purportedly, their children could have better opportunities. Such claims, however, are rarely based on the kind of data that follow such decisions across a community's diversity but rather imagined as already achieved by a community as if united. In the background of my thinking in this paper is an example used by Sally in language contact class and referenced in *Language Contact: An Introduction* (Thomason 2001). Thomason cites Kilpatrick's work in the Isthmus of Tehuantepec. Kilpatrick contrasted Zapotec language maintenance in the city of Juchitán with language shift in nearby rural highlands. This story resonated with a comparison I was working on in graduate school between the larger town of Lachixío, which had at that point resisted the waves of language shift across Oaxaca in the latter twentieth century, and the small frontier town of Asunción Mixtepec where Zapotec was already moribund during my PhD work (subsequently published as Sicoli 2011). Both cases inverted a common understanding of language shift where more remote towns were shifting to Spanish but more cosmopolitan centers were maintaining Zapotec. In an e-mail to Thomason, Kilpatrick reported being told that local women had decided to speak only Spanish so that children could get jobs at a cement factory as explanation for why no one under forty spoke the language any more (see also Falconi [2011] for insight on this, as far as I can tell, unpublished example). This left me with many questions, including what decision making looks like in situations of language use? How did the decision become shared over time? How did the women have agency as a group? How and whether it was contested in its process of becoming? Retrospective narrative data may tend to gloss over the diversity of stances people took on a language practice during its historical development. While I have heard of cases where a town has voted at a general assembly to stop speaking an Indigenous language and have published on the case of Lachixío Parents-of-Students Association voting to keep speaking Zapotec as a home language (Sicoli 2011), it is more often the case that a mosaic of family choices accumulate to shift language socialization practices over time (see Kulick 1992), and that contact between families may be what Paul Kroskrity called *sites of ideological struggle* (2009: 71, and cited in Rinehart 2011). The community may never have made a collective decision but one may appear so, emergent over time from the accumulated effect of many shifts in socialization styles in the experience near, and morally accountable, order of everyday conversation. The story I present here is one of the moral contestation of an emerging pattern of language use.

This paper takes a close look at family conversation styles that have consequence for understanding language shifts in a Zapotec region of Oaxaca, Mexico. I take the position that language shift, as well as the resistance to shift, is achieved through talk in interaction and that expanding the linguistic study of conversational interaction to studying language endangerment, and the practice of language documentation to include interactional linguistics, can yield insights into processes that develop the collective achievement of cultural and linguistic change. This research then brings together language documentation and language contact in examination of language change in progress. These data were recorded through my fieldwork when I was a member of the Language and Cognition Department of the Max Planck Institute for Psycholinguistics. The corpus was built through participatory methods where people of Lachixío recorded daily life activities ranging from events like cooking and eating together to gardening and construction projects. All videos in this paper were recorded by my collaborator Pedro Martinez García without my presence (I was living in Lachixío but did not meet these families until after the recordings were made). The video materials were transcribed and translated through work with Zapotec speakers supported by a fellowship from the Documenting Endangered Languages Program (a partnership between the NEH Division of Preservation and Access and NSF Dynamic Language Infrastructure). My work with this corpus also developed into my book *Saying and Doing in Zapotec* (2020), which depicts Lachixío Zapotec language through conversational interaction and works to better understand language change as dialogically emergent process.

2. Lachixío and Lachixío Zapotec in Oaxaca

Lachixío Zapotec is a West Zapotec language spoken in a region characterized by several mutually unintelligible Zapotec, Mixtec, and Chatino languages. All are Eastern Otomanguean languages. Speakers of Lachixío can be found across Mexico, United States, and Canada with most of the population distributed in pueblos of the first mountain ridges southwest of the Oaxaca Valley of Zimatlán. Since 1997, I have conducted fieldwork primarily in a town called *Xe'yyò* in Zapotec (Santa Maria Lachixío in Spanish) and *Zhílìì* (San Vicente Lachixío) and have also surveyed languages to various degrees with people of the neighboring towns and villages in this mountainous region (San Miguel, San Mateo, and Santa Cruz Mixtepec; San Pedro Totomachapam; San Pedro, San Antonino, and San Andres el Alto; and the land tenancy (*ejido*) villages of the Lachixíos (San Pablo el Rincón and Palo Verde). While close to Oaxaca City by line of sight (this mountain ridge can be seen from Monte Albán), the sierra provides for a remoteness from the central valleys of the Oaxaca capital.

Oaxaca is one of the southernmost states of Mexico and has one of the highest percentage Indigenous populations with some sixty

Indigenous languages spoken in an area about the size of the U.S. state of Virginia. The area of this fieldwork is in the southwest of the state near the border of the Zimatlán and Sola de Vega districts. The southernmost West Zapotec variety known as Solteco spoken around Sola de Vega went out of use without documentation beyond some vocabulary collected around 1900 by Antonio Peñafiel (Smith-Stark 1999; Sullivant 2016). The furthest to the northwest is Totomachapan, known to have just a couple of elders remaining who can remember the language, but no one speaks it in daily life. I worked with one of the last fluent speakers from San Andres el Alto in 1998, only older people in San Pedro can speak the language today, and no one younger than about fifty years currently speaks the language in San Antonino. The last speaker I knew of from Santa Cruz died about 2005. So at the time of this fieldwork, Santa María, San Vicente, San Miguel, and San Mateo were the towns where children were being socialized to and through Zapotec.

3. Speaking Correct Zapotec: Speaking Beautifully

The first video extract that I will discuss is a speech event where we see a family socializing a boy into the expected use of the Zapotec Respect Register (described in my dissertation as *speaking beautifully, as if to God* [Sicoli 2007:147]). The boy sitting on the log is Little Leo. His paternal grandmother Sabina is with him in the middle, his father Flavio on the left sharpening his chainsaw, his mother Kacha is in the back, and a couple of his siblings are present. In the recent past before this video was made, Little Leo made a gaffe in which he didn't speak to an elder in the Zapotec respect register and used an improper term of address. Several members of his family tease him about this, and the grandmother goes on to model the correct behavioral norm, animating the beautiful way to speak to elders in Lachixío Zapotec.

Figure 1.1 Family Socializing Child to Correct Zapotec

Falsetto voice is one of several voice registers that I have described for Lachixío Zapotec and which are used to frame conversational moves as positioned to fit particular participation frameworks, and for taking several stances on what is being said. High pitch and falsetto depict respect, low pitch and breathy voice depict authority and assertiveness, whisper frames important speech and sets up exclusionary participation frames (sort of like a first-person exclusive pronoun but using a public whisper combined with gaze to exclude an overhearer from being ratified as an addressee [Sicoli 2010]), and creaky voice is used to seek commiseration or empathy with another speaker. I am not focusing on voice qualities in this paper (see rather Sicoli 2010, 2015), but several voice registers are represented in the data. Since the high-pitched voice is the implicit topic of this socialization event, I'll mention a few points about how its use ties sound iconicity to social iconicity. In conversations and psycholinguistic field tasks conducted for a comparative project on categories of perception (Majid et al. 2018; Shayan, Özturk, and Sicoli 2011), a high pitch was described as being *nelettze* 'thin' or *me'e'* 'small', which is contrasted with low pitch described as *nerokko* 'thick' and *zxenne* 'big'. The same vocabulary is used to describe small people, like babies *endoh me'e'*, with low social status, in contrast to *benné zxenne* 'big people', high-social-status individuals, usually elders who have a record of community service. The use of high-pitched voice depicts a speaker as smaller than the addressee. Socialization to this Zapotec way of speaking is also socialization to Zapotec social relations. Respectful falsetto is used with particular addressees like God and deceased ancestors, godparents and compadres, religious and municipal authorities, daughter-in-law to mother-in-law, and generally to any elders. There are also expectations for terms of address that co-occur with respectful voice and multimodal actions, like averting eye gaze and making one's body smaller by bowing as well. Consider the transcript in example 1 where the register is being depicted and socialized to Little Leo.

(1)[2]

1 Sabina: Xaa nii lò loo xoo Líkkò? (0.37)
xa ni=lò lo x(ey)o Líkò
what say=2s face uncle Fred
What do you say to uncle Fred?

2 Sabina: ^<Maa lò né xe:yyo>^ ellò: ^{v}>te Líkkò zxa' nna<^{v}
Ma=lò=né xeyo elò te Líkò zxa'na
greeting=2s=ACT3o uncle where DIM Fred tiny
^Greetings Uncle.^ Where (you say) ^{v}>Hey Tiny Fred<^{v}

3 [Laughter (0.92)

4 Kacha: [Eskye kalla nii txee.
eske kala ni txe
like.this truly say then
That's what he said.

In this example, see some common features of Zapotec language socialization for this register. The use of the register is depicted rather than explained. In turns 1 and 2, the grandmother enacts a dialogue that includes both the question 'What do you say to uncle Fred?' and then answering it as if the child. In line 2, she voices the normative expectation of a shift to the falsetto voice and expanded delivery of the respect register. She contrasts this with a lowered pitch and a compressed delivery with which she constructs Little Leo's dialogue when he improperly greeted his uncle. One of the co-occurrence features for falsetto voice is respectful terms of address like 'uncle' or 'aunt' used for any elder. Little Leo instead used a derogatory nickname *Líkkò Zxa'nna* like 'Tiny Fred.' In Lachixío, there is a common person-reference practice of using of derogatory nicknames for individuals who are absent (third-person reference), but these same terms are not used as terms of address (in second person, or when the person is an overhearer). This evokes laughter from the group (at little Leo's expense and intended benefit). In line 4, his mother confirms that he really said this.

(2)

```
6 Sabina: ^^Maa lò [né xe:yyo]^^ nii á loo xoo Líkkò zxa'nna nii.
          Ma=lò=né            xeyo  ni=á  lo   x(ey)o Líkò zxa'na ni
          greetings=2s=ACT3o uncle say=1s face uncle Fred tiny say
          ^^Greetings Uncle^^ I will say to Uncle Fred, say.

7 Flavio:            [Xhii eskye Leyitto]?
                     xhi  eske       leyito]
                     how  like.this  Leoncito
                     Is that how it was little Leo?

8         (2.84)

9 Sabina  vv°Xoo Líkkò zxa'nnavv jlee nze'e nii ì°
          x(ey)o  Líkò  zxa'na jle       nze'e ni=ì
          uncle   Fred  little calls     there say=3s
          Tiny Fred he calls him there, he said.
```

In line 6 then, the grandmother models the falsetto voice for a second time. From her choice of using first-person pronoun we can see that she is animating how a younger person should speak, voicing a future Little Leo who would embody the moral ideal of speaking to an elder in correctly framed Zapotec. The father then asks the boy if that's how it went. To which there is still no response and the grandmother confirms in line 9 the gaffe Little Leo made. The topicalization is of correct Zapotec speech, even if mostly achieved indirectly and through depiction. In a bit of a lucky break from a documentary perspective, the net we cast by video recording daily life interactions caught an example of socialization to the respect register and the metalinguistics around its use. I had only previously been able to report on the register through reflections on participant observations where I heard it used and learned to use it myself, and some audio-recorded examples depicting its use (Sicoli 2007, 2010). Register shifting plays a role in contrasting 'speech to' and 'speech about' the child, but in both child- and adult-directed speech in this family, the language code is consistently Zapotec. At issue in the interaction are Zapotec ways of speaking. Voicing the behavioral ideal for/as the child is seen to be an important socialization device, as is teasing and shaming.

4. Addressing and Directing Children in Spanish

Now let's contrast a socialization style from the home of another Lachixío family with children of the same age. The family is sitting in the shade sharing the daily chore of shelling corn (removing dried kernels from the cob) for making tortillas (figure 1.2). A boy (Brendon) and girl (Iveth) about three years old are in the middle of frame, the girl's mother, Mary, is in the white shirt, and her mother, Sofia, is to her left, the boy's grandparents are on the right, and the boy and girl are cousins. The grandfather (Raul) grabs a vine and tells the boy to

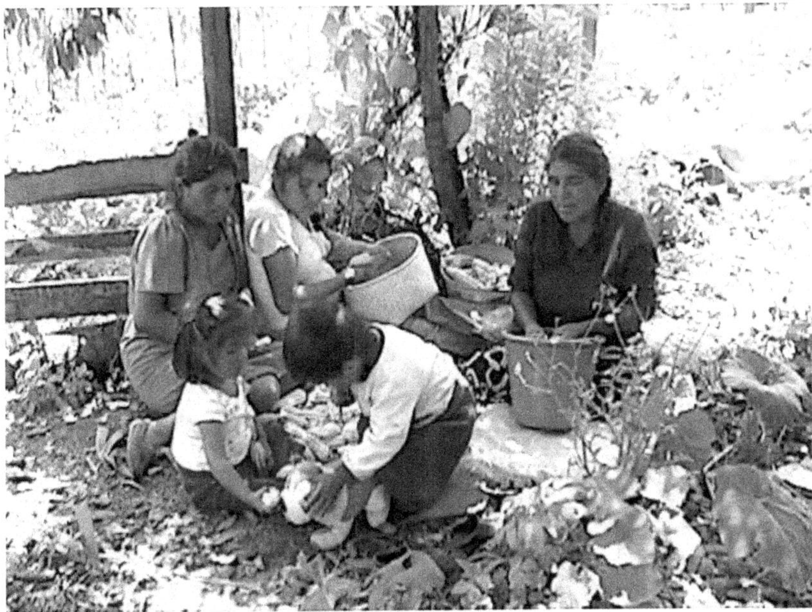

Figure 1.2 Code Shifting Socialization Style

give it to a pig in a pen out of frame to the left. The grandfather shifts to Spanish when he addresses the boy. There is a short sequence between the grandparents who address each other in Zapotec: the grandmother (Alfonsa) asks if it is safe to send the boy on this errand since the pig bites. Convinced enough by Raul that it is OK, she then code shifts to Spanish to also tell the boy to put the vine in the pig pen. After her Spanish-language utterance, the grandmother then tries to use some Zapotec with the child, but gives up when he does not respond to it, and then comments to the others in Zapotec that the boy doesn't understand her when she talks 'like this' (meaning speaks Zapotec). The boy ultimately responds to a Spanish-language utterance in Spanish and proceeds on the errand. The sequence of example (3) begins with a question-response adjacency pair between Alfonsa and Sofia related to some ongoing gossip (in Zapotec) and then Raul does an *outloud* in Zapotec commenting that nobody is giving the herbs growing on the patio to the pig to eat. He then turns his gaze to the boy Brendon and addresses him directly in Spanish to issue a directive to give a vine he pulled to the pig (Spanish speech represented in Italics).

(3)

1 Alfonsa: **Lèkka endò’ niyyo ì la?**
lèka endò’ niyo=ì=la
also child male=3O=Q
Is he also his son?

2 Sofia: **Áwwà.**
Yes

3 Raul: **Ka’a tzyáà no’o’ waññi noo xhìkki lò waññi àkko kúcchì lò**
ka’a tzyáà no’o’ wani no xhìki=lò wani àko
here just there.is herb and afraid=2S herb eat
kúchì=lò
pig=2S
Here there are herbs and you’re afraid to give them to the pig to eat.

4 Raul: ***Agarra ésta y dale para kúcchì pâ***
--|R turns gaze to Brendon hold plant out toward him
Brendon engaging with Iveth (not attending to Raul)
Grab this and give it to the pig my son.

5 Raul: ***Ten.***
-Raul shakes plant
-Brendon turns gaze to Raul
Here.

6 Alfonsa: **Kaa ràkko kye’e’ yaà endò’? Nee [ràkko kye’e’ í.**
-----------------------------|A head turn to Raul
ka r-àko ke’e’ yà endò’ ne r-àko
NEG HAB-eat tooth hand child because HAB-eat
ke’e’=í
tooth=3ANIM
It’s not going to bite the child’s hand? Because it bites.

7 Raul: [A'a::.
No.

8 Alfonsa: *Ponte ésa adentro.=*
-|Alfonsa head turn to Brendon
Put that inside.

9 Raul: *=Ponte ésa adentro.*
-|Raul gaze to and nods at Iveth
Put that inside.

10 Brendon: **Eé?**
Huh?

11 Raul: ***Ponte ésa adentro de kúcchì.***
-------------Raul offers plant to Brendon (Fig. 2)
Put that inside of the pigpen.

12 **(0.38)**
Brendon slowly takes plant from Raul

13 Raul: **Áà doo í lò loo kúcchì pâ.**
Brendon turns with plant to take to the pig
------------------------------|Alfonsa turns gaze to Brendon
áà do=í=lò lo kúchì pâ
yes give=3ANIM=2S face pig my.son
Yes, you give it to the pig, my son.

14 Alfonsa: **^Liññi korálle too é pâ. Liññi koralle kíà too é pâ. Loo kúcchì kwa' é.**
-------------|Brendon leaves frame
----------|Alfonsa points to pig-then drops point
lini korale k-do=é pâ lini korale
belly corral CAUS-insert=3O my.son belly corral
kíà k-do=é
go.and CAUS-insert=3O
pâ lo kúchì kwa'=é
my.son face pig that=3O
Put it inside the corral my son. Go and put it inside the corral my son. Of that pig.

15 Brendon: **Eé?**
Huh?

16 Raul: ***Allí en el kúcchì ése .***
-|Raul points to pig---|returns hand
There in the pigpen (with) that.

16 Alfonsa: **Liññi korálle doo é pâ.**
Alfonsa gazing to Brendon
lini korále do=é pâ
belly corral insert=2INAN my.son
Put in in the corral my son.
((E's action is out of frame))

17 Alfonsa: **°Toòno ndicchì ro'o lò.° Laa yenne' lò nóo nya'á**
-|Alfonsa looks down to work
toòno n-dichì ro'o=lò la yene'=lò nó ni=á
ideo STA-shit mouth=2S NEG hear=2S that say=1S
Damn you. You don't hear what I say.

This pattern that code shifts to Spanish in child-directed speech is consistent across multiple videos. In another video with the same family (example 4), we see the grandmother (Alfonsa) shift to Spanish to address the little girl Iveth to send her on an errand to get the grandmother's shawl. In the first turn, Alfonsa speaks Zapotec to issue a directive as *an outloud* (similar to Raul in example 3, line 2). Everybody could hear this but it was not clearly directed to anyone particular by reference. Young Iveth is present in the scene while Sofia washes clothes and Alfonsa and her other daughter Fabiola sit to talk.

(4)

1 Alfonsa: **Kíà chii yaà tome'e' báyyo á kaa ndxokko loo ákkà nisso lò enzí chò' ótto á nee jròlla á.**
kíà chi#yà te-me'e' báyo=á ka ndxoko lo
go.and bring a.little shawl=1S where is.piled face
ákà niso=lò
tree aunt=2S

enzí#chò' H*-oto=á ne r-ròla=á
over.there POT-cover=1S because HAB-be.cold=1S
Go and bring my little shawl that is by your aunt's tree so I can cover up because I'm cold.

((3 turns of unrelated conversation with Sofia omitted))

2 Alfonsa: **°Jre'tte á.°**
-|Alfonsa head turn toward tree/shawl
r-re'te'=á
HAB-be.lazy=1S
I'm feeling lazy.

3 Alfonsa: ***^Dame mi reboso pues mâ.***
-----------------------------|Alfonsa head/gaze turn to girl
Get me my shawl, my daughter.

4 Alfonsa: ***Dame mi rebozo. Está allí.***
---------|Alfonsa points right-----|Alfonsa points right
Get me my shawl. It's over there (by you).

5 Alonsa: ***Esta vieja no quiere ir.***
-------|Alfonsa head turn front
This old lady doesn't want to go.

6 Fabiola: ***Vete a dar su reboso de mi mama.***
Go and get the shawl of my mother.

7 ((girl gets shawl))

Now we turn to a transcript of the little girl Iveth and her father Pedro receiving an offer of a drink when visiting a neighbor. The transcript clearly illustrates the pattern of language choice alternating between speech about the child when the child is present (in Zapotec) and speech directly addressed to the child (in Spanish). Pedro and Iveth are visiting the household of the traditional family of example 1. Pedro is also my collaborator, who has been visiting relatives and neighbors as a project videographer. As a visitor, he was in a position to receive offers of hospitality (Sicoli 2020). Prior to the beginning of the transcript, Pedro was asked if he wanted water. He turned down the offer for himself, but in line 2, he expands upon his response to request water for his daughter. Note the shift to the creaky voice register marked by tildes in lines 2 and 4, and which solicits the commiseration of Kacha (see Sicoli 2010, 2015). The turns of talk where the adults address each other here are all in Zapotec, but in line 5, Pedro shifts his participant frame to address his daughter and concordantly shifts to Spanish.

(5)

2 Pedro: **Eerò i'ñña tome'e' inzá wà ~we'e' endò' á txee ra Kacchà~**
erò i'na tome'e' inzá=wà we'e' endò'=á txe=ra Kachà~
but ask a.little water=2PL drink child 1S then=EXC Kacha
But, I ask you for a little of your water for my daughter then!, Kacha?

3 Kacha: **^Áà we'e' ndxò é:^**
----------------Kacha gives cup to Pedro
áà we'e'=ndxò=é
yes drink=3F=3INAN
Yes that she drinks it.

4 Pedro: **^Áà txee ~Kacchà~^**
-Pedro takes cup
áà txe Kachà
yes then Kacha
Yes then, Kacha.

5 Pedro: ***ᵛTen ahora mija toma agua ahora ᵛ.***
Here now, my daughter, drink water now.

6 **(6.0)** Pedro gives water to Iveth who drinks

```
7 Kacha:  Skwa' rebi~cchi ndx[ò~
          skwa' rebichi=ndx[ò
          like.this dry.throat=3F
          She's so thirsty.
```

As Iveth drinks Kacha and Pedro continue talking in Zapotec and then when Iveth finishes, Pedro checks with her that she's doesn't want more and then closes the sequence by returning the cup to Kacha. As he returns the cup, he represents the physical action of returning the cup with a resonating spoken proposition 'here's your cup'.

(6)

```
21 Pedro:  …áwwà ni'i á ((to Kacha))
           áwà '-ni=á
           yes ACT-say=1S
           Yes, I do say.

22 Pedro:  Quieres mas mija? (3.0)
           Do you want more, my daughter?

23 Pedro:  Ya ahora (0.9) así no mas ahora hija (3.3)
           That's it now, just like this, no more now, daughter.

24 Pedro:  Che'ttza lá lò [ningyè' básso lò oora Kacchà]
           -------------------------|Pedro offers cup to Kacha
           che'tza=lá=lò     ningyè' báso=lò ora Kachà
           Thanks=already=2S thing   cup=2S  now Kacha
           Thank you, here's your cup, Kacha.

25 Kacha:                       [Áà Bettò (0.3)] ^áà:
                                -K takes cup from P
                                Áà  Bettò áà
                                yes Pedro yes
                                Yes, Pedro. Yes.
```

With this socialization style, code alternation co-occurs with addressee shifts: when a person directs a linguistic action to a child, they also shift language codes from Zapotec to Spanish. The corpus shows consistency within the family as the father, mother, and grandparents all display the style. But at the time these videos were recorded, there was no consistency *across* families in Lachixío (as we saw in example 1, which is contemporaneous with the others). A little later Kacha's mother-in-law Sabina arrives and observes Pedro code-switching with his daughter. Sabina topicalizes the girl's language abilities, and more generally the code-switching socialization style displayed in her interactions with her father.

5. Contesting Choices and Motives

In the (anonymized) interactional scene pictured in figure 1.3, the little girl Iveth is seated in a chair, her father Pedro is behind her dressed in black, and they are visiting Flavio (in white on the left) and his family. You can see here the grandmother Sabina and little Leo seated in the back and Kacha, Leo's mother, in the upper right. Pedro is shifting to Spanish for all speech directed toward his daughter. Sabina takes notice of this and she first tries to engage Iveth in Zapotec. When she gets no response, she turns to Pedro and says (in Zapotec), 'She doesn't understand Zapotec, Pedro?' The question makes a response relevant about the code-shifting style of talking to children. Pedro's response includes, in various ways, his ethnotheory of language acquisition (what would have been the subject or object of prior conversations between Pedro and his family, through which they converged on the same code-alternation pattern of child-directed speech). Flavio then himself shifts to Spanish to try to engage the girl. Iveth does not respond to Spanish either. Not responding to either Zapotec or Spanish, the grandmother initiates an exchange

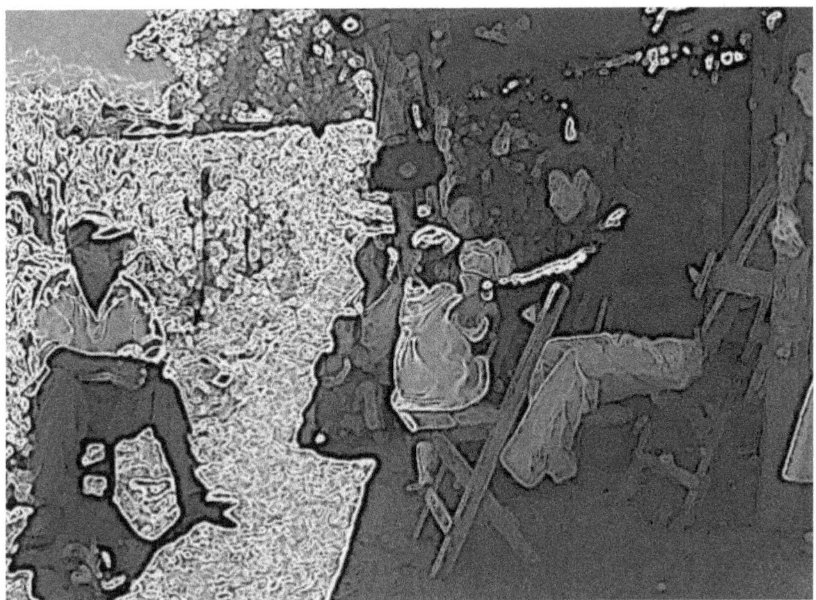

Figure 1.3 Two Families Together[3]

throughout which, I argue, she does not buy into Pedro's language acquisition theory, and which we will look at the line-by-line details a little further on.

(7)

1 Sabina:	**Laa yenne ndxò [dia'lò la Bettò? (0.3)** la yene=ndxò dia'lò=la Betò no listen=3F Zapotec=Q Pedro ***She doesn't understand Zapotec, Pedro?***
2 Flavio:	**[ni'i á í** ni'i=á=í ACT.say 1S 3ANIM ***I do say!***

3 Pedro: <Lè'kka:: no'o'> (.) tzyáà nóo ryenne ndxò nisso
lè'ka no'o' tzyáà nó ryene=ndxò niso
good there.is a.little that listens=3F aunt
Well, there is a little that she understands, aunt

From this transcription of the question response sequence between Grandma Sabina and Pedro, it is apparent that the question is evoking something delicate or controversial. The question is asked in the negative (line 1) marking 'not speaking Zapotec' as out of the ordinary. Flavio's talk in line 2 is part of an overlapping but unrelated sequence of talk between Pedro and Flavio. Between the question and its response in 3 is a pause, and then Pedro begins to respond slowly with hesitation (indicated <...>). Stivers et al. (2009), Pomerantz (1984), and others have demonstrated that negative responses show longer turn-transition times, and the hesitancy in Pedro's delivery conveys a parallel message. *Lè'kka* (a token that literally means 'good') functions here like 'well' would in English. Schegloff and Lerner (2009) described well-prefaced responses as 'general alert that indicate nonstraightforwardness in responding'. Such cross-cultural lexical-functional parallels are surprisingly common in the developing comparative conversation analysis literature.

After Grandma Sabina topicalized the code-switching, Pedro and she begin to talk and at the same time Flavio tries to engage the girl in a Spanish-language baby talk register characterized by asking known-answer questions in high-pitched melodic prosodies.

(8)

21 Flavio: ***Así te llamas?***
Is that your name?

22 Flavio: ***Iveth te llamas?* (5.0)**
Iveth is your name?

23 Sabina: **(a hu ha)** ((laughter))

24 Sabina: **Nii á [nóo jnii beè endò' distillà.**
ni=á nó r-ni bè endò' di.stilà
say=1S that HAB-speak PL child Spanish
I say that children speak Spanish

25 Flavio: **[(a hu hu)** ((laughter))

26 Pedro: **Ai: áwwà nóo le'kka=**
Ai áwà nó le'ka
INT yes that good
Yeah yes that's good

Flavio goes through his baby talk routine in Spanish trying to involve the girl in a conversation. I'll just mention here that baby talk like this is associated with Spanish and not Zapotec because the high-pitch prosodic feature overlaps with the high pitch of the Zapotec respect register and would thus be dissonant with the social roles (cf., findings of Ochs and Schieffelin on Samoan and Kaluli [1984] for parallel examples). After a five-second pause in which the child doesn't respond (which itself would depart from norms of politeness and respect for elders), Sabina chuckles followed quickly by a chuckle from Flavio during which the grandmother says, 'I say that children speak Spanish' in 24. Her proposition resonates with the irony of the situation, perhaps sarcastically, given that the child has not responded to either Zapotec or Spanish. Pedro didn't seem to catch the irony. He responds with an emphatic agreement to the literal meaning of the proposition, 'that children speak Spanish', and not the ironic twist. The equals sign at the end of Pedro's turn in 26 and beginning of Sabina's turn in 27 shows that Sabina's response comes immediately latched onto Pedro's turn and where she displays what she interprets as Pedro's position.

(9)

27 Sabina: **=Laa niì benné dia'llò loo beè endò'.**
la ni bené dia'lò lo bè endò'
no say people Zapotec face PL child
People shouldn't speak to children in Zapotec.

28 Pedro: **Áww:à nisso:. (0.3)**
áwà niso
yes aunt
Yes, aunt.

29 Pedro: **Rekkà beè endò’ tónnò nzaa niì nzaa niì benné distillà beè endò’ no’o’.**
rekà bè endò’ tónò n-tza nì n-tza nì bené
know PL child if STA-go speak STA-go speak people
di.stilà bè endò’ no’o’
Spanish PL child there.is
The children learn (it) if the people speak to them in Spanish.

30 **(0.5)**

31 Pedro: **Ai rekkà beè endò’ nee ri’yya á. (‘u ha)**
Ai rekà bè endò’ ne ri’ya=á (‘u ha)
INT know PL child IRR see=1S
Yeah I see that the children would learn. (‘u ha)

32 Sabina: **#Rekk[:à beè endò’ nee ri’yya niì á# (.) a[^ai::::**
Rekkà bè endò’ ne ri’ya nì=á ai
know PL child IRR see say=1S INT
#I see that the children would learn# . a^ai::::

Is line 27, Sabina provides a caption to the image she has gotten from Pedro’s code-switching and stance taking: ‘People shouldn’t speak to children in Zapotec’ she says. Pedro responds to this as if it is an understanding check. Pedro then expands on his response in line 29: ‘The children learn (it) if the people speak to them in Spanish’. This is followed by a pause (sequentially a gap of no response from the Grandmother). In 31, Pedro provides a response to himself, ‘Yeah I see that the children would learn’, followed by a couple of laugh syllables. In 32 Sabina repeats Pedro’s proposition from 30, ‘I see that the children would learn’, in a harsh breathy voice (shown bracketed with the number signs #. . .#). The reader may remember that the breathy voice register frames authority and assertiveness. On repeated discourse like this, I have described breathy voice as "demanding expansion" on the truth value of the proposition because something is interpreted as surprising or not easily believable. These sequences predictably continue in the form of a third-position repetition of the proposition followed by a fourth-position expansion providing some account or evidence (Sicoli 2010, 2020) as depicted in the next few turns of example 10.

(10)

```
33 Pedro:    [Rekkà beè endò' nee ri'yya á noo uh
             rekà bè endò' ne ri'ya=á no  uh
             know PL child  IRR see=1S  and um
             I see that children would learn and, um

34 Pedro:    tonno jnii kà benné dia'lò le'kka enza'
               [lakka rekkà beè endò' txee.
             tono r-ni   kà   bené   dia'lò  le'ka enza'    laka
             if   HAB-says true people Zapotec also direction down
               rekà       bè endò' txe
               knowledge PL child then
             if the people speak truly in Zapotec too, the
               children take this in then

35 Sabina:     [Aà puurò enze'e nee nii txee
               à  purò enze'e ne ni  txe
               oh just this   IRR say then
               Oh, just like that they'll speak, then?

36 Pedro:    Áwwà nisso[:
             áwà niso
             yes aunt
             Yes, aunt.

37 Sabina:                [Mm ta'ccha lá lokko ndxò xhoobe zekkà
                            zaà beè nokwà né, Béttò?
```

```
mm ta'cha=lá          loko=ndxò xhobe    zekà.zà
INT beautiful=already shoe=3F   how.much cost
  bè     nokwà=né     Pedro
  PL     this=ACT3O   Betò
```

Mm her shoes are very pretty. How much do they cost, Pedro?

Indeed, the sequence REPETITION+EXPANSION follows the challenge of the breathy-voiced repeat of line 32. In line 33, Pedro does a repeat followed by the expansion in 34, that he thinks that if Zapotec is spoken in the children's presence that they will internalize Zapotec as well. Grandma Sabina responds 'Oh, just like that they'll speak, then' in 35. Sabina's move is interpreted as an understanding check of what 33 and 31 are doing, which we can infer in Pedro's affirmative response in 36. Sabina then, beginning in slight overlap with Pedro's affirmation, abruptly changes the topic of their conversation to start a new sequence by asking about the little girl's pretty shoes. There are several sequential and grammatical considerations that show Grandma Sabina does not buy into Pedro's argument.

Pedro's socialization style and the justifications that he gives are contested by Sabina in the positive evidence of morphosyntax and the negative evidence of deviation from expected sequence organization. The evidence I pointed to in the transcriptions are found in the original negative formulation of Grandma's question, the contrary-to-fact statement of the grandmother that 'children speak Spanish' after the little girl failed to demonstrate that she does, and the breathy-voiced repeat that suggests the proposition being animated by Sabina is contrary to her belief or experience. One other place to look is the sequence organization of affirmation, which would not be apparent without attending to discourse practices of Zapotec within the Mesoamerican *sprechbund* (discourse area) (where Campbell, Kaufman, and Smith-Stark [1986] focus on a *sprachbund* [linguistic area] using isoglosses and typological features). Some accompanying *sprechbund* features of interactional discourse have been presented in Sicoli (2010) and Brown, Sicoli, and Le Guen (2010).

In the sequence organization that involves affirmative answers, the normative sequence across much of Mesoamerica is in three parts: first, a *question* or *declaration*; second, an *affirmation* by the second party; and then third, the *acknowledgment*[4] of the affirmation by the first speaker now responding in third position. This sequence organization is illustrated in example (11) here. Line 1 is a question. The affirmation is given as a modal voiced repeat of the proposition. The acknowledgment is displayed with a minimal news uptake token Aà 'oh' here. Showing agreement with a third repeat is also possible in this sequential position (Sicoli 2020).

(11)

```
1 Jorge:  ¿Kássi laa dò'o' zxa (i') íña'a txaa?
          kási   la dò'o'=zxa      í#na'a   txa
          almost no cultivate=3DIS ag.fields then
          They don't plant corn much then?

2 Pedro:  Káss:i laa dò'o' zxa íña'a.
          Pedro head shake
          kási   la dò'o'=zxà      íña7a
          almost no cultivate=3DIS ag.fields
          They don't plant much corn.

3 Jorge:  Aà:
          Oh
```

We have also seen this sequence organization in transcripts I have already presented as in example 5, lines 2–4, where Pedro affirms Kacha's affirmative response to his request for water for his daughter.

Returning to Pedro and Sabina's conversation, we see this sequence is left *unclosed* multiple times. Consider example 12 (containing a sequence from example 9). Line 27 is an assessment that is responded to with an affirmation in 28, to which we would now expect the third-position acknowledgment but instead we get a pause, notable at 0.3 seconds given the pace of turn and response in this interaction and which is thus off from the rhythm of the interaction represented in the transcript where we do not otherwise see pauses like this. In the absence of Sabina's response Pedro himself takes third position, going on with his evidence in pursuit of acknowledgment. I take this lack of third-position acknowledgment on Sabina's part as evidence that she has not and is not coming around to Pedro's position on language socialization.

(12)

```
27 Sabina:   =Laa niì benné dia'llò loo beè endò'.
             la ni  bené   dia'lò  lo   bè endò'
             no say people Zapotec face PL child
             People shouldn't speak to children in Zapotec.

28 Pedro:    Áww:à nisso:. (0.3)
             áwà niso
             yes aunt
             Yes, aunt.

29 Pedro:    Rekkà beè endò' tónnò nzaa nii nzaa nii benné
               distillà beè endò' no'o'.
             rekà bè endò' tónò n-tza ni     n-tza nì    bené
             know PL child if   STA-go speak STA-go speak people
               di.stilà bè endò' no'o'
               Spanish  PL child there.is
             The children learn (it) if the people speak to
               them in Spanish.
```

We can see a parallel sequence in example 10. A sarcastic assessment 'Oh, just like that they'll speak, then?' by Grandma in 35 is issued as an understanding check of Pedro's declaration in 34, 'if the people speak truly in Zapotec too, the children take this in then'. This receives an affirmative response by Pedro in 35. Rather than Grandma acknowledging Pedro's position with some token of agreement like a repetition or an affirmative interjection, she rather abruptly changes the subject here.

In this short sequence then we find quite a bit of evidence to support an argument that the socialization style that uses code alternation to shift to Spanish for child-directed speech was contested within the community in 2008 when it was incipient, and that the particular beliefs held by Pedro, on which he motivates his behavior, were not shared. There is always a lot at stake in everyday dialogues where language can be both the means of discourse and a public moral object to be evaluated. Little Leo is sitting on his grandmother's lap observing this exchange and his siblings, who all attend a public school in Spanish and have peers who are children socialized in Spanish outside of the classroom, are present as well. At issue are questions of whether to be bilingual or monolingual, of language shift, and of how to raise one's children in Lachixío in 2008 when this was recorded. There is one other thing I want to point to about this segment before closing, and that is that like so many other conversations, it echoes previous conversations, and becomes an echo later in the future-present. This temporality of language is not something that we can get from the transcripts directly, but is something grounded in a longitudinal perspective from long-term ethnographic engagement. Evidence for this position bears out in the next section.

6. Conversations That Depict or Refer to Deliberate Decisions in Language Use

In an article called "Shadow Conversations," Judith Irvine (1996) discussed the indeterminacy of participant roles in any particular speech event, based in part on the notion that so much of what we do with language is to bring speech forward from prior speech events, and that the chain of participation extends back into the past as well as forward to an indeterminate future. As speakers we animate others' speech, through processes that Greg Urban (1996) described as decontextualization and recontextualization. These particular authors were themselves recontextualizing prior authors, like Bakhtin's and Voloshinov's concepts of dialogicality (Bakhtin 1981; Voloshinov 1986), and Pete Becker's notion of *prior text*, which he characterized by saying, "Every utterance is to some extent speaking the past and to some extent deviating from it" (Becker 1995).

Five years before this conversation between Sabina and Pedro, I recorded a series of narratives from several towns in the region about the arrival of the schoolteachers (who generally are Spanish monolinguals that come from large urban centers, like the state capital of Oaxaca City). Across the region it has been common since the 1950s for schoolteachers to suggest that parents stop using Zapotec at home with their children. In Lachixío, adults held meetings on several occasions to discuss this and for many years resisted such attempts with a unified response, arguing for a structured bilingualism where Zapotec was used in the home and Spanish in the schools—that it was the teacher's job to teach Spanish rather than the parents. In a paper titled, "Agency and ideology in language shift and language maintenance" (2011), I reported on a deliberate decision conveyed to me in interviews and narratives characterizing a vote in Lachixío by the parents of schoolchildren in council meetings. Those conversations are in the background history of Sabina and Pedro's conversation. Their conversation can be seen as another iteration of this discourse, in an ongoing dialogue balancing coexisting trajectories of language shift and language maintenance. It may not surprise you to learn that Pedro worked as a teacher's assistant and that he voiced in these speech events the ideological position of that social network here (the one other schoolteacher who is from Lachixío has also raised his children in the code-alternation style [children several years older than Pedro's and who were outliers in the earliest days of my fieldwork]). The new socialization style that took hold at the turn of the twenty-first century represented a deviation from the previously unified and organized response of the parents and as I have shown here was being contested at the same time that it progressed into the daily practices of a young generation of parents (and as we saw in examples 3 and 4, sometimes also by their parents). The new mosaic in Lachixío was one where children had widely varying levels of competence in Zapotec, some only with the passive familiarity of a heritage language. Language variation in code choice was then playing out on the playgrounds and other social settings where children of different families with different linguistic repertoires interacted.

Formally, the alternations between languages pattern in a similar way as the alternations between voice registers that we saw in examples 1 and 2. With both, people's social identities are in part constructed by the varieties of language addressed to them. Judith Butler (2002) referred to address as hailing or interpolation of identity. The use of a respectful voice marks the type of person being addressed and their relationship to the speaker. The use of Spanish here does this as well, ratifying children as Spanish speakers and also as non-Zapotec speakers. Zapotec itself became transformed for this new generation from being the language of everyday life to being a heritage language spoken by parents and grandparents. The agency for this sociolinguistic transformation was emergent in interactions and distributed between the adults and the children with consequences beyond any intentions the participants could reflect on.

A lasting impression of Sally Thomason as a scholar from my earliest days working with her as a graduate student in linguistics is her commitment to working with a community over the long term, returning year after year to the Montana Salish community. I have worked to emulate this long-term commitment in my work with the Lachixío Zapotec community. It is only across the decades that a longitudinal perspective on language change and language shift can be developed. Ten years after the video recordings described in this chapter, there had been time for the child-directed speech patterns of 2009 to grow along with the children who were then teenagers. By 2018, the pattern of addressing children in Spanish had become commonplace among families entering childbearing age, and the mosaic of language socialization styles had shifted from predominantly Zapotec language child socialization to predominantly a style of socialization shifting to Spanish for child-directed speech. Like the young man from 2008, the young parents in 2018 have told me that they suspect that enough Zapotec is still spoken around the children in the Lachixío environment that they will go on to speak later. Perhaps some will (as Meek [2010] has written about for a Northern Athabaskan community), but something implicitly creative was also going on in ordering code alternation in parallel with intergeneration participant roles. Ten years after the videos we examine in this chapter, Little Leo continues to speak Zapotec. The children whose family code-switched to Spanish for child-directed speech, however, told me that while they generally understand Zapotec, they are not comfortable speaking Zapotec. The discourse pattern aligning addressee to language choice through code alternations in the repeated interactions of daily life ratified those children as speakers of Spanish and nonspeakers of Zapotec, producing a new category of Zapotec as the *heritage* language for a new generation in Lachixío. Deliberate decisions can have unintended consequences.

Endnotes

1. An early version of this paper was given as a job talk to the Faculty of Linguistics at Georgetown University, one of many job applications over the years for which Sally served as a reference.

2. Glossing conventions: 1S = first-person singular, 1PLX = first-person plural exclusive, 1PLI = first-person plural inclusive, 2S = second-person singular, 2PL = second-person plural, 3M = third-person masculine, 3DIS = third-person distal (respect), 3F = third-person feminine, 3ANIM = third-person animal, 3INAN = third-person inanimate (object), ACT3O = active indefinite subject acting on object, PL = plural, DIM = diminutive, HAB = habitual aspect, CMP = completive aspect, STA = stative aspect, POT = potential mood, IMP = imperative mood, IRR = irrealis, CAUS = causative, EXC = exclamative, Q = polar question particle, INT = interjection, IDEO = ideophone. In the conversational transcripts, numbers in parentheses indicate pauses in speech, colons indicate nonphonemic or nonstress template-based lengthening, square brackets co-occurring between lines indicate that speech

is in overlap (where there are multiple overlaps in the same line, subscript co-indexing is used), and angle brackets pointed outward (<. . .>) indicate slowed speech rate. Upward (^) and downward (v) arrows point to raised and lowered pitch. Raised circles (°...°) bracket quiet speech. Each line, or utterance, of the transcripts is represented in a block of multiple tiers: (1) phonetic with CA transcription (in bold text with Spanish language indicated by italics), (2) action descriptions in regular density text. The pipe symbol within a description <|> indexes the onset of the action aligned to the phonetic tier, (3) morpho-phonemics, (4) morpheme-by-morpheme gloss (3 and 4 are in regular density), (5) English free translation (in bold, italic).

3. A contrast between the two families can be seen in the difference of consent: the Spanish-language socializing family granting use of photos and traditional family requesting anonymization of photos in publications.

4. What I am calling here "acknowledgment," I've referred to as "uptake" in talks on this topic. But considering the cultural metaphor represented in example 10, line 34 *enza' lakka rekkà* (lit: direction down knowledge) that knowledge is embodied downward in Lachixío Zapotec, "uptake" would be dissonant. What the third-position move does is create a public sign acknowledging the proposition and stance of the other.

References

Bakhtin, Michael M. 1981. Discourse in the novel. In Michael Holquist (Ed.), *The dialogic imagination*, 259–422. Austin: University of Texas Press.

Becker, A. L. 1995. *Beyond translation: Essays toward a modern philology*. Ann Arbor: University of Michigan Press.

Brown, Penelope, Mark A. Sicoli, and Oliver Le Guen. 2010. *Cross-speaker repetition in Tzeltal, Yucatec, and Zapotec conversation*. Paper presented at ICCA 10: International Conference on Conversation Analysis, July 8, Mannheim, Germany.

Butler, Judith. 2002. *Excitable speech: A politics of the performative*. New York: Routledge.

Campell, Lyle, Terrence Kaufman, and Thomas C. Smith-Stark. 1986. Meso-America as a linguistic area. *Language*, 62(3): 530–70.

Falconi, Elizabeth Anne. 2011. *Migrant stories: Zapotec transborder migration and the production of a narrated community* (PhD dissertation). University of Michigan, Ann Arbor.

Goffman, Erving. 1967. *Interaction ritual: Essays in face-to-face behavior.* New York: Pantheon Books.

Goffman, Erving. 1981. The interaction order. *American Sociological Review*, 48(1): 1–17.

Irvine, Judith T. 1996. Shadow conversations: The indeterminacy of participant roles. In Michael Silverstein and Greg Urban (Eds.), *Natural histories of discourse*, 131–59. Chicago, IL: University of Chicago Press.

Kroskrity, Paul. 2009. Narrative reproductions: Ideologies of storytelling, authoritative words, and generic regimentation in the village of Tewa. *Journal of Linguistic Anthropology*, 19(1): 40–56.

Kulick, Don. 1992. *Language shift and cultural reproduction: Socialization, self and syncretism in a Papua New Guinean village.* Cambridge: Cambridge University Press.

Majid, Asifa, Seán Roberts, Ludy Cilissen, Karen Emmorey, Brenda Nicodemus, Lucinda O'Grady, Bencie Woll, Barbara LeLan, Hilário de Sousa, Brian L. Cansler, Shakila Shayan, Connie de Vos, Gunter Senft, N. J. Enfield, Rogayah A. Razak, Sebastian Fedden, Sylvia Tufvesson, Mark Dingemanse, Ozge Ozturk, Penelope Brown, Clair Hill, Olivier Le Guen, Vincent Hirtzel, Rik van Gijn, Mark A. Sicoli, and Stephen C. Levinson. 2018. The differential coding of perception in the world's languages. *Proceedings of the National Academy of Sciences*, 115(45): 11369–376. www.pnas.org/cgi/doi/10.1073/pnas.1720419115.

Meek, Barbra. 2010. *We are our language: An ethnography of language revitalization in a Northern Athabaskan community.* Tucson: University of Arizona Press.

Ochs, Elinor, and Bambi Schieffelin. 1984. Language acquisition and socialization: Three developmental stories and their Implications. In Richard Shweder and Robert LeVine (Eds.), *Culture theory: Essays on mind, self, and emotion*, 276–320. New York: Cambridge University.

Pomerantz, Anita. 1984. Agreeing and disagreeing with assessments: Some features of preferred/dispreferred turn shapes. In J. Maxwell Atkinson and John Heritage (Eds.), *Structures of social action: Studies in conversation analysis*, 57–101. Cambridge: Cambridge University Press.

Pomerantz, Anita, and John Heritage. 2012. Preference. In Jack Sidnell and Tanya Stivers (Eds.), *The handbook of conversation analysis*, 210–28. Hoboken, NJ: Wiley-Blackwell.

Rinehart, Melissa A. 2011. The agency of language ideologies in Miami Indian Recovery. In Tania Granadillo and Heidi Orcutt-Gachiri (Eds.), *Ethnographic contributions to the study of endangered languages: A linguistic anthropological perspective*, 7–110. Tucson: University of Arizona Press.

Schegloff, Emanuel A., and Gene H. Lerner. 2009. Beginning to respond: Well-prefaced responses to Wh-questions. *Research on Language & Social Interaction*, 42(2): 91–115.

Shayan, Shakila, Özge Öztürk, and Mark A. Sicoli. 2011. The thickness of pitch: Crossmodal iconicity in three unrelated languages; Farsi, Turkish and Zapotec. *Senses and Society*, 6(1): 96–105.

Sicoli, Mark A. 2007. *Tono: A linguistic ethnography of tone and voice in a Zapotec region* (PhD dissertation). University of Michigan, Ann Arbor.

Sicoli, Mark A. 2010. Shifting voices with participant roles: Voice qualities and speech registers in Mesoamerica. *Language in Society*, 39(4): 521–53.

Sicoli, Mark A. 2011. Agency and ideology in language shift and language maintenance. In Tania Granadillo and Heidi Orcutt-Gachiri (Eds.), *Ethnographic contributions to the study of endangered languages: A linguistic anthropological perspective*, 161–76. Tucson: University of Arizona Press.

Sicoli, Mark A. 2015. Voice registers. In Deborah Tannen, Heidi E. Hamilton, and Deborah Schiffrin (Eds.), *The handbook of discourse analysis, 2nd edition*, 105–26. Chichester, UK: John Wiley & sons, Ltd.

Sicoli, Mark A. 2020. *Saying and doing in Zapotec: Multimodality, resonance, and the language of joint actions*. Bloomsbury Studies in Linguistic Anthropology. London: Bloomsbury Press.

Smith-Stark, Thomas C. 1999. *El solteco y el zapotec occidental: Un aprecio a partir de los vocabularios de Peñafiel*. Paper presented at the V Congreso Nacional de Lingüística, Monterrey.

Stivers, Tanya, N. J. Enfield, Penelope Brown, Christina Englert, Makoto Hayashi, Trine Heinemann, et al. 2009. Universals and cultural variation in turn-taking in conversation. *Proceedings of the National Academy of Sciences*, 106(26): 10587–592.

Sullivant, J. Ryan. 2016. Reintroducing Teojomulco Chatino. *International Journal of American Linguistics*, 82: 393–423.

Thomason, Sarah, G. 2001. *Language contact: An introduction*. Washington DC: Georgetown University Press.

Urban, Greg. 1996. Entextualization, replication, and power. In Michael Silverstein and Greg Urban (Eds.), *Natural histories of discourse*, 21–44. Chicago, IL: University of Chicago Press.

Voloshinov, Valentin N. 1986 [1930]. *Marxism and the philosophy of language* (L. Matejka and I. R. Titunik, trans.). Cambridge, MA: Harvard University Press.

CHAPTER 2

Code-Switching as a Way of Speaking—From Language Shift to Language Maintenance

Carmel O'Shannessy

1. Background

There has been considerable debate about the role of code-switching practices in contact-induced language change, especially as to whether they contribute to a path of language loss, and whether they could lead to the emergence of mixed languages. But the role of code-switching practices as a factor contributing to the maintenance of a language has been discussed much less. In this chapter, I show that although code-switching practices among one community of speakers at first played a role in partial language shift through leading to the emergence of a mixed language (O'Shannessy 2005, 2012, 2013), a new configuration of code-switching practices assists in maintaining aspects of the traditional language, by enabling verbs in the traditional language to remain easily accessible to the speakers. The new language, Light Warlpiri, uses few verbs from Warlpiri, and does not include full Warlpiri morphology. Code-switching into Warlpiri requires use of Warlpiri verbs and verbal morphology. Accessibility of the lexical items and morphology is increased through increased frequency of use, as higher-frequency items are more accessible and easier to process than lower-frequency items (e.g., Becker 1979; Forster 1976; Levelt, Roelofs, and Meyer 1999; Morton 1976).

In this paper, I present data showing (a) the presence of restructured Warlpiri-derived verb stems in Light Warlpiri and (b) speakers code-switching between Warlpiri and Light Warlpiri. I argue that the two ways of speaking—on the one hand, Light Warlpiri, with Warlpiri-derived verb stems, and on the other hand practices of switching between Light Warlpiri and Warlpiri—are mutually supportive in maintaining speakers' knowledge of, and psycholinguistic access to, Warlpiri verbs, and therefore maintenance of Warlpiri.

Mixed languages combine a significant amount of lexical and/or grammatical material from more than one source language, largely unchanged, in a systematic, conventionalized way, and consequently do not have only one parent language, but two or more (Matras and Bakker 2003; Thomason and Kaufman 1988: 12). An example of the recently emerged Australian mixed language, Light Warlpiri, is given in (1).

(1) *junga* *mayi* *nyuntu* yu-m go *karnta-kurl*
true Q 2SG 2SG-NFUT go woman-COM
'Is it true that you went with the woman?' (Light Warlpiri, O'Shannessy 2012: 305)

Example (1) shows the verb *go*, from English and/or Kriol (an English-lexified Creole), an innovative auxiliary form, *yu-m* '2SG-NONFUTURE', and elements other than the verb and auxiliary from Warlpiri.

Until recently, research was divided as to whether a mixed language could be the result of conventionalized community code-switching practices, as there was no direct evidence of the process occurring (Matras and Bakker 2003; Thomason 2003). Some researchers considered that the linguistic structures seen in code-switched speech differed from those of mixed languages and that code-switching could not lead to a mixed language (Backus 2003; Bakker 2003; Matras and Bakker 2003). Others hypothesized that ordinary processes of language contact could conventionalize to the extent that they could form a systematized, mixed language (e.g. Auer 1999; Thomason 2003: 26). Thomason (1995, 2001, 2003) uses the term bilingual mixed languages (as opposed to pidgin and Creole languages, which are also mixed, but in a different way, and due to different histories of emergence) and sees that different processes may operate in the emergence of different languages. She sees at least a partial role for code-switching in the development of the mixed languages, Michif, which combines Cree and French (Bakker 1994, 1997), and Media Lengua, which combines Quechua and Spanish (Muysken 1994, 1997), but not in Mednij Aleut, which combines Aleut and Russian (Golovko 1994; Vakhtin 1998). The reasoning is based on how closely the structures of source language combination in the mixed languages match those seen in documented code-switching practices.

It is now known that code-switching can lead to the formation of a mixed language, with direct evidence from the recently documented mixed languages in Australia, Light Warlpiri (O'Shannessy 2005, 2013) and Gurindji Kriol (McConvell and Meakins 2005). Evidence of code-switching between Gurindji, a Pama-Nyungan language, and Kriol, an English-lexified creole, in the 1970s, is given in Dalton, Edwards, Farquarson, Oscar, and McConvell (1995) and shows the same structure and type of language combination as in Gurindji Kriol today (McConvell and Meakins 2005). For Light Warlpiri, code-switching evidence is present in the speech of those who are older than the age cohorts who speak the mixed language, and again the structures are almost the same, with the exception that Light Warlpiri also shows structural innovation in the verbal auxiliary system that is not present in its sources, as detailed later in the text. The innovation and the observation that the innovative structure is used only by Light Warlpiri speakers point to a two-stage process of language emergence. Older speakers code-switched consistently in a specific pattern, consistent with Thomason's hypothesis, and younger speakers conventionalized the code-switching and added innovations. These observations add new insight into the stages involved in relatively abrupt language creation (O'Shannessy 2012, 2013).

Linked to the idea that code-switching could conventionalize to become a systematic linguistic system is the notion of the age group of speakers who would undertake the systematization process. There is widespread agreement that mixed languages are created by bilinguals, and Thomason suggests that the bilinguals who conventionalize their way of speaking into an independent linguistic system would be adults, or at least speakers who are not young children. This is because they would need to have developed their linguistic knowledge to the extent that they can retain the morphosyntactic system of one or both languages in the new language with little or no change (Thomason 2003: 32). In partial agreement and partial contrast, the emergence of Light Warlpiri through a two-stage process shows that adult bilinguals play a crucial role in the first stage of the process by code-switching in a systematic manner in their speech to young children, and then the young children also play a crucial role by further conventionalizing the speech they hear.

Early research into the motivations for conversational code-switching identified identity-related and social discourse motivations (Gumperz 1982). Identity-related motivations are those that link the use of a language to the speakers' language identities. Discourse motivations include packaging information for the listener in a certain way, or indicating a change in the contextualization of the interaction, termed metaphorical code-switching. Examples include switching language to emphasize a point, for repetition, for a quotation, or to qualify a point. Another motivation is to express a semantic nuance that is more precisely expressed by a word or phrase in one language, termed *mot juste* 'right word' by Poplack (1980).

In situations of language endangerment, code-switching practices have largely been viewed through two perspectives. One is as an indicator of the intrusion of an incoming language, or new way of speaking, into domains where only the heritage language was previously used (e.g., Crystal 2000; Fishman 1972; Haugen 1949), and the other is as practices of sociopragmatic and sociopolitical negotiation in a complex multilingual arena (Gal 1988; Hill 1993; Hill and Hill

1980; McConvell 1988; O'Shannessy 2015). The second perspective draws on analyses of motivations for code-switching that view the practices as sophisticated usage of linguistic resources to convey intentions that both bilingual speakers in the interaction understand, for instance, the identity-related and discourse motivations suggested by Gumperz (1982). The usages and understandings are shaped by historical, social, and political forces (Gal 1988). In situations of language endangerment, while code-switching can mean the intrusion of a dominant language into the domains of the other language, it can also have the positive language maintenance effect of keeping the elements of the endangered language accessible to speakers by using them frequently, even if not speaking the language all of the time (e.g., Dorian 1982).

2. Light Warlpiri

Code-switching practices were a major contributor to the development of Light Warlpiri, a recently emerged mixed language spoken in a remote Warlpiri community in northern Australia (O'Shannessy 2005, 2012, 2013). Light Warlpiri systematically combines the nominal structure of Warlpiri, a Pama-Nyungan language, with the verbal structure of Kriol (an English-lexified Creole) and English, with some dramatic innovations (O'Shannessy 2013). It can be thought of as a new language in the sense that it is not mutually intelligible with any of its sources, because a significant grammatical and lexical component is derived from each type of source, that is, from Warlpiri or from Kriol and/or English. It can also be thought of as a new variety of Warlpiri, which is how it is viewed by its speakers. It is spoken only in one Warlpiri community, and is part of the legacy of forced relocation of people by the government in the late 1940s, to the site that became their community. In the new site where they had to live, adults worked on cattle stations, in mines, and in the army, interacting with speakers of many different languages as well as English, and probably using the then-newly emerging *lingua franca* Kriol to do so.

Light Warlpiri developed through a two-stage process. In the first stage, adult speakers frequently code-switched between Warlpiri and Kriol and/or English in a consistent pattern when speaking to very young children, as part of a baby talk register (O'Shannessy 2012). Adults code-switched when speaking to each other, as well as when speaking to children, but when speaking to young children a specific code-switching pattern was used consistently (O'Shannessy 2012: 327). The pragmatic motivation for adults to code-switch in the pattern that was used to young children was likely due to conventionalization of a speech style through speech accommodation practices, where families heard each other interacting and spoke in the same style. An ideology that English and Kriol verbs were easier for young children to learn may also have played a role. In the second stage, the young children conventionalized the code-switching patterns into a new linguistic system, and added innovations in the verbal structure that were not in the speech of the adults. Examples (2) and (3) show how elements of Warlpiri, Kriol, and English combine in Light Warlpiri, with examples of Warlpiri given in (4) and (5). In the examples elements from Warlpiri are in italics, and from Kriol and/or English in plain font.

Discourse motivations that were present when the older cohort first began code-switching when talking to each other, that is, to other adults, and to children, would have been lost once the system was conventionalized, and the patterns of the new way of speaking became the expected way for the younger speakers to communicate with each other (cf. Auer 1999; Thomason 2003). In turn, this way of speaking came to index the identity of the younger speakers. In the examples, elements from Warlpiri are in italics and from English and Kriol in plain font.

(2)	*nganimpa-ng*	wi-m	go	luk-raun	*wardapi-k*	*Nungarrayi-k*
	1PL.EXCL-ERG	1PL-NFUT	go	look-round	goanna-DAT	sub.sect-DAT

'We went looking around for a goanna for Nungarrayi.'

(Light Warlpiri, Elicit_A21_AC58_2015)

(3) yu-m pud-im-on *mayi* *nyampu* *ngaju-nyang*
2SG-NFUT put-TR-on Q DET 1SG-POSS
'You put it on, did you, mine?' (Light Warlpiri, C06_14)

(4) *nganimpa-rlu-rnalu* *warru-rnu* *wardapi-k* *Nungarrayi-k*
1PL.EXCL-ERG-1PL.EXCL.S look.for-PST goanna-DAT sub.sect-DAT
'We looked around for a goanna for Nungarrayi.' (Warlpiri, constructed by author)

(5) *Yirra-rnu-npa-nyanu* *mayi* *nyampu* *ngaju-nyangu*
put-PST-2SG.S-REFLEX Q DET 1SG-POSS
'You put it on, did you, mine?' (Warlpiri, constructed by author)

Examples (2) and (3) show how Light Warlpiri systematically combines verbal structure of English and Kriol with the nominal structure of Warlpiri. A Kriol transitive affix is seen on the transitive verb 'put' in (3), consistent with its marking on most transitive verbs. In morphology, an ergative case marker occurs on the overt subject of a transitive clause, *nganimpa* '1PL.EXCL' in (2), dative case marking occurs on *wardapi* 'goanna' and the subsection term, or name, *Nungarrayi* in (2), and possessive marking occurs in (3). Constructed equivalent Warlpiri sentences are given in (4) and (5). Examples (2) and (3) also show the innovation brought into the verbal auxiliary structure of Light Warlpiri, explained in detail in O'Shannessy (2013). Briefly, the pronoun system from Kriol (*im* '3SG', *dem* '3PL') and the English contracted form *I'm* '1SG.PRES' were reanalyzed so that the bilabial nasal present in *im*, *dem*, and *I'm* came to have a separable meaning, of nonfuture temporality, incorporating present and past time, or realis mode. This element attaches to all of the pronominal elements (except second-person dual and plural), creating the structure seen in (2) and (3). This is summarized in table 2.1.

The structure of the reanalyzed pronominal-plus-tense-mood-aspect (TMA) element is present throughout the Light Warlpiri auxiliary system, as shown in table 2.2. When talking about events that occurred before the time of speech, the Kriol and Aboriginal English

Table 2.1 Pronominal Forms and Structure in Light Warlpiri (Adapted from O'Shannessy [Forthcoming])

Person and Number	*Form in English and/or Kriol*	*New Structure in Light Warlpiri*		*Sample Clause*
		Pronoun	*TMA Element*	
1SG	I'm	a	m	a-m going 'go-PROG'
3SG	im	i	m	i-m faind-im 'find-TR'
3SG	im	i	m	i-m laf-ing 'laugh-PROG'
3PL	dem	de	m	de-m ged-im 'get-TR'
1PL	wi	wi	m	wi-m ged-im 'get-TR'
2SG	yu	yu	m	yu-m ged-im 'get-TR'

Table 2.2 Detail of the Light Warlpiri Verbal Auxiliary System, Using 1SG as the Pronoun Form (Adapted from O'Shannessy [Forthcoming])

	1SG	*1PL*	*2SG*	*3SG*	*3DU/PL*	*2DUAL*
Future	a-l	wi-l	yu-l	i-l	de-l	yutu/yumob garra
Future/ Should	a-rra	wi-rra	yu-rra	i-rra	de-rra	yutu/yumob garra
Might/ Should	a-rra	wi-rra	yu-rra yu mada	i-rra	de-rra	yutu/yumob beta / mada
Might/ Should	a gada	wi gada	yu gada	i gada	dei gada	yutu/yumob gada
Want to	a-na	wi-na	yu-na	i-na	de-na	yutu/yumob wana
Nonfuture (i.e., present or past)	a-m	wi-m	yu-m	i-m	de-m	yutu/yumob / yutu/yumob bin
Past completed	a bin	wi bin	yu bin	i bin	dei bin	yutu/yumob bin

	1SG	*1PL*	*2SG*	*3SG*	*3DU/PL*	*2DUAL*
Past progressive	a was	wi was	yu was	i was	dei was	?
Might	a mait	wi mait	yu mait	i mait	dei mait	yutu/yumob mait
Past Negative	a neban	wi neban	yu neban	i neban	dei neban	?
Present Negative	a neba	wi neba	yu neba	i neba	dei neba	yutu/yumob neba
Future Negative	a won	wi won	yu won	i won	dei won	yutu/yumob won

form *bin* 'PST' occurs only rarely, and the Light Warlpiri construction of pronoun-plus- -*m* 'NONFUTURE' occurs frequently. The *bin* 'PST' form occurs consistently in the contact languages spoken in the region, including Kriol (Sandefur 1991; Schultze-Berndt, Meakins, and Angelo 2013) and varieties of Aboriginal English (Butcher 2008; Harkins 1994).

The emergence of Light Warlpiri shows both a partial shift away from speaking Warlpiri as the younger speakers' primary language and a partial maintenance of Warlpiri under great pressure to shift, as Light Warlpiri contains a significant amount of Warlpiri syntax, morphology, lexicon, and discourse pragmatics (O'Shannessy forthcoming), and can be considered a new variety of Warlpiri. It reflects not only speakers' negotiation of pressure on them from the wider Australian arena to speak more English but also the importance of speaking Warlpiri, and resistance to the domination of English (cf. Gal 1988: 249).

The cohort that conventionalized and brought innovations into Light Warlpiri is now around thirty to forty years old, and there is a third generation of Light Warlpiri speakers in some families (the third generation is aged under approximately five years at the time of writing). For these speakers Light Warlpiri is their primary everyday language, and they also learn Warlpiri from birth, and tend to increase the amount that they speak Warlpiri as they grow up. In everyday interactions, Light Warlpiri speakers hear and interact in Warlpiri as well as in Light Warlpiri. While only younger speakers speak Light Warlpiri, speakers of all ages interact in Warlpiri to different extents. Light Warlpiri speakers also learn English at school, and have an awareness and understanding of the ways of speaking of people in other communities in the region.

A conversation involving Light Warlpiri speakers often includes both Light Warlpiri and Warlpiri, with switching between clauses, and the diagnostic of each variety is the verb structure. I identify a clause as Warlpiri if it contains the Warlpiri auxiliary and verb structure, as in (6), and as Light Warlpiri if it contains the Light Warlpiri auxiliary and verb structure, as in (7) and (8), regardless of whether the verb has a Warlpiri (7) or English/Kriol (8) stem.

(6)	*maliki-ji*	lada-*ng*	*katu-rnu*	*yalyu-kurra*
	dog-TOP	ladder-ERG	press.down.on-PST	blood-ALL

'The ladder squashed the dog, until it bled.'
(Warlpiri, ERGstory_WiWC20)

(7)	bat	i-m	*katirn*-im	*jarntu*	*yalyu-kurra*
	but	3SG-NFUT	press.down.on-TR	dog	blood-ALL

'But it squashed the dog until it bled.'
(Light Warlpiri, ERGstory_LA58)

(8)	i-m	flaten-im
	3SG-NFUT	flatten-TR

'It flattened it.' (Light Warlpiri, ERGstory_LA64)

2.1. Light Warlpiri Verb Structure

An interesting feature of Light Warlpiri is that although most verbs are derived from Kriol and/or English, Warlpiri verb stems are also part of the Light Warlpiri verb system, reanalyzed to fit Light Warlpiri verbal structure (Meakins and O'Shannessy 2012). This is noteworthy because most verbs in Light Warlpiri are drawn from English and

Kriol, and the use of Kriol verbal lexicon and morphology is one of the defining features of Light Warlpiri (O'Shannessy 2005). In (6) the verb *katirn-im* is a restructured Warlpiri verb. In Warlpiri the verb form is *kati-rni* 'press.down.on-NPST.' In Light Warlpiri the final vowel is deleted and the stem reanalyzed to include part of the tense inflection, making it consonant-final, and a Kriol transitive suffix is attached to the reanalyzed stem (cf. Meakins and O'Shannessy 2012).

Additionally, Warlpiri verbs can be complex verbs, consisting of a coverb and an inflecting verb. Most coverbs cannot occur independently of an inflecting verb and do not take inflections themselves (Nash 1982). The entire complex verb forms a single phonological phrase (Meakins and O'Shannessy 2012; Pentland and Laughren 2005). Examples are given in (9), where both *rdurrkurl-jirri-rni* 'make. noise-NPST' and *kurnta-ngarri-rni* 'shame-tell-NPST' are complex verbs, formed from a coverb and inflecting verb.

(9) *Kaji* *yapa-ngku* *rdurrkurl-jirri-rni* *ngurra-kari-rla*
REL.COMP person-ERG make.noise-NPST camp-other-LOC
'When someone makes a lot of noise in another camp'

yapa-kari-rli *kapi* *kurnta-ngarri-rni.*
person-other-ERG FUT.COMP shame-tell-NPST
'another person will tell him off.'
(Warlpiri dictionary database, author's gloss)

Both types of Warlpiri verb, simplex and complex, are present in Light Warlpiri, with restructuring. The differences in the verbal constructions between Warlpiri and Light Warlpiri, and the two types of verb source in Light Warlpiri, are summarized in table 2.3.

The presence of Warlpiri verb stems in Light Warlpiri, and the use of code-switching practices between the two varieties leads to the question of the relationship between the two types of practice, especially in terms of contributing to the maintenance of Warlpiri. The following data show (a) the occurrence of restructured Warlpiri-derived verb stems in Light Warlpiri and (b) code-switches between

Table 2.3 The Types of Verbal Construction in Light Warlpiri and Warlpiri

Light Warlpiri		*Warlpiri*	
Kriol-derived verbs (auxiliary restructure)	*Warlpiri-derived verbs (verb restructure)*	*Warlpiri simplex verb*	*Warlpiri complex verb*
wi-m puk-im 1PL-NFUT poke-TR	wi-m *pantirn*-im 1PL-NFUT poke-TR	*panti-rni ka-rlipa* poke-NPST PRES-1PL	*kari-nya-nyi ka-rna* other-see-NPST PRES-1SG
wi-m hit-im 1PL-NFUT hit-TR	wi-m *pakarn*-im 1PL-NFUT hit-TR	*paka-rni ka-rlipa* hit-NPST PRES-1PL	*kurnta-ngarri-rni ka-rna* shame-tell-NPST PRES-1SG

Warlpiri and Light Warlpiri. The two ways of speaking—Light Warlpiri, with Warlpiri-derived verb stems, and practices of switching between Light Warlpiri and Warlpiri—both support speakers' knowledge of, and psycholinguistic access to, Warlpiri verbs, and therefore maintenance of these aspects of Warlpiri.

In the next section the data collection for the study is described, and the data are presented in section 4. In section 5, I discuss the data and implications for language maintenance.

3. Data Collection

The data for this study are part of a longitudinal project on the emergence and development of Light Warlpiri, and speakers' bilingualism in the two languages. Specifically, data for this paper are of two types. One type is elicited data from discussions of the use of verbs in Light Warlpiri with two speakers, aged in their twenties and thirties. The two speakers are accustomed to discussing Light Warlpiri with me, and have been doing so for several years. Drawing on Hale (1982), speakers were asked how they talked about specific Warlpiri verbal concepts when they speak Light Warlpiri. In response to this prompt, the speakers created scenarios in which they would use the concepts and gave examples of their use in Light Warlpiri. The second type of data are narratives told from picture stimuli. A series of wordless picture books were used, designed to elicit a range of constructions (O'Shannessy, 2004), and to investigate grammatical categories relevant to social cognition (San Roque et al. 2012). In the case of the social cognition picture stimuli, two speakers interacted with each other, talking about the pictures and narrating the story from different perspectives, for example, from a third-person perspective, and then from a first-person perspective as part of a role play. Speakers create their own narrative from the picture stimuli. The method allows speakers to speak naturally in their own style, with the pictures prompting informational content and language function. The method enables comparability across speakers because all speakers are responding to the same sets of pictures. Speakers were not prompted to speak in any specific style or variety; they were only asked to speak the way they usually do.

Twenty adult Light Warlpiri speakers have been recorded undertaking this task since 2004, and the data presented in this paper are from recordings of speakers in 2015. Data presented in this paper, by five speakers, are believed to be representative of Light Warlpiri.

4. The Data

This section presents the illustrative data. The two ways of speaking in focus in this paper are represented—the presence of restructured Warlpiri verb stems in Light Warlpiri and code-switching between Light Warlpiri and Warlpiri.

4.1. Reanalyzed Warlpiri Verb Stems in Light Warlpiri

Examples 10 to 13 show the presence of restructured Warlpiri verb stems in Light Warlpiri, from picture stimuli and elicited data. Names have been removed to preserve anonymity.

(10a)	maja-wan	*inya*	i-m	*kurnta-ngarrirn*-im
	mother-one	DEM	3SG-NFUT	shame-tell-TR

'that mother there she told him off'

(b)	wel	*nyuntu-ng*	na	*waja*
	DIS	2SG-ERG	DIS	EMPH

'well you, really,'

(c)	yu-rra	shut-im	*wurnturu-waja*	puluku-*k waja*
	2SG-FUT	shoot-TR	far-EMPH	bullock-DAT-EMPH

'you should shoot the bullock from far away'

(ERGstory_LA92_2015) Picture stimuli data

In (10), the Warlpiri complex verb *kurnta-ngarri-rni* 'shame-tell-NPST' is restructured to *kurnta-ngarrirn-im* 'shame-tell-TR', with the final vowel deleted and the Kriol transitive suffix attached to the reanalyzed verb stem. The verb is transitive in Warlpiri, and accordingly is transitive also in Light Warlpiri. A transitive verb with the Kriol transitive suffix attached is the most frequently occurring transitive verb structure in Light Warlpiri.

(11a)	[name]	yu	sidan	*yartiwaji-rla-juk*	anis
	name	2SG	sit.down	TV-LOC-still	DIS

'[name] you just sit there watching TV'

(b)	yu	kaan	kam	aut-*rlang*
	2SG	can.not	come	out-also

'you don't come outside'

(c) an [name] mam *nyiya-janga* *wara-parnpim* *ngaju-k-juku?*
CONJ name mum what-ABL call.attention.to 1SG-DAT-YET
'and [name], 'Mum why are you picking on me?'
(Elicit_A21_AC58_2015) Elicitation data

In (11), the speaker explains the use of the verb *wara-parnpim* 'call. attention.to', from the Warlpiri complex verb *wara-parnpi-mi* 'call. attention.to-NPST'. The verb has been restructured with the final vowel deleted. In the case of this verb, once the final vowel is deleted the word-shape fits the structure of Light Warlpiri verbs, ending in the word-final *im*, and a transitive marker from Kriol (that would be an additional *-im*) is not added. This is presumably a phonotactic constraint in Light Warlpiri (Meakins and O'Shannessy 2012).

(12) Lajamanu stail, "ah a-m *kari-nyan* yu *wiyarrpa*"
Lajamanu style DIS 1SG-NONFUT other-see 2SG affect
'In Lajamanu Style, "ah, I didn't recognize you, poor thing" '.
(Elicit_A21_AC58_2015) Elicitation data

In (12), the Warlpiri complex verb *kari-nyanyi* 'not recognise' (lit. 'other-see') is restructured by final vowel deletion. In this case also there is no Kriol transitive marker attached, and the reason for this is not yet clear.

(13a) [name] i-m *japird*-ing bo yu *nyuntu-k* na
name 3SG-NFUT threaten-PROG DAT 2SG 2SG-DAT DIS
'[Name] he's threatening you, you know'

(b) i-rra hit yu *inya-ng*
3SG-FUT hit 2SG DEM-ERG
'he'll hit you, he will!' (Elicit_A21_AC58_2015) Elicitation data

In example (13), the Warlpiri verb *japirdi-pinyi* 'threaten-attack' is restructured so that only the Warlpiri coverbal element is present as a verb in Light Warlpiri, with the English progressive affix *-ing* attached. This structure of producing only a Warlpiri coverb as an inflecting verb in Light Warlpiri is so far rare in the data.

4.2. Warlpiri Verbs in Code-Switching Data

The following examples show speakers code-switching between Light Warlpiri and Warlpiri. In the examples, the clauses that I identify as being Warlpiri clauses are underlined and in italics, to show that these are not categorized as Light Warlpiri.

(14a)	A:	na	*walku*	a-m	gib-im	*wumara*	de	*inya-ku-ju*
		NEG	NEG	1SG-NFUT	give-TR	money	DET	DEM-DAT-TOP

'no, it's not true, I gave money to that one there'

(b)	B:	*walku*	yu	trik-in	baga
		NEG	2SG	trick-PROG	bugger

'no, you're lying'

(c)	B:	*ka-rna-ng*	*paka-rn*
		pres-1SGS-2SG.O	hit-NPST

'I'll hit you' (FamArgStory_A53_A54) Picture stimuli data

Example (14) is from a recording of two speakers role-playing characters represented in the social cognition picture set and speaking in the first person. Speaker A speaks in Light Warlpiri in (14a), identified by the combination of the Light Warlpiri auxiliary *a-m* '1SG-NFUT', and the Kriol transitive verb *gib-im* 'give-TR'. In (14c), the speaker switches to Warlpiri with the clause *ka-rna-ng paka-rn* 'pres-1SGS-2SG.O hit-NPST'. In the realization of this clause, the Warlpiri object auxiliary form *-ngku* '2SG.O' is reduced to *-ng*, and the verb *pakarni* 'hit-NPST' has the final vowel deleted. This example shows that in Warlpiri sometimes final vowels are deleted or not voiced (Bavin and Shopen 1985; O'Shannessy 2016), and this was likely part of the pathway for the reanalysis of the verbs in Light Warlpiri. The clause is identified as Warlpiri because of the presence of the Warlpiri auxiliary, and because when this verb occurs in a Light Warlpiri clause it does take the Kriol transitive suffix, -*im*, not present here.

(15a) laik [name1] bin kuk-im *kuyu* sapa
like name PST cook-TR meat supper
'like [name1] cooked meat for supper'

(b) an *[name2]-k-rla yirra-rnu*
CONJ name-DAT-DAT put-PST
'and put it out for [name2]'

(c) an *jarntu-ng-rla marlaja-nga-rnu*
CONJ dog-ERG-DAT assoc-eat-PST
'and the dog ate it on her'

(d) an [name1] mait shaut "Wara! [name2] neba waj-im *kuyu*"
CONJ name might shout DIS name NEG watch-TR meat
'and [name1] might shout "Oh no! [name2] didn't watch the meat"'

(e) *marlaja-nga-rnu-rla jarntu-ng*
assoc-eat-PST-DAT dog-ERG
'The dog ate it on her!' (Elicit_A21_AC58_2015) Elicitation data

In (15), the speaker gives an example of the use of the Warlpiri coverb *marlaja*- glossed as 'because of', or 'associated with'. She paints a scenario of someone leaving food out and not paying attention to the presence of a dog, who eats the food. The use of this verb invokes the meaning of a negative consequence for an entity that is neither the agent nor recipient of the action depicted by the verb. The case array of this Warlpiri verb is ergative-dative. The verb selects ergative case to occur on the transitive agent, and dative case on the nominal that references the affected entity (-*ku*/-*ki*), and in the verbal auxiliary (-*rla*). The speaker employs both ergative and dative case marking (in lines 15b, c, and e) in keeping with Warlpiri conventions (cf. Hale et al. 1995: 1431). This shows that although the speaker's primary way of speaking is Light Warlpiri, when she speaks Warlpiri she includes full Warlpiri verbal and nominal morphology.

(16a) a-m tok "[name] go shop-*kirra*"
1SG-NFUT talk name go shop-ALL
'I said "[name] go to the shop" '

(b) an [name] mait tok bo me
CONJ name might talk DAT me
'and [name] might say to me'

(c) mam *nyiya-jangka nyuntu* yu *warungka*? *nyurru* a-m go shop.
mum what-ABL 2SG 2SG crazy finished 1SG-NFUT go shop
'Mum, why are you crazy? I already went to the shop.'

(d) ah well *ngayi-rna waparlku-wangka-ja*
DIS well DIS-1SGS not.knowing-speak-PST
'Ah! well I just talked without knowing'

(e) a did-n nou yu-m go shop
1SG did-NEG know 2SG-NFUT go shop
'I didn't know you went to the shop'

(f) yeh *yi-rna waparlku-wangka-ja kula-ngana lawa-juk*
yes so-1SGS not.knowing-speak-PST NEG.COMP-allegedly NEG-YET
'yeh I just talked without knowing, I wrongly thought you hadn't gone'

(g) *kala ya-nu*
DISJ go-PST
'but you had gone'

(h) a did-n nou yu bin go shop
1SG did-NEG know 2SG PST go shop
'I didn't know you had gone to the shop.'
(Elicit_A21_AC58_2015) Elicitation data

In example (16), the speaker creates a scenario in which she might use the Warlpiri complex verb *waparlku-wangka-* 'not.knowing-speak'.

In the scenario she asks her daughter to go the shop, not realizing that her daughter had already been to the shop. By way of explanation she explains that she talked without knowing. In the example, she switches between Light Warlpiri and Warlpiri clauses, each with its full syntactic and morphological structure.

The final example, (17), also shows switches between Light Warlpiri and Warlpiri clauses, each with full syntactic and morphological structure.

(17a) [name] mait tok
name might talk
'[name] might say'

(b) mam, *parda-rni-rlipa-rla Nungarrayi-ki*
mum, wait-NPST-1PL.INCL-DAT sub.sect-DAT
'Mum, we'll wait for Nungarrayi'

(c) wi weit *waja Nungarrayi-k*
1PL wait EMPH sub.sect-DAT
'we'll wait for Nungarrayi'

(d) *parda-rni-rlipa-rla Nungarrayi-ki*
wait-NPST-1PL.INCL-DAT sub.sect-DAT
'we'll wait for Nungarrayi' (Elicit_A21_AC58_2015) Elicitation data

In example (17), the speaker creates a scene in which her daughter suggests that they wait for the speaker's grandmother, whose subsection term, or skin name, is Nungarrayi. The Warlpiri verb *parda-* 'wait for', takes an ergative-dative case array, with the dative occurring both in the verbal auxiliary (*-rla*) and on the nominal referencing the entity being waited for (*-ku/-ki*). In the example the agents of waiting, the speaker and her daughter, are not referenced by overt transitive nominals, so there is no opportunity for ergative case marking to occur in the clauses. But the dative is obligatory in the verbal clauses, and accordingly does occur, in lines 17b and 17d.

It also occurs on the nominal *Nungarrayi*, in the same lines. Both Warlpiri and Light Warlpiri share the convention of using subsection terms, or skin names, as the most frequent form of reference to people in the third person.

5. Motivations for the Reanalyzed Constructions and for Code-Switching

Taking an emic perspective, the speakers explained that switching between languages fluidly is part of what they call "Lajamanu Style" or "our language." It is part of their whole languages repertoire and part of being speakers of Warlpiri from one specific community. I draw on O'Shannessy (2015) in surmising that these ways of speaking indicate that the speakers are members of overlapping communities of practice (cf. Eckert and McConnell-Ginet 2007; Wenger 1998). Speaking Warlpiri shows membership of the wider Warlpiri community of practice, along with other Warlpiri communities (where Light Warlpiri is not spoken), and speaking Light Warlpiri shows membership of the local Light Warlpiri-speaking community of practice.

Turning to an etic perspective, the motivations appear to be the discourse motivations frequently identified in code-switching research (e.g., Gumperz 1982; Poplack 1980). The discourse motivations of repetition, emphasis, and contextual orientation are present, as well as that of semantic nuance or Poplack's *mot juste*, which is also part of conventionalization, becoming the regular or expected way of expressing a specific meaning.

The role of both semantic nuance and conventionalization of expression is seen in all of the examples of Warlpiri verbs in Light Warlpiri. These include example (10) *kurnta-ngarrirn*-im 'shame-tell-TR', example (11) *wara-parnpim* 'call.attention.to', (12) *kari-nyan* 'not.recognize,' and (13) *japird*-ing 'threaten-PROG'. Each of these verbs encapsulates a meaning that is expressed by a verb in Warlpiri, and would be expressed differently in English or Kriol. In principle, an option for the speakers would be to always use a reanalyzed verb in a Light Warlpiri clause, on analogy with other reanalyzed verbs, but the conventionalized preference of speakers is to sometimes use a full Warlpiri clause. Using a Warlpiri verb invokes a sense of being Warlpiri and speaking in Warlpiri, and is the conventionalized expression among the speakers (cf. Poplack 1980). Similarly, I propose the same motivation for the reanalyzed Warlpiri verbs in a Light Warlpiri clause—this kind of construction has become conventionalized among the speakers, has a Warlpiri identity element, and is *mot juste* 'just right'(cf. Poplack 1980) for speakers in the context of each occurrence.

In example 17, three consecutive clauses express the desire to wait for Nungarrayi, using clauses that alternate between Warlpiri, with the Warlpiri verb *parda-rni* 'wait-NPST', and Light Warlpiri, using the Kriol/English verb *wait*. The change in language between clauses highlights both the repetition and its emphatic function (e.g., Gumperz, 1982). The emphasis is also made clear in the use of a Warlpiri word *waja* 'emphasis' in the Light Warlpiri clause (17c).

Example 14 shows a switch between languages at the point where an accusation changes to a threat (14b–c). In the role-play scenario based on picture stimuli, using the first-person perspective, Speaker B accuses Speaker A of lying in 14b. In line 14c, Speaker B threatens to hit the other speaker, and a change from Light Warlpiri to Warlpiri coincides with the change of utterance function.

Both styles of speaking, integrating Warlpiri verbs into Light Warlpiri, and code-switching between Light Warlpiri and Warlpiri, help to keep Warlpiri verbs psycholinguistically accessible to speakers. Both styles are beneficial in achieving this result. Frequently using Warlpiri verbs in Light Warlpiri means that they are readily accessible when a speaker wants to switch to Warlpiri, because higher-frequency items are more accessible and easier to process than lower-frequency items (e.g., Becker 1979; Forster 1976; Levelt et al. 1999; Morton 1976; Strijkers, Costa, and Thierry 2010). The speaker needs to utilize the Warlpiri verbal morphology and syntax selected by the verb, but the root word is more readily available. Similarly, switching to Warlpiri for small amounts of time, for instance for a single clause, which entails the use of a Warlpiri verb with its full morphology, also means that the verbs and the morphology are used more frequently, and are therefore more readily accessible should the speaker want to use them. It also means that the verbs are available for use in Light Warlpiri, helping to keep more Warlpiri content in Light Warlpiri. The limited data drawn on here do not show the same lexical items used in both Light Warlpiri (with restructuring) and Warlpiri, but I argue that the use of some Warlpiri verbs in either style of interaction is helpful in making other verbs accessible.

6. Conclusion

In this chapter I have presented data illustrating the use of reanalyzed Warlpiri verb stems in Light Warlpiri, and code-switching between Light Warlpiri and Warlpiri, identified by the use of Warlpiri verbs and verbal morphology. The reanalyzed verbs are especially interesting because most verbs in Light Warlpiri are drawn from English and Kriol, and use of Kriol verbal lexical items and morphology is one of the defining features of Light Warlpiri. The code-switching data show that although Light Warlpiri represents a partial shift away from Warlpiri as the speakers' primary everyday language, Light Warlpiri speakers also speak Warlpiri and use both ways of speaking to indicate sophisticated semantic and discourse nuances in their everyday interactions.

There is a clear morphological distinction between the use of restructured Warlpiri verb stems in Light Warlpiri, where transitive verbs may take a Kriol transitive marker, *-im* 'TR', and the use of full Warlpiri verbal morphology in Warlpiri clauses, instances of code-switching. The use of these verbs in both Light Warlpiri and when code-switching helps to make them more accessible for subsequent use in Warlpiri (cf. Dorian 1982).

Earlier code-switching practices led to the development of the mixed language, Light Warlpiri. Yet now, fluid code-switching practices help to keep Warlpiri verbs accessible to speakers, and therefore are a strategy for the maintenance of Warlpiri.

Acknowledgments

Funding: National Science Foundation #1348013 "Documentation and acquisition of Light Warlpiri and Warlpiri"

Lajamanu community members and research assistants, especially Deanne Burns Napanangka† (deceased) and Tanya Hargraves Napanangka; David Nash; participants of the Australian Languages Workshop, Australian National University, 2015.

Abbreviations

1	first person
2	second person
ABL	ablative case
AFFECT	AFFECTION
AGR	Agreement
ALL	ALLATIVE CASE
COM	comitative case
COMP	complementizer
CONJ	CONJUNCTION
DAT	dative
DEM	demonstrative
DET	determiner

DIM	Diminutive
DIS	discourse marker
DISJ	DISJUNCTION
DL	dual
EMPH	emphatic
ERG	ergative case
EVIT	EVItative case
EXCL	exclusive
FOC	FOCUS
FUT	future
INCL	inclusive
INTENS	INTENSIFIER
ITER	ITERATIVE
LOC	locative case
NEG	NEGATIVE
NFUT	nonfuture
NMLZ	nominalizer
NS	NONSUBJECT
O/OBJ	object
PERF	PERFECTIVE
PERL	PERLATIVE CASE
PL	plural
POSS	POSSESSIVE CASE
PRO	PRONOUN
PROG	PROGRESSIVE
PST	PAST
Q	INTERROGATIVE
REDUP	REDUPLICATED
S	subject
SG	singular
TOP	TOPIC
TR	transitive
V	VERB

References

Auer, Peter. 1999. From code-switching via language mixing to fused lects: Toward a dynamic typology of bilingual speech. *International Journal of Bilingualism*, 3(4): 309–32.

Backus, Ad. 2003. Can a mixed language be conventionalized alternational code-switching? In Yaron Matras and Peter Bakker (Eds.), *The mixed language debate*, 237–70. Berlin: Mouton de Gruyter.

Bakker, Peter. 1994. Michif, the Cree-French mixed language of the Metis buffalo hunters in Canada. In Peter Bakker and Maarten Mous (Eds.), *Mixed languages: 15 case studies in language intertwining*, 13–33. Amsterdam: IFOTT.

Bakker, Peter. 1997. *A language of our own: The genesis of Michif, the mixed Cree-French language of the Canadian Metis* (vol. 10). Oxford: Oxford University Press.

Bakker, Peter. 2003. Mixed languages as autonomous systems. In Peter Bakker and Yaron Matras (Eds.), *The mixed language debate*, 107–50. Berlin: Mouton de Gruyter.

Bavin, Edith L., and Tim Shopen. 1985. Warlpiri and English: Languages in contact. In M. Clyne (Ed.) *Australia, meeting place of languages*, 81–94. Canberra: Pacific Linguistics.

Becker, Curtis A. 1979. Semantic context and word frequency effects in visual word recognition. *Journal of Experimental Psychology: Human Perception and Performance*, 5(2): 252–59.

Butcher, Andrew. 2008. Linguistic aspects of Australian Aboriginal English. *Clinical Linguistics and Phonetics*, 22(8): 625–42.

Crystal, Daivd. 2000. *Language death*. Cambridge: Cambridge University Press.

Dalton, Lorraine, Sandra Edwards, Rosaleen Farquarson, Sarah Oscar, and Patrick McConvell. 1995. Gurindji children's language and language maintenance. *International Journal of the Sociology of Language*, 113: 83–98.

Dorian, Nancy C. 1982. Language loss and maintenance in language contact situations. In R. D. Lambert and B. F. Freed (Eds.), *Loss of language skills*, 44–59. Rowley, MA: Newbury House.

Eckert, Penelope, and Sally McConnell-Ginet. 2007. Putting Communities of practice in their place. *Gender and Language*, 1(1): 27–37.

Fishman, Joshua. 1972. *The sociology of language*. Rowley, MA: Newbury House.

Forster, Ken. 1976. Accessing the mental lexicon. In R. Wales and E. Walker (Eds.), *New approaches to language mechanisms*, 257–87. Amsterdam: North-Holland.

Gal, Susan. 1988. The political economy of code choice. In Monica Heller (Ed.), *Code-switching: Anthropological and sociolinguistic perspectives*, 245–64. Berlin: Mouton de Gruyter.

Golovko, Evgeniy V. 1994. Mednij Aleut or Copper Island Aleut: An Aleut-Russian mixed language. In Peter Bakker and Maarten Mous (Eds.), *Mixed languages: 15 case studies in language intertwining*, 113–21. Amsterdam: IFOTT.

Gumperz, John J. 1982. *Discourse strategies*. Cambridge: Cambridge University Press.

Hale, Kenneth. 1982. Some essential features of Warlpiri verbal clauses. In Stephen Swartz (Ed.), *Papers in Warlpiri grammar: In memory of Lother Jagst*, 217–314. Darwin: Summer Institute of Linguistics-Australian Aborigines Branch.

Hale, Kenneth., Mary Laughren, and Jane Simpson. 1995. Warlpiri. In J. Jacobs, A. von Stechow, W. Sternefeld, and T. Vennemann (Eds.), *An international handbook of contemporary research*, 1430–49. Berlin: Walter De Gruyter.

Harkins, Jean. 1994. *Bridging two worlds: Aboriginal English and crosscultural understanding*. St. Lucia: University of Queensland Press.

Haugen, Einar. 1949. Problems of bilingualism. *Lingua*, 2: 271–90.

Hill, Jane H. 1993. Spanish in the Indigenous languages of Mesoamerica and the Southwest: Beyond Stage Theory to the dynamic of incorporation and resistance. *Southwest Journal of Linguistics*, 12(1): 87–108.

Hill, Jane H., and Kenneth C. Hill. 1980. Mixed grammar, purist grammar, and language attitudes in modern Nahuatl. *Language in Society*, 9(3): 321–48.

Levelt, Willem J. M., Ardi Roelofs, and Antje S. Meyer. 1999. A theory of lexical access in speech production. *Behavioral and brain sciences*, 22(1): 1–38.

Matras, Yaron, and Peter Bakker. 2003. The study of mixed languages. In Yaron Matras and Peter Bakker (Eds.), *The mixed language debate*, 1–20. Berlin: Mouton de Gruyter.

McConvell, Patrick. 1988. Mix-im-up: Aboriginal code-switching, old and new. In Monica Heller (Ed.), *Codeswitching: Anthropological and sociolinguistic perspectives*, 97–124. Berlin: Mouton de Gruyter.

McConvell, Patrick, and Felicity Meakins. 2005. Gurindji Kriol: A mixed language emerges from code-switching. *Australian Journal of Linguistics*, 25(1): 9–30.

Meakins, Felicity, and Carmel O'Shannessy. 2012. Typological constraints on verb integration in two Australian mixed languages 1, 2. *Journal of Language Contact*, 5(2): 216–46.

Morton, John. 1976. Interaction of information in word recognition. *Psychological review*, 2: 165–78.

Muysken, Pieter. 1994. Media Lengua. In Peter Bakker and Maarten Mous (Eds.), *Mixed languages: 15 case studies in language intertwining*, 201–5. Amsterdam: IFOTT.

Muysken, Pieter. 1997. Media Lengua. In Sarah Grey Thomason (Ed.), *Contact languages: A wider perspective*, 365–426. Amsterdam: John Benjamins.

Nash, David. 1982. Warlpiri verb roots and preverbs. *Work papers of SIL-AAB*, 6: 165–216.

O'Shannessy, Carmel. 2004. *The monster stories: A set of picture books to elicit overt transitive subjects in oral texts.* Unpublished series. Nijmegen: Max Planck Institute for Psycholinguistics.

O'Shannessy, Carmel. 2005. Light Warlpiri: A new language. *Australian Journal of Linguistics*, 25(1): 31–57. doi:10.1080/07268600500110472.

O'Shannessy, Carmel. 2012. The role of code-switched input to children in the origin of a new mixed language. *Linguistics*, 50(2): 328–53.

O'Shannessy, Carmel. 2013. The role of multiple sources in the formation of an innovative auxiliary category in Light Warlpiri, a new Australian mixed language. *Language*, 89(2): 328–53.

O'Shannessy, Carmel. 2015. Multilingual children increase language differentiation by indexing communities of practice. *First Language*, 35(4–5): 305–26.

O'Shannessy, Carmel. 2016. Distributions of case allomorphy by multilingual children. *Linguistic Variation*, 16(1): 68–102.

O'Shannessy, Carmel. Forthcoming. Conventionalised creativity in the emergence of a mixed language: A case study of Light Warlpiri. In Enoch Aboh and Umberto Ansaldo (Eds.), *TBA*. Amsterdam: John Benjamins.

Pentland, Christina, and Mary Laughren. 2005. Distinguishing prosodic word and phonological word in Warlpiri: Prosodic constituency in morphologically complex words. In *Proceedings of the 2004 Conference of the Australian Linguistic Society*, Sydney.

Poplack, Shana. 1980. Sometimes I'll start a sentence in Spanish y termino en Espanol: Toward a typology of code-switching. *Linguistics*, 18: 581–618.

San Roque, Lila, Lauren Gawne, Darja Hoenigman, Julia Colleen Miller, Alan Rumsey, Stef Spronck, . . . , Nicholas Evans. 2012. Getting the story straight: Language fieldwork using a narrative problem-solving task. *Language Documentation and Conservation*, 6: 135–74.

Sandefur, John. 1991. A sketch of the structure of Kriol. In Suzanne Romaine (Ed.), *Language in Australia*, 204–12. Cambridge: Cambridge University Press.

Schultze-Berndt, Eva, Felicity Meakins, and Denise Angelo. 2013. Kriol. In Susanne Michaelis, Philippe Maurer, Martin Haspelmath, and Magnus Huber (Eds.), *English-based and Dutch-based languages*, 241–51. Oxford: Oxford University Press.

Strijkers, Kristof, Albert Costa, and Guillaume Thierry. 2010. Tracking lexical access in speech production: Electrophysiological correlates of word frequency and cognate effects. *Cerebral cortex*, 20(4): 912–28.

Thomason, Sarah Grey. 1995. Language mixture: Ordinary processes, extraordinary results. In Carmen Silva-Corvalán (Ed.), *Spanish in four continents: Studies in language contact and bilingualism*, 15–33. Washington, DC: Georgetown University Press.

Thomason, Sarah Grey. 2001. *Language contact: An introduction*. Edinburgh: Edinburgh University Press.

Thomason, Sarah Grey. 2003. Social factors and linguistics processes in the emergence of stable mixed languages. In Yaron Matras and Peter Bakker (Eds.), *The mixed language debate*, 21–40. Berlin: Mouton de Gruyter.

Thomason, Sarah Grey, and Terrence Kaufman. 1988. *Language contact, creolization, and genetic linguistics*. Berkeley: University of California Press.

Vakhtin, Nikolai. 1998. Copper Island Aleut: A case of language "resurrection." In Lenore A. Grenoble and Lindsay J. Whaley (Eds.), *Endangered languages*, 317–27. Cambridge: Cambridge University Press.

Wenger, Etienne. 1998. *Communities of practice: Learning, meaning, and identity*. Cambridge: Cambridge University Press.

CHAPTER 3

Dynamics of Language Contact

On Similarities, Divergences, and Innovations in the Emergence of Creole Languages[1]

Marlyse Baptista

1. Introduction[2]

To the nonlinguist, a set of languages like English, French, Japanese, and Navajo may seem like very disparate, distinct entities that offer no ground for comparison given the different phonologies, lexicons, and grammatical structures they exhibit on the surface. This perception appears to be supported by the fact that English, French, Japanese, and Navajo belong to different language families (Germanic, Romance, Japonic, and Athabaskan, respectively) that have followed distinct historical and developmental paths.

As I discuss later, several subfields of linguistics (historical linguistics, contact linguistics, typology, generativism, and creolistics) have the opposite perspective on world languages and have made it part of their core mission to investigate the *similarities* between linguistic systems, establishing correspondences and connections among them and bringing to light the commonalities that unite them.

This paper focuses on the nature of similar features across languages and specifically on the role that such similarities may play in the emergence of Creole languages. In this respect, an examination of historical linguist Hugo Schuchardt's work provides insights about how early contact linguists may have dealt with the observable similarities among Creoles and between Creoles and their source languages.

At the outset, one must recognize that similarity itself is a vague and elusive notion. What does it mean to say that languages share similar features? How does one define similarity? To what degree and at what levels (phonological, lexical, structural) are languages similar? In a contact setting, can the notion of similarity be considered from both diachronic and synchronic perspectives? In other words, can languages become more similar to each other when they remain in contact over a long period of time, yet initially share similar features that are optimized by speakers at the onset of contact?

These are the research questions driving my inquiry into various angles from which the notion of linguistic similarities can be approached and developed. In section 2, I explore commonalities that seemingly disparate subfields of linguistics share in their attempt to identify similarities among languages. In section 3, I focus on work by Hugo Schuchardt, showing that similarities among Creoles and between Creoles and their source languages did not escape his keen sense of observation. I discuss how he originally detected the similar, congruent features that source languages may have contributed to particular Creoles like São Tomé and Cape Verdean. I also report on his observations of similarities between Creoles and non-Creoles, showing how his work straddled the subfields of historical linguistics, contact linguistics, typology, generativism, and creolistics. In section 4, I present Sally Thomason's framework of contact-induced change. I first discuss the significance of her theoretical framework in helping linguists ascertain that a particular feature is indeed the result of contact with a particular source language(s); I then proceed to show in section 5 how her framework could be potentially adapted to congruence. Section 6 summarizes the main points of this paper and provides the conclusion.

2. In Search of Similarities among World Languages

2.1. The Common Ground of Various Subfields of Linguistics

Though most would say that historical linguistics, language contact, typology, generativism, and creolistics are quite disparate, embodying distinct linguistic endeavors, driven by distinct research questions, founded on distinct theoretical assumptions, and at times holding antagonistic viewpoints on language, in this section I briefly consider what these subfields have in common.

Among other objectives, *historical linguistics* studies language change, reconstructs languages, and determines their relatedness, grouping them into language families whenever they display correspondences. In such cases, similarities are observed because languages belong to the same language family. On this topic, Lyle Campbell's (1998) definition of historical linguistics eloquently captures the way it intersects with other subfields:

> What is historical linguistics? Historical linguists study language change. . . . A very important reason why historical linguists study language change and are excited about their field is because historical linguistics contributes significantly to other sub-areas of linguistics and to linguistic theory. For example, human cognition and the human capacity for language learning are central research interests in linguistics, and historical linguistics contributes significantly to this goal. As we determine more accurately what can change and what cannot change in a language, and what the permitted versus impossible ways are in which language can change, we contribute significantly to the understanding of universal grammar, language typology and human cognition in general—fundamental to understanding our very humanity.
>
> (Campbell 1998: 1–2)

I revisit this point later when I show how Joseph Greenberg's view on language overlaps with Campbell's but from the standpoint of typology. Such comparisons clearly show how the various subfields under study intersect.

It is worth emphasizing that historical linguistics focuses both on crosslinguistic similarities that are due to a common ancestor and on similarities that are due to contact—similarities represented by Crowley's (1992) and Joseph's (1983, 2010) work, respectively. To start with Crowley:

> If we compare two different words used by two different groups of people speaking different languages, and we find that they express a similar (or identical) meaning by using similar (or, again, identical) sounds, then we need to ask ourselves this simple question: why? Maybe it is because there is some natural connection between the meaning and the form that is being used to express it. On the other hand, maybe the similarity says something about some kind of historical connection between the two languages.
>
> (Crowley 1992: 22)

Consider the languages illustrated in table 3.1 (Crowley 1992: 23). Crowley explains that it is reasonable to assume that a historical link connects all five languages. The observed similarities could have arisen because four of these languages copied a fifth or because all five copied a sixth; or one could surmise that these forms all derive from a single set of original forms that diverged in different ways (Crowley 1992: 23). As these languages are spoken in areas distant

Table 3.1 Crosslinguistic Similarities in Five Languages

Bahasa Indonesia		*Tolai*	*Paamese*	*Fijian*	*Maori*
'two'	dua	aurua	elu	rua	rua
'three'	tiga	autul	etel	tolu	toru
'four'	əmp	aivat	ehat	va	fa
'five'	lima	ailima	elim	lima	rima
'stone'	batu	vat	ahat	vatu	kofatu

from one another, Crowley concludes that 'the most likely explanation for their similarity in these widely dispersed languages is that each of these words is derived from a single original form (issued from an original protolanguage)' (Crowley 1992: 24).

Now, what about the similarities that emerge due to contact? Indeed, as observed by linguists, languages can develop similar features over time due to intense, long-term contact in an area of convergence, or *Sprachbund* (see Joseph 1983, 2010). The Balkans, where Albanian, Serbo-Croatian, Greek, Romanian, and Bulgarian (among others) have had prolonged contact in contiguous geographic areas, is a famous case of areal convergence. The long-term contact is assumed to have led to shared features across multiple grammatical domains of these languages. In another well-known case, reported by John Gumperz and Robert Wilson (1971), long-term contact in the Kupwar region of India between multilingual speakers of the dialects of the Dravidian language Kannada and the Indic languages Urdu and Marathi has gradually led to the elimination of their core differences, giving rise to complete intertranslatability. A single grammar has emerged from Kannada, Urdu, and Marathi, with three distinct lexicons that are retained as markers of social and ethnic identity.

For *historical linguists* and *contact linguists* studying areal convergence, the focus is on the process that allows distinct languages that evolve in the same general region to develop crosslinguistic similarities that originate from one or several possible language sources. In this scenario, similar features are disseminated through long-term contact among contiguous languages, leading to contact-induced change in these languages. Crucially in this case, such features were absent in the languages prior to contact and the exact source of the features is not always known. The study of language contact and contact-induced change has laid the groundwork for the development of important theoretical frameworks accounting for how and why languages change and the range of possible outcomes (Thomason 2001a; Thomason and Kaufman 1988). This is a point I revisit in section 4.

Though *typology* is also concerned with the diversity among world languages, one of its main objectives is to describe and account for the properties that languages have in common, whether or not they belong to the same language family. In other words, investigating the properties that some languages have in common allows linguists to classify them as belonging to the same 'type' of language.

On this topic, Cooreman and Goyvaerts (1980: 615) note that human beings have long been puzzled by the many differences and similarities among languages—in sum, by 'the paradox of being one and the same in one sense and being strikingly different in another.' These authors also capture the ironic parallels between the views of the language faculty held by *typology* and *generative syntax*, two subfields that typically do not see eye to eye when it comes to defining the nature of language. On this topic, they cite Greenberg (1976):

> Language universals are by their very nature summary statements about characteristics or tendencies shared by all human speakers. As such they constitute the most general laws of a science of linguistics. . . . [T]his study of language universals is intimately connected with the establishment of scientific laws in the linguistic aspects of human behavior.
>
> (Greenberg 1976: xv, xxv)

Elsewhere, Greenberg notes that beyond the surface differences that languages display, similar principles seem to be regulating them:

> The problem of universals in the study of human language as in that of human culture in general concerns the possibility of generalizations which have as their scope all languages or all cultures. *The question is whether underlying the diversities which are observable with relative ease there exist valid general principles*. Such invariants would serve to specify in a precise manner the notion of "human nature" whether in language or in other aspects of human behavior. They would, in effect, on the lowest level correspond to the "empirical generalization" of the natural sciences. On higher levels, they may be

> dignified by the name of laws. The search for universals, therefore, coincides on this view with the search for laws of human behavior, in the present context more specifically those of linguistic behavior.
> (Greenberg 1966: 10; my emphasis)

Cooreman and Goyvaerts (1980: 616) compare Greenberg's view of universals with that of generative grammarians, who also highlight the explanatory power of universals:

> We are looking for explanations of the facts of individual languages, embodied in grammars, and we are looking for explanations for these explanations, a general theory of language.
> (Bach 1974: 156)

A central goal of *generative syntax* is to show that no matter how dissimilar they may seem on the surface, there is a finite set of rules and principles that can account for the syntax of all the world's languages. Like Greenberg (but the comparison stops here), Noam Chomsky envisions a theory of language that organizes observable linguistic data based on certain systematic criteria and that additionally can explain adequately essential principles underlying the cognitive capacity of humans. Any genuine theory must be able to capture general properties of language (Chomsky 2000: 8).

As for *Creolistics*, many scholars have investigated the linguistic features that a given Creole has in common with one or several of the languages that contributed to its genesis. More specifically, Creolists like Chris Corne (1999) have noted that the structurally congruent, similar features that source languages have in common are more likely to be selected by speakers to contribute to the grammatical makeup of a Creole language. Focusing on new French varieties and French-based Creoles spoken in territories that include New Caledonia, Reunion Island, Louisiana, the West Indies, French Guiana, and Mauritius, Corne identifies grammatical domains (to be illustrated later) where he argues that congruence between source languages like Bantu languages and French nonstandard varieties has occurred. He also explores the constraints that may play a role in which variants are retained, and he takes into account speakers' attitudes (Thomason 1999, 2001, 2007). Methodologically, he provides a comparative study of the languages that he knows were present in a given contact situation and notes that congruence may have taken place between substrates and lexifiers or between substrates alone.

2.2. Corne and the Quest for Syntactic Similarities

Corne (1999) argues that in various grammatical domains of contact languages like Creoles, congruence between source languages has occurred; at the same time, he explores the constraints that may contribute to determining which variants are retained. Among other domains, he discusses verb fronting, sentence-final question words, and consecutive constructions involving conjunctionless or asyndetic coordination,[3] which he attributes to the 'fortuitous congruence of both Malagasy and Bantu languages' (1999: 8). For reasons of space, I focus here solely on verb fronting, a particular case of congruence that is representative of Corne's approach.

In both Isle de France Creole (IFC) and Reunion Creole, Corne (1999: 8) observes a high frequency of verb fronting (often featuring subject-verb inversion) to express emphasis, as in *rode Zan* 'seek John' in (1) (verb fronting is signaled with boldface). Corne proposes that this may result from congruence between Bantu languages and French nonstandard varieties.

(1) **rode Zan** ti ape rod so lisyeri, me li pa fin truv li. (Mauritian)
seek John PAST PROG seek his dog but he NEG find it
'Although he was looking everywhere for his dog, John couldn't find it.' (Corne 1999:191)

The Bantu languages, which include Swahili (2), Haya (3), and Makhuwa (4), use similar verb fronting to express emphasis. They display verb nominalization via an infinitive prefix whose role is to highlight the idea expressed by the verb (Corne 1999:193):

(2) **ku-cheza tu-**li-cheza kutwa (Swahili)
INF-play we-PAST-play all.day
'We played all day long.'

(3) **oku-lya** tu-ka-lya (Haya)
INF-eat we-PAST-eat
'We really ate!', 'As for what we ate! (unbelievable!)'

(4) **o-lya** **ni-**ho-lya (Makhuwa)
INF-eat we-PAST-eat
'As for what we *ate*!' (Corne 1999: 193)

Corne makes the case that congruence between Bantu languages and French dialects of the seventeenth and eighteenth centuries (as in (5)), could have favored verb fronting with an emphatic interpretation in IFC and Reunion Creole:

(5) **Chanter**, par Dieu je chanteray. (French)
to.sing by God I will.sing
'By God, I will sing'. (Corne 1999: 195)

Corne (1999: 23–24) is careful to note that congruence may take place not just between substrates and lexifiers but in fact between substrates alone. For instance, he argues that in the case of Tayo, congruent structures from the Kanak languages Drubéa and Cèmuhi resulted in Kanak-type patterns that overlapped with syntactic input from the French lexifier, leading to the emergence of novel structures. Corne proposes that the innovations emerging from this particular contact situation are based not on the 'highest common factor' of the French and Kanak grammars but on a selection of features from the source languages interwoven in a novel way. The Kanak languages being typologically similar, this would have allowed their speakers to use French words with Kanak structures that were relatively distant from French but still understandable. Not inhibiting communication in a major way would have favored their reinforcement and ultimate retention in the emerging interethnic vehicular language.

In this seminal work reporting on several cases of congruence across French varieties and French-based Creoles, Corne offers a number of concepts that are precursors to recent developments in Creolistics. He proposes that transfers from source languages will contribute to a variational pool to the extent that the selected variants that are retained in the new language are subject to constraints/principles such as frequency, transparency (the meaning is easily recoverable), and simplicity (Corne 1999: 43/230). Other linguistic factors favoring the selection of certain features over others are salience or ease of perception, transparency (one form, one meaning), and congruence between substrates and superstrates or (as we have seen) among substrates alone (Corne 1999: 230). Corne is cautious to add that the characteristics of the languages in contact dictate which constraints/principles drive the selection of a given set of features (Corne 1999: 230). This means that congruence may or may not play a role and when it does not, the lexifier could take over; specifically, Corne states, the less congruence there is among the source languages, the more influences the superstrate can exert on the local linguistic ecology via leveling, dialectal mixture, and other processes (Corne 1999: 174).

Corne's proposal also takes into account external factors that carry different weights, hence lead to different outcomes in terms of which features are selected. These factors are the demographics of the population, the type of economy (plantation vs. settlement colony), continued or disrupted contact with the lexifier, typological traits of the languages in contact, how quickly the speakers need to devise an interethnic means of communication, prestige of one language over another, and power relationships between speakers (master vs. enslaved population) (Corne 1999: 230).

In summary, Corne (1999) has two objectives. He shows how congruence manifests itself by comparing the same syntactic structures and their meaning among the languages in contact; and in so doing, he presents a set of internal and external factors that play a role in which features are selected to participate in the emergence of a new language variety and/or Creole while also allowing for innovations.

Corne's analysis of syntactic structures in languages in contact shows not only that similar syntactic constructions are probabilistically more likely to be selected by the emerging language but also, crucially, that similarities between languages in contact do not entail that structures present in the source languages are copied exactly (see Babel and Pfänder 2014; Thomason 2014); rather, the emerging language displays some degree of divergence and innovation.

Just as Corne investigates syntactic similarities between languages contributing to the formation of a new language variety and/or Creole, Schuchardt detected such similarities at the morphological and lexical levels, as we will see next.

3. Schuchardt (1882, 1883, 1885, 1888, 1909): In Search of Morphological and Lexical Similarities

Just as speakers have been noted to select certain similar syntactic structures in source languages to contribute to the creation of a new language (i.e., a Creole), they can also detect congruent forms in other domains, such as the phonology, morphology, and lexicon.

In this section, I discuss observations by Hugo Schuchardt (1882: 19–20), who was among the first to note the presence of similar morphemes and lexemes in languages in contact and the role they can play in Creole emergence. Many Creolists since then have examined or made passing observations about congruence in Creoles. To mention a handful of scholars, John Holm (1988), Peck (1988), Kihm (1990), Chris Corne (1999), Kouwenberg (2001), Mufwene

(2001), Rougé (2006), Intumbo (2008), and Aboh (2015) have all made insightful observations regarding congruent forms that individual Creoles may have inherited from their source languages. In Baptista (2020), I report on such studies and provide a crosslinguistic survey of morphological, syntactic, and lexical congruence in twenty pidgins and Creoles across nineteen grammatical/lexical domains, while proposing an algorithm and model accounting for how congruence may operate (see Baptista [2007] for a preliminary analysis of congruent features in Creoles).

We will see how Schuchardt's thinking about the role of congruent forms in language emergence evolved, reaching at first tentative conclusions about the source and function of certain Creole forms. As a historical linguist, he proposes that similar lexemes from distinct languages are possibly related, draws comparisons between distinct Creoles based on their similar features, and compares some of the Creole forms with those of their source languages.

3.1. Schuchardt's Quest for Morphological Similarities

I begin with Schuchardt's (1882) study of the pronominal systems of Portuguese-lexified Creoles, which include Cape Verdean Creole (Upper-Guinea Creole) and São Tomense (Gulf of Guinea Creole). Schuchardt was the first to note the similarity between pronominal forms (morphemes) in these two Creoles and their presumed source languages.

Consider tables 3.2–3.4, which display the pronominal systems of Cape Verdean and São Tomé Creoles, some northwestern African languages, and some southwestern African languages, respectively. All three tables are drawn from Schuchardt 1882. The original German text and its translation can be found in the Appendix.

Schuchardt uses these tables to demonstrate correspondences between languages: for instance, for the first-person singular pronoun, São Tomé and Cape Verde both have the morpheme *a* (highlighted in bold) and share it with African languages like Efik and Hereró.

Table 3.2 Pronominal Systems of São Tomé and Cape Verde Creoles

São Tomé		*Cape Verde*
Sing.	1. *mi, **a** mí, **a** mú*, conj. *um*	*mi, min, men, **a**min*, conj. *en, in*[4]
	2. *bô*	*bó, abó*, conj. *bu*
	3. *ê*	*ê*, conj. *Ê*
Plur.	1. *Nom*	*nós*, conj. *nu*
	2. *inancé, nancé*	*nhôs*
	3. *inem, nem*	*Ês*

Table 3.3 Pronominal Systems of Some Southwestern African Languages

	Yoruba	*Fante*	*Efik*	*Twi*	*Akra*
Sing	1. *emī*	*eme*, conj. *me*	***a**mi*, conj. *m, n*	*mé*	*mī*
	2. *iwọ*	*ewo*	*afü*, conj. *(a), u*	*wó*	*bo*
Plur.	1. *awa*	*ehyen*, conj. *nye*		*yéṅ*	*wo*
	2. *èyì*	*ehom*, conj. *hom*		*mó (hom)*	*nye*
	3. *awõ*	*ewon*, conj. *wo*		*wóṅ*	

Table 3.4 Pronominal Systems of Some Southwestern African Languages

		Angolese		*Hereró*	
		Abs.	*Conj.*	*Abs.*	*Conj.*
Sing.	1.	*emme (emmi)*	*Nghi*	***a**mi (o**a**mi)*	*dyi*
	2.	*eiê*	*U*	*ove*	*u*
Plur.	1.	*êtu*	*Tu*	*ete (oete)*	*tu*
	2.	*ênu*	*Nu*	*ene (oene)*	*mu*

As the German text and the English translation discussed later indicate, Schuchardt focuses specifically on the morpheme *a* and speculates on its functions and origins. Indeed, Schuchardt finds the São Tomense pronominal forms of 'extraordinary interest' when compared with those of Cape Verdean. He notes the similar form and different functions of the morpheme *a*- in distinct source languages, including the Portuguese (and Spanish) accusative pronoun *a*, emphatic pronouns in São Tomense (**a***mí*) and Cape Verdean (**a***min*), and pronouns in northwestern (Yoruba, Fante, Efik (**a***mi*), Twi, and Akra) and southwestern African languages (Angolese, Hereró (**a***mi*)). The comparisons he draws clearly highlight the correspondences between the languages in contact and the Creoles. However, it is important to note that although Schuchardt explicitly observes the partially similar forms, he makes no categorical statements about the source of the similar morpheme. He simply states that 'although at first this reminds one of the Span.-Port. accusative[5] pronoun *a*, I am inclined not to entirely exclude [the possibility of] the crossover of an African demonstrative pronoun' (Schuchardt 1882: 19).

It is worth noting that Schuchardt's analysis focuses heavily on the suffix *a* and does not delve much into a comparison of other pronominal morphemes like *mi* 'I/me' and *bo* 'you' that also happen to be shared by São Tomé Creole, Cape Verdean Creole, and (for instance) Akra (see tables 3.2 and 3.3). Nor does Schuchardt report that the prefix *a* can be found in Cape Verdean Creole throughout the strong pronoun paradigm:[6] **a***mi* 'me,' **a***bo* 'you,' **a***el* 'him/her/it,' **a***nos* 'we,' **a***nhos* 'you (all),' **a***es* 'they.' It is also interesting that Fante (table 3.3) exhibits a similar prefix (*e*) throughout its pronominal paradigm (**e***me* 'I,' **e***wo* 'you,' **e** *hyen* 'we,' **e***hom* 'you (all),' **e***won* 'they'), just as Cape Verdean Creole does today. Of course, this does not mean that the two pronominal systems are necessarily related; rather, it indicates that similarities between the pronominal systems of the Creoles and their potential source languages are detectable at various levels.

We have seen that Schuchardt explicitly observes partially similar forms between the two Creoles and African languages that may have contributed to their formation[7] but remains tentative in his conclusions about *a* in terms of its source, function, and etymology. Nor does Schuchardt comment on the notion of congruence among the languages in contact. This is a leap that John Holm (1988) makes a bit over 100 years later, when he claims more assertively that in light of Schuchardt (1882), the emphatic pronouns found in Príncipe (São Tomé)[8] result from congruence between the Portuguese superstrate and the African substrates. Holm states, 'The emphatic *a mim* construction [from Portuguese] is clearly the source of the Príncipe CP stressed forms such as *amí*, although there may have been some convergence with partially similar forms in Yoruba, Fante, Efik, Twi and certain Bantu languages (Schuchardt 1882: 906)' (Holm 1988: 203). Like Holm, Incanha Intumbo interprets Schuchardt's statements as pointing to some kind of convergence process: 'Schuchardt (1882: 906) points out that there may have been convergence with partially similar forms in some African languages' (Intumbo 2008: 275).

From Schuchardt's quest for morphological similarities among languages, I now turn to his quest for lexical ones.

3.2. Schuchardt's Quest for Lexical Similarities[10]

In his quest to identify similarities between languages, Schuchardt makes many connections between related and unrelated languages, between Creoles and their source languages, between superstrates and substrates, or just between substrates. As we will see, some of the correspondences he draws are expected and well-grounded whereas others appear somewhat random; however, they all attest to his sensitivity to similarities among world languages.

In what follows, I illustrate the various lenses and approaches Schuchardt adopted in his study of language. I show that in addition to him being a historical linguist, some of his comments would make him a good fit for today's circles of typologists, contact linguists, Creolists, and even universalists/generativists.[11] His erudition and curiosity about world languages made him an opportunist willing to tackle his study of language from a variety of angles, while pursuing his relentless search for similarities among the languages he encountered.

Studying the lexicon of the French-lexified Réunionnais, Schuchardt (1885) views the language through the lens of the *historical linguist* (his specialty) and notes that the Réunionnais lexeme *cacailler* is derived from French *cailleter* 'to do small talk,' which he argues is reminiscent of Spanish *carcarear* and German *gackern* (Schuchardt 1885; translated in Markey 1979: 16). He connects the same lexeme across languages belonging to distinct families (Romance and Germanic).

Wearing the hat of a *contact linguist*, Schuchardt (1883) notes that Portuguese *bicho de mar* 'sea snail' is passed on to French as *bêche de mar*, then passed on to English as *beech de mer*, and finally transformed into Melanesian English *beche le mer* (Schuchardt 1883; translated in Markey 1979: 20). With this example, he shows how the same term can be modified and adapted to various languages in contact, including the contact language itself (Melanesian English), which transforms the term in its own way.

When looking at Creoles from a *Creolist's* point of view, Schuchardt seeks similarities along four dimensions: (1) similarities between disparate Creoles, (2) similarities between Creoles and their source languages, (3) similarities between substrates, and (4) similarities between superstrate and substrates.

Regarding the *first* dimension (similarities between disparate Creoles), Schuchardt notes that some Creoles from different lexifiers share similar lexemes, which leads him to infer that those lexemes were borrowed from African languages. For instance, for the verb 'squat, cower, hunch down,' Schuchardt connects Cape Verde Portuguese *zongutú/zongotó* to São Thiago *djṹgurnidu*, Senegal Creole Portuguese *djongotó*, Curaçao Creole Spanish *jongotá*, Guyanese Creole French *diokoti/guiokoti*, and Sranan *djokotó/djokodón* (Schuchardt 1914; translated in Markey 1979: 77). Schuchardt makes similar types of connections between Lingua Franca and other contact languages. Indeed, in his 1909 work on Lingua Franca, he notes that the preposition *per* appears in Lingua Franca and a number of other contact languages:

> A striking phenomenon appears in Lingua Franca: the direct object is marked by "per." *Mi mirato* **per** *ti* "I have seen you" *mi ablar* **per** *ti* "I tell you," this use of "for" is unknown in Dutch creole but it is found in Malayo Portuguese *eu já olhá* **per** *vos*, *eu té fallá* **per** *vos* and in Cape Dutch *ek't* **fer** *jou gesien*, *ek sè* **fer** *jou*.
>
> (Schuchardt 1909; translated in Markey 1979: 29)

With respect to the *second* dimension (similarities between Creoles and their source languages), Schuchardt (1883) makes tentative connections between the plural-marking and tense-mood-aspect (TMA) systems of Melanesian Pidgin and the Melanesian languages in its linguistic ecology. For instance, he notes that *him fellow all* means 'they,' *other day he stop* 'there was,' and *by and by he come* 'he will come' and tentatively relates these forms to Melanesian languages where 'all' is used to convey plurality, and to the Sesake language of Epi (New Hebrides) in particular, which expresses the preterite with 'previously' and future events with 'soon.' Though he makes tentative associations between Melanesian Pidgin and the Melanesian languages, Schuchardt remains prudent in his conclusions and cautions against tracing features that are similar to a specific source or specific population. Incidentally, with respect to the first dimension mentioned earlier, Schuchardt observes that similar plural markers and TMA markers can also be found in Pidgin English. He shrewdly notes that Pidgin English also uses 'all' to express 'they' *he* **allo** *chow-chow medcin* 'they take medicine,' 'before time' to express preterite **before time** *you plenty hearee* 'they heard enough of it' (preterite), and *my by* to express the future **'mby** *catchee he* 'I will get it' (future) (Schuchardt 1883 translated in Markey 1979: 22).

Regarding the *third* dimension (similarities between substrates), Schuchardt links the same lexeme in Sranan Black English (his label for Sranan) to multiple substrates. For instance, he proposes that Sranan Black English *fugufugu*, *fokofoko* 'lungs' is onomatopoeic and is related to Congolese *lufulu*, Ashanti *flufla*, Ewe *foflokodzo*, Efik *obufre*, Kanuri, Hausa *fufu*, and Vai *vovo*. Similarly, he proposes that

Trinidadian Creole French *gogo* 'namesake(s)' derives from semantically equivalent Efik *koko*, Ewe *doko*, and Ibo *agù* (Schuchardt 1914; translated in Markey 1979: 76–77).

With respect to the *fourth* dimension (similarities between superstrate and substrates), Schuchardt's view was that communication between the masters and the enslaved population necessarily involved compromise: 'To the master as well as the slave it was solely a matter of the one making himself understood to the other . . ., they met in the middle' (Schuchardt 1914; translated in Markey 1979: 74). Speakers and languages met in the middle,[12] resulting at times in congruent forms that could be viewed as compromises between substrates and superstrates. In this regard, Schuchardt identifies in Lingua Franca several lexemes that he argues result from congruence between Romance and Arabic words:

> The Romance vocabulary of Lingua Franca appears to have been enriched by a number of Arabic words. . . . Many give the impression that they were introduced *due to similarity* [my emphasis] with corresponding Romance forms, e.g. *cašana* < *hezana* "cupboard/cabinet" ~ *cassa*, *maréia* < *meraia* "mirror" ~ Southern French *miralh*, *mirai*.
> (Schuchardt 1909; translated in Markey 1979: 30)

In other words, Schuchardt seems to assume that some of the lexicon of Lingua Franca may have made its way into that language because these words share similar forms in Arabic[13] and Romance languages like French. This could be viewed as a case of the type of lexical congruence documented in works by Peter Mühlhäusler (1997) and Chris Corne (1999).

Schuchardt can also be considered the *typologist* or *universalist* of his time. Referring to Black Creole Dialects, which include Creole Portuguese, Creole Spanish, Creole French, Creole Dutch, and Creole English,[14] Schuchardt states that 'we have no divergence, but parallelism: they are formed out of different material *according to the same plan and in the same style* [my emphasis]' (Schuchardt 1914; translated in Markey 1979: 77). Here, he seems to suggest that Creoles belong to the same type of language. Elsewhere, he refers explicitly to the universal linguistic features of Creoles: 'They are customarily regarded as products of very peculiar or extreme mixture but what distinguishes them is rather, if I dare say so, their universal linguistic features' (Schuchardt 1914; in Derek Bickerton's introduction to Markey 1979: xiv).

Schuchardt made countless insightful and descriptive observations regarding assumed lexical, morphological, and structural contact-induced changes across numerous languages. However, it was not until the publication of Thomason and Kaufman (1988) and Thomason (2001) that the field of contact linguistics benefitted from a rigorous methodology and theoretical framework, allowing researchers to ascertain that contact-induced change has genuinely occurred. In the next section, I introduce the model of contact-induced change developed by Sally Thomason and Terrence Kaufman and discuss how the model could also accommodate congruence.

4. A Framework to Identify Contact-Induced Change

Sally Thomason (2001: 91–94; 2010: 34) proposes a framework for identifying and determining contact-induced structural change. She focuses on structural change because, as she puts it (Thomason 2001: 91), loanwords that easily reveal their origin and occur among the nonbasic vocabulary are easy to identify. Detecting them is of course useful because their existence enables linguists to safely assume that contact took place between two or more languages, but it is much more challenging to detect structural interference. Determining whether a particular structural feature is native to a given language or the product of contact-induced change is far from straightforward. Thomason proposes a rigorous framework that, when applied stepwise, allows one to ascertain that structural contact-induced change has indeed taken place.

First, she recommends examining the receiving language (the language undergoing change) as a whole in order to detect several domains in which the same source (donor) language affected the same receiving language, as it is unlikely that a source language would pass on just one feature. Hence, the robustness of the evidence for contact-induced change lies in number of contact features (features whose emergence is solely due to contact between two [or more] languages). Second, a source language must be identified, ideally one that can be shown to have been in intense, long-term contact with the receiving language. Intensity and length of contact are two key factors promoting structural interference or contact-induced change. Thomason recognizes that in situations where the source language is no longer spoken in a given environment because the speakers have shifted to the receiving language, such a contact is not always easy to demonstrate (this is typically the case of creole languages). Third, it must be possible to list a number of shared features between the source and receiving languages—though the fact that the features are shared does not mean that they are identical in form, function, and syntactic distribution. Fourth, one must show that the contact feature was *absent* in the receiving language prior to contact with the source language. Finally, one must show that the contact feature was *present* in the source language prior to contact with the receiving language.

This rigorous methodology could be applied to test whether the changes that Schuchardt observed were genuinely contact-induced. In the next section, I show how Thomason and Kaufman's (1988) and Thomason's (2001) model can be adapted to also account for congruence.

5. Adapting Thomason and Kaufman's and Thomason's Model to Congruence

Keeping in mind that Thomason and Kaufman's and Thomason's model of contact-induced change focuses on structural change, my aim here is to expand it to morphological change and to adapt it so that it may also account for cases of congruence. Based on the assumption that congruent forms can arise in contact languages due to the similarity of features between distinct languages, we can reasonably argue that such features are contact-induced, and could therefore find some representation in Thomason and Kaufman's and Thomason's model of contact-induced change. With respect to congruence, which is also the result of contact, recall that Schuchardt seems to suggest that the morpheme *a* present in the pronominal systems of Cape Verdean and São Tomé Creoles may have been derived from the Spanish/Portuguese accusative pronoun *a*, and he does not 'entirely exclude [the possibility of] the crossover of an African demonstrative pronoun' (Schuchardt 1882: 19). This would be a case of morphological congruence. With respect to lexical congruence, he seems to suggest that some lexemes made it into the lexicon of Lingua Franca because lexemes similar to one another were present in both Arabic and Romance languages like French. One could therefore argue that those lexemes of Lingua Franca were preserved and retained in the contact language because they were *present* in both sources, and their presence is therefore also due to contact. If this reasoning is on the right track, one could add to the rigorous model and methodology that contact linguistics inherited from Thomason and Kaufman (1988) and Thomason (2001) that in order to assert that feature x in language C (the contact language) results from congruence between languages A and B (source languages), one must provide evidence that feature x was *present in both languages* at the time of contact (see Baptista, 2020). For instance, in the case of the morpheme *a* that made its way into the pronominal systems of Cape Verdean and São Tomé Creoles due to its presence in Spanish/Portuguese and African languages like Hereró, one must ascertain that this morpheme was indeed *present in both superstrates and substrates* at the time of contact. In the case of Cape Verdean and São Tomé Creoles, this would mean the fifteenth/sixteenth centuries.

The same condition would need to apply to cases of lexical congruence. Recall that in this regard, Schuchardt seems to have identified in Lingua Franca several lexemes that he argues result from congruence between Romance and Arabic words. For instance, he proposes that many of the vocabulary items of Lingua Franca seems to have been introduced to the language due to the similarity between Arabic and Romance forms. However, one should first make sure that the lexemes he attributes to similar forms in Arabic and Romance languages like French were indeed present and widely used at the time of contact. This is not an easy feat but a prerequisite to ensuring that the lexeme is present in the contact language due to congruent forms in its source languages. This is the type of work that Mühlhäusler (1997) and Corne (1999) conducted when arguing for lexical congruence in Tok Pisin and French-based creoles, respectively.

In summary, Schuchardt's work is deeply enlightening because he provides forms and lexemes that are shown to be present in the languages in contact in the nineteenth century. As slavery ended in the Senegambian region approximately in the 1850s, it would be reasonable to assume that a good number of the languages in contact Schuchardt assumed were present at that point in time may have contributed to some of the congruent forms Creolists have argued for in the scholarly literature. The prevalence of congruence as a grammar-building device in Creole languages (Kihm 1990) could help make a case to add one more layer to Thomason and Kaufman's (1988) and Thomason's (2001) framework of contact-induced change: for one to assume that feature x in language C (the contact language) results from congruence between languages A and B (source languages), one must provide evidence that feature x was *present in both languages* at the time of contact.

6. Conclusion

Going back to the quest for similarities among world languages that led Schuchardt to wear different hats, it is clear that though the subfields of historical linguistics, contact linguistics, Creolistics, typology, and generativism represent very different endeavors driven by distinct research questions, theoretical assumptions, and methodologies, they have this in common: among the many objectives that each subfield pursues is an abiding interest in the similarities among languages, whether those similarities are inherent to the linguistic systems being studied or inherited from other languages with which they have come in contact. As illustrated here, in some cases similarities exist because languages belong to the same family and go back to a common ancestor. In other cases, the similarities are due to contact. In the latter situation, saying that languages share a 'similar' feature clearly does not mean that the feature is an exact copy or identical in all the languages that happen to have it. Inherent in the dynamics of language contact seems to be the fact that languages may converge in such a way that features from each of them give rise to a similar feature that in turn develops in its own fashion, resulting in innovation. Such are the complexities of language contact that Thomason's life work has greatly illuminated.

Endnotes

1. It is a true honor to take part in this festschrift paying tribute to the countless, influential advances that Sally Thomason has made in the field of language contact. She single-handedly transformed this field by contributing rigorous theoretical frameworks and methodologies that have stood the test of time and greatly furthered our understanding of the processes and outcomes of language contact. Had Sally's pioneering work not equipped us with the right tools and insights, the field of language contact would not be where it stands today, recognized as a fertile and productive area of study. I am personally deeply indebted to her for her invaluable support, guidance, and cherished friendship over the years.

2. As a tribute to Sally, this paper focuses on work by the nineteenth-century linguist Hugo Schuchardt who, like Sally, was a specialist in historical linguistics, contact linguistics, pidgins, and Creoles and who was among the first linguists to consider Creoles as a fruitful area of investigation.

3. An example of a consecutive construction is (i), from IFC:

Mama-m dodine mwen, bo-m, karese mwen
mother/my/dandle/me/kiss/me/ caress/me
'my mother dandled me, kissed me, caressed me.' (Corne, 1999: 146)

4. Note that though Schuchardt provides a set of variants for the same pronoun, he does not elaborate on what patterns the variation follows.

5. Note that Schuchardt postulates that *a* on the pronouns reminds him of the Spanish and Portuguese accusative pronoun *a* but pronouns such as *ami* can only be found in subject positions and never in object positions.

6. This omission is no fault of Schuchardt's, as he depended on fellow linguists/correspondents abroad to pass along to him information regarding various Creoles and other languages.

7. These were the languages that Schuchardt believed had been in the linguistic ecology of these Creoles.

8. Schuchardt (1882) and Holm (1988) refer to São Tomé and Príncipe, respectively, but these terms refer to the same two-island archipelago, today called São Tomé and Príncipe.

9. Strong pronouns (like *mi* "me") are pronouns that can occur in isolation and can be coordinated (*mi ku bo* "me and you") whereas, in contrast, weak pronouns cannot do so and must lean against another element (typically a verb) when they appear (**N** bai "I went").

10. In this section, I use the names of the languages that Schuchardt used in his studies, though the names of some of the Creoles have now changed.

11. As a reviewer points out, the current subfields of linguistics today may represent reductionistic silos that may have been produced by the twentieth-century postwar modernist shift. In contrast, Schuchardt's works demonstrate that linguists of his time were inclined to study linguistic phenomena by adopting a much more holistic approach.

12. As pointed out by a reviewer, the power relationship between masters and the enslaved population that was present in those colonial settings could cast doubt on the possibility that meeting in the middle could possibly take place. One cannot make strong generalizations, as each Creole emerged and developed in distinct linguistic ecologies but in the right setting, one can imagine cases where the need and urgency to communicate could motivate both masters and slaves "to meet in the middle."

13. Note that speakers of African languages like Wolof were early on familiarized with Arabic, as Islam has been present in Senegal since the eleventh century.

14. These are broad labels that Schuchardt uses to refer to clusters of Creoles that are lexified by the same superstrate.

References

Aboh, Enoch. 2015. *The emergence of hybrid grammars*. Cambridge: Cambridge University Press.

Babel, Anna, and Stefan Pfänder. 2014. "Doing copying: Why typology does not matter to language speakers." In Juliane Besters-Dilger, Cynthia Dermarkar, Stefan Pfänder, and Achim Rabus (Eds.), *Congruence in contact-induced language change: Language families, typological resemblance and perceived similarity*, 239–57. Berlin: DeGruyter.

Bach, Emmon. 1974. "Explanatory inadequacy." In D. Cohen (Ed.), *Explaining Linguistic Phenomena*. Washington, D.C.: Hemisphere Publishing Corporation.

Baptista, Marlyse. 2007. "Feature selection and competition in creole formation: A case study." *Penn Working Papers in Linguistics* 13.2. Paper selected from the conference proceedings of NWAV, 35, 38–50.

Baptista, Marlyse. 2020. Competition, selection and the role of congruence in creole genesis and development. *Language* , 96(1): 160–99.

Campbell, Lyle. 1998. *Historical linguistics: An introduction*. Cambridge: MIT press.

Chomsky, Noam. 2000. *New Horizons in the Study of Language and Mind*. Cambridge: MIT Press.

Crowley, Terry. 1992. *An introduction to historical linguistics*. Oxford: Oxford University Press.

Cooreman, A., and D. Goyvaerts. 1980. Universals in human language: A historical perspective. In *Revue belge de philologie et d'histoire, tome 58, fasc. 3, 1980. Langues et littératures modernes—Moderne taal- en letterkunde*, 615–38. Brussels: Percée.

Corne, Chris. 1999. *From French to Creole*. London: Battlebridge Publications (Westminster Creolistics).

Greenberg, Joseph. 1966. Synchronic and diachronic universals in phonology. Language, 42(2): 508–17.

Greenberg, Joseph. 1976. Universals of Language (2nd Ed.). Cambridge: MIT Press.

Gumperz, John J., and Robert Wilson. 1971. Convergence and creolization: A case from the Indo-Aryan/Dravidian border in India. In Dell Hymes (Ed.), *Pidginization and creolization of languages*, 151–67. Cambridge: Cambridge University Press.

Holm, John. 1988. *Pidgins and creoles: Theory and structure*. Cambridge: Cambridge University Press.

Intumbo, Incanha. 2008. The pronominal system of Balanta, Guinea-Bissau Creole and Portuguese. In Susanne Michaelis (Ed.), *Roots of creole structures: Weighing the contributions of substrates and superstrates* [Creole Language Library 33], 263–78. Amsterdam/Philadelphia: Benjamins.

Joseph, Brian. 1983. *The synchrony and diachrony of the Balkan infinitive: A study in areal, general, and historical linguistics*. Cambridge: Cambridge University Press.

Joseph, Brian. 2010. Language contact in the Balkans. In Raymond Hickey (Ed.), *The handbook of language contact*, 618–33. Malden, MA: Wiley-Blackwell.

Kihm, Alain. 1990. Conflation as a directive process in creolization. InJan Koster (Ed.), *Bochum Essener Kolloquium*, 111–37. Bochum: Brockmeyer.

Kouwenberg, Silvia. 2001. Convergence and explanations in Creole genesis. In Norval Smith and Tonjes Veenstra (Eds.), *Creolization and contact*, 219–39. Amsterdam: John Benjamins.

Markey, Thomas. 1979. *The ethnography of variation: Selected writing on pidgins and creoles*. Ann Arbor, MI: Karoma.

Mufwene, Salikoko. 2001. *The ecology of language evolution*. Cambridge: Cambridge University Press.

Mühlhäusler, Peter. 1997. *Pidgin and Creole linguistics*. London: Westminster.

Peck, Stephen. 1988. *Tense, aspect, and mood in Guinea-Casamance Portuguese Creole* (Dissertation).UCLA, Los Angeles, CA.

Rougé, Jean-Louis. 2006. L'influence manding sur la formation des creoles du Cap-Vert et de Guinée-Bissau et Casamance. In Jürgen Lang, John Holm, Jean-Louis Rougé, and Maria João Soares (Eds.), *Cabo Verde: Origens da sua sociedade e do seu crioulo*, 63–74. Tübingen: Gunter Narr Verlag.

Schuchardt, Hugo. 1882. Kriolische Studien I. Ueber das Negerportugiesische von S. Thomé. Zitzungsberichte der philosophisch-historisch Classe der kaiserlichen Akademie der Wissenschaften in Wien. 101-889-917.

Schuchardt, Hugo. 1883. Kriolische Studien V. Ueber das MelanesoEnglische. Zitzungsberichte der philosophisch-historisch Classe der kaiserlichen Akademie der Wissenschaften in Wien. 105-151-61.

Schuchardt, Hugo. 1885. *Über die Lautgesetze. Gegen die Junggrammatiker.* Berlin: Oppenheimer.

Schuchardt, Hugo. 1888. Beiträge zur Kenntnis des kreolischen Romanisch III. Zum Negerportugiesischen Kapverden. *Zeitschrift für romanische Philologie,* 12:312–22.

Schuchardt, Hugo. 1909. Romanisch bast-. *Zeitschrift für romanische Philologie*, 33: 339–46.

Schuchardt, Hugo. 1914. Zum Negerholländischen von St. Thomas. *TNTL*, 33: 123–35.

Schuchardt, Hugo. 1979: *The ethnography of variation: Selected writings on pidgins and creoles.* Edited and translated by T. L. Markey; Introduction by Derek Bickerton. Ann Arbor, MI: Karoma.

Thomason, Sarah, And Terrence Kaufman. 1988. *Language contact, creolization, and genetic linguistics.* Berkeley: University of California Press.

Thomason, Sarah. 1999. Speakers' choices in language change. *Studies in the Linguistic Sciences*, 29(2): 19–43.

Thomason, Sarah. 2001a. *Language contact: an introduction.* Edinburgh: Edinburgh University Press.

Thomason, Sarah. 2001b. Speakers' attitudes in language change, contact-language genesis, and language preservation. *Estudios de Sociolingüística*, 2(2): 13–26.

Thomason, Sarah. 2007. Language contact and deliberate change. *Journal of Language Contact*, 1: 41–62.

Thomason, Sarah. 2010. Contact explanations in linguistics. In Raymond Hickey (Ed.), *The handbook of language contact*, 31–47. Oxford: Blackwell.

Thomason, Sarah. 2014. Contact-induced language change and typological congruence. In Juliane Besters-Dilger, Cynthia Dermarkar, Stefan Pfander, and Achim Rabus (Eds.), *Congruence in contact-induced language change: Language families, typological resemblance, and perceived similarity*, 201–18. Berlin: De Gruyter.

APPENDIX

Translation (Babel Linguistics, Inc.)

Of extraordinary interest are the forms of the personal pronouns, which I have juxtaposed with those of the Cape Verdean language:

	São Tomé:	Cape Verde:
Sing.	1. ***mi*** , ***amí***, *amú*, **conj.** ***Um***	***mi***, *min*, *men*, ***amin***, conj. ***en, in***
	2. *bô*	*bó*, *abó*, conj. *bu*
	3. *ê*	*ê*, conj. *ê*
Plur.	1. *nom*	*nós*, conj. *nu*
	2. *inancé*, *nancé*	*nhôs*
	3. *inem*, *nem*.	*ês*.

Coelho said nothing about the difference in usage of the Cape Verdean forms that stand next to each other; however, his examples make this difference clear (*mi en staba* 'moi j'étais'). All that I have been able to document for São Tomé is the opposition between strong and weak forms.[9] This difference exists in the Curaçao Creole as well; cf. Gospel of St. Matthew XIX, 9: *I. a mi, mi ta bisa bosonan.* Civilisadó July 29, 1871: *Sji Rosali, amí? mi no a papia nada*. The strong form *mi* becomes even more pronounced through a prefixed *a* (in Cape Verdean in the second-person singular, as well). Although at first this reminds one of the Span.-Port. accusative pronoun *a*, I am inclined not to entirely exclude (the possibility of) the crossover of an African demonstrative pronoun. In Cape Verdean, it seems possible for a relative pronoun to follow forms such as this, hence *Amí qu'é bóde* (cu son um valentão) would actually mean: 'It (is) I who am a huge fellow.' But in São Tomé, *amí* can also occur after prepositions: *cu amí*. Compare the northwestern African languages:

	Yoruba	Cape Coast Fante	Efik	Twi	Akra
Sing.	1. ***emī***	*eme*, conj. ***me***	***ami***, conj. ***m*** , ***n***	***Mé***	***mī***
	2. *iwọ*	*ewo*	*afü*, conj. (*a*), *u*.	*wó*	*bo*
Plur.	1. *awa*	*ehyen*, conj. *nye*		*yéṅ*	*wo*
	2. *èyì*	*ehom*, conj. *hom*		*mó* (*hom*)	*nye*.
	3. *awõ*	*ewon*, conj. *wo*		*wóṅ*	

In the southwestern languages:

		Angolese		Hereró	
		Abs.	Conj.	Abs.	Conj.
Sing.	1.	*emme* (***emmi***)	*nghi*	***ami (oami)***	*dyi*
	2.	*Eiê*	*u*	*ove*	*u*
Plur.	1.	*Êtu*	*tu*	*ete* (*oete*)	*tu*
	2.	*ênu*.	*nu*.	*ene* (*oene*).	*mu*.

Regarding the Hereró forms, Hahn states (§ 102): 'In the 1st person singular, the initial *a* unmistakably displays the genitive form, which however has come to be used as the nominative. In the 2nd person singular, as well as in the 1st and 2nd person plural, contraction has caused the genitive form to become more blurred.' An even more striking correspondence with the genitive seems to me to be demonstrated in the prefixed *o*. Nevertheless, we are not dealing here with forms that were originally genitives. *A* is a widespread particle of weak demonstrative meaning, which occurs in manifold functions, especially in copula, as of course otherwise tend to be used in this fashion both in the demonstratives of native African languages as well as in the African patois. Thus in Angolese 'The man is ugly' is *ri-ala ri-a hiba*, actually '(prefix) man (prefix) he ugly.' But the utterances 'The man who is ugly,' 'the ugly man' are expressed in exactly the same way. For this reason, *a* is especially considered to be a relative particle that serves to demonstrate the genitive.

English version from German: Babel Linguistics, Inc.

das Pronomen der 3. Pers. Plur. vor, z. B.: *inem moço* ,die Knaben'.[1] Ganz entsprechend im Negerenglischen von Surinam: *dem boi;* im Curazoleñischen wird das Pronomen nachgestellt: *moso-nan.* Theilweise auch im Negerfranzösischen Westindiens. Im Capverdischen ist der organische Plural noch nicht ganz ausgestorben.

Von diesem Falle abgesehen, wird der bestimmte Artikel nicht wiedergegeben; der Gebrauch von *ũa* scheint nicht allzuweit über den des Zahlwortes hinauszugehen.

Aeusserst interessant sind die Formen der Personalpronomina, denen ich die capverdischen zur Vergleichung gegenüberstelle:

	S. Thomé:	Capverden:
Sing. 1.	*mi, amí, amú,* conj. *um*	*mi, min, men, amin,* conj. *en, in*
2.	*bô*	*bó, abó,* conj. *bu*
3.	*ê*	*êl,* conj. *ê*
Plur. 1.	*nom*	*nós,* conj. *nu*
2.	*inancé, nancé*	*nhôs*
3.	*inem, nem.*	*ês.*

Coelho hat sich über den Gebrauchsunterschied der nebeneinanderstehenden capverdischen Formen nicht ausgesprochen, seine Beispiele aber machen ihn deutlich (*mi en staba* ,moi j'étais'). Für das Santhomensische ist mir nur in der 1. Pers. der Gegensatz der starken und schwachen Form bezeugt. Auch im Curazoleñischen existirt der Unterschied; vgl. Ev. S. Matth. XIX, 9: *I. a mi. mi ta bisa bosonan.* Civilisadó 29. July 1871: *Sji Rosali, ami? mi no a papia nada.* Die starke Form *mi* wird durch ein vorgesetztes *a* (im Capverdischen auch in der 2. Pers. Sing.) noch mehr verstärkt. Obwohl man hiebei zunächst an die span.-port. Accusativpräposition *a* denken wird, so bin ich doch geneigt, den Uebertritt eines afrikanischen Demonstrativums nicht für ganz unmöglich zu halten. Im Capverdischen scheint nach solchen Formen ein Relativum stehen zu können, so dass *amí qu'é bóde* (eu sou um valentão) eigentlich heissen würde: ,Es (ist) ich, der ein Riesenkerl ist'. Doch im Santhomensischen

[1] Sogar bei Zahlwörtern findet sich *inem,* so: *inem doço sapé dji bô* ,deine beiden Hüte'.

findet sich *amí* auch nach Präpositionen: *cu amí.* Man vergleiche in den nordwestlichen Negersprachen:

	Yoruba:	Fante von Cape Coast:	Efik:
Sing. 1.	*emī*	*ẹme,* conj. *me*	*ami,* conj. *m, n*
2.	*iwọ*	*ẹwo*	*afü,* conj. *(a), u.*
Plur. 1.	*awa*	*ẹhyen,* conj. *nye*	
2.	*ẽyī*	*ẹhom,* conj. *hom*	
3.	*awõ.*	*ẹwọn,* conj. *wọ.*	

	Tšwi:	Akra:
Sing. 1.	*mé*	*mī*
2.	*wó*	*bo*
Plur. 1.	*yẹ́ñ*	*wọ*
2.	*mó (hom)*	*nye.*
3.	*wọ́ñ.*	

In den südwestlichen Sprachen:

	Angolensisch:		Hereró:	
	abs.	conj.	abs.	conj.
Sing. 1.	*emme (emmi)*	*nghi*	*ami (oami)*	*dyi*
2.	*eiê*	*u*	*ove*	*u*
Plur. 1.	*êtu*	*tu*	*ete (oete)*	*tu*
2.	*ênu.*	*nu.*	*ene (oene).*	*mu.*

Hahn §. 102 sagt bezüglich der Hereróformen: ‚Bei der 1. Pers. Sing. zeigt das anlautende *a* unverkennbar die Genitivform an, die sich aber als Nominativ eingebürgert hat. Bei der 2. Pers. Sing. und 1. und 2. Pers. Plur. ist durch Contraction die Genitivform mehr verwischt.‘ Noch schlagender scheint mir die Uebereinstimmung mit dem Genitiv durch das vorgesetzte *o* dargethan zu werden. Um ursprüngliche Genitive handelt es sich dennoch nicht. *A* ist eine weitverbreitete Partikel von schwacher demonstrativer Bedeutung, welche in den mannigfachsten Functionen auftritt, besonders in der der Copula, wie ja auch sonst in den Negersprachen Demonstrativa gern auf diese Weise verwandt werden und nicht minder in den Negerpatois. So heisst auf Angolensisch ‚der Mann ist hässlich‘: *ri-alu ri-a hiba,* eigentlich: ‚(Präf.) Mann (Präf.) er hässlich‘. Ganz ebenso aber wird ausgedrückt: ‚der Mann, welcher hässlich ist‘, ‚der hässliche Mann‘. Daher gilt das *a* insbesondere als Relativpartikel, mit deren Hilfe der Genitiv dargestellt wird, z. B.:

CHAPTER 4

Contact-Induced Change in the Inflectional Systems of Immigrant Languages in the United States

Differential Change in Noun and Verb Inflection

Anna Fenyvesi

To Sally: my professor, advisor, mentor, academic role model, and friend.

1. Introduction

Research into immigrant language use, that is, the language use of European immigrants to the United States and of their descendants goes back to approximately the beginnings of modern bilingualism research, namely, the early 1950s. Immigrant language use is heavily affected by language contact in both its lexicon and structure. Besides the direct influence of English, immigrant language use is also affected by language attrition due to limitations of the minority language situation (since speakers use it only in some domains of language use, usually in the private domains). Separating the effects of contact and attrition is not the aim of the present paper, however. Instead, I want to discuss the linguistic results of these influences in the inflectional systems of nine immigrant languages documented in detailed descriptions.

In addition to supplying a wide variety of contact-induced changes, U.S. immigrant languages also provide a "language-contact laboratory" type of issues, that is, what happens when the same majority language, English, affects a range of immigrant minority languages: what kinds of similar changes are produced and what kind of differences, and how we can explain these.

The present paper focuses on one small aspect of the wide range of changes that most immigrant languages undergo: the way the inflectional systems of nouns versus verbs are affected in nine U.S. immigrant languages of European origin spoken in the United States, namely, Hungarian, Finnish, Polish, Slovak, Czech, Russian, Serbo-Croatian,[1] Dutch, and Greek, as described in detailed works of these languages as spoken in the United States. The question the paper seeks to answer is what similarities and differences are there in the changes observed in these languages, and what patterns emerge overall?

A cataloging of changes in noun inflection (specifically, case) and verb inflection (specifically, person/number marking) in the immigrant languages under investigation demonstrates that considerable change occurs in the marking of case in all investigated immigrant languages compared to their Old World counterparts: (1) the number of cases used decreases; (2) prepositions begin to govern nouns in the nominative; (3) considerable variability develops in the use of case affixes; and (4) relatively rarely used cases are lost. In contrast, person/number marking in verbs is preserved unchanged in most of the investigated languages (Greek, Polish, Czech, Slovak, Serbo-Croatian, Finnish, and Hungarian), whereas it changes considerably in American Russian (AR) and American Dutch.

In the final part of the paper, answers are sought (and partly found) to explain the difference in changes in AR and American Dutch versus in the other immigrant languages and to find why noun and verb inflection systems so drastically differ in immigrant languages in the United States.

2. Previous Studies on Immigrant Languages

The description of U.S. immigrant languages of European origin started in the early 1950, with Einar Haugen's *The Norwegian Language in America* (1953) meticulously describing the bilingualism and language use of Norwegians in the United States, and continued with several others, focusing on various other groups and their languages, as well as, later, their sociolinguistic situations.

Descriptions of U.S. immigrant languages were first, in the late 1950s and 1960s, typically dissertations (Meyerstein 1959: Slovak; Hasselmo 1961: Swedish; Lyra 1962: Polish; Lehtinen 1966: Finnish; Jutronić 1971: Serbo-Croatian), in which authors described the U.S. varieties of their own first languages through the language use of immigrant communities. Such comprehensive works continued to sporadically appear later as well, resulting in a considerable number of contact linguistic works by now (Seaman 1972: Greek; Albin and Alexander 1972: Serbo-Croatian; Henzl 1975: Czech; Sahlman-Karlsson 1976: Finnish; Jutronić-Tihomirović 1985: Croatian; Arnbjornsdottir 1991: Icelandic; Justman 1984 and Kučera 1990: Czech; Hammerová and Ripka 1994: Slovak; Andrews 1989, 1998 and Polinsky 1997: Russian; Smits 1996: Dutch, etc.), together with brief accounts (Benson 1957, 1960: Russian; Lewis 1973: Swiss German; Correa-Zoli 1981: Italian; Clausing 1986: German and Icelandic, etc.) and papers focusing on particular details (Gilbert 1965: loanwords in German; Benson 1967: loanwords in Serbo-Croatian; Meyerstein 1959: use of prepositions in Slovak; Larmouth 1974: cases in Finnish; Correa-Zoli 1973, 1974: gender assignment in loans and lexical interference in Italian; Karttunen 1977: language change in one generation in Finnish; Juričić and Kess 1978: address forms in Croatian; Henzl 1982: immigrant language use and children's language in Czech; Filipović 1982, 1984: Croatian dialects; Preston and Turner 1984 and Preston 1986: case use in Polish; Bauer 1984: Croatian syntax; Rakusan 1985, 1988: the semantics of loanwords in Czech; Salmons 1988, 1990, 1991: vocabulary issues in German; Schatz 1989: lexical borrowing in Dutch; Haller 1981, 1987: creole features in Italian; van Marle and Smits 1989, 1993, 1995: morphological erosion in Dutch, 1997: loanwords in Dutch; Cohen 1989: language loss in Portuguese; Andrews 1990, 1993: the semantic categorization of loanwords and intonation in Russian; Martin 1990: loan verbs in Finnish; Jönsson-Korhola 1990: Finnish syntax; Hirvonen 1992, 1995: vowel and consonant oppositions, and morphological change in Finnish; Lauttamus 1990, 1991, and Lauttamus and Hirvonen 1995, 2011: lexical and structural borrowing in Finnish; Hirvonen 2001: codeswitching in Finnish; Moen 1988, 1991: pronunciation in Norwegian; Dumitrescu 1993: contact phenomena in Romanian; Hatzidaki 1994: lexical borrowing in Greek; Hjelde 1996: the gender of loans in Norwegian; Rabeno and Repetti 1997: the gender of loan nouns in Italian, etc.).

In the past three decades, the description of U.S. immigrant languages extended beyond languages of European origin (e.g., Blair 1991: changes of Iranian names in Los Angeles; Daher 1992: Lebanese Arabic in Cleveland; Rouchdy 1992: borrowing in Arabic etc.).

Beginning with the 1960s, immigrant varieties in other countries have been described (Clyne 1967, 1972, 1978, 1997: Australian German; Clyne 1991: Australian German and Dutch; De Bot and Clyne 1994: language loss in Australian Dutch; Endrődy 1971: Australian German and Hungarian; Dearmond 1971: the phonology of Canadian Ukrainian; Surdučki 1978: Serbo-Croatian in Canada; Sussex 1982: the phonetics of Australian Polish; Kouzmin 1982: grammatical change in Australian Russian; Stoffel 1983: address forms in New Zealand German; Clivio 1986: loanwords in Toronto Italian; Bettoni 1986, 1989, 1990, 1991: language loss in Australian Italian; Tamis 1991: Greek in Australia; Kinder 1993: subordination and coordination in Australian Italian; Papademetre 1994: discourse marking in Australian Greek; Watson 1995, 1996, 1999, and Lauttamus et al. 2007: Australian Finnish; Søndergaard 1997: the syntax of Australian Danish; Janurik 2011: the online use of Canadian Estonian; Backus and Boeschoten 1998: language change in immigrant Turkish in Europe, etc.). This listing is not comprehensive and does not contain any of the literature on

Spanish in the United States, since the sociolinguistic context of the speakers of Spanish varieties in the United States is greatly different from those of the other typical immigrant languages. (For comprehensive discussions of Spanish in the United States, see, for instance, Silva-Corvalán 1994a, 1994b, 1998, 2004, while de Fina 2003 provides a discourse analytical approach to the study of Mexican immigrant identity in the United States.)

It is a curious fact that very few works deal with the English language use of immigrants (Hirvonen 1982, Lauttamus 1990, Linn 2006: American Finns; Moen 1988: American Norwegians; Watson 1996 Australian Finns).

The immigrant language in the focus of my own previous investigations, American Hungarian (AH), had sporadic early treatments detailing "linguistic oddities" (Balassa 1928, 1936; Reményi 1934, 1937; Rubinyi 1921; Spissák 1906; Zsoldos 1938), followed by modern linguistic studies of dialectological focus by Bako (1961a, 1961b) and Kálmán (1970). Even though both these authors collected large amounts of recorded interview data (Bakó interviewed 124 speakers and recorded seventy hours of interviews, while Kálmán interviewed 78 and recorded sixteen hours, cf. Kálmán 1970: 381–82), neither of them systematically analyzed all of their materials. Bakó's data have been donated to Debrecen University, Hungary, digitized, and made freely available to researchers (http://mnytud.arts.unideb.hu/bako/index.php).

The first comprehensive study of AH language use was done by Kontra in South Bend, Indiana, in 1980–1981, who published a detailed monograph (in Hungarian) based on eighty hours of sociolinguistic interviews with forty speakers in 1990. Bartha (1993b) analyzed the lexical material of her investigation of Detroit, Michigan, Hungarians (using fifteen hours of interviews). Besides these overviews, both authors also published further papers based on various aspects of AH (cf. Bartha 1992, 1993a, 1993b, 1995; Kontra 1984, 1984–1985, 1985, 1986, 1988a, 1988b, 1989, 1990–1995, 1993a, 1993b; Kontra and Gósy 1988; Kontra and Nehler 1981a, 1981b). The third larger sociolinguistic and contact linguistic investigation with published results was carried out by myself in McKeesport, Pennsylvania, in 1993, based on about twelve hours of interviews with twenty speakers (Fenyvesi 1995a; with further papers dealing with specific aspects of AH being Fenyvesi 1995b, 1995/1996, 1998a, 1998b, 2000). A sizeable book chapter (Fenyvesi 2005a) overviews the characteristics of AH language use as described by Kontra (1990), Bartha (1993b), and Fenyvesi (1995). Further analyses, individual or coauthored, were published as Fenyvesi (2005b, 2006) and Fenyvesi and Zsigri (2006, 2007, 2010, 2011). Code-switching in AH was analyzed by Myers-Scotton and Bolonyai (2001) and Bolonyai (1998, 2000) as well as Kovács (2018). In recent years, Szabó (2018a, 2018b) provided discourse analytical approaches to AH. Australian Hungarian (and Australian Finnish) language use was described in Kovács's dissertation (Kovács 2001a) and other publications (Kovács 1996, 1997, 2001b, 2001c, 2002, 2005). The language use of Hungarians in the United Kingdom was analyzed by Benkő (2000), whereas Huber (2013, 2016) and Molnár and Huber (2013) analyzed Canadian Hungarian language use.

U.S. immigrant languages have two dictionaries, an American Finnish (AF) (Virtaranta 1992), and an AH (Vázsonyi 1995, compiled by Miklós Kontra using Endre Vázsonyi's data).

3. Sources

This paper, then, analyzes patterns of change in the systems of noun and verb inflection in nine immigrant languages of European origin used in the United States. The languages chosen for the analysis all have detailed descriptions of the changes in the inflectional system. They are the following: AH—Bartha (1993b), Fenyvesi (1995, 1995/1996), Kontra (1990); AF—Hirvonen (1995), Jönsson-Korhola (1990), Larmouth (1974), Lehtinen (1966); American Polish (AP)—Lyra (1962), Preston (1986); American Slovak (ASk)—Hammerová and Ripka (1994), Meyerstein (1959); American Czech (AC)—Henzl (1982), Justman (1984), Kučera (1990); AR—Polinsky (1997); American

Serbo-Croatian (ASC)—Albin and Alexander (1972), Jutronić (1971); American Dutch—Smits (1996); and American Greek—Seaman (1972).

A detailed discussion of the methodological similarities of and differences between the sources is beyond the scope of this paper, but, in brief, it is safe to state that they all analyze empirical spoken language data produced by active bilingual speakers, recorded and transcribed by the researchers/authors. The speakers are typically of two kinds: first-generation speakers, that is, immigrants, dominant in the immigrant language, and second-generation, U.S.-born speakers dominant in English. The only exception is Polinsky's 1997 paper, which specifically focuses primarily on the language attrition aspects of U.S.-born semi-speakers with reduced language (Polinsky 1997: 371–72)—this will be of relevance later in the text.

4. The Inflectional Systems of Immigrant Languages

4.1. Nominal Inflection: Cases

The sources on the nine immigrant languages under investigation show that the noun inflection systems of these languages, specifically, their case systems, undergo considerable change: case inflection is lost and/or replaced to a great extent. The number of cases used decreases compared to the old-world varieties of the languages.

In AR two major cases, the nominative and the accusative, evolve, with the nominative being used more frequently, including in arguments governed by verbs (1–3) (Polinsky 1997: 378, 380) and in adjuncts (Polinsky 1997: 378). (Throughout this paper I provide examples in the form given in the sources, underlining the part of the example affected by change.)

(1) AR *i eta ženščina ona imela sekretnaja žizn'* "and this woman had a secret life" (cf. R *sekretnuju žizn'*, Acc)

(2) AR *rasskazal devočku istorija* "he told the girl a story" (cf. R *devočke*, Dat; *istoriju*, Acc)
(3) AR *ja ne čitaju russkaja kniga* "I do not read Russian books" (cf. R *russkix knig*, Gen)

In AC all cases erode except for the nominative and the accusative, which are often realized in old-world Czech (C) by a zero morpheme:

(4) AC *používá vydličku* (Acc) "he uses the fork" (cf. C *vidličky*, Gen; Justman 1984: 127)
(5) AC *podobá se muž* "she resembles the man" (cf. C *muži*, Dat; Justman 1984: 127)
(6) AC *toužil po dívka* "he longed for the girl" (cf. C *dívkě*, Loc; Justman 1984: 128)
(7) AC *volal chlapci* "he called in the boys" (cf. C *chlapce*, Acc; Justman 1984: 128)

According to Justman (1984: 139), in AC only one case is used instead of two if the same preposition can govern arguments (producing different meanings):

(8) AC *na* + Loc (cf. C *na* + Acc [where to?], *na* + Loc [when?])

na stole "onto the table" (cf. C *na stol*, Acc)

In ASk, the nominative occurs in place of other cases:

(9) ASk *chcela pes* "she wanted a dog" (cf. Sk *psa*, Acc; Hammerová and Ripka 1994: 73)
(10) ASk *o deň* "about the day" (cf. Sk *dni*, Loc; Meyerstein 1959: 95)
(11) ASk *od jednich ludé* "from some people" (cf. Sk *ľudí*, Gen; Meyerstein 1959: 98)

In AP, each one of the six cases of Polish (P) can be replaced by the nominative or the accusative (rarely, by the genitive) (Lyra 1962: 151–70):

(12) AP *gram tenis* "I play tennis" (Nom, cf. P *tenisa*, Acc; Lyra 1962: 151)

(13) AP *znać innego języka* "know another language" (Acc, cf. P *język*, Gen; Lyra 1962: 152)
(14) AP *on nie wierzy moje słowo* "he doesn't believe my word" (Nom, cf. P *mojemu słowu*, Dat; Lyra 1962: 153)
(15) AP *o tych ludzi* "about those people" (Nom/Acc, cf. P *ludziach*, Loc; Lyra 1962: 156)
(16) AP *nie mog wierzyć swoich oczów* "I couldn't believe my eyes" (Gen, cf. P *oczom*, Dat; Lyra 1962: 155)

Both Preston (1984) and Lyra (1962: 195) mention the loss of the dative in AP due to it being a rarely used case.

In ASC, non-nominative forms are replaced by nominative ones:

(17) ASC *pokupiti janci* "to collect the lambs" (cf. SC *jance*, Acc; Jutronić 1971: 67)
(18) ASC *on je saranio pokojnego muž moj* "he buried my deceased husband" (cf. SC *muža moja*, Gen; Albin and Alexander 1972: 63)
(19) ASC *kolovoz jedanastog* "11th of August" (cf. SC *kolovoza*, Gen; Jutronić 1971: 66)
(20) ASC *pomoc klanovci* "help the members" (cf. SC *klanovcima*, Dat/Loc; Jutronić 1971: 68)
(21) ASC *imali hrvatski učitelice* "we had Croatian teachers" (cf. SC *hrvatske*, Acc; Jutronić 1971: 78)
(22) ASC *u naši knjigi* "in our book" (cf. SC *našoj*, Dat/Loc; Jutronić 1971:79)

Levine (1995) reports that in American Yiddish definite articles only occur in the nominative (unfortunately, I have not found a comprehensive description of this immigrant language).

At least two authors (Jönsson-Korhola 1990: 74; Lehtinen 1966: 33) state that in AF partitive subjects occur in the nominative (23), and the subject of the verb expressing possession is in the nominative (rather than in the adessive, as in old-world Finnish) (24):

(23) AF *tämä kaupunki enään ole* "this town does not exist anymore" (cf. F *tätä kaupunkia*, Part; Jönsson-Korhola 1990: 74)
(24) AF *isä oli seitsämän lasta* "father had 7 children" (cf. F *isällä*; Ade; Jönsson-Korhola 1990: 74)

In AF, nominative forms replace other case-marked forms, such as the allative in (25) and the accusative in (26):

(25) AF *me tultii Itämeri ja Pohjanmeri* "we came to the Baltic Sea and the North Sea" (cf. F *Itämerelle ja Pohjanmerelle*, All; Jönsson-Korhola 1990: 74)
(26) AF *muistan poika jonka nimi oli Billy* "I remember a boy whose name was Billy" (cf. F *pojan*, Acc; Hirvonen 1995: 188)

AH is characterized by the loss of various cases (Fenyvesi 1995/1996) (in the examples of AH all data are from my McKeesport interviews:

(27) AH *tudja Goldie Szarka?* "do you know Goldie Szarka?" (cf. H *Ismeri Goldie Szarkát?* Acc)
(28) AH *akkor találkoztam a férjem* "that's when I met my husband" (cf. H *férjemmel*, Instr)
(29) AH *azt hívtuk a magyar negyed* "we called it the Hungarian district" (cf. H *negyednek*, Dat)
(30) AH *elmentünk a liget* "we went to the park" (cf. H *ligetbe*, Illative)
(31) AH *egyszer egy hónap* "once a month" (cf. H *hónapban*, Inessive)

4.1.1 Cases Governed by Prepositions/Postpositions

In the immigrant languages under-investigation prepositions/postpositions tend to govern the nominative case.

In AR, prepositions govern the nominative rather than the prepositional, the accusative, or the dative:

(32) AR *v kitajskij restoran* "in the Chinese restaurant" (cf. R *v kitajskom restorane*, Prep; Polinsky 1997: 380)
(33) AR *bez vrač* "without a doctor" (cf. R *bez vrača*, Acc; Polinsky 1997: 380)
(34) AR *na mirovaja vojna* "in the world war" (cf. R *na mirovoj vojne*, Dat; Polinsky 1997: 379)

In ASC, prepositions similarly govern the nominative rather than the accusative, the genitive, the dative/locative, or the instrumental cases:

(35) ASC *u Jugoslavija* "to Yugoslavia" (cf. SC *u Jugoslaviju*, Acc; Jutronić 1971: 66)
(36) ASC *do leto* "by summer" (cf. SC *do leta*, Gen; Jutronić 1971: 66)
(37) ASC *po noč* 'at night' (cf. SC *po noči*, Dat/Loc; Jutronić 1971: 66)

In ASk also, prepositions govern the nominative instead of the accusative, the genitive, or the locative (38–40), just like in AC, instead of the genitive, locative, or the instrumental (41–43):

(38) ASk *na policija* "to the police" (cf. Sk *policiu*, Acc; Meyerstein 1959: 94)
(39) ASk *v male mestečko* "in a small town" (cf. Sk *v malom mestečku*, Loc; Hammerová and Ripka 1994: 74)
(40) ASk *okolo krk* "around [her] neck" (cf. Sk *krku* Gen; Hammerová and Ripka 1994: 74)
(41) AC *okolo to dítě* "around that child" (cf. C *toho dítěte*, Gen; Henzl 1982: 43)
(42) AC *v lednice* "in the fridge" (cf. C *v lednici*, Loc; Henzl 1982: 43)
(43) AC *se Československo* "with Czechoslovakia" (cf. C *se Československem*, Instr; Henzl 1982: 43)

Prepositions govern the nominative rather than the genitive in AP (44), and the accusative in American Greek (45):

(44) AP *do szkoła* "to school" (cf. P *szkoły*, Gen; Lyra 1962: 152)
(45) AG *ména ánqropos* "with a man" (cf. G *ánqropo*, Acc; Seaman 1972: 149)

Postpositions govern the nominative instead of the genitive or the partitive in AF (46–47) and instead of the instrumental in AH (48):

(46) AF *ikkuna läpi ~ läpi ikkuna* "through the window" (cf. F *ikkunan*, Gen; Larmouth 1974: 359)
(47) AF *tauni kohti ~ kohti tauni* "toward the town" (cf. F *taunia*, Part; Larmouth 1974: 360)
(48) AH *harmincöt év ezelőtt* "thirty-five years ago" (cf. H *évvel*, Instr)

4.1.2. Variability in Case Usage

Besides the loss of non-nominative cases and their replacement with the nominative, variability in case usage develops where the cases are not completely lost. Some examples from American Greek are as follows:

(49) AG *edo éxome énas ierefs* "here we have a priest" Nom (cf. G *éna ieréa*, Acc; Seaman 1972: 149)
(50) AG *íne just tu driver mésa* "there is just the driver inside" Gen (cf. G *to*, Acc; Seaman 1972: 150)
(51) AG *ke metaksí ta dío speakers* "between the two speakers" Acc (cf. G *ton*, Gen; Seaman 1972: 150)

In ASk, in prepositional phrases cases replace each other in various combinations: nominative or accusative is used where old-world Slovak has locative, and accusative or locative is used in place of genitive (Meyerstein 1959: 86–103).

Jönsson-Korhola (1990: 77) reports great variability in case use in AF.

In AH, cases expressing locative meanings often replace each other in such a way that their directionality (movement to, position at, or movement from) is preserved (52–53), but other kinds of replacement also occur (54–56) (Fenyvesi 1995/1996):

(52) AH *mindenki a tükörbe akart egyszerre menni* "everyone wanted to go to the mirror at the same time" (cf. H *tükörhöz*; illative instead of allative)
(53) AH *nem messze New York-ból* "not far from New York" (cf. H *New York-tól*; elative instead of ablative)
(54) AH *a magyar istentiszteleten járok* "I go to the Hungarian church service" (cf. H *istentiszteletre*; superessive instead of sublative)
(55) AH *angol templomban járnak* "they go to an English church" (cf. H *templomba*; inessive instead of illative)
(56) AH *jól tudta a szlovákon* "she spoke Slovak well" (cf. H *szlovákul*; superessive instead of essive)

4.2. Verb Inflection: Person/Number Marking

In contrast with what we have seen in the noun inflection, in connection with verb inflection—specifically, the person and number marking on the verb—authors do not report change, with the exception of American Dutch and AR. In all the other immigrant languages, verbal person/number marking is unchanged.

Unfortunately, from the perspective of the present analysis, most authors do not usually explicitly mention that person/number marking is unchanged, this can be deduced implicitly: they do not mention such change because no such change occurs. Only Seaman (1972: 165) remarks that "*errors* [*sic!*] *are rare*" in person/number marking in American Greek. Even though the sources the present analysis is based on are detailed and exhaustive, no mention is made about change in person/number marking in AP (Lyra 1962), Czech (Henzl 1982; Kučera 1990), Slovak (Meyerstein 1959), Finnish (Hirvonen 1995; Jönsson-Korhola 1990), and Serbo-Croatian, the latter at least not in Albin and Alexander (1972). Jutronić (1971: 100–1) mentions only two examples of the "mixing" of verbal inflections: in one case, the speaker used a first- rather than a third-person plural ending, and another where the speaker used a third- rather than a first-person plural ending. In AF, third-person plural endings are sometimes used instead of third-person singular ones (Pekka Hirvonen, 1999, personal communication), but the same phenomenon is also there in spoken Finland Finnish, so this feature cannot be regarded as a characteristic of AF only.

I have found no examples of changes in person/number marking of AH verbs in my own McKesport data, or Kontra's South Bend interviews (the transcripts of which he kindly shared with me), or among Bartha's (1993b) examples. Benkő (2000) reports no occurrence of such change either in her work on London Hungarians.

My McKeesport interviews contain many examples of speakers selecting a definite conjugation suffix instead of an indefinite one

(57–58) or vice versa (59–60),[2] but even when they do this, the person/number marking is retained:

(57) AH *de nem érted mindent* "but you don't understand everything" (H: *értesz*)
(58) AH *az öregek meghalták* "the old people died" (H: *meghaltak*)
(59) AH *bezártak a gyárt* "they closed the factory" (H: *bezárták*)
(60) AH *egymást ütöttünk* "we were hitting each other" (H: *ütöttük*)

In stark contrast, AR and American Dutch exhibit a very different picture regarding the person/number marking of verbs. In AR, Polinsky (1997: 382) reports a considerable erosion of subject–verb agreement in gender, number, and person:

(61) AR *moi roditeli oni kupil rugoj dom* "my parents bought another house" (R *kupili*)

In American Dutch, based on her research carried out with van Marle, Smits (2000) reports great variability in person/number marking: Table 4.1 summarizes her findings, showing what forms were replaced by what other forms by her interviewees. (The present tense paradigm of old-world Dutch monosyllabic verbs, illustrated through *zwemmen* "swim," is in 62.)

Table 4.1 Iowa Dutch, 1966 (Conversations): Deviation from Standard Dutch Present Tense Forms of Monosyllabic Verbs (Smits 2000)

	Total n	*Stem %*	*Stem + t %*	*Stem + en %*	*Schwa Addition %*
1Sg	*22*	59.1	**40.9**	**0**	n.a.
2Sg	*26*	**3.8**	88.5	**7.7**	n.a.
3Sg	*110*	**0.9**	99.1	**0**	n.a.
1Pl	*40*	**12.5**	**0**	57.5	**30.0**
3Pl	*59*	**1.7**	**0**	89.8	**8.5**

(62) *zwemm-en* "swim"

1Sg:	*zwem*	1Pl:	*zwemm-en*
2Sg:	*zwem-t*	2Pl:	*zwemm-en*
3Sg:	*zwem-t*	3Pl:	*zwemm-en*

As we can see in the table, in the percentages marked in bold, many verbs are marked with a person/number inflection, which is not the one that would be required in old-world Dutch—basically, the system collapses.

5. A Comparison of Noun versus Verb Inflection Systems

To summarize, what we see earlier is the development of great variability and case loss in the noun inflection of immigrant languages, and basically a lack of change in the person/number marking of verbs in the same languages, with the exception of American Dutch and AR.

Even though I have not been able to find a theoretically based explanation for this contrast, later in the text I want to forward some empirical observations that could explain the reason for why it may occur.

As we know, a case inflection does not have one individual meaning and, thus, does not have one single equivalent in another language. Even though the primary meaning of, for instance, the accusative case is marking the direct object, the accusative can also express other meanings: in some Slavic and Germanic languages, it can be governed by a preposition and mark a locative (cf. example 38, Slovak *na policiju* "to the police"), or in Hungarian it can mark an adjunct and express the extent of an activity (*ezer métert úszik* "swim a thousand meters"). That is, in the case of cases, there is no one-to-one correspondence between form and meaning—either within the languages under investigation or in comparison to English. Instead, there is great variability in matching forms and meanings both within and between languages.

In contrast, in the person/number marking of verbs, the languages under investigation have the same categories (first vs. second vs. third person, and singular vs. plural) and, with the exception of Dutch, six distinct suffixes for the six slots of the paradigm—basically, a one-to-one correspondence between each form and its meaning. See, for instance, Russian present-tense forms in (63) or Hungarian present tense forms in (64) for both the indefinite and definite paradigms of the same verb:

(62) Russian: *čitát'* "read"

1Sg: *čitáju*	1Pl: *čitájem*
2Sg: *čitáješ'*	2Pl: *čitájete*
3Sg: *čitájet*	3Pl: *čitájut*

(64) Hungarian: *olvas* "read"

indefinite conjugation:

1Sg: *olvasok*	1Pl: *olvasunk*
2Sg: *olvasol*	2Pl: *olvastok*
3Sg: *olvas*	3Pl: *olvasnak*

definite conjugation:

1Sg: *olvasom*	1Pl: *olvassuk*
2Sg: *olvasod*	2Pl: *olvassátok*
3Sg: *olvassa*	3Pl: *olvassák*

Even in English, where, seemingly, the standard variety has only five person/number pronoun forms (with *you* expressing both singular and plural since the times that *thou* "2Sg" was lost), many nonstandard and/or regional varieties do have the distinction between the singular and plural second-person pronouns by creating second-person plural forms to fill this gap: cf. colloquial American English *you guys*, U.S. southern *you all* and *y'all*, Pittsburgh area *you'unz* and *yinz*, U.S. regional *yous(e) guys*, colloquial British English *you lot*, Irish, Scottish (and some English) English *yous(e)*, and British regional *yees*.

The six person/number slots exist in English (with pronouns) and in the immigrant languages under investigation (with pronouns and inflections) in such a way that, with the exception of Dutch, one-to-one correspondence exists between each verbal inflection and the person/number expressed by it (at least in the present-tense paradigm). In Dutch, as we have seen, three inflected forms are distributed over the six slots–with no one-to-one correspondence between person/number versus inflection. This lack of one-to-one correspondence in old-world Dutch, then, might be the reason why the system collapses in American Dutch, producing the variability (see Table 4.1).

AR, on the other hand, exhibits the collapse of the system despite the one-to-one correspondence between inflections and their meanings in old-world Russian. This, in my opinion, is due to the fact that Polinsky's speakers (second-generation semi-speakers) are more advanced in their language attrition than the speakers in the other (Polish, Slovak, Finnish, Hungarian, Greek, etc.) studies. We can only hypothesize that the same collapse of the verbal inflection paradigms could have been found in the communities of the latter groups at a later stage, when language attrition had become more apparent.

One word about the immigrant Hungarian system of verbal inflections. As we have seen, the person/number marking on verbs was retained in AH, while the marking of definiteness versus indefiniteness collapsed—maybe because of its unusual, marked status, or maybe because of the lack of the distinction in English. According to Campbell and Muntzel (1989), both markedness and the lack of a distinction can lead to the loss of a linguistic feature in a contact situation.

It seems, then, that variability develops in the inflectional systems of the languages under investigation when there is no one-to-one correspondence between form and meaning, as is the case in the noun inflection systems of the languages in question as well as in the American Dutch verb inflection system. Importantly, no variability seems to develop in those cases where one-to-one correspondences exist—at least at the stage of immigrant bilingualism prior to massive language attrition.

6. Conclusion

As we have seen in the analysis presented in this paper, the nine immigrant languages investigated here demonstrate stark differences in how their noun inflection (case) systems versus verb inflection (person/number marking) systems change due to contact with English. Empirical observations have been presented to explain possible reasons for the differences, while systematic, theoretically grounded explanations should be sought by future research.

The most important empirical observation is that there seems to be a great contrast in how noun inflection (case marking) and verb inflection (person and number marking of subject) is affected by language contact in the immigrant languages under investigation. Language contact-induced change produces great variability in cases where no one-to-one correspondence between form and meaning exists, namely, in noun inflection as well as in the verb inflection of American Dutch, whereas contact does not affect verb inflection in all the other investigated immigrant languages, where the form and meaning of person/number marking inflection are in a one-to-one correspondence. The only exception to the latter phenomenon is AR as described by Polinsky (1997), likely due to the fact that her speakers were second-generation semi-speakers rather than fluent first- and second-generation speakers like in the other immigrant language studies. It is quite possible that results similar to Polinsky's would have been achieved regarding verb inflection if semi-speaker subjects had been investigated for the other immigrant languages as well.

Endnotes

1. Since the work I rely on, Jutronić (1971), talks about *Serbo-Croatian*, I use this designation in this paper also, even though of course distinguishing between *Serbian* and *Croatian* has been the norm since the breakup of Yugoslavia in the early 1990s.

2. Hungarian marks all finite verbs for definiteness (in case of a definite object) or indefiniteness (in case of an indefinite object or no object), cf. Kenesei et al. (1998: 256–59, 290–97, 322–26).

References

Albin, Alexander, and Ronelle Alexander. 1972. *The speech of Yugoslav immigrants in San Pedro, California*. The Hague: Nijhoff.

Andrews, David. 1989. *The how and why of some borrowings from English in third-wave emigré Russian* (PhD dissertation). Georgetown University, Washington, DC.

Andrews, David. 1990. A semantic categorization of some borrowings from English in third-wave emigré Russian. In Margaret Mills (Ed.), *Topics in colloquial Russian*, 157–74. New York: Peter Lang.

Andrews, David. 1993. American intonational interference in emigré Russian: A comparative analysis of elicited speech samples. *Slavic and East European Journal*, 37: 162–77.

Andrews, David R. 1998. *Sociocultural perspectives on language change in diaspora: Soviet immigrants in the United States*. Amsterdam: Benjamins.

Arnbjornsdottir, Birna. 1991. *North American Icelandic: The linguistic and social context of vowel mergers* (Dissertation).University of Texas, Austin.

Backus, Ad, and Hendrik Boeschoten. 1998. Language change in immigrant Turkish. In Guus Extra and Jeanne Maartens (Eds.), *Multilingualism in a multicultural context: Case studies on South Africa and Western Europe*, 221–37. Tilburg: Tilburg University Press.

Bako, Elemer. 1961a. *American Hungarian dialect notes: Goals and methods of Hungarian dialectology in America*. New Brunswick, NJ: Rutgers University.

Bako, Elemer. 1961b. Hungarian dialectology in the USA. *Hungarian Quarterly*, 1: 48–53.

Balassa, József. 1928. Az amerikai magyarok nyelve. *Nyelvőr*, 57: 62–63.

Balassa, József. 1936. A magyar és a finn nyelv Amerikában. *Nyelvőr*, 65: 103–6.

Bartha, Csilla. 1992. A nyelvek közötti érintkezés univerzáléi: Néhány adalék a kódváltás kérdésköréhez [Universals of language contact: More on codeswitching]. In Sándor Géza Kozocs and Krisztina Laczkó (Eds.), *Emlékkönyv Rácz Endre hetvenedik születésnapjára* [*Festschrift for Endre Rácz on the occasion of his 70th birthday*], 19–28. Budapest: ELTE Mai Magyar Nyelvi Tanszék.

Bartha, Csilla. 1993a. "Mindég csak magyarú beszélünk ALL THE TIME"—Magyarnak lenni "túl a Kecegárdán" ["We always speak Hungarian ALL THE TIME": Being Hungarian "beyond the Castle Garden"]. *Magyar nyelvőr*, 117: 491–5.

Bartha, Csilla. 1993b. *Egy amerikai magyar közösség nyelvhasználatának szociolingvisztikai megközelítései* [*A sociolinguistic analysis of the language use of an American Hungarian community*] (Dissertation). Budapest.

Bartha, Csilla. 1995. A nyelvvesztés néhány rendszerbeli szimptómája amerikai magyarok nyelvhasználatában. In Krisztina Laczkó (Ed.), *Emlékkönyv Szathmári István hetvenedik születésnapjára* [*Festschrift for István Szathmári on the occasion of his 70th birthday*], 34–44. Budapest: ELTE Mai Magyar Nyelvi Tanszék.

Bauer, Ivan. 1984. Syntactic deviations in an American Croatian newspaper: An approach to the phenomena of linguistic borrowing. *Folia Slavica*, 6: 253–63.

Benkő, Annamária. 2000. *An analysis of British Hungarian: Some morphological features of Hungarian as used by Hungarian immigrants and their descendants in London*. Szeged: University of Szeged MA thesis.

Benson, Morton. 1957. American influence on the immigrant Russian press. *American Speech*, 32: 257–63.

Benson, Morton. 1960. American-Russian speech. *American Speech*, 35: 163–74.

Benson, Morton. 1967. English loanwords in Serbo-Croatian. *American Speech*, 42: 178–89.

Bettoni, Camilla. 1986. Italian language attrition in Sydney: The role of birth order. In Camilla Bettoni (Ed.), *Altro Polo: Italian abroad—Studies on language contact in English-speaking countries*, 61–86. Sydney: Frederick May Foundation.

Bettoni, Camilla. 1989. Language loss among Italians in Australia: A summary of current research. *ITL: Review of Applied Linguistics*, 83–84: 37–50.

Bettoni, Camilla. 1990. Italian language attrition in Sydney: The role of dialect. In M. A. K. Halliday, John Gibbons, and Nicholas Howard (Eds.), *Learning, keeping, and using language: Selected papers from the 8th World Congress of Applied Linguistics, Sydney, 16–21 August, 1987, vol. 2*, 75–89. Amsterdam: Benjamins.

Bettoni, Camilla. 1991. Language shift and morphological attrition among second generation Italo-Australians. *Rivista di Linguistica*, 3: 369–87.

Blair, Betty A. 1991. Iranian immigrant name changes in Los Angeles. In: Stephen Stern and John Allan Cicala (Eds.), *Creative ethnicity: Symbols and strategies of contemporary ethnic life*, 122–36. Logan: Utah State University Press.

Bolonyai, Ágnes. 1998. In-between languages: Language shift/maintenance in childhood bilingualism. *International Journal of Bilingualism*, 2(1): 21–43.

Bolonyai, Ágnes. 2000. "Elective affinities": Language contact in the abstract lexicon and its structural consequences. *International Journal of Bilingualism*, 4(1): 81–106.

Campbell, Lyle, and Martha C. Muntzel. 1989. The structural consequences of language death. In Nancy C. Dorian (Ed.), *Investigating obsolescence: Studies in language contraction and death*, 181–96. Cambridge: Cambridge University Press.

Clausing, Stephen. 1986. *English influence on American German and American Icelandic*. New York: Peter Lang.

Clivio, Gianrenzo P. 1986. Competing loanwords and loanshifts in Toronto's italiese. In Camilla Bettoni (Ed.), *Altro Polo: Italian abroad—studies on language contact in English-speaking countries*, 129–46. Sydney: Frederick May Foundation.

Clyne, Michael. 1967. *Transference and triggering: Observations on the language assimilation of postwar German-speaking migrants in Australia*. The Hague: Nijhoff.

Clyne, Michael. 1972. *Perspectives on language contact: Based on a study of German in Australia*. Melbourne: Hawthorn Press.

Clyne, Michael. 1978. Some (German-English) language contact phenomena at the discourse level. In Joshua Fishman (Ed.), *Advances in the study of societal multilingualism*, 114–28. The Hague: Mouton.

Clyne, Michael. 1991. German and Dutch in Australia: Structures and use. In Suzanne Romaine (Ed.), *Language in Australia*, 241–48. Cambridge: Cambridge University Press.

Clyne, Michael. 1997. The German of 3rd generation German-English bilinguals in Australia. In Wolfgang Wölck and Annick de Houwer (Eds.), *Recent studies in contact linguistics*, 36–44. Bonn: Dümmler.

Cohen, Andrew D. 1989. Attrition in the productive lexicon of two Portuguese third language speakers. *Studies in Second Language Acquisition*, 11: 135–49.

Correa-Zoli, Yole. 1973. Assignment of gender in American Italian. *Glossa*, 7: 123–28.

Correa-Zoli, Yole. 1974. Language contact in San Francisco: Lexical interference in American Italian. *Italica*, 51: 177–92.

Correa-Zoli, Yole. 1981. The language of Italian-Americans. In Charles Ferguson and Shirley Brice Heath (Eds.), *Language in the USA*, 239–56. Cambridge: Cambridge University Press.

Daher, Nazih Y. 1992. A Lebanese dialect in Cleveland: Language attrition in progress. In Aleya Rouchdy (Ed.), *The Arabic language in America*, 25–35. Detroit: Wayne State University Press.

De Bot, Kees, and Michael Clyne. 1994. A 16-year longitudinal study of language attrition in Dutch immigrants in Australia. *Journal of Multilingual and Multicultural Development*, 15: 17–28.

De Fina, Anna. 2003. *Identity in narrative: A study of immigrant discourse.* Amsterdam: John Benjamins.

Dearmond, Richard C. 1971. The phonology of Canadian Ukrainian. In Regna Darnell (Ed.), *Linguistic diversity in Canadian society*, 291–307. Edmonton: Linguistic Research.

Dumitrescu, Domnita. 1993. A preliminary approach to the contact phenomena found in the Romanian spoken by Romanian-Americans of the first generation. *Journal of the American Romanian Academy of Sciences*, 18: 161–86.

Endrődy, Tibor. 1971. *"Prepositional" interference and deviation in migrant German and migrant Hungarian in Australia.* Clayton: Monash University MA thesis.

Fenyvesi, Anna. 1995/1996. The case of American Hungarian case. Morphological change in McKeesport, Pennsylvania. *Acta Linguistica Hungarica*, 43(3–4): 381–404.

Fenyvesi, Anna. 1995a. Language contact and language death in an immigrant language: The case of Hungarian. *University of Pittsburgh Working Papers in Linguistics*, 3: 1–117.

Fenyvesi, Anna. 1995b. *How assimilation affects assimilations: The loss of some phonological processes in American Hungarian*. Presented at the Symposium on Language Loss and Public Policy, University of New Mexico, Albuquerque, June 30 to July 2, 1995.

Fenyvesi, Anna. 1998a. Nyelvkontaktus és nyelvvesztés az amerikai magyarban: A hasonulások sorsa a McKeesporti beszélők nyelvében [Language contact and language loss in American Hungarian: The fate of assimilations in the language use of McKeesport speakers]. In Klára Sándor (Ed.), *Nyelvi változó—nyelvi változás [Linguistic variables and language change]*, 89–102. Szeged: JGyTF Kiadó.

Fenyvesi, Anna. 1998b. Patterns of borrowing and language attrition: American Hungarian in McKeesport, Pennsylvania. In Casper de Groot and István Kenesei (Eds.), *Approaches to Hungarian 6: Papers from the Amsterdam conference*, 229–49. Szeged: JATE Press.

Fenyvesi, Anna. 2000. The affectedness of the verbal complex in American Hungarian. In: Anna Fenyvesi and Klára Sándor (Eds.), *Language contact and the verbal complex of Dutch and Hungarian: Working papers from the 1st Bilingual Language Use Theme Meeting of the Study Centre on Language Contact, November 11–13, 1999, Szeged, Hungary*, 94–107. Szeged: JGyTF Press.

Fenyvesi, Anna. 2005a. Hungarian in the United States. In Anna Fenyvesi (Ed.), *Hungarian language contact outside Hungary: Studies in Hungarian as a minority language*, 265–318. Amsterdam: Benjamins.

Fenyvesi, Anna. 2005b. A toledoi magyarok nyelve: Nonstandard nyelvhasználat vagy a nyelvkontaktus hatása? [The language of Toledo Hungarians: Nonstandard language use or the effect of language contact?] In Nóra Kovács (Ed.), *Tanulmányok a diaszpóráról [Studies on the diaspora]*, 58–73. Budapest: Gondolat és MTA Etnikai-nemzeti Kisebbségkutató Intézet.

Fenyvesi, Anna. 2006. Contact effects in Toledo Hungarian: Quantitative findings. In Greg Watson and Pekka Hirvonen (Eds.), *Finno-Ugric language contacts*, 157–77. Frankfurt am Main: Peter Lang.

Fenyvesi, Anna, and Gyula Zsigri. 2006. The role of perception in loanword adaptation: The fate of initial unstressed syllables in American Finnish and American Hungarian. *SKY Journal of Linguistics*, 19: 131–46.

Fenyvesi, Anna, and Gyula Zsigri. 2007. A percepció szerepe az angol kölcsönszavak hangsúlytalan szókezdő szótagjainak fonológiai adaptációjában az amerikai magyarban [The role of perception in the phonological adaptation of unstressed initial syllables of English loanwords in American Hungarian]. In Attila Benő, Fazakas Emese, and Szilágyi N. Sándor (Eds.), *Nyelvek és nyelvváltozatok: Köszöntő kötet Péntek János tiszteletére, I. kötet* [*Languages and varieties: Festschrift for János Péntek, vol. 1*], 315–24. Kolozsvár: Anyanyelvápolók Erdélyi Szövetsége.

Fenyvesi, Anna, and Gyula Zsigri. 2010. Hangsúlytalan szó eleji szótagok adaptációja amerikai magyar kölcsönszavakban: Elméleti vonatkozások [The adaptation of unstressed word initial syllables of loanwords in American Hungarian]. In Csilla Fedinec, Mariann Tarnóczy, Ildikó Vančoné Kremmer, and István Csernicskó (Eds.), *Utazás a magyar nyelv körül* [*Traveling around the Hungarian language*], 254–67. Budapest: Tinta Kiadó.

Fenyvesi, Anna, and Gyula Zsigri. 2011. The adaptation of English initial unstressed syllables in American Hungarian loans: Theoretical implications. *Americana (e-journal)*, 7. http://americanaejournal.hu/vol7ling/fenyvesi-zsigri, date of access: July 9, 2019.

Filipović, Rudolf. 1982. Serbo-Croatian in the United States: Croatian dialects in contact with American English. In Roland Sussex (Ed.), *The Slavic languages in emigré communities*, 23–32. Edmonton: Linguistic Research.

Filipović, Rudolf. 1984. Croatian dialects in the United States: Sociolinguistic aspects. *Folia Slavica*, 6: 278–92.

Gilbert, Glenn G. 1965. English loanwords in the German of Fredericksburg, Texas. *American Speech*, 40: 102–12.

Haller, Hermann W. 1981. Between Standard Italian and creole: An interim report on language patterns in an Italian-American community. *Word*, 32: 181–91.

Haller, Hermann W. 1987. Italian speech varieties in the United States and the Italian-American lingua franca. *Italica*, 64: 193–209.

Hammerová, Louise, and Ivor Ripka. 1994. *Speech of American Slovaks—Jazykové prejavy americkich slovákov*. Bratislava: Veda.

Hasselmo, Nils. 1961. *American Swedish: A study in bilingualism* (Dissertation).Harvard University, Cambridge, MA.

Hatzidaki, Aspassia. 1994. Lexical borrowing in immigrant varieties of Greek. In Irene Philippaki-Warburton, Katerina Nicolaidis, and Maria Sifianou (Eds.), *Themes in Greek linguistics: Papers from the first international conference on Greek linguistics, Reading, September 1993*, 365–72. Amsterdam: Benjamins.

Haugen, Einar. 1953. *The Norwegian language in America, I-II*. Philadelphia: University of Pennsylvania Press.

Henzl, Vera. 1975. *The cultivation and maintenance of literary Czech by American speakers* (Dissertation).Stanford University, Stanford, CA.

Henzl, Vera. 1982. American Czech: A comparative study of linguistic modifications in immigrant and young children speech. In Roland Sussex (Ed.), *The Slavic languages in emigré communities*, 33–46. Edmonton: Linguistic Research Inc.

Hirvonen, Pekka. 1982. Aspects of a fossilized interlanguage: The English of Finnish Americans. In Thorstein Fretheim and Lars Hellan (Eds.), *Papers from the 6th Scandinavian Conference on Linguistics*, 260–78. Trondheim: Tapir.

Hirvonen, Pekka. 1992. Vowel and consonant length opposition in American Finnish: An example of language attrition. In Jussi Niemi (Ed.), *Studia Linguistica Careliana: A festschrift for Kalevi Wiik on the occasion of his 60th birthday*, 21–38. Joensuu: University of Joensuu.

Hirvonen, Pekka. 1995. Phonological and morphological aspects of Finnish language attrition in the United States. In Wolfgang Viereck (Ed.), *ZDL-Beihefte 77. Verhandlungen des Internationalen Dialektologenkongresses Bamberg 1990*, 181–93. Stuttgart: Franz Steiner.

Hirvonen, Pekka. 2001. Doni finished—meni läpi—highskoulun. Borrowing, code-switching and language shift in American Finnish. In Sture P. Ureland (Ed.), *Global Eurolinguistics: European languages in North America—migration, maintenance and death*, 297–324. Tübingen: Niemeyer.

Hjelde, Arnstein. 1996. The gender of English nouns used in American Norwegian. In Sture P. Ureland and Iain Clarkson (Eds.), *Language contact across the North Atlantic*, 297–312. Tübingen: Niemeyer.

Huber, Máté. 2013. A magyar mint örökségnyelv generációk közötti továbbadása Kanadában: A hamiltoni magyar közösség makro-szociolingvisztikai vizsgálata [The intergenerational transmission of Hungarian as a heritage language: The macro-sociolinguistic analysis of the Hungarian community in Hamilton]. In Gábor Keresztes (Ed.), *Tavaszi szél 2013* [*Spring winds 2013*], 242–49. Budapest: Doktoranduszok Országos Szövetsége.

Huber, Máté. 2016. Analitikus szerkezetek egy kanadai magyar beszélõközösség nyelvhasználatában [Analytic constructions in the language use of a Canadian Hungarian speech community]. In Tamás Váradi (Ed.), *Doktoranduszok tanulmányai az alkalmazott nyelvészet körébõl: X. Alkalmazott Nyelvészeti Doktoranduszkonferencia* [*PhD students' papers in applied linguistics: 10th Applied Linguistics PhD Conference*], 31–44. Budapest: MTA Nyelvtudományi Intézet.

Janurik, Boglárka. 2011. Contact induced features of Canadian Estonian: An analysis of forum discussions of the online newspaper. *Eesti Elu. Americana (e-journal)*, 7. http://americanaejournal.hu/vol7ling/janurik, date of access: July 9, 2019.

Jönsson-Korhola, Hannele. 1990. American Finnish syntax. Some observations on the use of cases in second generation speech. In László Jakab, László Keresztes, Antal Kiss, and Sándor Maticsák (Eds.), *Congressus Septimus Internationalis Fenno-Ugristarum, Debrecen, 27 August—2 September, 1990, Linguistica*, 72–77. Debrecen: KLTE.

Juričić, Ž. B., and J. F. Kess. 1978. Sociolinguistic dimensions of respectful address: A comparative study of native and immigrant Croatian. In Zbigniew Folejewski (Ed.), *Canadian contributions to the 8th International Congress of Slavists*, 103–16. Ottawa: Carleton University.

Justman, Zuzana. 1984. *Changes in the word order and the case system of fifteen Czech speakers in the United States* (Dissertation).Columbia University, New York.

Jutronić, Dunja. 1971. *Serbo-Croatian and American English in contact. A sociolinguistic study of the Serbo-Croatian community in Steelton, Pennsylvania* (Dissertation). Pennsylvania State University, State College.

Jutronić-Tihomirović, Dunja. 1985. *Hrvatski jezik v SAD* [*The Croatian language in the USA*]. Split: Logos.

Kálmán, Béla. 1970. Amerikai magyarok [American Hungarians]. *Magyar Nyelvőr*, 94: 377–85.

Karttunen, Frances. 1977. Finnish in America: A case study in monogenerational language change. In Ben G. Blount and Mary Sanchez (Eds.), *Sociocultural dimensions of language change*, 173–84. New York: Academic Press.

Kenesei, István, Robert Vago, and Anna Fenyvesi. 1998. *Hungarian* (Routledge Grammars). London: Routledge.

Kinder, John C. 1993. Coordination and subordination in second generation Australian Italian: A case study. *Rivista di Linguistica*, 5: 31–53.

Kontra, Miklós. 1984–1985. Egy—amerikai magyarok körében használt—kérdőívről [About a questionnaire used among American Hungarians]. *Magyar Nyelvjárások*, 36–37: 57–67.

Kontra, Miklós. 1984. Virág Roza jött Amerikába [Roza Virág came to America]. *Magyar Nyelv*, 80: 344–49.

Kontra, Miklós. 1985. Hungarian-American bilingualism: A bibliographic essay. *Hungarian Studies*, 1: 257–82.

Kontra, Miklós. 1986. Az amerikai-magyar kétnyelvűség kutatásának áttekintése (1906–1984) [An overview of research into American Hungarian bilingualism]. *Magyar Nyelvőr*, 110: 237–55.

Kontra, Miklós. 1988a. Az amerikai magyar nyelv néhány hangtani kérdéséről [Some phonological issues of American Hungarian]. In Jenő Kiss and László Szűcs (Eds.), *A magyar nyelv rétegződése* [*The stratification of the Hungarian language*]. Budapest: Akadémiai Kiadó, 573–83.

Kontra, Miklós. 1988b. Névtani megjegyzések a South Bend-i (Indiana, USA) magyarokról [Onomastic remarks on Hungarians in South Bend, Indiana]. *Magyar Nyelv*, 84: 58–93.

Kontra, Miklós. 1989. Túl sok-e az angol szó az amerikai magyarban? [Are there too many English words in American Hungarian?]. *Magyar Nyelvőr*, 113: 204–11.

Kontra, Miklós. 1990. *Fejezetek a South Bend-i magyar nyelvhasználatból* [*The Hungarian language as spoken in South Bend, Indiana*]. Budapest: MTA Nyelvtudományi Intézet.

Kontra, Miklós. 1990–1995. Changing names: Onomastic remarks on Hungarian-Americans. *Journal of English linguistics*, 23: 114–22.

Kontra, Miklós. 1993a. Communicative interference and failure: A classification with examples from Hungarian Americans. *Review of Applied Linguistics*, 101–2: 79–88.

Kontra, Miklós. 1993b. The messy phonology of Hungarians in South Bend: A contribution to the study of near-mergers. *Language Variation and Change*, 5: 225–31.

Kontra, Miklós, and Mária Gósy. 1988. Approximation of the standard: A form of variability in bilingual speech. In Alan R. Thomas (Ed.), *Methods in dialectology*, 442–55. Philadelphia, PA: Multilingual Matters.

Kontra, Miklós, and Gregory Nehler. 1981a. Language usage: An interview with a Hungarian American. *Hungarian Studies Review*, 8: 99–117.

Kontra, Miklós, and Gregory Nehler. 1981b. Ethnic designations used by Hungarian-Americans in South Bend, Indiana. *Ural-Altaische Jahrbücher*, 53: 105–11.

Kouzmin, Ludmilla. 1982. Grammatical interference in Australian Russian. In Roland Sussex (Ed.), *The Slavic languages in emigré communities*, 73–88. Edmonton: Linguistic Research.

Kovács, Magdolna. 1996. Tulajdonnevek használata az ausztráliai magyar nyelvben [The use of proper nouns in Australian Hungarian]. In Edit Mészáros (Ed.), *Ünnepi könyv Mikola Tibor tiszteletére* [*Festschrift for Tibor Mikola*], 198–201. Szeged: JATE.

Kovács, Magdolna. 1997. Language attrition in Australian Hungarian: A case study. In , László Borsányi and Edit Szőke (Eds.), *International Conference of PhD Students: University of Miskolc, Hungary, August 11–17, 1997. Section Proceedings. Humanities*, 114–21. Miskolc: Miskolci Egyetem.

Kovács, Magdolna. 2001a. *Code-switching and language shift in Australian Finnish in comparison with Australian Hungarian*. Åbo: Åbo Akademi Förlag.

Kovács, Magdolna. 2001b. Code-switching and case marking in Australian Finnish and Australian Hungarian. In Tõnu Seilenthal, Anu Nurk, and Triinu Palo (Eds.), *Congressus Nonus Internationalis Fenno-Ugristarum, 7.-13.8.2000 Tartu. Pars V*, 139–44. Tartu: Eesti Fennougristide Komitee.

Kovács Magdolna. 2001c. "A szókincs az nekem nem annyira bő": Az ausztráliai magyarság nyelvének néhány lexikai sajátossága a nyelvfenntartás szempontjából ["The vocabulary is not so wide for me": Some lexical features of the language of Australian Hungarians from the perspective of language maintenance]. *Néprajz és Nyelvtudomány*, 41: 135–48.

Kovács, Magdolna. 2002. Hatalom és nyelv: Fokozatos nyelvváltás az ausztráliai magyarok körében [Power and language: Gradual language shift among

Australian Hungarians]. In István Hoffmann, Dezső Juhász, and János Péntek (Eds.), Hungarológia és dimenzionális nyelvszemlélet: Előadások az V. Nemzetközi Hungarológiai Kongresszuson [Hungarian studies and the dimensional perspective on language: Papers from the 5th International Congress of Hungarian Studies]. Debrecen/Jyväskylä, 339–49.

Kovács, Magdolna. 2005. Hungarian in Australia. In Anna Fenyvesi (Ed.), *Hungarian language contact outside Hungary: Studies in Hungarian as a minority language*, 319–50. Amsterdam: Benjamins.

Kovács, Tímea. 2011. How optimality theory works for bilingual grammar: On the applicability of optimality theory for bilingual grammar for the description of English-Hungarian code-switching patterns. *Americana (e-journal)*, 7. http://americanaejournal.hu/vol7ling/kovacs, date of access: July 9, 2019.

Kovács, Tímea. 2018. *Codeswitching and optimality*. Budapest: L'Harmattan.

Kučera, Karel. 1990. *Česky jazyk v USA* [*The Czech language in the USA*]. Praha: Univerzita Karlova.

Larmouth, Donald W. 1974. Differential interference in American Finnish cases. *Language*, 50: 356–66.

Lauttamus, Timo. 1990. Code-switching and borrowing in the English of Finnish Americans in an interview setting. *Studies in Languages*, 20: 1–56.

Lauttamus, Timo. 1991. Borrowing, code-switching, and shift in language contact: Evidence from Finnish-English bilingualism. In Muusa Ojanen and Marjatta Palander (Eds.), *Language contacts east and west*, 32–53. Joensuu: Joensuun yliopiston monistuskeskus.

Lauttamus, Timo, and Pekka Hirvonen. 2011. American English and Finnish in contact. *Americana (e-journal)*, 7. http://americanaejournal.hu/vol7ling/lauttamus-hirvonen, date of access: July 9, 2019.

Lauttamus, Timo, and Pekka Hirvonen. 1995. English interference in the lexis of American Finnish. *The New Courant*, 3: 55–65.

Lauttamus, Timo, John Nerbonne and Wybo Wiersma. 2007. Detecting syntactic contamination in emigrants: The English of Finnish Australians. *SKY Journal of Linguistics*, 20: 273–307.

Lehtinen, Meri. 1966. *An analysis of a Finnish-English bilingual corpus* (Dissertation).Indiana University, Bloomington.

Levine, Glenn. 1995. *Elderly second-generation speakers of Yiddish: Toward a model of L1 loss, incomplete acquisition, competence an control*. Presented at the Symposium on Language Loss and Public Policy, University of New Mexico, Albuquerque, June 30 to July 2, 1995.

Lewis, Brian A. 1973. Swiss German in Wisconsin: The impact of English. *American Speech*, 48: 211–28.

Linn, Michael. 2006. Language change in the English of three generations of American Finns on the Iron Range of Minnesota. In Greg Watson and Pekka Hirvonen (Eds.), *Finno-Ugric language contacts*, 27–38. Frankfurt am Main: Peter Lang.

Lyra, Franciszek. 1962. *English and Polish in contact* (Dissertation).Indiana University, Bloomington.

Martin, Maisa. 1990. On the morphological distribution of English loan verbs in American Finnish. In László Jakab, László Keresztes, Antal Kiss, and Sándor Maticsák (Eds.), *Congressus Septimus Internationalis Fenno-Ugristarum, Debrecen, 27 August—2 September, 1990, Linguistica.* Debrecen, 68–71.

Meyerstein, Goldie Piroch. 1959. *Selected problems of bilingualism among immigrant Slovaks* (Dissertation).University of Michigan, Ann Arbor.

Moen, Per. 1988. The English pronunciation of Norwegian-Americans in four Midwestern states. *American Studies in Scandinavia*, 20: 105–21.

Moen, Per. 1991. The influence of a Norwegian substratum on the pronunciation of Norwegian-Americans in Upper Midwest. In Botolv Helleland (Ed.), *Norsk språk i Amerika/Norwegian language in America*, 97–115. Oslo: Novus.

Molnár, Tímea, and Máté Huber. 2013. Hungarian in Canada: A macro-sociolinguistic analysis. In Rudolf Muhr, Carla Amosor Negre, and Carmen Fernández Juncal (Eds.), *Exploring linguistic standards in non-dominant varieties of pluricentric languages*, 303–18. Wien: Peter Lang Verlag.

Myers-Scotton, Carol, and Ágnes Bolonyai. 2001. Calculating speakers: Codeswitching in a rational choice model. *Language in Society*, 30: 1–28.

Papademetre, Leo. 1994. Discourse marking in Australian Greek: Code interaction and communicative resourcing. In Irene Philippaki-Warburton, Katerina Nicolaidis, and Maria Sifianou (Eds.), *Themes in Greek linguistics: Papers from the first international conference on Greek linguistics, Reading, September 1993*, 349–56. Amsterdam: Benjamins.

Polinsky, Maria. 1997. American Russian: Language loss meets language acquisition. In Wayles Browne, Ewa Dornsich, Natasha Kondrashova, and Draga Zec (Eds.), *Annual Workshop on Formal Approaches to Slavic Linguistics: The Cornell Meeting 1995*, 370–406. Ann Arbor: Michigan Slavic.

Preston, Dennis R. 1986. The case of American Polish. In Dieter Kastovsky and Aleksander Szwedek (Eds.), *Linguistics across historical and geographical boundaries: In honor of Jacek Fisiak on the occasion of his fiftieth birthday. Volume 2—descriptive, contrastive and applied linguistics*, 1015–23. New York: Mouton de Gruyter.

Preston, Dennis R., and Michael Turner. 1984. The Polish of Western New York: Case. *Melbourne Slavonic Studies*, 18: 135–54.

Rabeno, Angela, and Lori Repetti. 1997. Gender assignment of English loan words in American varieties of Italian. *American Speech*, 72: 373–80.

Rakusan, Jaromira. 1985. The function of English loanwords in Canadian Czech. *Canadian Slavonic Papers*, 27: 178–87.

Rakusan, Jaromira. 1988. Sociosemantics of ethnic lexicon: Evidence from American Czech. *American Speech*, 63: 99–111.

Reményi, József. 1934. Rokontalan magyarok Amerikában [Hungarians without relatives in America]. *Magyar Szemle*, 20: 187–91.

Reményi, József. 1937. Az amerikai magyar nyelv [The American Hungarian language]. *Nyugat*, 30: 184–88.

Rouchdy, Aleya. 1992. Borrowing in Arab-American speech. In Aleya Rouchdy (Ed.), *The Arabic language in America*, 35–49. Detroit: Wayne State University Press.

Rubinyi, Mózes. 1921. Amerikai magyarság [American Hungarians]. *Magyar Nyelvőr*, 50: 11–13.

Sahlman-Karlsson, Siiri. 1976. *Specimens of American Finnish: A field study of linguistic behavior*. Uppsala: University of Uppsala.

Salmons, Joe. 1988. The question of a German-American vocabulary. In Elmer H. Antonsen and H. H. Hock (Eds.), *German linguistics II*, 102–11. Bloomington: Indiana University Linguistics Club.

Salmons, Joe. 1990. Bilingual discourse marking: Code switching, borrowing, and convergence in some German-American dialects. *Linguistics*, 28: 453–80.

Salmons, Joe. 1991. Register evolution in an immigrant language. The case of some Indiana German dialects. *Word*, 42: 31–57.

Schatz, Henriette. 1989. Code-switching or borrowing? English elements in the Dutch of Dutch-American immigrants. *ITL: Review of Applied Linguistics*, 83–84:125–62.

Seaman, David P. 1972. *Modern Greek and American English in contact*. The Hague: Mouton.

Silva-Corvalán, Carmen. 1994a. *Language contact and change: Spanish in Los Angeles*. Oxford: Clarendon.

Silva-Corvalán, Carmen. 1994b. The gradual loss of mood distinctions in Los Angeles Spanish. *Language Variation and Change*, 6: 255–72.

Silva-Corvalán, Carmen. 1998. On borrowing as a mechanism of syntactic change. In , Armin Schwegler, Tranel Bernard, and Uribe Uribe-Etxebarria (Eds.), *Romance linguistics: Theoretical perspectives*, 225–46. Amsterdam: Benjamins.

Silva-Corvalán, Carmen. 2004. Spanish in the southwest. In Edward Finegan and John R. Rickford (Eds.), *Language in the USA: Themes for the twenty-first century*, 205–29. Cambridge: Cambridge University Press.

Smits, Caroline. 1996. *Disintegration of inflection: The case of Iowa Dutch*. The Hague: North Holland Graphics.

Smits, Caroline. 2000. On the efficacy of "surface regularity" in disintegrating languages: The shape of verb forms in Iowa Dutch. In Anna Fenyvesi and Klára Sándor (Eds.), *Language contact and the verbal complex of Dutch and Hungarian: Working papers from the 1st Bilingual Language Use Theme Meeting of the Study Centre on Language Contact, November 11–13, 1999, Szeged, Hungary*, 164–76. Szeged: JGyTF Press.

Søndergaard, Bent. 1997. Syntactic interference in Australian Danish. In Wolfgang Wölck and Annick de Houwer (Eds.), *Recent studies in contact linguistics*. Bonn: Dümmler, 349–55.

Spissák, Ferenc. 1906. Az amerikai magyarság nyelve. *Magyar Nyelvőr*, 2: 259–63.

Stoffel, G. M. 1983. Forms of address amongst German-English bilinguals in New Zealand. *General Linguistics*, 23: 79–93.

Surdučki, Milan. 1978. *Srpohrvatski i engleski u kontaktu: Rečnik i morfoložska analiza engleskih pozajmljenica u standardnom srpohrvatskom jeziku srba i hrvata iseljenika u kanadi* [*Serco-Croatian and English in contact: A dictionary and morphological analysis of English loanwords in the standard Serbo-Croatian language of Serbian and Croatian immigrants in Canada*]. Novi Sad: Matice Srpska.

Sussex, Roland. 1982 The phonetic interference of Australian English in Australian Polish. In , Roland Sussex (Ed.), *The Slavic languages in emigré communities*, 141–53. Edmonton: Linguistic Research.

Szabó, Gergely. 2018a. *"Mit mixolod itt a lengvidzseket?" Amerikai magyar iskolák osztálytermi interakcióinak szociolingvisztikai vizsgálata*. Paper presented at the 20th Conference of Hungarian Sociolinguistics, Budapest, Hungary.

Szabó, Gergely. 2018b. A migráció és a többnyelvûség narratívái amerikai magyarok körében. *Magyar Nyelv*, 142(1): 1–21.

Tamis, Anastiosis. 1991. Modern Greek in Australia. In Suzanne Romaine (Ed.), *Language in Australia*, 249–63. Cambridge: Cambridge University Press.

van Marle, Jaap, and Caroline Smits. 1989. Morphological erosion in American Dutch. In , Norbert Boretzky (Ed.), *Viefalt der Kontakte*, 37–65. Bochum: Brockmeyer.

van Marle, Jaap, and Caroline Smits. 1993. The inflectional systems of Overseas Dutch. In Henk Aertsen and Robert J. Jeffers (Eds.), *Historical linguistics 1989 Papers from the 9th International Conference on Historical Linguistics, Rutgers University, 14–18 August 1989*, 313–28. Amsterdam: John Benjamins.

van Marle, Jaap, and Caroline Smits. 1995. On the impact of language contact on inflectional systems: The reduction of verb inflection in American Dutch and American Frisian. In Jacek Fisiak (Ed.), *Linguistic change under contact conditions*, 179–206. Berlin: Mouton de Gruyter.

Vázsonyi, Endre. 1995. *Túl a Kecegárdán: Calumet-vidéki amerikai magyar szótár [Beyond the Castle Garden: Calumet region American Hungarian dictionary*]. Budapest: Teleki László Alapítvány.

Virtaranta, Pertti. 1992. *Americansuomen sanakirja: A dictionary of American Finnish*. Turku: Institute of Migration.

Watson, Greg. 1999. Sveitsi's ja Tenoris: Code-switching and borrowing in the English of first generation, non-fluent bilingual Finnish-Australians. *SKY Journal of Linguistics*, 12: 195–217.

Watson, Gregory John. 1995. A corpus of Finnish-Australian English: A preliminary report. In P. Muikku-Werner and J. Julkunen (Eds.), *Kielten väliset kontaktit. AFinLAn vuosikirja 1995. Suomen soveltavan kieltieteen yhdisteyken (AFinLA) julkaisuja no. 53*, 227–46. Jyväskylä: AFinLA.

Watson, Gregory John. 1996. The Finnish-Australian English corpus. *ICAME Journal*, 20: 41–70.

Zsoldos, Benő. 1938. Az amerikai magyarok nyelve. *Magyarosan*, 7: 135–36.

CHAPTER 5

The "Why" of Social Motivations for Language Contact

Anna M. Babel

In this chapter, I argue that the way that speakers perceive language lies at the heart of language contact effects. This is an argument that I first laid out in an article coauthored with Stefan Pfänder in 2013, in which we argued that the meaning of grammatical structures is emergent in interaction and that speakers "build bridges" between languages through perceived similarity, even when the two languages are typologically dissimilar. In this chapter, I examine speakers' use and perception of two nonstandard Spanish diminutives, linking their use of variants of this linguistic feature to their positioning with respect to social categories such as gender, authenticity, and upward mobility. These social positionings lead speakers to largely reject the urban variant of the diminutive despite its grammatical transparency and social pressures to assimilate to an urban norm, factors that would generally favor transfer. I frame this analysis within the context of decades of work in linguistic anthropology showing that language contact is intimately embedded in social structures, and that the motivations for linguistic change are deeply and fundamentally social. Thomason's field-defining work insists on attention to these social factors. Her most famous contention, that *any* contact outcome is possible given the right social factors and regardless of the grammatical characteristics of the languages in contact, has been vigorously debated and challenged (e.g., Mufwene 2003; Thomason 2003) but has ultimately emerged as mainstream in the field of language contact.

Thomason writes that 'in its simplest definition, language contact is the use of more than one language in the same place at the same time' (2001: 1). However, she argues that this definition tends to overgeneralize to trivial cases of language contact that are unlikely to result in language change. Contact effects in language, on the other hand, occur 'if it is less likely that a particular change would have happened outside a specific contact situation' (2010: 32). While this definition appears quite loose at face value, Thomason goes on to enumerate a number of conditions that must be met in order to establish that a linguistic change is due to language contact.

(1) Is there evidence of contact effects throughout the grammar?
(2) Is there a potential source language?
(3) Is there a structural feature in the proposed source language and in the proposed receiving language?
(4) Was the feature NOT present in the receiving language before it came into contact with the source language?
(5) Was the feature present in the source language before it came into contact with the receiving language?
(6) Can the change be better explained by language-internal factors?

Paraphrased from Thomason (2001: 93–94)

These criteria tend to work better for some types of contact—specifically, borrowing, whether lexical or morphosyntactic—than others. In other types of contact, such as convergence, it works less well, and criterion 4 in particular can be tricky to establish. For example, most of the morphosyntactic contact effects that have been described in Andean Spanish are cases of structural convergence (Calvo Pérez 2000; Escobar 2000). This is true despite the fact that Quechua and Spanish are extremely divergent typologically (Muysken 2004). If we cleave strictly to criterion 4, we would exclude many linguistic features that have a strong argument in favor of contact.

However, considering changes in the distribution, frequency, pragmatics, or morphosyntactic behavior of particular features can open up a wider set of realistic possibilities (see also chapters by Baptista and Mithun, this volume).

Regardless of typological differences, speakers who regularly use the two languages perceive them to be similar, and gradually "build bridges" or wear possible paths of convergence (Babel and Pfänder 2013). This argument fits well with work suggesting that language contact effects are most likely to occur where languages converge, rather than where they diverge (Jarvis and Pavlenko 2008; Johanson 2008; Palacios 2007; Palacios and Pfänder 2014). The key question here is how speakers *see* similarity, and how speakers perceive grammar in ways that may ultimately result in convergence, or—as in the present case—may have the opposite effect.

Thomason suggests that the ultimate goal of the study of language contact is not to predict where and how change will unfold in contact situations, but to better understand the processes that lead to change through a detailed understanding of linguistic and social factors (2010: 33). While Thomason, in her work, has examined the large-scale forces that bring languages and their speakers together, I have focused on the small-scale interactional dynamics in which we can find the motivations for borrowing and structural convergence between languages. I believe that these dynamics, and detailed attention to social categories and how people inhabit and enact them, hold the key to understanding what language means to people, and therefore how and why language contact effects occur and persist, even under pressure from standardized varieties of language.

1. Language Contact as Speakers in Contact

Some of the most fundamental work in language contact has come from the field of linguistic anthropology, despite the fact that the two disciplines are too rarely read together. Beginning in the early days of the subdiscipline of linguistic anthropology, scholars moved away from an emphasis on the study of language as an abstract code, and toward the study of the use of linguistic repertoires by communities and social groups. Groundbreaking work by Hymes (1972), Gumperz (1968), Jackson (1974), and other scholars redefined the object of study away from essentializing concepts like "tribe," "nation," and "language" and toward an analysis of *interaction* in social spaces. These approaches are surprisingly up-to-date in an era in which new and different modes of interaction (Bonilla and Rosa 2015; Dauphinais 2018; Squires 2010) have once more brought the concept of a community under scrutiny.[1]

Meanwhile, scholars influenced by Labov's variationist framework (1972) turned toward the role of social meaning produced through interaction using patterns of language and dialect features (Eckert 2012; Milroy and Milroy 1992; Rickford 1985). An intense interest in the relationship of language and political economy gave rise to a group of foundational studies that closely examined the relationship between large-scale ideologies of language and individual speakers' choices, giving rise to studies of language-level contact outcomes and language shift as superstructures (Dorian 1994; Gal 1988; Irvine and Gal 2000). Recognition of multilingualism, mobility, and globalization brought a new generation of scholars to question the ways in which 'community,' particularly in the linguistic sense, is constructed and understood (Blommaert 2010; Morgan 2004, 2015). Scholars have sought new understandings of linguistic and repertoires and communities under the rubrics of linguistic ecologies of communities (Dil 1972; Kramsch and Whiteside 2008; Ludwig et al. 2010) and multilingual repertoires of individuals (Blommaert and Backus 2013).

Thomason's work must be seen in the context of these increasingly sophisticated approaches to the study of languages, communities, and ultimately speakers in contact. Scholars like Jaffe (1999), examining attitudes toward Corsican, language shift, and practices that work to distinguish the minority language from French; Duranti (1994), closely analyzing the grammatical encoding of agency in establishing authority through political discourse; and Hill and Hill (1986), reading divergent linguistic ideologies of Mexicano (Nahuatl) through a meticulous study of code-switching practices in discourse provide the necessary links between linguistic codes, social contexts, and individual identities and aspirations that help to elucidate the motivations behind contact effects.

Recent studies draw on decades of work in linguistic anthropology that takes the way that people understand language, and its place in a symbolic system, as the starting point for analysis of language and social structure. These studies examine the way that people construct languages as being appropriate for their own use, or not (Grammon 2018; Narayanan 2018; Sicoli 2011). The use of different codes brings into being the possibility of different types of community and socialization (Emlen 2015). Contexts of use—genres and registers—affect the way that contact features are used and the way that they travel through language (Babel 2011; Emlen 2019; Mannheim 1998; Sicoli 2010). And speakers can use intentional practices to control and influence the way that language contact plays out, particularly through discourses of purism (Barrett 2008; Swinehart 2012; Thomason 2007).

Many of these studies have engaged as a matter of course with situations of language contact. Yet, since these studies are not always grouped in the subfield of "language contact," they are often ignored and undercited in the current social turn in the fields of language and dialect contact (Erker 2017; Rodríguez-Ordóñez 2019). I hold, and have implemented in my work, that the key to understanding language contact processes is deep ethnographic work in particular communities and with particular speakers, describing and understanding the social systems and patterns of language use that people use to orient themselves with respect to contact features. As Thomason points out, this is generally a post hoc endeavor; we cannot predict with any degree of certainty language contact outcomes, because of the complexity and indeterminacy of the social systems that they respond to. However, we can understand why people make the choices that they do, and make probabilistic guesses about how contact outcomes will develop under a given set of social circumstances.

2. Contact in the Andes

Andean Spanish is the result of long-term contact between Spanish, brought to Latin America by colonists and invaders beginning in the sixteenth century, and Quechua, an indigenous language that was first used by the Inka and then spread by European colonizers as a lingua franca in the Andes (Durston 2007; Mannheim 1991). The 500 years of close contact between Quechua and Spanish and the continuing vitality of the Quechua-speaking population in Bolivia have resulted in fascinating convergence effects between the two languages—from the use of aspirates and ejectives in Spanish, primarily but not exclusively on Quechua loanwords (Babel 2017), to morphosyntactic convergence (Babel 2010; Escobar 2000; Pfänder et al. 2009), to semantic and pragmatic influences (Babel 2009; De los Heros and Montes 2008). However, the fact of contact does not explain the choices that individual speakers make to use contact variables and varieties.

In my more recent work, I have turned toward the questions of how people become aware of difference in the way that they speak, specifically through the process of migration. The contact variety of Spanish that I study is stigmatized in urban and educated spheres. Speakers from rural areas, who interact primarily with those who speak the same dialect, may not be aware that the way they speak is "different" or Quechua-influenced until they come into contact with a dialect that does not have the same characteristics. In interviews that I carried out with urban migrants in 2015, young women working in professional office jobs in the city were more likely to say that they modified the way that they spoke because of external pressures, in contrast to consultants who were working class and/or male. Indeed, the young women reported being shamed by coworkers, employers, and professors for using their rural dialect. In order to access the social mobility offered by education and the professional jobs they sought, they quickly learned to assimilate to the urban norm. Given that essentially all higher education and most job opportunities were in the city, young women typically adapted linguistically to their new surroundings. At the same time, on visits home they felt pressure in their home community not to act as if they were too good for their hometown and particularly for their families. Eva, one of the few young women who held a full-time professional job in Saipina, put this succinctly:

41:31
E: La familia, e, nos critica. Critica la forma de hablar. Ellos están acostumbrados, y ellos quieren que vayamos a Santa Cruz, o a España, o adonde sea, y que volvamos, y que hablemos igual. Porque estamos en Saipina.

E: The family, um, criticizes us. Criticizes our way of speaking. They're used to [a certain way], and they want us to go to Santa Cruz, or to Spain, or wherever, and for us to come back, and speak the same way. Because we're in Saipina.

Rural-urban migrants like Eva were quite specifically aware of dialect differences due to language contact and of perceptions of appropriateness in different spheres. Carlos, another migrant, performed a particularly fluent rendition of the difference between the urban and the rural dialects, utilizing prosody and voice quality as well as lexical and morphosyntactic differences in order to demonstrate the contrast between the two.

27:05
C: *¿Qué hacés por acá?* te dicen [en la ciudad]. Su forma de hablar es así. Pero el valluno, pues, te dice, *Qué hacés por, Qué has hecho?* Nada, así cortante es. *¿Aunde [es]tás yendo?* te dice el valluno. Y el camba te dice, *¿Pa'dónde vas?*, te dice. Son así palabras, costumbres que tienen. Eso.

C: *What're you up to?* they say [in the city]. Their way of speaking is like that. But a person from the [rural] valleys says, *What're you, Whatcha doing?* So, kind of cut-off. *Where ya goin'?* the valley person says. And the camba [from Santa Cruz] says *Where to?*, they say. Those are the words, the customs they have. Like that.

Despite his fluent dialect-switching, high degree of linguistic consciousness, and the fact that he had lived in the city since he was an adolescent and had strong ties with the urban sphere, Carlos's control was imperfect; he admitted that his country accent gave him away sometimes, showing through the urban dialect that he cultivated. He added that city people took his accent as an opportunity to mock him and call him names, underlining the tacit social and political power of the urban sphere.

Hegemonic standard language ideologies could cut both ways. Eva, a young professional who was strongly oriented toward the rural sphere, defended her use of local language forms by appealing to "correctness," pointing out that the urban form *acá* 'here' is not the written Spanish standard, *aquí* 'here'. While she admitted that she "corrected" her Spanish when she was aware that she was using Quechua words, she appealed to broader notions of correctness in defending her local, rural use of *aquí*, in contrast to the urban norm.

37:08

E: Yo trato de corregir, cuando es la palabra incorrecta. Por ejemplo, qué sé yo, el *khuchi*.[2] O sea, *khuchi*, yo sé que no es, es en Quechua, no es cierto. Por ejemplo, yo siempre, con otro, no, no voy a decir *khuchi*, siempre voy a decir *chancho*. Pero *aquí, aquí,* yo siempre digo *aquí* porque no es una palabra incorrecta *aquí*. Así yo siempre digo *aquí*.

E: I try to correct [myself], when the word is incorrect. For example, I dunno, *khuchi* 'pig.' So *khuchi*, I know it's not, it's in Quechua, right. For example, I always, with someone else, I'm not, I'm not going to say *khuchi*, I'm always going to say *chancho* 'pig'. But *aquí* 'here', *aquí*,

I always say *aquí* because *aquí* is not a word that is incorrect. So I always say *aquí*.

Rural-to-urban migrants who had experience with both a rural, Quechua-influenced dialect of Spanish and a powerful urban variety navigated language choice as part of their personal identification and positioning, using conceptions of place and context appropriateness in explaining their choices of codes and linguistic features. In doing so, they monitored their use of features linked to rural dialects, including not only Quechua contact features but also a range of lexical, prosodic, and grammatical contrasts.

3. Diminutives

The Spanish of the Andes has been described as being characterized by a widespread use of diminutive forms, which are widely considered to be reflective in some way of Quechua and Aymara grammar and/or pragmatics (Lipski 2007: 312). In Andean Spanish, the use of the diminutive extends to a variety of grammatical categories, including nouns, verbs, adjectives, adverbs, and even gerunds and imperative verb forms (Bustamante-López and Niño-Murcia 1995). This is considered unusual in comparison to European Spanish, which remains the hegemonic standard variety due to colonial ideologies. For example, in one study, 95 percent of educated respondents in Peru thought that the use of a diminutive on the temporal adverb *ahorita* 'right now+DIM' "sounds good," while 0 percent of respondents in Spain accepted the form (Talavera 1988: 71, cited in Pfänder et al. 2009: 198).

From a prescriptive point of view, these diminutive uses are often characterized as 'excessive' (Callisaya Apaza 2012: 43), marking a variety of Spanish that is in some way defective or nonstandard with respect to European Spanish (Callisaya Apaza 2012: 104; Pfänder et al. 2009: 198; Rendón 2008: 138). For example, the use of *ahoritita* 'right away+DIM+DIM', with a double diminutive marker *-it -ita*, is described as a 'barbarism' in a book dedicated to Bolivian dialectology (Muñoz Reyes 1982: 44).

From a descriptive point of view, the diminutive in Spanish in contact with Andean languages has been characterized as 'familiar' (Muñoz Reyes 1982: 44); affectionate or intensifying (Coello Vila 1996); modest or courteous (Escobar 2011: 332); polite (Bustamante-López and Niño-Murcia 1995; Calvo Pérez 2000: 345); and extending to a sense of warning or danger (Mendoza 1991). These uses are in line with the use of diminutives and other politeness strategies in Quechua and Aymara (Escobar 2001).

However, the question of whether, and how, the diminutive is linked to contact with indigenous languages is rather a fuzzy one. The extended use of diminutives has been characterized not only as a feature of Spanish in contact with Quechua but also of Spanish in contact with indigenous languages (Escobar 2012: 80), and indeed of Spanish in the Americas in general (Quilis 2001: 103). As Pfänder et al. note, in Bolivia, the extended use of the diminutive is present even among people who are entirely monolingual (Pfänder et al. 2009: 198). At the same time, it is widely noted that the use of the diminutive in Andean varieties, including Bolivian Spanish, is both distinctive and historically attested (Ramirez Luengo 2016).

Feke holds that the extended use of the diminutive in Andean Spanish can be linked to a calque of the Quechua first-person possessive suffix, which indicates affection and politeness (Feke 2004: 181, citing Lipski 1996: 213–14). Other authors, more straightforwardly, hold that it is a calque of the Quechua diminutive *-cha*, now entirely replaced in Bolivian Spanish by Spanish *-ito/a* (Muysken 2001). However, given the complicated back-borrowing and the extreme levels of contact between Quechua and Spanish in Bolivia, it can be difficult to establish directionality of contact influence with any precision.

The link between the diminutive and indigenous language contact is not limited to Spanish and Andean languages. The increased use of the diminutive relative to non-contact varieties of Spanish has been observed in Spanish in contact with Nahuat (Flores Farfán 2013), as well as Spanish in contact with Yucatec Mayan, Quechua, and Guaraní (Escobar 2012: 75). Escobar sums up the argument in favor of considering the diminutive to be a contact effect:

> In analyzing the functions that the diminutive has in these contact varieties of Spanish, it is clear that in addition to size, the diminutive is used to express courtesy and modesty, functions found in the Amerindian languages as well, and consistent with universal tendencies of diminutive expressions. These pragmatic functions suggest that the higher frequency of use of the diminutive in these Spanish varieties is a way of serving the discursive functions necessary in communication in such communities, especially in oral discourse. In addition, discourse markers in Guarani, Quechua, and Mayan are highly complex and relevant in face-to-face communication. Discourse constraints seem to also influence and account for other discourse-related functions, such as evidential meanings, and possession.
>
> Escobar (2012: 80)

In other words, the Spanish diminutive was available for pragmatic uses that were, and are, important in the areal context of indigenous languages of the Americas. We can observe that the diminutive is used more frequently in varieties of Spanish that are in contact with indigenous languages than in non-contact varieties, and we can hypothesize that this is due to contact influence and to pragmatic needs. However, given that the diminutive also marks informal registers of Spanish, it seems likely that this is a matter of grammatical convergence rather than unidirectional transfer (as argued by Fernández Lávaque and del Valle Rodas [1998] for northwestern Argentine Spanish).

The other principal variant of the Bolivian diminutive, *-ingo/a*, is used primarily in the eastern lowland department of Santa Cruz (Callisaya Apaza 2012: 82, 105, 317; Coello Vila 1996; Sanabria Fernández 1965, 1975). Coello Vila speculates that the suffix is 'presumably' borrowed from Tupí-Guaraní languages (1996: 173–74), but gives no evidence to support this supposition.[3] Indeed, the Guaraní diminutive suffix *-í* is more widely used in Paraguay (Escobar 2012). While the *-ingo/a* diminutive is rarely used in written language,[4] it seems to be less stigmatized than the Andean Spanish diminutive, probably because of the relative wealth and social status of the lowland speakers who use it.

Although the *ingo/a* diminutive stretches from the eastern Bolivian lowlands as far west as Vallegrande, in the Santa Cruz valleys, it is the use of diminutives on deictics (*estito* 'this little thing', *esito* 'that little thing', *aquellita* 'that little thing over there', *allacito* 'right over there') and on adverbs (*ahoritita* 'right away', *igualito* 'exactly the same', *rapidito* 'very quickly', *despuescito* 'right afterwards') that is particularly associated with the Santa Cruz valleys (Callisaya Apaza 2012: 326–27, citing Sanabria Fernández 1965). This observation was echoed by my consultants, as I explain in more detail later.

My interviewees commented on different forms of the diminutive explicitly, indicating that they were aware of variation in the diminutive at a conscious level. In interviews, the *-ingo/a* diminutive was one of a consistent set of linguistic features that stood out to my consultants as being typical of Santa Cruz. Other aspects of dialectal differentiation that were available at a metalinguistic level included the use of a distinctive variant of *pues* (see Babel 2014a), lexical differences (e.g., *hueco* vs. *hoyo* vs. *agujero* 'hole'), prosodic differences, and the use of augmentative *-ango/a*.

The diminutive is a particularly interesting case of variation in terms of standard language ideologies, since the urban form *-ingo* is not a standard Spanish diminutive. It is true that the rural *-ito/a* diminutive is used in nonstandard ways—particularly in the sense that it is licensed to modify more grammatical categories than in canonical Spanish, it may be doubled or tripled, and the extensive use of the diminutive is considered a sign of Quechua contact influence. However, it takes the same form as the canonical Spanish diminutive, while the urban variant is rather idiosyncratic, indeed quite uncommon in the Spanish-speaking world.

4. Methods and Data

In the summer of 2015, I spoke with twenty-eight *Saipineños*, natives of the town of Saipina in western Santa Cruz, Bolivia. I have carried out long-term ethnographic fieldwork in this region since 2002 and have extensive contacts in the area (see Babel 2018). The participants in this study were selected in order to represent a range of experience in the urban center of Santa Cruz, from a low of zero months to a high of twenty-five years in the city. The participants were recruited via existing participant networks and included thirteen men, ranging in age from eighteen to forty-three, and fifteen women, ranging in age from fourteen to forty-five. Eight of the participants were residents of Santa Cruz at the time of the interview, nineteen were residents of Saipina at the time of the interview, and one was living in a different city in eastern Santa Cruz. A summary of the participants is given in Table 5.1.

The interviews mainly took the form of questions about language and language ideologies, though a few consultants interpreted the interview context as an opportunity to give me their life history. Since the length of the interviews varied, I analyzed the use of diminutives in the first thirty minutes of the interview, though nine interviews were a few minutes short of that length (see Table 5.1). I did not ask specifically about diminutives, but I did ask about differences between the way that people in Saipina talked versus the way that people in Santa Cruz talked. Of twenty-eight interviewees, every single person used multiple diminutives in the course of a half-hour recording. The speakers with the highest rates of diminutives met or exceeded the rate of one diminutive for every minute of the recording. Nine of the respondents, without prompting, explicitly identified diminutives as a relevant difference between the urban Santa Cruz dialect and the dialect of the rural valleys.

Several consultants discussed *-ito/a* diminutives explicitly, linking them to a valley identity. Here and in all following transcripts, *-ito/a* diminutives are <u>underlined</u> and **-ingo/a** diminutives are in **boldface**.

Table 5.1. Participant Data for Diminutive Study

Participant #	*Age*	*Gender*	*Years in SCZ*	*Current Residence*	*ITO Diminutives (Metalinguistic)*	*INGO Diminutives (Metalinguistic)*	*Minutes Analyzed*
1	37	M	1	Saipina	16		30
2	43	M	14	Saipina	6		30
3	35	M	5.5	Saipina	10		30
4	30	M	9	Santa Cruz	14 (4)	1	30
5	25	F	15	Saipina	12	(4)	24
6	39	M	9	Saipina	38	2	30
7	24	M	4.5	Santa Cruz	11	1(1)	30
8	23	F	5	Santa Cruz	16		30
9	25	F	11.5	Other city	12		30
10	35	F	17	Saipina	35		30
11	18	M	0.5	Saipina	12		22
12	25	F	7	Saipina	22 (3)		28
13	28	F	7	Saipina	10		30
14	40	F	5	Saipina	21	(7)	27
15	45	F	25	Santa Cruz	4		30

16	14	F	0	Saipina	22	(1)	27
17	37	M	0	Saipina	22		30
18	23	M	0	Saipina	8		30
19	37	F	10	Saipina	27		30
20	17	F	0	Saipina	4	(2)	29
21	18	M	0.5	Santa Cruz	9		30
22	36	F	0.5	Saipina	16		27
23	36	M	7	Saipina	17 (1)	(4)	28
24	23	M	11	Santa Cruz	7	2	30
25	27	M	6	Saipina	10	1	30
26	35	F	11	Saipina	7		30
27	24	F	16	Santa Cruz	24 (5)	(2)	30
28	23	F	4.5	Santa Cruz	14	1	26

Participant 4 (Male; SCZ resident; nine years in SCZ)[5]

13:00
B: A los vallunos por ejemplo allá en Saipina ... eh, preguntan por ejemplo '¿dónde queda la, la plaza principal?' dicen
A: Ah-hah
B: Y si es, si es Saipina, el, la persona que responde dice ahiʃito dicen, ahiʃito
A: Uh-huh
B: Quiere decir 'está ahí, ahí, ahí, ahí cerca' digamos, 'está, está, está ahicito' dicen (laughter)
A: Uh-huh, y ¿aquí no dicen eso?
B: Y aquí dicen diferente, o sea, no conocen, o sea, conocen esa palabra pero saben que somos de aquí de ... que es, digam, una palabra valluna digamos

B: About the valley people, for example, there in Saipina . . . uh, they ask for example, 'Where is the plaza, the central plaza?' they say
A: Uh-huh
B: And if it's, if it's Saipina, the, the person who answers says 'right over there+DIM' they say, 'right over there+DIM'
A: Uh-huh
B: That means, 'it's there, there, there, there nearby,' let's say, 'it's, it's, it's right over there+DIM' they say (laughter)
A: Uh-huh, and they don't say that here [in Santa Cruz]?
B: And here they say it differently, that is, they don't know, like, know that word but they know that we're from here from . . . what is, it, you know, a word from the valleys for example.

14:00
B: Uhh varias, varias veces ... siempre digo ... hasta ahorita, eh, yo trabajo con clientes, con mis clientes, y a veces me dicen 'Oiga usted, ¿de dónde es pues?' me dicen. 'Yo soy de los valles cruceños' les digo, 'de ahiʃito' les digo. 'Ah valluno es Usted, no,' me dicen, 'con razón su forma de hablar es diferente' me dicen.

B: Uhh many, many times . . . I always say . . . up to right now, uh, I work with clients, with my clients, and sometimes they say to me, 'Listen, where are you [formal] from anyway? ' they say. 'I'm from the Santa Cruz valleys,' I say, 'from right over there+DIM,' I say. 'Oh, you [formal] are from the valleys,' they say, 'No wonder your way of speaking is different,' they say.

Young women related being mocked or criticized for using diminutives such as *allacito* 'over there+DIM,' *aquicito* 'right here+DIM,' *ahoritita* 'right away+DIM+DIM,' and so forth.

Participant 12 (Female; Saipina resident; seven years in SCZ)

5:25
J: La verdad, un poco mezclado será pues, no, con el Quechua, digamos, uno siempre habla, En cambio, allá [en la ciudad], es un poco, ya, más mejor p' que uno habla. No, que uno se equivoca, también.

The truth, it's a little mixed up I guess, with Quechua, you know, [as] one always speaks,, On the other hand, over there [in the city], it's a little, *better* that one speaks. Right? And one makes mistakes, also.

6:10
J: Por ejemplo, allá. Allacito uno dice por acá, no ve? Y en cambio allá [en la ciudad], digamos, es diferente.

For example, 'over there'. 'Right over there+DIM' one says around here, right? And on the other hand over there [in the city] it's different.

6:20
J: Pueden decir allá, digamos [en la ciudad]. Y nosotros decimos allacito o aquicito, digamos. Entonces eso uno trato de cambiar digamos.

> They might say 'over there', for example [in the city]. And we say 'right over there+DIM' or 'right over here+DIM', for example. So one tries to change, you know.

Participant 13 (Female; Saipina resident; seven years in SCZ)

> 31:28
> M: Y todo el tiempo él se hacía la burla de, de, de algunas palabras que yo hablaba, por ejemplo a veces me, me, me decía que se lo haga algo, yo le decía 'Ahoritita!' 'Ahoritita voy!' O 'Un ratito!' Y todo el tiempo él, él, lo disfrutaba escuchar esas palabras.
>
> And all the time he made fun of, of, of some words that I spoke, for example sometime he, he, he told me to do something, and I would say 'Right away+DIM+DIM!' 'I'll be right there+DIM+DIM!' or 'One sec+DIM!' And all the time, he, he, enjoyed hearing those words.

Participant 27 (Female; Santa Cruz resident; sixteen years in SCZ)

> 22:24
> V: Y también el 'ahorita' dicen aquí, que allá dicen '**ahoringa**'. (se ríe) No ve? O dicen también 'ahicito'. Aquí es 'en ahicito.' Y allá cuando uno dice 'ahicito' se ríen. Ah hah, se ríen, se reían. Unas compañeras de la universidad se reían. '¿Dónde?—Ahicito!—Wa ja jajaja.' Dicen '**ahicingo**', o 'aquí', digamos.
>
> And also people use 'right away+DIM' here, where over there [in the city] they say '**right away+DIM**'. (laughs) Right? Or they also say 'right there+DIM'. Here it's 'right in there+DIM.' And over there when someone says 'right there+DIM' they laugh. Uh-huh, they laugh, they used to laugh. Some of my classmates at the university used to laugh. 'Where?—right there+DIM!—Bwa ha hahaha.' They say '**right there+DIM**' or 'here', for example.

Interestingly, the contexts in which consultants mentioned or used the *-ingo* diminutive were not strikingly different in morphosyntactic terms from the contexts in which the *-ito* form was used; indeed, they reported hearing or using *ahoringa* 'right away+DIM', *ahicingo* 'right over there+DIM', *rapidingo* 'very quickly+DIM', *un ratingo* 'one sec+DIM', the same temporal and spatial adverbs that are commonly linked to Quechua contact. In particular, *ahoringa* 'right away+DIM' was pointed out as a stereotypical aspect of urban Santa Cruz speech.

Despite their high level of awareness, the interviewees, even those that identified very strongly with Santa Cruz, had lived there in childhood, and indicated that they planned to live in Santa Cruz in the future, rarely used the *-ingo* diminutive outside of metalinguistic contexts (see Table 5.1). When they did use the *-ingo* diminutive, it was typically men rather than women who used it, and it generally appeared in contexts in which they were orienting themselves to the city.

Participant 4 (Male; Santa Cruz resident; nine years in SCZ)

> 20:00 El seis ... a la mano izquierda hay una canchita que se llama canchita de [vidrio]. **Todingo** por ahí viven puros saipineños
>
> The sixth [ring] . . .[6] on the left-hand side there's a field+DIM that's called the field+DIM of [glass]. **All+DIM** around there it's purely Saipineños.

Participant 6 (Male; Saipina resident; nine years in SCZ)

> 08:50 Claro, al **ratingo** se le nota su hablar pues. [speaking of urban migrants]
>
> Of course, **right away+DIM** you notice their way of speaking.

Participant 7 (Male; Santa Cruz resident; 4.5 years in SCZ)

> 16:35 El papa. Mmm, **lleningo** va a estar pues la ciudad.
>
> The pope. Mmmm, the city's going to be **full+DIM**.

Participant 24 (Male; Santa Cruz resident; eleven years in SCZ)

> 3:15 Era llorar, y llorar, y llorar, y llorar, **todingo** los días. Era difícil. [speaking of his first weeks in Santa Cruz]
>
> [I was] was crying, crying, crying, crying, **every+DIM** day. It was hard. [speaking of his first weeks in Santa Cruz]

Participant 25 (Male; Saipina resident; six years in SCZ)

> 17:00 Un globo **asicingo**! (G: Quieren hacer doler.) Ese es el chiste pues. [speaking of Carnaval in Santa Cruz]
>
> A balloon **like this+DIM**! (G: They want to cause pain.) That's the joke. [speaking of Carnaval in Santa Cruz]

Participant 28 (Female; Santa Cruz resident; 4.5 years in SCZ)

> 10:45 Por donde venden para cumpleaños de niños? **Ahicingo** es. [describing the location of her home in the city.]
>
> Where they sell things for children's birthdays? It's **right there+ DIM**. [describing the location of her home in the city.]

In these excerpts, consultants used the *-ingo* diminutive when speaking of locations and activities that took place in the city—the location of a football field (participant 4) or a home (participant 28); experiences of feeling homesick in the city (participant 24) or visiting for Carnaval (participant 25); the supposition that the city will be full of people during the Pope's visit (participant 7) and a commentary on the manner of speaking of urban migrants (participant 6).

All of these consultants, however, used the *-ito* diminutive primarily and more consistently than the *-ingo* diminutive (Table 5.1). While men were more likely than women to use the *-ingo* diminutive, women were more likely than men to mention it explicitly, indicating that they recognized the form and were able to use it, though they generally chose not to. This was true even of women who expressed a strong identification with the city and a positive attitude toward the urban dialect.

Another illustration that may provide context for the tendency of my consultants to avoid the *-ingo* diminutive comes in the form of a joke that surfaced in one of my interviews. Reina was talking about people who move to the city and instantly change their style of speech, and she recounted the following story:

> 16:05
> R: De allá volvieron en las vacaciones vuelta a su pueblo dice. 'Ay mamá!' le había dicho, no? 'Qué **animalucho** con su **paluchos** aquel,' le había dicho a la chiva. (laughs) A la chiva, pues! 'Qué animal, **animalingo** con su **palucho** aquel,' había dicho pues.
>
> R: So apparently they came back [from the city] during [school] vacations, returning to their town. 'Oh mama!' she said, right? 'What **animal+AUG** with its **sticks+AUG** is that one,' she said about the goat. (laughs) About the goat! 'What animal, **animal+DIM** with its **sticks+AUG** is that one,' she said.
>
> 16:58
> R: Ah, para el perro pues. El perro chiquito dijo no ve? Y ella le decía, '**Chiquitingo** la **pierringo**,' por decir que es chiquito el perrito, no ve. Ella no decía así. '**Chiquitingo** la **pierringo**,' así.
>
> R: Uh-huh, about the dog. The little+DIM dog, right? And she said, '**Tiny+DIM** little **dog+DIM**,' in order to say that the dog+DIM is little+DIM, right. She didn't say it like that. '**Tiny+DIM** little **dog+DIM**,' like that.

In this story, Reina tells of a young woman who returns from the city to her rural hometown in the countryside. In the countryside, she feigns ignorance at the common sight of a goat, calling it an animal with sticks on its head. In her telling, Reina uses a form of the augmentative that is uncommon in rural areas, *animal+ucho* 'great big animal' and *pal+ucho+s* 'great big sticks', then switches to the *-ingo* diminutive, *animal+ingo*. In a follow-up to the story, she relates that the young woman remarked on a dog's tiny size by using the *-ingo* diminutive, *chiquit+ingo la pierr+ingo.*[7] Here, both 'tiny' and 'dog' are marked with *-ingo* diminutives, but oddly, the reported speech also includes grammatical errors in Spanish, with a lack of gender concord (*la pierringo*, the+FEM dog+DIM+MASC) and an unexpected stem change on *perro* > *pierr-ingo*.[8] This is no speech error; Reina repeats the sentence twice, with emphasis. She even "translates" the sentence back into our common dialect, *por decir que es chiquito el perrito, no ve?* 'to say that the dog+DIM is little+DIM, right?' to make sure that I get the point.

Gender mismatches and vowel confusion, particularly the hypercorrection of *-ie* sequences, are typical features of Quechua-dominant speakers of Spanish (Babel 2010), and indeed the town in which Reina sets her story is a Quechua-dominant town near Saipina. Here, the young woman in the story seems to be caught between two undesirable stereotypes—that of a Quechua speaker who cannot truly make a claim to the Spanish language and that of an urban migrant who ostentatiously claims not to know what a goat is, even as she uses patently ridiculous augmentative and diminutive forms associated with lowland, Spanish-speaking Santa Cruz. In short, the parodic element lies in the contrast between the young woman's inability to control standard Spanish, at the same time as she lays claim to a relatively prestigious urban dialect.

Given the potential for ridicule when young women return from the city and are perceived as "putting on airs," coupled with the readiness of both rural and urban listeners to dismiss their Spanish dialect as illegitimate due to Quechua contact influence, is it any wonder that young women tend to avoid marked, nonstandard forms of the diminutive? The fact that they can, and do, discuss the use of the form indicates that they are perfectly aware of its existence. However, the young women are caught in a double bind—if they sound *too urban*, they will be accused of putting on airs (in local terms, being *refinidas* 'stuck up'), but if they sound *too rural*, they will be accused of speaking illegitimate, Quechua-influenced Spanish and being country bumpkins. By and large, they stick to what they perceive as the most standard form of the diminutive, while avoiding forms like *ahoritita* 'right now, right away' that people highlight as nonstandard.

The case of the diminutive provides an interesting example of dialect contact between a rural, Quechua-influenced variety of Spanish and a powerful urban lowland variety. The diminutive appeared to be quite a salient linguistic feature in that speakers recognized it and discussed it explicitly. Speakers were aware of the variation, relating stories about being mocked or made fun of because of their use of their native, rural variant. Young women, who were more socially mobile but also more vulnerable than young men, controlled their use of the diminutive form carefully, avoiding both usages that were markedly rural and those that were markedly urban. Young male migrants used the urban form occasionally, but it appeared primarily in contexts in which they were orienting spatially or thematically to the urban center.[9] Ideologies of standard language came into conflict with the general power of the lowland dialect, and my consultants balanced a complicated field of power, prestige, loyalty, and authenticity as they controlled their usage of the diminutive.

5. Discussion

In this article, I discuss the *why* of contact effects—why do they persist, even in contact with more prestigious varieties of Spanish? The answer to this question involves a complex intersection of awareness, social identification, and context.

Awareness. My consultants were very aware of the contrast between *-ito* and *-ingo* forms of the diminutive. They mentioned them explicitly, urban migrants told of being corrected or made fun of because of their use, and they used the diminutive to tease or lampoon other speakers. However, they had less awareness of the morphosyntactic aspects of the diminutive. Both *-ingo* and *-ito* forms of the diminutive were used in similar grammatical slots, and both were available for doubling. This is particularly visible in participant 27's comments earlier—the urban equivalent of *ahorita* is ***ahoringa***, and the urban equivalent of *ahicito* is ***ahicingo***. That is, the use of diminutives on adverbs of time and place was not the problem, from the speakers' point of view; the problem was the form itself. While the *-itito* doubled diminutive was stigmatized, *-it**ingo*** was not flagged as having nonstandard morphosyntax. Rather, the ***-ingo*** lexical entry was marked as being citified or urban.

Social identification. The use of the *-ingo* diminutive sent strong social signals. In general, people who used the *-ingo* diminutive were those who had current ties to the city. In general, they were men. While these observations describe tendencies, not absolutes, they do cohere with the expectation that young, upwardly mobile women are under particular pressure to sound "standard" and unaccented, both in Bolivia (Babel 2018) and as has been shown more broadly (Gal 1978; Labov 1972). Part of the construction of a "professional" persona for young women includes the avoidance of marked dialect features. This illustrates the links between gender, class mobility, and language use in the transfer of dialect features.

Context. There was a strong tendency for the rural diminutive to appear when people were feeling particularly relaxed or speaking of topics that were close to home, showing affection or pity. Interviews that I felt went particularly well were often those in which many diminutives were found. This is an excellent example of the pragmatic uses of a contact feature—in this case, the diminutive—that leads to its portability due to its links with a particular register of speech (Babel 2011; Emlen 2019; Sicoli 2010). On the other hand, consultants used the urban diminutive specifically when discussing topics that were oriented toward the spatial or social realm of the city, as shown earlier in the text.

Along with speakers' attitudes, Thomason identifies *markedness* as one of the key factors affecting the transfer of linguistic material due to language contact. She refers to 'universal markedness' in a linguistic sense (2010: 43–44). Rather than subscribing to a universal view of markedness, I believe that we must shift this discussion to a view of what speakers perceive as marked—in other words, the extent to which speakers are aware of particular features, and are able to mobilize, control, or suppress them (Irvine and Gal 2000). The process of becoming aware of difference has a great effect on our use of language (Babel 2016; see also Erker 2017, which uses the term *salience*). The way that we perceive social groups affects the way that we understand their language use (Babel 2014b; McGowan and Babel 2020), and the way that speakers understand difference and similarity in their languages affects the way they perceive linguistic features as portable or not (Babel and Pfänder 2013). However, there is an interplay between individual positioning and social structure that constrains or enables particular possible outcomes of language contact (Narayanan 2018; Sicoli 2010). Most importantly, these are often emergent possibilities, rather than stable, established structures (Babel 2017; Babel and Pfänder 2013).

6. Conclusion

This paper considers the *why* of contact effects. Why do speakers use local, contact-inflected linguistic features, even as they come into contact with more prestigious varieties of Spanish? Why do people use particular features at all—because they feel like home, because they feel like an identity in which people feel comfortable? Or because of appropriateness to a particular context? Being a bidialectal or bilingual speaker means having two linguistic homes, two linguistic selves. Yet all speakers move back and forth between different styles of speech to some extent, without necessarily finding themselves in any great crisis of identification.

All language is language contact, whether between individual speakers or between codes on a large scale. I argue in this paper, as I have argued elsewhere, that speakers perceive similarity in the different codes that they control, whether to a greater or a lesser extent. The pragmatic needs of communities shape the linguistic material that speakers borrow or transfer between dialects and codes, and affective links with particular forms of language may lead them to retain contact features for particular discourse purposes (Babel 2014c, 2016). At the same time, people take ownership of linguistic features based on personal positioning and goals—the extent to which they feel that it "fits" themselves and their aspirations. Even when people have strong ties to the urban sphere, even when they're made fun of for using the local diminutive, they don't necessarily embrace urban forms of language, in part because of ideologies of standard language that mark the urban diminutive as nonstandard. Because affective links to language are personal and individual as much as they are large-scale and societal, they can produce surprising effects. The case of Quechua-Spanish contact in the Andes is a case in point of Thomason's contention that under the right social conditions, *anything* can happen—whether it is convergence and similarity between two typologically extremely divergent codes, as described in Babel and Pfänder (2013), or whether it is the choice *not* to adopt a linguistic feature despite its high social prestige and grammatical similarity, as in the case of the diminutive that I describe here.

The social life of language is at the heart of language contact, as it is at the heart of linguistics. Language contact is most likely to occur where people perceive similarity, whether in emergent structures or in well-established parallels. However, the question of whether features are ultimately transferred depends on the social identifications and beliefs of speakers. The case of dialect contact between two different forms of the diminutive in rural and urban forms of Bolivian Spanish, and the hesitancy with which rural speakers take up the urban diminutive despite its considerable economic and social power, demonstrates the extent to which individual attitudes toward particular linguistic features can both constrain and enable language contact effects.

Endnotes

1. While scholars once thought of communities as bounded geographical entities, characterized by social ties between individuals, current research examines communities as complex, dynamic entities that may be constituted in digital, moral, action-centered, or physical realms.

2. The word *khuchi* is actually a back-borrowing from Spanish *cochino*.

3. It is possible that this supposition is based on the possibility of a borrowing of the Guaraní emphatic marker *-ngo*, which has been borrowed into dialects of Spanish in contact with Guaraní; however, in these dialects the diminutive *-í* is typically what is borrowed into Spanish as a diminutive marker (Justin Pinta, personal communication, August 22, 2019)

4. Callisaya Apaza reports the use of the diminutive in online forums, although they seem to be used to index a jocular or informal style of speech (2012: 318)

5. The individual quoted has a slight stutter, accounting for apparent dysfluencies in the transcript.

6. Santa Cruz is laid out on a ring pattern, so locations within the city are commonly described with respect to which ring they lie on or between; the oldest Saipineño colony is on the sixth ring, well outside the city center.

7. An alert reader will notice that *chiquit-ingo* is actually formed with two diminutives, *chic+it+ingo*, and that the first diminutive suffix is the normative diminutive *-it(o)*. This is broadly true of diminutive doubling in the lowland Santa Cruz dialect; for example, *ahor+it+inga* 'right away' is also attested, and is apparently less stigmatized than the *ahor+it+ita* variant of the valleys.

8. Typically, this stem change would occur only on certain classes of verbs, never on a noun.

9. Perhaps it is relevant that I carried out all but four of the interviews in Saipina. The exceptions were participants 8 (F), 15 (F), 24 (M), and 4 (M)—the latter two of whom used the *-ingo* diminutive in the recorded material that I analyzed for this paper.

References

Babel, Anna M. 2009. Dizque, evidentiality, and stance in Valley Spanish. *Language in Society*, 38: 487–511.

Babel, Anna M. 2010. *Contact and contrast in valley Spanish*. Ann Arbor: University of Michigan. http://deepblue.lib.umich.edu/bitstream/handle/2027.42/77866/ambabel_1.pdf?sequence=1.

Babel, Anna M. 2011. Why don't all contact features act alike? Contact features as enregistered features. *Journal of Language Contact*, 4: 56–91. http://www.ingentaconnect.com/content/brill/jlc/2011/00000004/00000001/art00004. http://dx.doi.org/10.1163/187740911X558806.

Babel, Anna M. 2014a. Stereotypes versus experience: Indexing regional identity in Bolivian Valley Spanish. *Journal of Sociolinguistics*, 18(5): 604–33.

Babel, Anna M. 2014b. The role of context in interpreting linguistic variables. *Boletín de Filología de la Universidad de Chile*, XLXIX: 49–85.

Babel, Anna M. 2014c. Time and reminiscence in contact: Dynamism and stasis in contact-induced change. *Spanish in Context*, 11: 311–44.

Babel, Anna M. 2016. Affective motivations for borrowing: Performing local identity through loan phonology. *Language and Communication*, 49: 70–83.

Babel, Anna M. 2017. Aspirates and ejectives in Quechua-influenced Spanish. *Spanish in Context*, 14: 159–85.

Babel, Anna M. 2018. *Between the Andes and the Amazon: Language and social meaning in Bolivia*. Tucson: University of Arizona Press.

Babel, Anna M., and Stefan Pfänder. 2013. Doing copying: Why typology doesn't matter to language speakers. In Besters-Dilger, C. Dermarkar, S. Pfänder, and A. Rabus (Eds.), *Congruence in contact-induced language change: Language families, typological resemblance, and perceived similarity*. Berlin: De Gruyter.

Barrett, Rusty. 2008. Linguistic differentiation and Mayan language revitalization in Guatemala 1. *Journal of Sociolinguistics*, 12: 275–305.

Blommaert, Jan. 2010. *The sociolinguistics of globalization*: Cambridge: Cambridge University Press.

Blommaert, JME, and Aad Backus. 2013. Repertoires revisited: "Knowing language" in superdiversity. In *Working Papers in Urban Language and Literacies*. London: Kings College, 67: 1–26.

Bonilla, Yarimar, and Jonathan Rosa. 2015. # Ferguson: Digital protest, hashtag ethnography, and the racial politics of social media in the United States. *American Ethnologist*, 42: 4–17.

Bustamante-López, Isabel, and Mercedes Niño-Murcia. 1995. Impositive speech acts in Northern Andean Spanish: A pragmatic description. *Hispania*, 78: 885–97.

Callisaya Apaza, and Gregorio Marcelino. 2012. *El español de Bolivia: contribución a la dialectología ya la lexicografía hispanoamericanas* (Doctoral dissertation). Universidad de Salamanca.

Calvo Pérez, Julio. 2000. *Partículas en el castellano andino. Teoría y práctica del contacto: el español en América en el candelero*, edited by J. Calvo Pérez, 73–112. Madrid: Iberoamericana/Vervuert.

Coello Vila, Carlos. 1996. *Bolivia. Manual de dialectología hispánica: El español de América*, edited by M. Alvar, 169–83. Barcelona: Editorial Ariel.

Dauphinais, Ashlee. 2018. *A Comunidade de Guerreriras: Production of community in a group for Turner Syndrome*. Columbus: Ohio State University.

De los Heros, Susana, and Cecilia Montes. 2008. Una primera aproximación al habla de contacto en dos peluquerías limeñas. *Oralia*, 11(1): 169–90.

Dil, Anwar S. 1972. The ecology of language: Essays by Einar Haugen. Stanford, CA: Stanford University Press.

Dorian, Nancy. 1994. Varieties of variation in a very small place: Social homogeneity, prestige norms, and linguistic variation. *Language*, 70: 631–96.

Duranti, Alessandro. 1994. Politics and grammar: Agency in Samoan political discourse. *American Ethnologist*, 17: 646–66.

Durston, Alan. 2007. *Pastoral Quechua: The history of Christian translation in colonial Peru*. Notre Dame, IN: University of Notre Dame Press.

Eckert, Penelope. 2012. Three waves of variation study: The emergence of meaning in the study of sociolinguistic variation. *Annual Review of Anthropology*, 41: 87–100.

Emlen, Nicholas Q. 2015. Public discourse and community formation in a trilingual Matsigenka-Quechua-Spanish frontier community of Southern Peru. *Language in Society*, 44: 679–703.

Emlen, Nicholas Q. 2019. The poetics of recapitulative linkage in Matsigenka and mixed Matsigenka-Spanish myth narrations. *Bridging Constructions*, 24: 45.

Erker, Daniel. 2017. The limits of named language varieties and the role of social salience in dialectal contact: The case of Spanish in the United States. *Language and Linguistics Compass*, 11: e12232.

Escobar, Anna María. 2000. *Contacto social y linguístico: El español en contacto con el quechua en el Perú*. Lima: Pontificia Universidad Católica del Perú.

Escobar, Anna María. 2001. Semantic and pragmatic functions of the Spanish diminutive in Spanish in contact with Quechua. *Southwest Journal of Linguistics*, 20: 135–49.

Escobar, Anna María. 2011. Spanish in contact with Quechua. In M. Diaz-Campos (Ed.), *The handbook of hispanic sociolinguistics*, 321–52. Malden, MA: Wiley Blackwell.

Escobar, Anna María. 2012. Spanish in contact with Amerindian languages. In JI Hualde, A. Olarrea, and E. O'Rourke (Eds.), *The handbook of hispanic linguistics*, 65–88. Malden, MA: Wiley Blackwell.

Feke, Marilyn. 2004. Quechua to Spanish cross-linguistic influence among Cuzco Quechua-Spanish bilinguals: The case of epistemology (PhD dissertation). University of Pittsburgh.

Fernández Lávaque, Ana María, and Juana del Valle Rodas. 1998. Español y quechua en el noroeste argentino: contactos y transferencias: Consejo de Investigacion Universidad Nacional de Salta.

Flores Farfán, and José Antonio. 2013. El español en contacto con lenguas indígenas mexicanas: Documentación, descripción, y cuestiones aplicadas. In Ana Kuzmanovic Jovanovic (Ed.), Estudios hispánicos en el siglo XXI. Belgrade: Department of Philology, University of Belgrade.

Gal, Susan. 1978. Peasant men can't get wives: Language change and sex roles in a bilingual community. *Language in Society*, 7: 1-16-1-16.

Gal, Susan. 1988. The political economy of code choice. In M. Heller (Ed.), *Code-switching: Anthropological and sociolinguistic perspectives*, 245–64. Berlin: Mouton de Gruyter.

Grammon, Devin. 2018. *Acquiring Cuzco: Marginalized language, ideology, and study abroad in Peru*. Columbus: Ohio State University.

Gumperz, John. 1968. The speech community. In P. P. Giglioli (Ed.), *Language and Social Context*, 219–31. Harmondsworth: Penguin.

Hill, Jane H., and Kenneth C. Hill. 1986. *Speaking Mexicano: The dynamics of syncretic language in Central Mexico*. Tucson: University of Arizona Press.

Hymes, Dell. 1972. Models of the interaction of language and social setting. In J. Gumperz and D. Hymes (Eds.), *Directions in sociolinguistics: The ethnography of communication*, 35–71. New York: Holt, Rinehart, and Winston.

Irvine, Judith T., and Susan Gal. 2000. Language ideology and linguistic differentiation. In P. Kroskrity (Ed.), *Regimes of Language*, 35–83. Santa Fe: School of American Research Press.

Jackson, Jean. 1974. Language identity of the Colombian Vaupes Indians. In R. Bauman and J. Sherzer (Eds.), *Explorations in the Ethnography of Speaking*, 50–64. Cambridge: Cambridge University Press.

Jaffe, Alexandra. 1999. *Ideologies in action: Language politics on Corsica*. Berlin: Mouton de Gruyter.

Jarvis, Scott, and Aneta Pavlenko. 2008. *Crosslinguistic influence in language and cognition*. New York: Routledge.

Johanson, Lars. 2008. Remodeling grammar: Copying, conventionalization, grammaticalization. In P. Siemund and N. Kintana (Eds.), *Language contact and contact languages*, 60–80. Amsterdam: John Benjamins.

Kramsch, Claire, and Anne Whiteside. 2008. Language ecology in multilingual settings: Towards a theory of symbolic competence. *Applied Linguistics* 29: 645–71. http://applij.oxfordjournals.org/content/29/4/645.abstract.

Labov, William. 1972. *Sociolinguistic patterns*. Philadelphia: University of Pennsylvania Press.

Lipski, John M. 1996. *El español de América*. Madrid: Ediciones Cátedra.

Lipski, John M. 2007. El español de América en contacto con otras lenguas. In *Lingüística aplicada del español*, 309–45. Madrid: Arco/Libros.

Ludwig, Ralph, Peter Mühlhäusler, and Steve Pagel. 2010. *Linguistic ecology and language contact: Overview and perspectives*. Cambridge: Cambridge University Press.

Mannheim, Bruce. 1991. *The language of the Inka since the European invasion*. Austin: University of Texas Press.

Mannheim, Bruce. 1998. Semantic couplets in Quechua verse. *Michigan Discussions in Anthropology*, 13: 238–81.

McGowan, Kevin, and Anna Babel. 2020. Perceiving isn't believing: Divergence in levels of sociolinguistic awareness. *Language in Society*, 49(2): 231–56.

Mendoza, José G. 1991. El castellano hablado en La Paz: sintaxis divergente: Tall. Gráf. de la Facultad de Humanidades y Ciencias de la Educación.

Milroy, Lesley, and James Milroy. 1992. Social network and social class: Toward an integrated sociolinguistic model. *Language in Society*, 21: 1–26.

Morgan, Carrie Ann. 2015. *Language ideologies in TirOna*. Columbus: Ohio State University.

Morgan, Marcyliena. 2004. Speech community. In A. Duranti (Ed.), *A companion to linguistic anthropology*, 3–22. Malden, MA: Wiley Blackwell.

Mufwene, Salikoko S. 2003. Genetic linguistics and genetic creolistics: A response to Sarah G. Thomason's "Creoles and Genetic Relationships." *Journal of Pidgin and Creole Languages*, 18: 273–88.

Muñoz Reyes, Jorge. 1982. *Diccionario de bolivianismos y semántica boliviana*. La Paz: Librería Editorial "Juventud."

Muysken, Pieter. 2001. Spanish grammatical elements in Bolivian Quechua. In K. Zimmerman and T. Stoltz (Eds.), *Lo propio y lo ajeno en las lenguas austronesicas y amerindias*, 59–82. Prensa Iberoamericana: Vervuert.

Muysken, Pieter. 2004. Two languages in two countries: The use of Spanish and Quechua in songs and poems from Peru and Ecuador. In G. Delgado and J. Schecter (Eds.), *Quechua verbal artistry: The inscription of Andean voices*, 35–60. Bonn: Institut fur Altamerikanistik und ethnologie.

Narayanan, Sandhya Krittika. 2018. Are we one?: Quechua-Aymara contact and the challenges of boundary maintenance in Puno, Peru. *Language and Communication*, 62: 145–55.

Palacios, Azucena. 2007. ¿Son compatibles los cambios inducidos por contacto y las tendencias internas al sistema? In Martina Schrader-Kniffki and Morgenthaler Laura (Eds.), *Lenguas en interacción: Entre historia, contacto y política. Ensayos en homenaje a Klaus Zimmermann*, 259–79. Frankfurt: Vervuert.

Palacios, Azucena, and Stefan Pfänder. 2014. Similarity effects in language contact. Congruence in Contact-Induced Language Change: Language Families, Typological Resemblance, and Perceived Similarity 27.219.

Pfänder, Stefan, Juan Ennis, Mario Soto, and España Villegas. 2009. *Gramática Mestiza. Presencia del quechua en el castellano*. La Paz: Academia Boliviana de la Lengua and Editorial Signo.

Quilis, Antonio. 2001. Notas gramaticales sobre la lengua española de Bolivia. *Lexis*, 25: 201–21.

Ramirez Luengo, José Luis. 2016. El diminutivo en la Bolivia andina de la primera mitad del siglo XIX: valores y funciones en el "Diario" de JS Vargas. *Cuadernos de Investigación Filológica*, 42: 111–27.

Rendón, Jorge Gómez. 2008. *Typological and social constraints on language contact: Amerindian languages in contact with Spanish*. Utrecht: Netherlands Graduate School of Linguistics.

Rickford, John R. 1985. Standard and non-standard language attitudes in a creole continuum. *Language of inequality* 36: 145.

Rodríguez-Ordóñez, Itxaso. 2019. The role of linguistic ideologies in language contact situations. *Language and Linguistics Compass*, 13(10): e12351.

Sanabria Fernández, Hernando. 1965. El habla popular de la Provincia de Vallegrande. Santa Cruz, Bolivia: Librería Juventud.

Sanabria Fernández, Hernando. 1975. El habla popular de Santa Cruz. Santa Cruz, Bolivia: Librería Juventud.

Sicoli, Mark A. 2011. Agency and ideology in language shift and language maintenance. InS.D. Penfield (Ed.), *Ethnographic contributions to the study of endangered languages*, 161–76. Tucson, AZ: University of Arizona Press.

Sicoli, Mark A. 2010. Shifting voices with participant roles: Voice qualities and speech registers in Mesoamerica. *Language in Society*, 39: 521–53.

Squires, Lauren. 2010. Enregistering internet language. *Language in Society*, 39: 457–92.

Swinehart, Karl F. 2012. Metadiscursive regime and register formation on Aymara radio. *Language and Communication*, 32: 102–13.

Talavera de Dávila, Rosario. 1988. *El diminutivo en español: Productividad del sufijo ito/a* (unpublished manuscript).

Thomason, Sarah G. 2001. *Language contact: An introduction*. Washington, DC: Georgetown University Press.

Thomason, Sarah G. 2003. A response to Mufwene's response. *Journal of Pidgin and Creole Languages* 18: 289–98.

Thomason, Sarah G. 2007. Language contact and deliberate change. *Journal of Language Contact*, 1: 41–62.

Thomason, Sarah G. 2010. Contact explanations in linguistics. In R. Hickey (Ed.), *The handbook of language contact*, 31–47. Malden, MA: Wiley Blackwell.

CHAPTER 6

Typology, Contact, and Explanation

The Surprising Wappo Case

Marianne Mithun

1. Introduction

A fundamental question in linguistics has been why languages are the way they are, why certain structures and constellations of structures appear in language after language, and why some are rare. Sally Thomason's work has led the way in deepening our understanding of how languages take the shape they do, demonstrating not only the role of common processes of language change but also the potentially powerful effects of language contact. She has shown in detail how contact can affect not just vocabulary but all other areas of language structure. Of course, the kinds of evidence available for establishing the role of contact are not uniform across domains. Transferred vocabulary can be identified with relative confidence when words in one language closely match those in a neighbor in form and meaning, particularly if the languages are not related genealogically. Where the languages are related, the first signal might be matches that are too close, when words in one of the languages fail to show the effects of regular sound changes known to have occurred during the course of development of that language. And the longer the words, the less likely it is that the resemblances are due to chance. In the realm of pure structure, by contrast, the identification of contact effects can be more challenging, particularly in the absence of deep philological records. The only basis for positing contact effects may be circumstantial evidence. The first signal might be structural parallelisms between languages whose speakers are known to have been in contact. But structures are not always transferred precisely. And they may continue to evolve after they have been copied. The case for contact-induced grammatical development can be strengthened if the structures in question are not shared by relatives of the recipient language. Significantly, the more unusual the structures typologically, the less likely the resemblances are due to chance.

It is becoming ever clearer that particular typological patterns can often be understood as the result of not only the processes of grammatical change but also language contact. Here this possibility is illustrated with an apparent anomaly in case marking. As is well known, in languages with case inflection, if one case marker is zero, this is normally the nominative or absolutive. Other case inflections are often based on this form. But Wappo, a language indigenous to Northern California, is described as having an unmarked accusative case, while the nominative case is marked by an enclitic *=(y)i*. Additional case forms are built on the unmarked accusative. A likely explanation for this typologically rarity may lie in the history of its development, stimulated by contact and perhaps subsequent processes of language change.

2. Wappo

The traditional homeland of the Wappo is north of San Francisco. There is documentation of their language from just two communities, the Mishewal of Alexander Valley and Knights Valley and the Mayacama of the upper Napa Valley (Golla 2011: 191; Radin 1929: 7). The locations of these two communities can be seen in figure 6.1.

The Wappo language is generally thought to be remotely related to just one other language, Yuki to the north, but the two have not been in contact for some time, perhaps several millennia, apparently separated by the intrusion of Pomoan peoples.

Figure 6.1 Northern California

Source: Adapted from Heizer, Robert F. 1978. *California: Handbook of North American Indians 8*. Washington: Smithsonian Institution, ix

There are no longer any first-language Wappo speakers. In addition to some early wordlists there are, however, a set of Wappo texts and a detailed grammar compiled by Radin (1924, 1929), based on work carried out with two speakers in 1918, Jim Tripo and Joe McCloud, as well as a lexicon and grammatical notes (Sawyer 1965, 1991), articles on subjects (Li and Thompson 1976; Li, Thompson, and Sawyer 1977), a reworking of a Radin text (Sawyer and Somersal 1977), and a grammar (Thompson, Park, and Li 2014), all from work with one of the last speakers, Laura Fish Somersal.

The Radin materials are especially valuable because they are based on unscripted connected speech. They date from a time before phonemic principles were well established, so the transcription does not always match that of the more modern materials. Here Radin's original transcriptions are retained for the most part, with substitution of a few symbols used in the modern Wappo sources for some of his earlier conventions to facilitate comparisons, specifically <š> for his <c>, <č> for his <tc>, and <c> for his <ts>. Distinctive glottalization and aspiration were not always noted in his transcriptions, but they have not been restored.

3. Wappo Cases

Thompson et al. list the Wappo case enclitics, which are attached to determiner phrases, as in (1).

(1) Wappo case enclitics: Thompson et al. (2014: v)

Nominative	*=i*
Accusative	=Ø
Dative	*=t^hu*
Benefactive	*=ma*
Instrumental	*=t^hiʔ*
Comitative	*=k'a*

There are also locative enclitics, with meanings 'on top of' (as a house), 'downstream from/below', 'behind', 'in front of', 'across', 'upstream from/above', 'beside', 'inside', 'under', 'away from', 'near', 'on top of' (as a stove), 'on/in/by', 'off', and 'out of'.

Some examples of case marking are in (2) from the opening of a tale about two characters, Gray Squirrel and his father Old Rock. The subjects 'Gray Squirrel' and 'Old Rock' are marked with the enclitic *=i*, the object 'his father' is unmarked for case, and his companion, his grandmother, is marked with the comitative case enclitic *=k'a*.[1]

(2) Wappo case use: Radin (1929: 151)

K'ana-mót'a kon	*nóm-ki*	*méhwa-o-lele*
St. Helena-mountain HRSY	live-PAST	grapevine-NMLZ-flat

'At St. Helena Mountain in the Grapevine flatland, it is said,'

hot=i	***me-pápa =ka***	*wima-méte=**ka**.*
gray.squirrel=NOM	3R.POSS-mother's.mother=COM	animal-woman=COM

'**Gray Squirrel** (NOM) lived **with his grandmother Wima** (COM).'

Pata	*hela*	***lél-has=i***	*te-kútiya-k-tsel*
And	first	rock-old=NOM	3R-small-VBLZ-SUBORD

'Now (long) before that **Old Rock** (NOM), when (the boy) was still young,'

te-me-'aya	*t'óh-ta.*
3R-POSS-father	kill-PAST

'had killed **his father** (UNMARKED ACC).'

The enclitic *=(y)i* appears on determiner phrases that are translated as subjects whether their referents are animate or inanimate, definite or indefinite, and specific or nonspecific, and whether the clause is transitive or intransitive. Radin (1929: 131–32) describes the phonologically determined alternations in form. The enclitic appears as *=i* after consonants (*k'ew, k'ew=i* 'man', *k'éš, k'és=i* 'deer', *mey, mey=i* 'water', *huʔ, huʔ=i* 'head') and after most stems ending in a vowel, with loss of that vowel (*háyu, hay=i* 'dog', *šáwo, sáw=i* 'bread', *náʔa, náʔ=i* 'mother'). It is generally *=yi* after stems ending in *e*, with shift of the *e* to *a*: (*mét̯'e, mét̯'a=yi* 'woman'). There are some nouns with alternate forms (*holophút̯'e, holopút̯'=i/holopút̯'a=yi* 'basket').

Intervocalically *o* becomes a glide (*ʔéo*, *ʔéw=i* 'fish'), and there is some syncope (*yéníš, yénš=í* 'rabbit').

Based on sentences elicited from Mrs. Somersal, Li et al. (1977) conclude that subjects are marked as nominative whether they are semantic agents, experiencers, inanimate causers, patients of adjectival verbs, or patients of passives. They are unmarked, however, in subordinate clauses: complement clauses of various types, embedded questions, relative clauses, and adverbial clauses.

(3) Wappo main clause case: Li et al. (1977: 86)
Ce ***k'ew=i*** *ce* *ʔew* *hak'šeʔ.*
that man=NOM that fish like
'**The man** (NOM) likes the fish.'

(4) Wappo complement clause: Li et al. (1977: 86)
ʔah *[ce* ***k'ew*** *ʔew* *ṭ'oh-taʔ]* *haṭiskʰiʔ.*
I [that man fish catch=PAST] know
'I know [**the man** (unmarked) caught a fish].'

(5) Wappo relative clause: Li et al. (1977: 88)
ʔah ***[ce*** ***k'ew*** ***ce*** ***cʰica*** *ṭ'a-taʔ]* *naw-taʔ.*
I [that man that bear kill-PAST] see-PAST
'I saw [**the man** (unmarked) who killed **the bear** (unmarked)].'
= 'I saw **the bear** (unmarked) that **the man** (unmarked) killed.'

Li et al. also report that the nominative case is used in existential constructions.

(6) Wappo existential: Li et al. (1977: 91)
C'ic'=i *hol-č'ola=h* *yoʔkʰiʔ.*
bird=NOM tree-hollow=LOC exist/stay
'There's **a bird** (NOM) in the tree' = '**The bird** (NOM) is in the tree.'

The case paradigm is, however, surprising typologically. Normally, if any case in a language is unmarked it is the nominative or absolutive, and this unmarked form is the base on which other case forms are built. In Wappo the unmarked case is the accusative, and it is this form that serves as the basis for the other case inflections. This pattern is not shared with its only proposed relative, Yuki. Yuki case marking follows an agent/patient organization for both lexical determiner phrases and pronouns, and it is the agent case that is unmarked, in keeping with usual expectations (Balodis 2016).

4. The Wappo Nominative

Radin had noted that in Wappo, 'a few nouns make no change for the subjective case; the overwhelming majority, however, do' (1929: 131). There are in fact some sentences in his published texts (approximately 150 pages including translations) in which subjects carry no nominative enclitic.

Loanwords do not generally carry nominative inflection in the Radin texts. In his dictionary, Sawyer lists several words for 'dog', among them *čú:ču?*.

(7) Wappo 'dog': Sawyer (1965: 31)
'dog' *čú:ču?* (Central American *chucho*; Napa dialect). The occurrence of *čú:ču?* in the Napa dialect is the sort of evidence that suggests that Napa Wappo had more contact with Spanish than the Russian River Wappo. The Napa people were closer to the mission at Sonoma.

(Jesús Olguin Martínez informs me that this term is used in rural areas of Mexico in reference to street dogs, often pejoratively.)

Frequent in the Radin texts are quotative constructions, 'X said' and 'said X'. In both of these, the subject is usually inflected with the nominative enclitic, as in (8).

(8) Radin (1924: 23.161)
*Cel kalila? **holoṭ'éw=i** hah-ta, "..."*
then after.all ant=NOM say-PAST
'Then after a while **the ant** (NOM) said, "..." '

But in the same construction in (9), the loanword 'dog' is uninflected.

(9) Wappo: (Radin 1924: 18.81)
Kalila? ***cucu?*** *hah-ta, "..."*
after.all dog say-PAST
'Then **the dog** (uninflected) said, "..." '

The native noun *yéniš* 'rabbit' carries the enclitic =*i* in this Radin text.

(10) Wappo: Radin (1924: 22.171)
Maihucátite? *cé-u-pi* *atri* ***yénš=i***
will.jump.away that-in-from soon rabbit=NOM
'**A rabbit** (NOM) will immediately jump out.'

In the same construction a few sentences later, the loanword 'chicken' is uninflected.

(11) Wappo: Radin (1924: 173)
Maihucátite? *cé-u-pi* ***kayína*** *šái?isi*
will.jump.away that-in-from chicken jump.out
'**A chicken** (uninflected) will jump out of it.'

Interestingly, in a sentence elicited by Thompson et al. from Mrs. Somersal, the same loanword 'chicken' does carry the enclitic.

(12) Wappo: Thompson et al. (2014: 37)
Káyi:na?=i *nale?-ša?.*
chicken=NOM angry-dur
'**The chicken** (NOM) is behaving angrily.'

Other differences in marking can also be seen between the texts collected by Radin from Jim Tripo and Joe McCloud, both born around 1850, and material collected by Sawyer and by Li and Thompson from Laura Somersal, born in 1890. The 1918 story cited earlier in (2) continued with Gray Squirrel going out to hunt for deer. He came to a plateau. Deer were standing around there, identified in the text by a noun unmarked for case.

(13) Wappo: Radin (1929: 152)
'To a country where it was flat all around there he arrived.'
'Beautiful it looked.'

K'éšu *hólalo-ki*
deer stand.around
'**Deer** (unmarked) were standing (all) around.'

(The verb in (13) is finite, ending in the suffix *-k^hiʔ*, glossed by Sawyer [1965] as Verb Definite and by Thompson et al. [2014] as Stative.) In sentences elicited more recently by Li and Thompson from Mrs. Somersal, the same noun appears in a similar context, but here it is inflected with the nominative case enclitic.

(14) Wappo: Thompson et al. (2014: 81)
Ceta ***k'eš=i*** *lepu-k^hiʔ.*
there deer=NOM stand-STAT
'**The deer** (NOM) is standing there.'

As noted earlier, Radin had stated that a specific/nonspecific distinction made no difference. The discrepancies could be the result of minor errors in transcription or simply reduced pronunciation. There may, however, be more going on.

The variation could suggest, for example, that the case marking was still in flux. In some languages, marked nominatives have been shown to have developed from ergatives. In ergative systems, ergative arguments (corresponding to subjects of transitives in languages like English) usually carry case markers, while absolutives (corresponding to intransitive subjects and transitive objects) are usually unmarked. Craig (1976) shows that in Jacaltec Mayan (Popti'), for example, original ergative pronominal affixes were extended to intransitive subjects, but only in subordinate clauses unmarked for aspect. Larsen and Norman (1979) and Bricker (1981) show that in some other Mayan languages, ergative markers were extended to intransitive subjects in certain tenses and aspects formed with auxiliary verbs, constructions that are traced to subordinate clause constructions, perhaps involving nominalization. Such sources for the Wappo nominative case seem unlikely, because it is precisely in Wappo subordinate clauses that nominatives are unmarked.

5. Another Possible Scenario

Northern California is known as a strong linguistic area, exhibiting extensive, deep structural parallels among neighboring but genealogically unrelated languages. Within this area, the region around Clear Lake, the homeland of the Wappo, is a particularly strong subarea. Communities have always been small and exogamy common, resulting in long-standing, early multilingualism. A closer view of the area is in figure 6.2 from Sawyer (1965). As can be seen from figures 6.1 and 6.2, the Wappo were adjacent to various Pomoan groups. Intermarriage continued to be common up to modern times. In fact, all three of the Wappo speakers who contributed to the documentation of the language, Jim Tripo, Joe McCloud, and Laura Fish Somersal, were bilingual in Wappo and a Pomoan language.

There is extensive evidence within Wappo of contact effects from Pomoan languages. There are a few obvious loanwords: one is a word *háyu* for 'dog', pervasive across the area (Mithun 2010), but there was less lexical transfer than might be expected, due to a cultural tradition throughout the area of not mixing languages. Structural similarities, however, are pervasive. The Wappo consonant inventory contains a series of aspirated obstruents (p^h, t^h, ṭ^h, c^h, č^h, k^h), unlike its only relative Yuki, but like the neighboring Pomoan languages, a series that can be reconstructed for Proto Pomoan. Wappo contains a series of apical affricates (c, c^h, c') that contrast with an alveopalatal series (č, č^h, č'), unlike Yuki but again like the neighboring Pomoan languages. Wappo has a five-vowel system, unlike Yuki, which contains an additional central nasalized vowel but like the Pomoan languages. First- and second-person pronouns were copied into Wappo from Pomoan languages (Mithun 2012). Some other effects are more subtle, involving structural patterns without replicated substance. There is lexical patterning (Mithun to appear). There is recent renewal of negation in Wappo via clause-final matrix verbs 'to not exist', common throughout the area, including in some neighboring Pomoan languages (Mithun 2018, In press). There is an additional third-person 'coreferential' category among the Wappo pronouns, as in the Pomoan languages (Mithun 2012). There are means/manner prefixes, pervasive throughout the area and particularly well developed in Pomoan (Mithun 2007, 2015). Often it was not the markers themselves that were copied from one language into another by bilinguals, but rather a propensity to specify certain distinctions or calques that, over long periods of time, became routinized in grammar.

Several Pomoan languages contain an enclitic that marks a significant topic shift. The examples here are from Central Pomo, where the topic shift marker is *=ya*. Two speakers, Mrs. Frances Jack of the Hopland Rancheria and Mrs. Florence Paoli of the Yokayo Rancheria, were discussing differences among languages and dialects in their area. (The full discussion was in Central Pomo, but the context is given here just in translation.)

(15) Central Pomo topic shift

FJ 'Those are stories for children, about the rat, the bear.'
'Did you learn any of those from the elders?'

FP ***Čáts'=ya*** *bač'ó-w-a:d-an ʔe,*
grandfather=TOPIC.SHIFT tell-PFV-IPFV.SG-IPFV.SG COP
'**My grandfather** used to tell'

šíyel=da ʔ=méṭi.
evening=at COP=such
'those kinds of stories in the evening.'

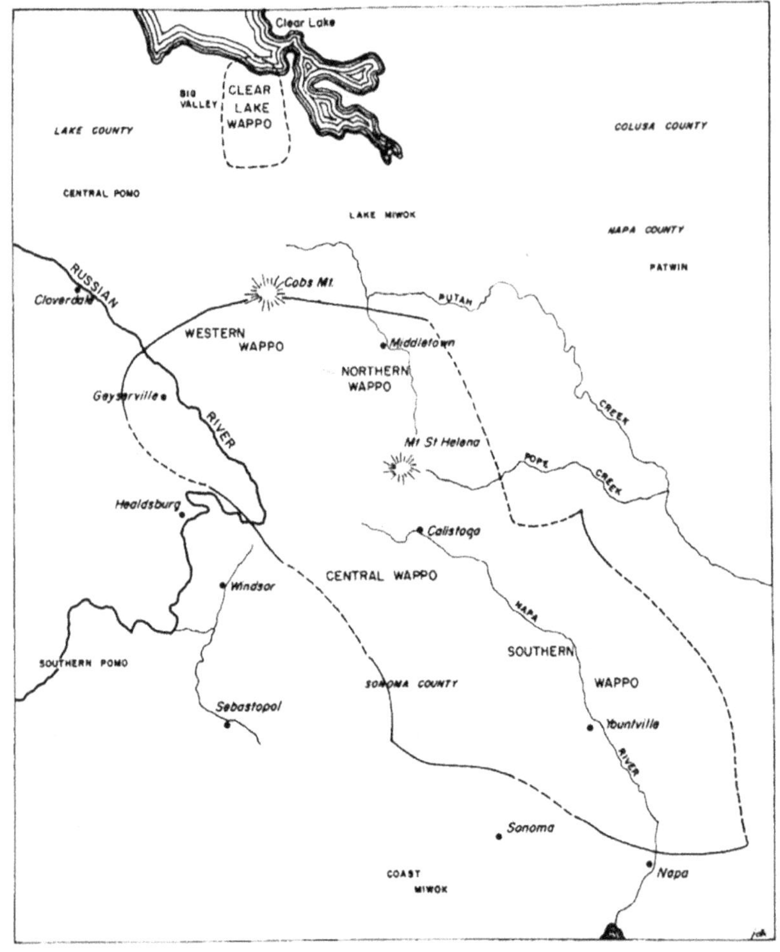

Approximate distribution of Wappo-speaking bands.

Figure 6.2 Wappo-Speaking Bands

Source: Sawyer (1965: xii).

In (16), 'we Hopland people' constituted a shift from 'you' (a Yokayo person).

(16) Central Pomo topic shift

FJ 'That word you used, *šán*.

FP *šan*.

FJ *Mu:l ʔe ya* ***Hópland=kʰe=ya***
that COP 1PL.AGT Hopland=from=TOPIC.SHIFT
'We Hopland people'

yús-t̪a-m tʰí-n.
use-MULT.EVENT-MULT.AGT not-IPFV
'don't use that word.'

The Central Pomo clitic does not appear every time there is a change in subject. It tends to be used primarily for human referents (or personified animals), presumably because they are more often discourse topics. The use of the topic shift clitic over a longer stretch of speech can be seen in (17).

(17) Central Pomo topic shifts: Frances Jack, speaker, p.c.

'My father's lady relative, it was said that she was about to die.'
'She was not getting well.'

Masá:n=ya, *nán-a:č';*
white=TOPIC.SHIFT be.unable-IPFV.PL
'The whitemen were unable to help her.'

'it was said there was no medicine.'

Mu:l=ʔt̪i bal híntil ***čá:č-ay=ya*** *qʰadí:ya-w šó:=ʔkʰe,*
that=but this Indian person-PL=TOPIC.SHIFT go.after-PFV south=from
'But then **the Indians** went after'

šó:=ʔkʰe čá:ʔ=yem hínt̪il,
south=from person=old Indian
'an old Indian man from the south,'

badó-:n čá:č' qʰadí:-ya-w.
doctor-IPFV.SG man go.after-PASS-PFV
'a healer.'

Mú:l=ya,
that=TOPIC.SHIFT
'That man'

maṭúl ʔ=mú:t̪u,
old.lady COP=3SG.PAT
'tied live waterdogs (lizards)'

šá:qawo:lo qašóy-ay,
waterdog live-DISTR
'to a hoop,'

daq'ó:=htol ščét̪-ba,
hoop=to tie.on-and
'and the old lady,'

mú:t̪u daq'ó: ʔ=mí:li mú:t̪u qó:bee-ya-w.
3SG.PAT hoop COP=there 3SG.PAT shove.through-PASS-PFV
'she was shoved through there.'

Cá:č yá=t̪ay ʔel=ya *p^hí-c^h-ma-ba*
person strong-DISTR the=TOPIC.SHIFT pick-up-MULT.AGT-and
'**Strong people** picked her up and'

'shoved her through, a large, heavy woman.'
'After quite a while, the old lady was well.'
'That lady lived a long time after that.'
'She never contracted any kind of disease.'

Hínt̪il=ya
Indian=TOPIC.SHIFT
'**Indian people**'

qaʔó h-šíla-w ʔ=do: mú:t̪u.
poison thrusting-serve-PFV COP=HRSY 3SG.PAT
'had poisoned her they say.'
'That's what happened to her.'

Čá:ʔ=yem ʔél =ya
person=old the=TOPIC.SHIFT
The old man'

t̪í: *mú:l* *pʰwí-w* *t̪i:* *qʰaʔán-t̪a-w.*
3R.AGT 3SG see-PFV 3R.AGT dream-MULT.EV-PFV
'he himself saw those things in a dream.'

Northern Pomo texts transcribed and analyzed by O'Connor and posted on the Northern Pomo language website (http://northern-pomolanguagetools.com/texts/index.php) show similar uses of the Northern enclitic *=yaʔ*.

In natural speech in most languages, there is usually a substantial overlap in the contexts in which full lexical determiner phrases denote shifted discourse topics, and those in which they function as syntactic subjects. Continuing topics are usually identified by unstressed pronouns or by nothing at all. The overlap between shifted discourse topics and lexical subjects can be seen in Wappo. In 1977, linguist Jesse Sawyer and Wappo speaker Laura Fish Somersal published a text reconstituted from one originally collected by Radin in 1918. The opening to their reconstituted version is in (18), with their translation. The **bolded nominals** are lexical subjects, inflected with the nominative enclitic **=(y)i**. The *underlined demonstratives* correspond to third-person pronouns in the translation. The pronouns in parentheses in the translation have no overt counterparts in the Wappo.

(18) Wappo passage: (Sawyer and Somersal 1977: 106–7)

1 *Lòkʰnomah nómkʰiʔ, kʰón', **Chíca:met'a:=yi**, meʔèw k'ěšu:hask'a.*
'Long ago at Goose Camp **Bear Woman** lived with her husband Deer.'

2 *Mèl yékʰahkʰiʔ, **teme:ʔéw=i.***
'**Her husband** used to go for acorns.'

3 *Holcàwuh mehyʔelkʰiʔ, mèl chék'miʔ.*
'(He) would climb to the top of a tree and knock acorns off.'

4 ***Chìca:meta:=yi** mèl páʔmiʔ.*
'**Bear Woman** always eats some of the acorns.'

5 *Cèl' **K'éšu:has=i**, "T^{h}àl ʔìs-**i** ma:mésa:siʔ", háhtaʔ.*
'And **Deer** said, "What are we going to take home?"'

6 *Cèl' **Chíca:met'a:=yi** "ʔi:cáhšiʔ mìʔ,*
'Then **Bear** said, "Why do you say that to me?'

ʔi:k'éyi:šiʔ" háhtaʔ.
'Why are you always scolding me?'

7 *"Toʔoyáʔel', toʔoyáʔel', ʔìs-i ma:wélelsiʔ.*
'Come down, Come down!. We'll go home.'

8 *ʔáh, mìma yàʔse:hol me:wíṭe:siʔ.*
'And I will hold the climbing stick for you.'

9 *Cèṭa lák^{h}u, ʔàh ʔúh, mahyáʔelk^{h}iʔ,*
'Indeed, I've already climbed up,'

k'otamàʔa mìʔ toʔoyá:seʔ, ʔàh mìma kàle:raʔ mewíṭe:siʔ."
'but I still will hold the ladder for you as you climb down."'

10 *Ówhistaʔ.*
'(He) motioned agreement.'

11 *Cèp^h-i toʔoyáʔelk^{h}iʔ,*
'He climbed down,'

***Chìca:met'a:=yi** teṭàʔuhpi tè temešút'taʔ, wéyh, tè mapáʔtaʔ.*
'and **Bear Woman** jerked him down by his legs and (she) ate him up.'

12 *Cèl' tehùʔ hèymah šukòloʔuh mawíltaʔ,*
'Then (she) put his head down in the bottom of her pack basket,'

wèyh p^{h}àʔma mehómtaʔ, cèt^{h}iʔ cè masót'taʔ.
'and then picked some soaproot by hand and covered it up with that.'

13 *Cèl' mawélelk^{h}iʔ.*
'Then (she) went home.'

14 *Cèl' **Nète?met'a:-yi** me?èyk'a:pit^{h}u céwista?, "?ìṭa:yoh mi:?éw?"*
'Then **Mole Woman** asked her daughter, "Where is your husband?" '

15 *"**Wal-i** ?ìsa:pi néy'ahk^{h}i?, wèyh ?ìsa č'a:pahk^{h}éy'ta?, **?i:èw-i** ṭ'ólk^{h}e."*
' "**The enemy** caught up with us, surrounded us, and **my husband** got killed." '

16 *"?ik^{h}ámta?yoh mìs-i?"*
' "What had the two of you done?" '

17 *"?ìs-i mèl pí?uh, cèṭa <u>cèp^h-i</u> ṭ'ólk^{h}e?.*
'"We were knocking acorns out of a tree, there where <u>he</u> was killed." '

18 *Cèl' **K'èšu mèt'a:-yi** kámi? me:?èpa.*
'Then **Deer Woman** cries her elder brother.'

All of the **bolded subjects**, marked with the enclitic =***(y)i*** in Wappo, are also shifted topics: '**Bear Woman** always eats some of the acorns. And **Deer** said, . . . ' The *demonstratives*, also marked with the enclitic =*i*, tend to occur where there is a slight shift in reference or potential ambiguity: 'We were knocking acorns out of a tree, there where *he* was killed.' All of the parenthesized pronouns, which are simply absent from the Wappo, represent continuing topics: 'Her husband used to go for acorns. (He) would climb to the top of the tree and (he) would knock acorns off'. The overlap between information structure and syntactic structure is nearly perfect.

There is, however, an intriguing difference between this Sawyer and Somersal version and the original Radin version. In the earlier Radin version, only some lexical subjects carry the =*(y)i* enclitic. There the first mention of Bear Woman in line 1 and of her husband Deer in line 2; both show the ending. But the second and third mentions of Bear Woman in lines 4 and 6 lack the ending, as does the second mention of Deer in line 5, though all were subjects. At those points, both characters were already part of the scene. The two versions of the opening of the text can be compared in (19), with first the Radin version in his original transcription, then the Sawyer and Somersal version in each line.

(19) Wappo passage: Radin (1924: 46), Sawyer and Somersal (1977: 106–7)

1 *lɔk·nomanɔ´mk·i’* ***tsitsa mɛta=i’*** *mɛ-ɛ·´oka k’ɛ´cu.*
Lòk^{h}nomah nómk^{h}iʔ, k^{h}ón’, ***Chíca:met’a:=yi,*** *meʔèw k’éšu:hask’a.*
‘Long ago at Goose Camp **Bear Woman** lived with her husband Deer.’

2 *mɛl yɛ´yak·* ***tɛmɛ-ɛ´ow=i.***
Mèl yék^{h}ahk^{h}iʔ, ***teme:ʔéw=i.***
‘**Her husband** used to go for acorns.’

3 *hɔl ts·a´wo meya´ɛl·k´ɛ, mɛl pi´’mi’*
Holcàwuh mehyʔelk^{h}iʔ, mèl chék’miʔ.
‘(He) would climb to the top of a tree and knock acorns off.’

4 ***tsitsa*** *mɛl pa´’ome’*
Chìca:meta:=yi *mèl páʔmiʔ.*
‘**Bear Woman** always eats some of the acorns.’

5 *tse’l* ***k’ɛ´cɛ,*** *“Ta’l mamɛ´s·asɛ?”*
Cèl’ ***K’éšu:has=i,*** *“T^{h}àl ʔìs-**i** ma:mésa:siʔ,” háhtaʔ.*
‘And **Deer** said, “What are we going to take home?” ’

When Bear Woman is mentioned sometime later in line 11, and still later in line 18, the enclitic is again present in the original version. The enclitic appears with the first mentions of Mole Woman in line 14 and the enemy in line 15. It also appears with ‘my husband’ in 15, but here it is within a quotation in which it constituted a first mention. The patterning of the enclitic in the Radin version of the text is not random. The fact that it does not appear on every lexical nominal serving as a subject, even across identical referents (Bear Woman, Deer), indicates that it was not a full-fledged nominative case marker, at least in 1918. It was apparently a topicalization marker, marking a topic shift. In the later 1977 Sawyer and Somersal version, by contrast, all lexical subjects carry the enclitic. Similarly, in all of the example sentences in the 1976 Li and Thompson and the 1977 Li, Thompson, and Sawyer articles, and the 2014 Thompson et al. grammar, all subjects carry the enclitic.

The data suggest at least two possible explanations for the typologically surprising Wappo nominative case marker. Both have the same point of departure. It is not unlikely that the Pomoan topic shift marker provided a stimulus for the development of the Wappo enclitic. Bilinguals, accustomed to signaling significant topic shifts in a Pomoan language, might have started marking comparable shifts when speaking Wappo. The form itself may or may not have been copied, but the propensity to mark significant topic shifts could have easily been transferred. The marking of a shift in topic appears to be exactly the function of the enclitic in the 1918 Wappo texts.

Over time, the overlapping distribution of topic shifts and lexical subjects could have led to a reanalysis of the function of the enclitic as a nominative case marker within Wappo. The crystallization of high-frequency discourse structures into syntactic structures is of course a common process cross-linguistically. Just such a development is proposed by Lehmann (1976) for Indo-European.

Alternatively, there may be another explanation for the surprising Wappo nominative case marker, perhaps ultimately related to a second wave of language contact. The later documentation process itself might have affected the record. While reconstituting the Radin text with its English translation, Sawyer and Somersal may have reinterpreted the function of the marker as corresponding to an English subject category. (Though she did not read or write, Mrs. Somersal did speak English.) They may have then regularized its occurrence accordingly as they polished the new written text, adding it to every lexical subject. The examples in the papers on Wappo subjects in Li et al. (1976), and Li et al. (1977), as well as the grammar in Thompson et al. (2014) were all drawn from single elicited sentences. Without a discourse context, the topicalization function could have been obscured; in isolation, each new sentence with a lexical subject could be understood as introducing a new topic.

6. Conclusion

As noted at the outset, it is generally assumed that in languages with case marking, if any case marker is zero it will be the nominative or absolutive. But in Wappo, it is the accusative that is unmarked. Wappo subjects are described as marked with an enclitic *=(y)i*. There are no longer any first-language speakers of Wappo, but modern descriptions indicate that the marker is well-installed in the grammar. Nearly all subject determiner phrases referring to semantic agents, patients, and experiencers carry the marker, whether these are animate or inanimate, definite or indefinite, and specific or nonspecific. The pattern is the same in transitive and intransitive clauses, and in passive and existential constructions. Subjects of subordinate clauses, however, are unmarked.

The fact that the marker does not occur in the only proposed related language, Yuki, suggests that it could have been an innovation in Wappo. Because its presence on lexical subjects is so consistent in the modern documentation, opportunities for unraveling its history via internal reconstruction seem at first limited. Texts collected early in the twentieth century, however, do show some lexical subjects without the marker. The gaps could be dismissed as artifacts of the challenging transcription process. The material collected by Radin over a few months in the spring and summer of 1918, long before audio recording was a possibility, was necessarily transcribed laboriously by hand. Speakers would have had to produce their accounts haltingly, phrase by phrase. The sound system was not yet fully understood. The gaps could also indicate that the use of the marker was still in flux at that time. The fact that it does not occur in subordinate clauses is suggestive, hinting that it might have originated not within the clause, but at a higher level of structure.

A likely stimulus for its development can be found in its Pomoan neighbors. Long-standing contact, intermarriage, and bilingualism throughout the area are well documented. Several Pomoan languages, among them an immediate neighbor, Central Pomo, contain an enclitic that marks topic shifts. The enclitic does not occur on all lexical phrases that might correspond to subjects, but it can be pervasive, marking shifts the speaker considers significant. A propensity to mark significant topic shifts could have been carried by bilinguals into Wappo. Given the strong correlation in spontaneous connected speech between shifted topics and lexical subjects, it would not be surprising if the topic shift marker was reanalyzed as a nominative case marker on lexical determiner phrases.

The apparent typological anomaly may, however, be the result of additional contact with English. The later documentation of Wappo was focused on the reconstitution of the earlier written Radin text and translation and the elicitation of words and isolated sentences, often as translations from English. The circumstances of elicitation could have resulted in higher frequencies of new topic marking. They could also have led analysts to conclude that the enclitic *=(y)i* was actually a nominative case marker. Their analyses could have led them in turn, as they polished their work, to ensure that all subjects were marked with the enclitic.

Unfortunately, since there are few if any modern recordings of spontaneous connected Wappo speech, it is difficult to know at this point to what extent the pattern was actually established in the language. A consideration of the role of language contact, however, brings us closer to understanding an apparent typological anomaly.

Endnote

1. The following abbreviations are used in glossing: AGT = grammatical agent, COM = comitative case, COP = copula, DISTR = distributive, DUR = durative, HRSY = hearsay, IPFV = imperfective aspect, LOC = locative case, MULT.AGT = multiple agent, MULT.EV = multiple event, NMLZ = nominalizer, NOM = nominative case, PASS = passive, PAT = grammatical patient, PFV = perfective aspect, PL = plural, POSS = possessive, R = coreferential, SG = singular, STAT = stative, SUBORD = subordinate, VBLZ = verbalizer.

References

Balodis, Uldis. 2016. *Yuki grammar, with sketches of Huchnom and Coast Yuki.* University of California Publications in Linguistics 151. Berkeley: University of California Press.

Bricker, Victoria. 1981. The source of the ergative split in Yucatec Maya. *Journal of Mayan Linguistics*, 2: 83–127.

Craig, Colette. 1976. Properties of basic and derived subjects in Jacaltec. In C. N. Li (Ed.), *Subject and topic*, 99–123. New York: Academic Press.

Golla, Victor. 2011. *California Indian languages.* Berkeley: University of California Press.

Larsen, Thomas, and Will Norman. 1977. Correlates of ergativity in Mayan grammar. In Frans Plank (Ed.), *Ergativity: Towards a theory of grammatical relations*, 347–70. New York: Academic Press.

Lehmann, Winfred P. Lehmann. 1976. From topic to subject in Indo-European. In Cherles N. Li (Ed.), *Subject and topic*, 445–56. New York: Academic Press.

Li, Charles N., and Sandra A. Thompson. 1976. Strategies for signaling grammatical relations in Wappo. *Papers from the 12th Regional Meeting of the Chicago Linguistic Society*, 450–57.

Li, Charles N., Sandra A. Thompson, and Jesse O. Sawyer. 1977. Subject and word order in Wappo. *International Journal of American Linguistics*, 43(2): 85–100.

Mithun, Marianne. 2007. Grammar, contact, and time. *Journal of Language Contact* (e-journal) THEMA, 1: 133–55. www.jlc-journal.org

Mithun, Marianne. 2010. Contact and North American languages. In Raymond Hickey (Ed.), *Handbook of language contact*, 673–94. Oxford: Blackwell.

Mithun, Marianne. 2012. Morphologies in contact: Form, meaning, and use in the grammar of reference. In Thomas Stolz, Martine Vanhove, Hitomi Otsuka, and Anna Urdzu (Eds.), *Morphologies in contact*, Studia Typologica 10, 15–36. Berlin: Akademia Verlag.

Mithun, Marianne. 2015. Morphological complexity and language contact. In Rik van Gijn and Fernando Zuñiga (Eds.), Special issue of *The diachronic stability of verbal morphology. Linguistic discovery* 13.2. 10.1349/PS1.1537-0852.A.466.

Mithun, Marianne. 2018. Shaping typology through grammaticalization: North America. In Heiko Narrog and Bernd Heine (Eds), *Grammaticalization from a typological perspective*, 309–36. Oxford: Oxford University Press.

Mithun, Marianne. To appear a. Stories behind post-verbal negation clustering. In Olga Krasnoukhova, Mily Crevels, and Johan van der Auwera (Eds.), *Postverbal negation: Synchrony, diachrony, areality*, Special Issue of *Studies in Language*.

Mithun, Marianne. To appear. Sitting and talking together: Packaging meaning into verbs with the neighbors. In Maria Koptjevskaja-Tamm, Antoinette Schapper, and Felix Ameka (Eds.), *Areal typology of lexico-semantics*, Special Issue of *Linguistic Typology*.

O'Connor, Mary Catherine. Northern Pomo stories and texts. http://northernpomolanguagetools.com/texts/index.php.

Radin, Paul. 1924. *Wappo texts*. University of California Publications in American Archaeology and Ethnology 19.1. Berkeley: University of California Press.

Radin, Paul. 1929. *A grammar of the Wappo language*. Berkeley: University of California Press.

Sawyer, Jesse O. 1965. *English-Wappo vocabulary*. University of California Publications in Linguistics 43. Berkeley: University of California Press.

Sawyer, Jesse O., and Laura Fish Somersal. 1977. Bear woman and her children (Wappo). In Victor Golla and Shirley Silver (Eds.), *Northern California texts*, Native American Texts Series, International Journal of American Linguistics 2.2, 105–13. Berkeley: University of California Press.

Sawyer, Jesse O. 1991. *Wappo notes*. Edited by Alice Schlichter. Survey of California and Other Indian Languages, 11–84. Berkeley: University of California Press.

Thompson, Sandra, Joseph Sung-Yul Park, and Charles Li. 2014. *A reference grammar of Wappo*, University of California Publications in Linguistics 138. Berkeley: University of California Press.

CHAPTER 7

Oblique Arguments in Montana Salish

Separating Agreement and Licensing

Nico Baier

1. Introduction

In Montana Salish, overt nominal arguments may be unmarked (1) or preceded by the oblique particle *t* (2):[1]

(1) *Unmarked argumentas*

a. *Subject of an intransitive*
Ø téšlš **Qeyqeyší**
3SBJ get.up Qeyqeyší
'Qeyqeyší got up.'

b. *Object of a transitive*
wíč-nt-Ø-s **sχʷélmn**
see-TR-3OBJ-3SBJ Devil
'He saw the Devil.'

c. *Goal of a ditransitive*
xʷíč-ši-t-Ø-s **Malí** t pus t Čoní
give-APPL-TR-3OBJ-3SBJ Mary OBL cat OBL Johnny
'Johnny gave Mary the cat.'

(2) *Oblique arguments*

a. *Subject of a transitive*

čɫíp-nt-Ø-s	sné	**t**	**Čoní**
hunt-TR-3OBJ-3SBJ	cow.elk	OBL	Johnny

'Johnny hunted a cow elk.'

b. *Object of an antipassive*

čn=	wíč-m	**t**	**qxmín**
1SG.SBJ=	see-ANTIP	OBL	antler

'I saw an antler.'

c. *Theme and subject of a ditransitive*

xʷíč-ši-t-Ø-s	Malí	**t**	**pus**	**t**	**Čoní**
give-APPL-TR-3OBJ-3SBJ	Mary	OBL	cat	OBL	Johnny

'Johnny gave Mary the cat.'

Unmarked determiner phrases (DPs) may function as the subject of an intransitive, (1a); the object of a transitive, (1b); or the goal of a ditransitive, (1c). Oblique *t* marks the subject of a transitive, (2a); the object of an antipassive, (2b); and the theme and subjects of a ditransitive, (2c).

Verbs in Montana Salish agree[2] with up to two of their arguments for person and number,[3] regardless of whether those arguments are overt or not. Intransitive verbs agree with their subject, as shown in (1a) and (2b). Transitive verbs agree with their subject and object, as in (1b) and (2a). Ditransitive agree with their subject and goal arguments, (1c) and (2c). Agreement for third-person intransitive subject and primary object is null.[4]

This paper examines the interaction of agreement and nominal marking in Montana Salish, focusing on the distribution of oblique nominals with regards to agreement. The distribution of agreement in relation to oblique marking is summarized in table 7.1. DPs and agreement are labeled with their grammatical function. Oblique arguments are boxed.

Two important generalizations can be derived from table 7.1. First, there is at most one unmarked overt argument in a clause (and

Table 7.1 Distribution of Agreement and Nominal Marking

Predicate Type	*Verb Form*	*Arguments*		
Intransitive	AGR_{sbj}=V	DP_{sbj}		
Antipassive	AGR_{sbj}=V-ANTIP	DP_{sbj}	*t* DP_{obj}	
Transitive	V-TR-AGR_{obj}-AGR_{sbj}	DP_{obj}	*t* DP_{sbj}	
Ditransitive	V-APPL-TR-AGR_{goal}-AGR_{sbj}	DP_{goal}	*t* DP_{theme}	*t* DP_{sbj}

that argument will be closer to the verb than any other). Second, both unmarked and oblique arguments can control agreement on the verb; however, subjects of transitive and ditransitive verbs are the only type of oblique argument that can control agreement.

The pattern of Montana Salish oblique marking is interesting both from a Salish-internal perspective and from a theoretical standpoint. First, while most (if not all) Salish languages have an oblique marker, outside of the Southern Interior branch of the family, oblique marking is in complementary distribution with agreement (Kroeber 1999).[5] This makes agreeing oblique transitive subjects in Montana Salish distinct.

Theoretically, the data discussed here bear on theories of the interaction of agreement, case, and licensing. Specifically, I argue that the Montana Salish pattern of oblique marking and agreement emerges because nominal licensing and agreement are distinct processes in Montana Salish. That is, not all agreement is able to license nominals in the language. I propose that all Montana Salish clauses include one probe that can license nominals, located on T. Nominals that do not Agree with T must be licensed in some other way, specifically, through oblique marking. I argue that oblique marking realizes the head of a case phrase (KP; Bittner 1994; Bittner and Hale 1996), and that KPs in Montana Salish are inherently licensed. I propose the licensing principle in (3).

(3) *Montana Salish nominal licensing*
A DP in Montana Salish is licensed through either
a. Agree with T or
b. Merge with K

The principle in (3) derives the generalizations that there is at most one unmarked nominal per clause, and that other nominal arguments are introduced by oblique *t*. The proposal here therefore supports work that argues that Agree does not necessarily involve licensing and that licensing does not always involve Agree (e.g., Bobaljik 2008; Levin and Preminger 2015).

The rest of the paper is structured as follows. In section 2, I give necessary background information about Montana Salish clause structure, transitivity, and agreement. Then, in section 3, I discuss why oblique transitive subjects in Montana Salish are puzzling from a theoretical perspective. Section 4 presents my analysis of the pattern. Section 5 concludes.

2. Background

2.1. Clause Structure and Transitivity

As in other Salish languages, in Montana Salish, transitivity is marked on the verb. Bare root verbs and those with an intransitive suffix are intransitive; verbs with a transitive suffix are transitive. Structurally, I take the locus of transitivity-related morphology to be *v*. Bare root verbs, like *tiyéš* in (4), are intransitive and have a null *v*. I assume the Unaccusativity Hypothesis, which holds that all roots in Salish are underlyingly unaccusative (Davis 1997; Davis and Matthewson 2009), as shown in (5).

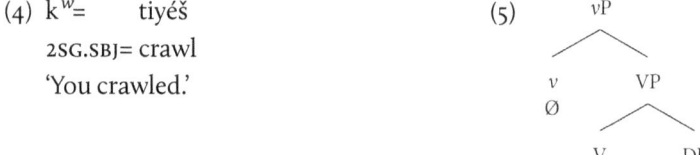

Verbs with the antipassive suffix *-m* are also formally intransitive, but may take an overt internal argument marked with oblique *t*, as shown in (6). I take that antipassive *-m* is a *v* head that introduces an external argument, as shown in (7).

(6) čn= wíč-m **t** **qxmín**
1SG.SBJ= see-ANTIP OBL antler
'I saw an antler.'

(7) 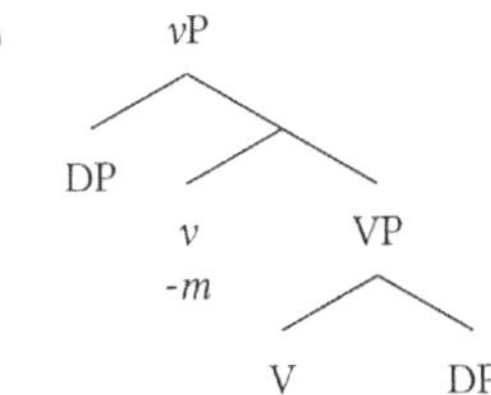

There are also a number of bare intransitive verbs that allow an overt oblique internal argument. I assume these verbs are structurally antipassive, with a null allomorph of the *v* in (7).

Verbs with one of the suffixes *-nt-* or *-st-* are transitive. Such verbs take object agreement and transitive subject agreement, as shown in (8). I assume that the transitive suffixes realize the *v* that introduces the external argument, which also hosts object agreement (see later in the text). Following Davis (2015), I assume transitive verbs also include an additional VoiceP layer, which hosts transitive subject agreement. This structure is shown in (9).

(8) wíč-nt-si-s
see-TR-2SG.OBJ-3.SBJ
'He saw you.'

(9) 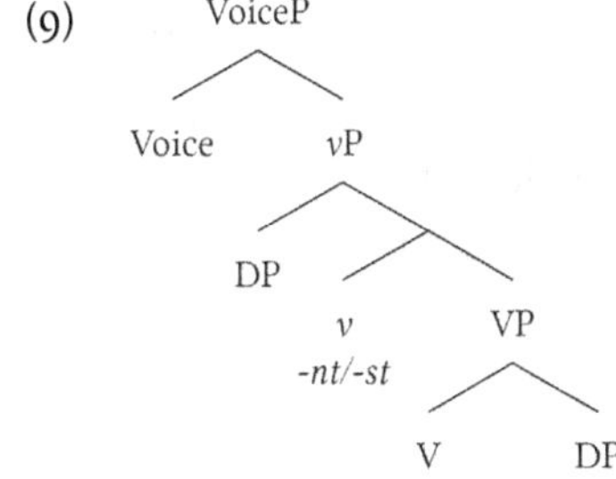

Ditransitive verbs are derived with an applicative suffix followed by the transitive suffix *-t*. There are two applicative suffixes, *-ši* and *-ɬ*, as shown in (10). I take the applicative suffix to be a high applicative (Pylkkänen 2008) between vP and VP that introduces the goal DP in its specifier. As in transitives, the external argument is introduced in Spec-vP and Voice hosts subject agreement. This structure is shown in (11).

(10) qʷo= xʷíc'-š-t-s t pús
ISG.OBJ= give-APPL-TR-3.SBJ OBL cat
'He gave me a cat.'

(11)

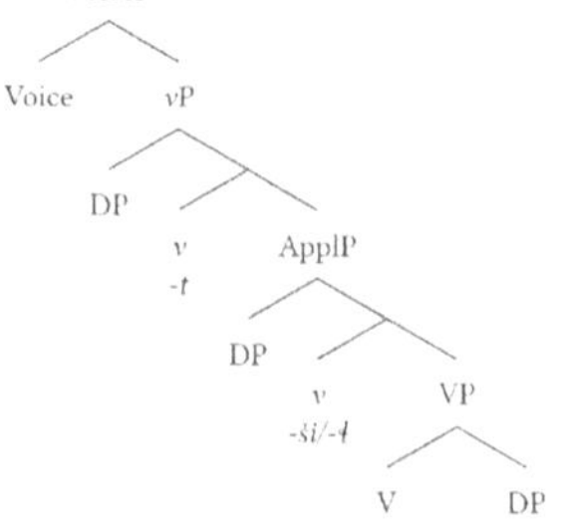

In the next section, I describe Montana Salish agreement and spell out my assumptions about its derivation.

2.2. Agreement and Verb Movement

Montana Salish has a rich system of person marking governed by transitivity. There are three series of person markers in Montana Salish relevant to the present discussion.[6] These are a set of proclitics used to mark intransitive subjects; a suffix series used to mark transitive subjects; and a mixed proclitic/suffix series used to mark transitive objects. All three series are shown in table 7.2.

I assume that agreement is derived in the syntax by the operation Agree, which pairs a φ-probe with a c-commanded goal, whose features are copied to the probe. I propose that there are potentially up to three φ-probes in the Montana Salish clause, as shown in (12).

Table 7.2 MSa Agreement Morphemes

	INTR SBJ	*TR OBJ*	*TR SBJ*
ISG	*čn=*	*kʷu=/qʷo=*	*-en*
2SG	*kʷ=*	*-sí-/-úm-*	*-exʷ*
IPL	*qeʔ=*	*qeʔ= ... -ɬul-l-*	*qeʔ=*
2PL	*p=*	*-ɬul-m-*	*-mp*
3	*Ø*	*Ø*	*–es*

(12) *Locus of agreement types*

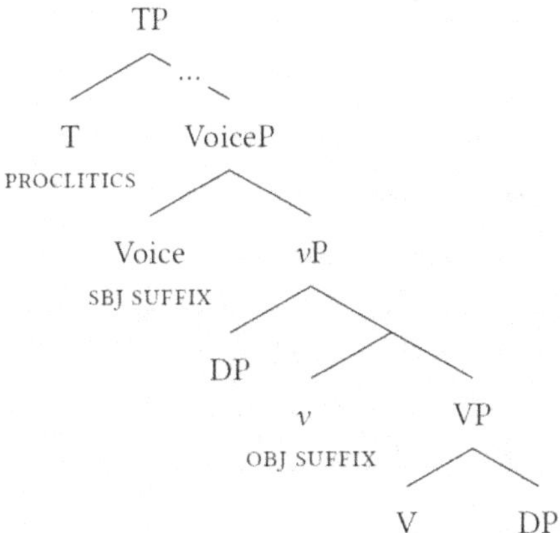

I assume proclitics are hosted on T (cf. Brandi and Cordin 1989). As I argue later in the text, T agrees with both intransitive subjects and transitive objects; this accounts for the fact that proclitics occur to mark both intransitive subjects and transitive objects.[7] Transitive subject agreement suffixes spell out a φ-probe on Voice, and transitive object agreement suffixes spell out a φ-probe on *v*.

Montana Salish is generally predicate initial. I assume that verb initial word order is derived by head movement of the verb along the clausal spine to a position above all arguments inside DP (Clemens and Polinsky 2017; McCloskey 1996; Ouhalla 1988). Here, tentatively, I propose that this position is Asp, which I take to occur between VoiceP and TP. This is shown in (13). Movement to Asp, but not T, accounts for the fact that agreement in T is always preverbal and more loosely bound to the verb than agreement suffixes.

(13) *Verb movement to Asp*

$[_{TP}$ T $[_{AspP}$ V+*v*+Voice+Asp $[_{VoiceP}$ DP t_{Voice} $[_{vP}$ t_v $[_{VP}$ *tv* DP]]]]]

The structure in (13) accounts for the fact that the verb precedes any overt arguments in unmarked word order. In transitive clauses, when there are two overt arguments, default word order is VOS. I will return to the derivation of this word order later in the text.

3. Obliques and Agreement

As shown in the introduction, only one type of oblique argument triggers agreement on the verb, namely the transitive subject. Other oblique arguments never control agreement. This pattern is repeated in table 7.3, with the modification of shading on the obliques that cannot control agreement.

This is not the case outside of Southern Interior Salish, where agreement and oblique marking are in complementary distribution. For example, in Island Halkomelem, transitive subjects may not be marked with oblique and trigger agreement (Donna Gerdts, p.c.):

(14) *niʔ q'ay-t-ʔəs ʔə tᶿə-nə sqeʔəq tᶿə yəx̌ʷəleʔ
AUX kill-TR-3SBJ OBL DET-1S.POS younger.sibling DET bald.eagle
'My younger brother killed the bald eagle.'

In Halkomelem, only unmarked DPs may control agreement on the verb, regardless of their grammatical function.

Whatever mechanism determines the distribution of oblique *t* in Montana Salish must be separate from the mechanism that determines the distribution of agreement. Therefore, an adequate

Table 7.3 Distribution of Agreement and Nominal Marking

Predicate Type	*Verb Form*	*Arguments*		
Intransitive	AGR_{sbj}=V	DP_{sbj}		
Antipassive	AGR_{sbj}=V-ANTIP	DP_{sbj}	*t* DP_{obj}	
Transitive	V-TR-AGR_{obj}-AGR_{sbj}	DP_{obj}	*t* DP_{sbj}	
Ditransitive	V-APPL-TR-AGR_{goal}-AGR_{sbj}	DP_{goal}	*t* DP_{theme}	*T* DP_{sbj}

account of the Montana Salish data discussed in this paper must be able to answer two key questions. First, what determines which overt arguments are marked with the oblique particle *t*? Second, why are oblique transitive subjects able to control agreement on the verb?

4. The Proposal

The core of the proposal rests on the idea that oblique marking is necessary when a DP cannot otherwise be licensed and that only some φ-probes in Montana Salish are capable of licensing a DP. That is, DP licensing and φ-agreement are two distinct processes in Montana Salish, in that not all φ-agreement is capable of licensing DPs. More concretely, I propose that there are two ways a DP are licensed in Montana Salish, as shown in (15).

(15) *Montana Salish nominal licensing*
A DP in Montana Salish is licensed through either
a. Agree with T or
b. Merge with K (oblique *t*)

The first clause of (15), that Agreeing with T is sufficient to licensing a DP, is essentially the same as saying that T is capable of assigning Case to a DP in Montana Salish, though I will remain agnostic about the role of abstract Case features in the grammar. The idea that Agree is capable of licensing nominals goes back to the first proposals regarding that operation in the literature (Chomsky 2000, 2001). The second clause of (15) allows for a DP not licensed by Agree with T to be licensed by merging with a K head. Here, I take this K head to be the oblique particle *t*. Thus, I follow proposals by Halpert (2012) and Levin (2015) that KPs are inherently licensed.[8]

In section 4.1, I show how this proposal can account for the distribution of unmarked DPs and agreement with those DPs. In section 4.2, I discuss the licensing of and agreement with oblique DPs.

4.1. Unmarked Licensing and Agreement

Recall that there is at most one unmarked overt DP in the Montana Salish clause. An unmarked DP may be the subject of an intransitive, (16a); the object of a transitive, (16b); or the goal of a ditransitive, (16c).

(16) *Unmarked arguments*

a. *Subject of an intransitive*

Ø	téšlš	**Qeyqeyší**
3SBJ	get.up	Qeyqeyší

'Qeyqeyší got up.'

b. *Object a transitive*

wíč-nt-Ø-s	**sχʷélmn**
see-TR-3OBJ-3SBJ	Devil

'He saw the Devil.'

c. *Goal of a ditransitive*

xʷíč-ši-t-Ø-s	**Malí**	t	pus	t	Čoní
give-APPL-TR-3OBJ-3SBJ	Mary	OBL	cat	OBL	Johnny

'Johnny gave Mary the cat.'

For bare intransitive clauses, the sole argument DP of the predicate is licensed by Agree with T, as shown in (17). The features of this argument are then spelled out as a proclitic on T.

(17) *T licenses intransitive subject*

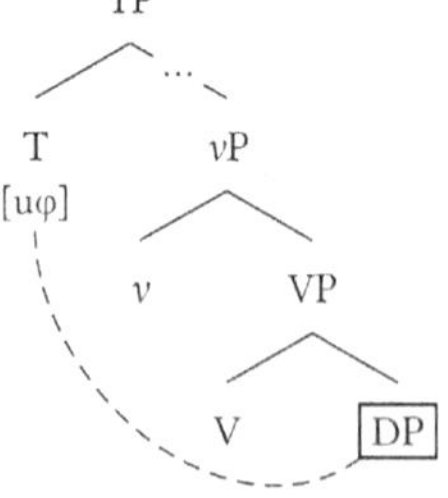

For verbs with the antipassive suffix *-m*, there are two arguments that need to be licensed. The φ-probe on T agrees with the external argument in Spec-*v*P, meaning that the internal argument must be a KP, to be discussed further later in the text. This is shown in (18).

(18) *T licenses external argument in antipassive*

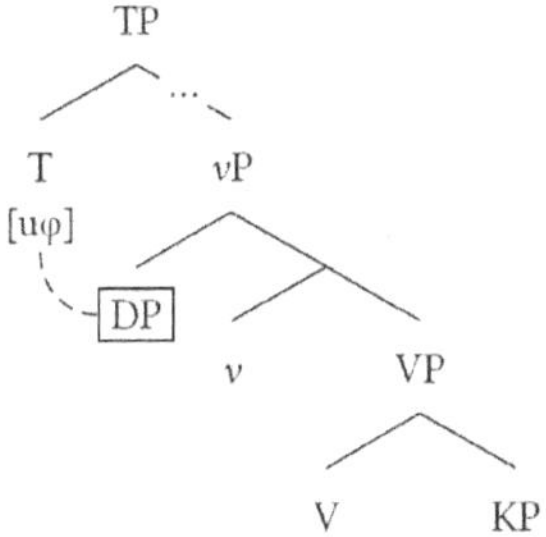

This derives the fact that the subjects of bare intransitives and of antipassives both control agreement on T.

Objects of transitive verbs are unmarked and control a separate paradigm of object suffixes that follow the transitive suffix directly. I assume object agreement spell out a φ-probe on *v*. As shown in (19), *v* agrees the object in its base position.[9]

(19) *Object agrees with v*

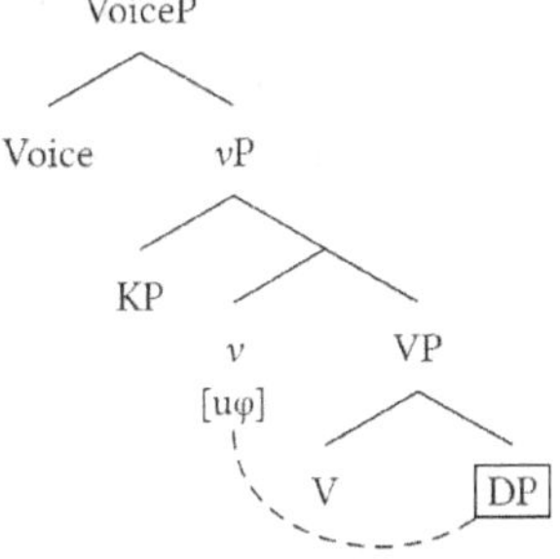

I assume that objects are not licensed by *v*, even though they enter into φ-agreement with that head. Instead, I propose that objects are licensed by Agree with T.[10] This is line with the idea that in some ergative languages, T assigns nominative case to both intransitive subjects and transitive objects (Legate 2008)

In order to be accessible to the φ-probe on T, objects must undergo object shift to the edge of VoiceP. I assume that this process targets the highest DP inside Voice's c-command domain. This step of the derivation is shown in (20).

(20) *T licenses shifted object*

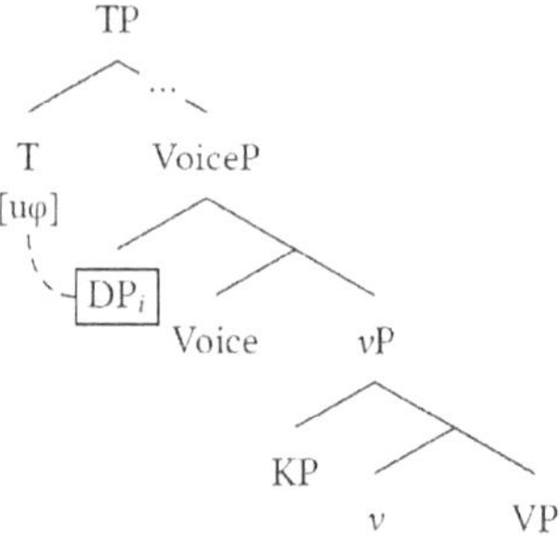

Support for this step of object shift comes from the fact that in transitive clauses with two overt arguments, the preferred word order is VOS. In addition, the fact that proclitics are present in the object agreement paradigm supports the idea that the object enters into an agreement relation with T, if this is the head that hosts agreement proclitics.

In ditransitive clauses, the goal is the unmarked argument, while the subject and the theme are oblique marked. As in transitive clauses, I assume that object agreement spells out a φ-probe on *v*, which in ditransitive clauses agrees with the goal argument in Spec-ApplP, as shown in (21).

(21) *Goal agrees with v*

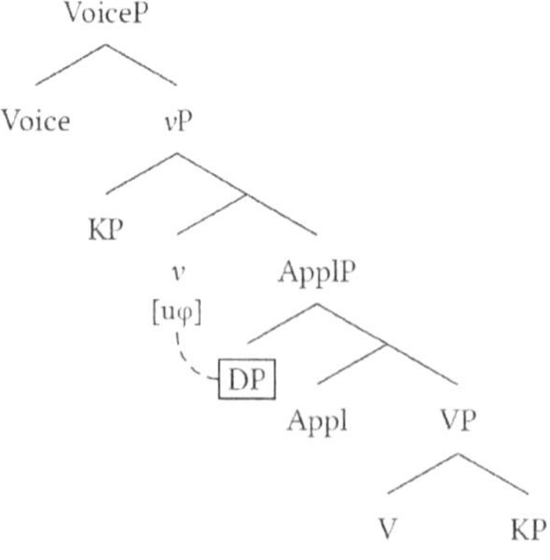

As in transitive clauses, the unmarked argument undergoes object shift to Spec-VoiceP, where it agrees with the φ-probe on T. This is shown in (22).

(22) *T licenses shifted goal*

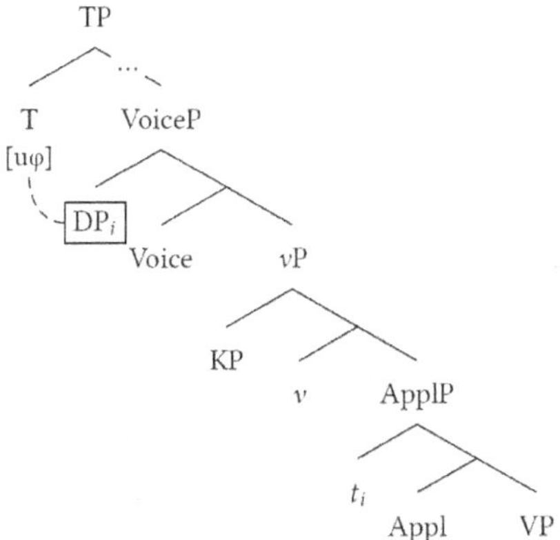

This analysis captures three important generalizations. First, because there is only one φ-probe that is capable of licensing a DP, namely on T, there will only ever be one unmarked DP. Second, because T always agrees with the highest argument in its c-command domain, the unmarked argument will always be closest to the verb after it raises to Asp. Third, because raising of a DP is triggered by the presence of Voice, transitive subjects will never be able to be licensed by T. They will always be lower than the argument that raises to Spec-VoiceP.

In the next section, I address the licensing of oblique phrases and agreement with transitive subjects.

4.2. Oblique Licensing and Agreement

There is only one φ-probe capable of licensing DPs in the Montana Salish clause, namely on T. Therefore, in clauses with more than one nominal, there will be arguments that remain unlicensed if they are merged as DP. The nominals in question are boxed in (23), where ✔ indicates a licensed argument and ✕ indicates an unlicensed argument.

(23) *Unlicensed DPs*

a. *Antipassive object*
$[_{\text{TP}}\ \text{T}\ [_{v\text{P}}\ \checkmark\text{DP}\ v\ [_{\text{VP}}\ \boxed{\times\,\text{DP}}\ ]]]$

b. *Transitive subject*
$[_{\text{TP}}\ \text{T}\ [_{\text{VoiceP}}\ \checkmark\text{DP}_i\ [_{v\text{P}}\ \boxed{\times\,\text{DP}}\ v\ [_{\text{VP}}\ t_i\ ]]]$

c. *Ditransitive subject and theme*
$[_{\text{TP}}\ \text{T}\ [_{\text{VoiceP}}\ \checkmark\text{DP}_i\ [_{v\text{P}}\ \boxed{\times\,\text{DP}}\ v\ [_{\text{ApplP}}\ t_i\ \text{Appl}\ [_{\text{VP}}\ \boxed{\times\,\text{DP}}\ ]]]]]$

Because there is no other φ-probe that is capable of licensing the boxed DPs in the structures mentioned earlier, they must be licensed some other way. I contend that the role of oblique *t* is to license these DPs. Specifically, I propose that *t* is a K head that is intrinsically licensed; it does not need to enter into an Agree relation to be licensed (see Halpert 2012 and Levin 2015 for proposals about KP along these lines). Oblique arguments have the structure shown in (24).

(24) *Oblique nominals are KPs*

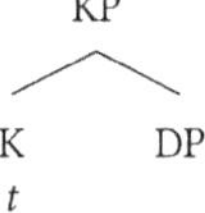

Support for the idea that the oblique marker serves a licensing function comes from the fact that it also introduces certain adjuncts, such as adverbs of time (25a) and instruments (25b).

(25) *Oblique adjuncts*

a. *Time adverbial*

t	**sq'sí**	u	es-wíč-st-Ø-n	Čoní
OBL	long.time	C	ASP-see-TR-3.OBJ-1SG.SBJ	Johnny

'It was a long time ago when I saw Johnny.'

b. *Instrumental*

púl-st-Ø-s	x̣amałtn	**t**	**čsṕmíntn**
die-TR-3.OBJ-1SG.SBJ	fly	OBL	fly-swatter

'She killed the fly with a fly-swatter.'

Assuming that nominals in adjuncts must be licensed just as arguments must be, the oblique marking of arguments and adjuncts receives a unified account in a theory where *t* heads an inherently licensed KP.

Because KP is inherently licensed, the structures in *unlicensed* can be repaired if the boxed DPs are instead merged as KPs, as shown in (26).

(26) *Licensed KPs*

a. *Antipassive object*
$[_{\text{TP}}\ \text{T}\ [_{v\text{P}}\ \checkmark\text{DP}\ v\ [_{\text{VP}} \boxed{\checkmark\text{KP}}\ ]]]$

b. *Transitive subject*
$[_{\text{TP}}\ \text{T}\ [_{\text{VoiceP}}\ \checkmark\text{DP}_i\ [_{v\text{P}} \boxed{\checkmark\text{KP}}\ v\ [_{\text{VP}}\ t_i\ ]]]$

c. *Ditransitive subject and theme*
$[_{\text{TP}}\ \text{T}\ [_{\text{VoiceP}}\ \checkmark\text{DP}_i\ [_{v\text{P}} \boxed{\checkmark\text{KP}}\ v\ [_{\text{ApplP}}\ t_i\ \text{Appl}\ [_{\text{VP}} \boxed{\checkmark\text{KP}}\ ]]]]]$

This part of the proposal answers the question of the distribution of oblique nominals: they are nominals that cannot enter into an Agree relation with the φ-probe on T. Therefore, these arguments must be merged as inherently licensed KPs.

Under this proposal, how is a transitive subject KP capable of controlling transitive subject agreement? I assume that because the KP is part of the extended nominal projection (Bittner and Hale 1996), the φ-features of the DP below it percolate up to the KP layer making the KP visible to Agree, as shown in (27).

(27) *φ-features on DP percolate to KP*

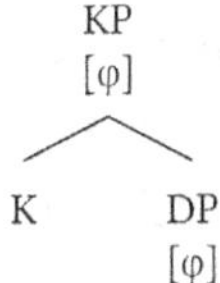

With (27) in place, deriving transitive subject agreement is straightforward. When Voice is merged, the φ-probe on that head searches

its c-command domain and finds the φ-features on the external argument KP in Spec-*v*P, as shown in (28).

(28) *Voice agrees with KP in Spec-vP*

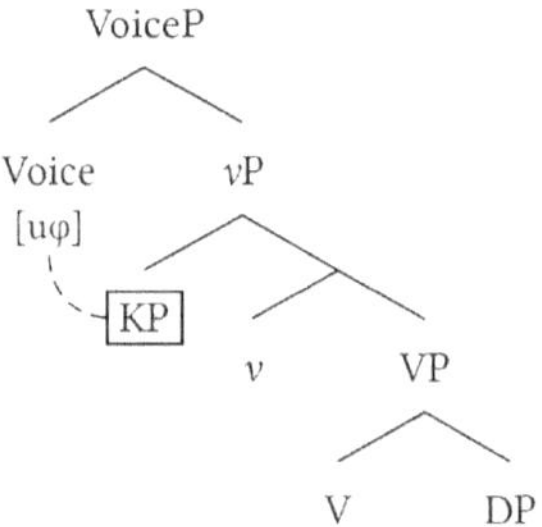

The agreement relation between Voice and the KP in Spec-*v*P occurs in both transitive and ditransitive clauses. Like the φ-probe on *v*, I argue the φ-probe on Voice does not license its goal. This is why the external argument of a clause containing a VoiceP layer must be a KP, and not a DP.

Support for the idea that Voice does not license its goal comes from passive clauses, which are formed with an invariant passive suffix -(ə)*m* in place of transitive subject agreement. As shown in (29), the subject of a passive is marked oblique.

(29) *Subject of a passive is oblique*

cú-nt-Ø-əm	ye	**t**	**sxʷmalyé**
say-TR-3.OBJ-PASS	this	OBL	doctor

'he was told by the doctor'

I assume that the passive suffix realizes a special passive Voice head, which lacks a φ-probe. The structure of (29) is therefore the same as a fully transitive clause, but the Voice head does not Agree with Spec-*v*P.

(30) *Passive Voice lacks [uφ]*

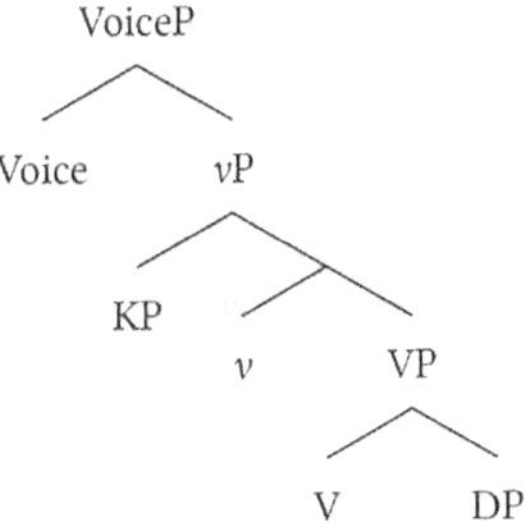

Under the current analysis, the lack of a φ-probe on Voice in passives has no effect on the licensing of the external argument, since in full transitives the presence of a φ-probe on that head does not license the external argument either.[11]

4.3. Summary

Table 7.4 summarizes the properties of the heads T, Voice, and *v*. Specifically, it shows whether or not a head has a φ-probe, and whether or not that head is capable of licensing its goal.

T is the only head capable of licensing the nominal that its φ-probe agrees with; Voice and *v* do not license nominals they enter into an Agree relation with. Nominals not licensed by T must be merged as oblique KPs. When combined with the assumption

Table 7.4 Heads and Their Properties

Head	*Φ-Probe?*	*Licenser?*
T	Yes	Yes
v_{TR}	Yes	No
Voice_{TR}	Yes	No
v_{INTR}	No	No
Voice_{PASS}	No	No

that Voice triggers movement of the highest DP in its c-command domain to its specifier derives the distribution of oblique and unmarked overt nominals.

An interesting property of the proposal is that the licensing behavior of heads in certain areas of the clause is uniform. Inside the extended VP, heads (Voice, *v*) do not license nominals, but they are capable of hosting φ-probes. Higher than VP, T is able to host a φ-probe *and* license nominals simultaneously.

5. Conclusions

In this paper, I examined the distribution of arguments marked by the oblique particle *t* and the interaction of oblique marking with agreement. I argued that the distribution of *t* is explained if it is a K head that licenses a DP otherwise unable to be licensed. Specifically, I proposed that there is only one licensing head in the clausal spine in Montana Salish, T, and that this limits the number of unmarked DPs that can appear in a clause to one.

Furthermore, I argued that φ-agreement and licensing are separate processes in Montana Salish. This conclusion emerges from the fact that transitive subjects are marked oblique in Montana Salish, yet are capable of controlling agreement. Concretely, I proposed that even if a head bears a φ-probe, it may not be able to license a nominal it agrees with. This is the case for transitive Voice, which hosts transitive subject agreement, and transitive *v*, which hosts transitive object agreement. Thus, the proposal here supports work that argues that Agree does not necessarily involve licensing (e.g., Bobaljik 2008).

Endnotes

1. This work would not be possible without Sally Thomason's long-term documentation work with elders of the Confederate Salish and Salish and Kootenai Tribes and the Salish-Pend d'Oreille Culture Committee. I would

like to deeply thank Sally for making her extensive corpus of Montana Salish fieldwork available to me. All data in this paper come from field notes or texts collected by her. Abbreviations used in this paper: 1 = first person, 2 = second person, 3 = third person, agr = agreement, antip = antipassive, appl = applicative, asp = aspect, goal = goal, obj = object, obl = oblique, pass = passive, sbj = subject, sg = singular, theme = theme, tr = transitive.

2. I use the term "agree" in both a pretheoretical sense of "crossreference" and a theoretical sense of the Minimalist operation Agree. Where Agree is capitalized, it refers to the operation.

3. The third-person paradigm does make a number distinction.

4. "Primary object" refers to the grouping of the object of a transitive and goal of a ditransitive together (Dryer 1986).

5. At least Colville-Okanagan in the Southern Interior branch shares this property with Montana Salish (Mattina 2004).

6. Here, I set aside side imperfective and irrealis agreement paradigms that are historically based on nominalization. The pattern of agreement that is relevant to the analysis here is the same in these cases.

7. I leave the appearance of the 1PL proclitic *qeʔ=* in the transitive subject paradigm to further work.

8. Similar proposals have been made for Okanagan (Lyon 2011) and for Halkomelem (Thompson 2012).

9. Recall the external argument is an oblique, therefore a KP in this structure.

10. In the terminology of Coon et al. (2014) for Mayan languages, Montana Salish is both a "high" and "low" absolutive language, in that it shows agreement with absolutive (=unmarked) arguments both inside the extended VP and from a high projection.

11. In this way, my analysis is similar to McKay's (2019) account of transitive subjects in Montana Salish. McKay argues that even agreeing transitive Voice is a "passive" in the language.

References

Bittner, Maria. 1994. *Case, scope, and binding*. Dordrecht: Kluwer.

Bittner, Maria, and Ken Hale. 1996. The structural determination of case and agreement. *Linguistic Inquiry*, 27: 1–68.

Bobaljik, Jonathan David. 2008. Where's phi? Agreement as a post-syntactic operation. In Daniel Harbour, David Adger, and Susana Béjar (Eds.), *Phittheory: Phi features across interfaces and modules*, 295–328. Oxford: Oxford University Press.

Brandi, Luciana, and Patrizia Cordin. 1989. Two Italian dialects and the null-subject parameter. In Osvaldo Jaeggli and Ken Safir (Eds.), *The Null Subject Parameter*. Dordrecht: Kluwer Academic.

Chomsky, Noam. 2000. Minimalist inquiries: The framework. In Roger Martin, David Michaels, and Juan Uriagereka (Eds.), *Step by step: Essays on Minimalist syntax in honor of Howard Lasnik*, 89–155. Cambridge, MA: MIT Press.

Chomsky, Noam. 2001. Derivation by phase. In Michael Kenstowicz (Ed.), *Ken Hale: A life in language*, 1–52. Cambridge, MA: MIT Press.

Clemens, Lauren Eby, and Maria Polinsky. 2017. Verb-initial word orders, primarily in Austronesian and Mayan languages. In Martin Everaert and Henk van Riemsdijk (Eds.), *The Wiley Blackwell Companion to Syntax*. Oxford: John Wiley & Sons.

Coon, Jessica, Pedro Mateo Pedro, and Omer Preminger. 2014. The role of case in A-bar extraction asymmetries: Evidence from Mayan. *Linguistic Variation*, 14: 179–242.

Davis, Henry. 1997. Deep unaccusativity and zero syntax in St'át'imcets. In Amaya Mendikoetxea and Myriam Uribe-Etxebarria (Eds.), *Theoretical issues at the morphology–syntax interface*. Bilbao: Universidad del Pas Vasco.

Davis, Henry. 2015. St'át'imcets and the nonexistence of T-S-V-O languages. Ms., UBC.

Davis, Henry, and Lisa Matthewson. 2009. Issues in Salish syntax and semantics. *Language and Linguistics Compass*, 3: 1097–1166.

Dryer, Matthew S. 1986. Primary objects, secondary objects, and antidative. *Language*, 62: 808–45.

Halpert, Claire. 2012. Argument licensing and agreement in zulu (Doctoral dissertation). MIT.

Kroeber, Paul D. 1999. *The Salish language family: Reconstructing syntax*. London: University of Nebraska Press.

Legate, Julie Anne. 2008. Morphological and abstract case. *Linguistic Inquiry*, 39: 55–101.

Levin, Theodore. 2015. Licensing without case (Doctoral dissertation). MIT, Cambridge, MA.

Levin, Theodore, and Omer Preminger. 2015. Case in Sakha: Are two modalities really necessary? *Natural Language and Linguistic Theory*, 33: 231–50.

Lyon, John. 2011. The semantics of determiner phrases in Okanagan. *ICSNL*, 46: 194–266.

Mattina, Anthony. 2004. The Okanagan transitive sentence prototype. In Donna B. Gerdts and Lisa Matthewson (Eds.), *Studies in Salish linguistics in honor of m. dale kinkade*, University of Montana Occasional Papers in Linguistics, 279–88. Missoula: University of Montana.

McCloskey, James. 1996. On the scope of verb movement in Irish. *Natural Language and Linguistic Theory*, 14: 47–104.

McKay, Isabel. 2019. Transitive subjects as adjuncts in Montana Salish. Poster presented at LSA 2019.

Ouhalla, Jamal. 1988. The syntax of head movement: A study of Berber (Doctoral dissertation). University College London.

Pylkkänen, Liina. 2008. *Introducing arguments*. Cambridge, MA: MIT Press.

Thompson, James J. 2012. Syntactic nominalization in Halkomelem Salish (Doctoral dissertation). UBC.

CHAPTER 8

'Gone Now Were the Days When All They Had to Eat Was Poor Food'

Temporal Participles in Meskwaki*

Lucy G. Thomason

1. Introduction

Meskwaki is a Central Algonquian language which is currently spoken in Iowa. A large body of texts—nearly 27,000 pages of manuscripts—written in the early twentieth century by native speakers of Meskwaki make it possible to identify some unexpected features of Meskwaki grammar which shed new light on the language as a whole. Temporal participles are one such startling-to-outsiders and yet defining outcropping of Meskwaki morphosyntax.

Two interesting facts about Meskwaki temporal participles are, first, that they exist, and, second, that most of them are in terms of surface morphology indistinguishable from certain types of verbs. Meskwaki aorist conjunct verbs, future conjunct verbs, changed conjunct verbs, iterative verbs, future iterative verbs, past verbs, future past verbs, changed past verbs, changed interrogative verbs, and future interrogative verbs are morphologically identical (on the surface) to various types of temporal participles. A significant amount of context is required—the whole sentence, or an even larger segment of discourse—in order to determine whether certain types of words are verbs or participles. And many ambiguities are inescapable: a sentence such as *i·ni=meko wi·h=we·pi·hko·neki wi·h=amo·neki* could mean either 'Then they'll start going after you, intending to eat you' (with *wi·h=we·pi·hko·neki* as one of two future conjunct verbs, the second modifying the first) or 'That is when they'll start going after you, intending to eat you' (with *wi·h=we·pi·hko·neki* as a temporal participle modified by a future conjunct verb). The difference in meaning between the two interpretations might be negligible in this case, but the underlying structures posited are quite different.

(1)	i·ni	=meko	wi·h=we·pi·hko·-neki	wi·h=amo·-neki.[1]
	then/that.inan.sg	=emph	fut=start.on-X>2s.conj	fut=eat-X>2s.conj
	then/that.inan.sg	=emph	ic.fut=start.on-X>2s.ppl(inan.sg)	fut=eat-X>2s.conj

'Then they'll start going after you, intending to eat you.'
Or: 'That is when they'll start going after you, intending to eat you'.[2]

It is even conceivable that temporal participles are the original source of some or all of the abovementioned ten Meskwaki verb moods. The changed conjunct mood and the iterative mood are especially difficult to distinguish semantically, as well as morphologically, from their corresponding temporal participles. To put this another way, some Meskwaki temporal participles have to be nominals rather than verbs, but there are no Meskwaki changed conjunct verbs or iterative verbs that can absolutely, incontrovertibly be proven to be verbs rather than temporal participles.

The rest of this paper lays out the case for the existence of twelve different types of Meskwaki temporal participles, ten of them morphologically indistinguishable (on the surface) from the ten abovementioned types of Meskwaki verbs, and eight of them morphologically indistinguishable (on the surface) from the various types of Meskwaki locative participles. In order to discuss Meskwaki temporal participles, I will first have to describe how Meskwaki participles work. In order to describe how Meskwaki participles work, I will have to give a brief overview of several aspects of Meskwaki grammar, under the headings of noun inflection, verb inflection, inflected versus uninflected arguments of verbs, verbal moods, relative roots and their complements, and heads of participles.[3]

2. Meskwaki Noun Inflection

Meskwaki is a polysynthetic language. Most Meskwaki noun stems and almost all Meskwaki verb stems are polymorphemic. Nonvocative and nonlocative Meskwaki nouns inflect for gender (animate or inanimate) and number (singular or plural). Animate nonvocative nonlocative nouns are moreover marked as either proximate (the currently most central, salient, or sympathetic third person in a discourse) or obviative (a currently less central, salient, or sympathetic third person in the discourse). Meskwaki nouns, including vocative and locative nouns, can also inflect for person and number of a possessor.

Examples of the possible nonvocative nonlocative noun inflections are given in 2. Meskwaki *ni·ča·p-* is an animate noun stem meaning 'doll', and Meskwaki *ošehki·ta·kan-* is an inanimate noun stem meaning 'garment' or 'clothing'.

(2)		
	ni·ča·p-a	'doll (prox.)'
	ni·ča·p-aki	'dolls (prox.)'
	ni·ča·p-ani	'doll (obv.)'
	ni·ča·p-ahi	'dolls (obv.)'
	ke-ni·ča·p-a	'your (sg.) doll (prox.)'
	ke-ni·ča·p-aki	'your (sg.) dolls (prox.)'
	ke-ni·ča·p-ani	'your (sg.) doll (obv.)'
	ke-ni·ča·p-ahi	'your (sg.) dolls (obv.)'
	ne-ni·ča·p-a	'my doll (prox.)'
	ne-ni·ča·p-aki	'my dolls (prox.)'
	ne-ni·ča·p-ani	'my doll (obv.)'
	ne-ni·ča·p-ahi	'my dolls (obv.)'
	o-ni·ča·p-ani	'his/her doll (obv.)'

o-ni·ča·p-ahi	'his/her dolls (obv.)'
ke-ni·ča·p-ena·n-a	'our (incl.) doll (prox.)'
ke-ni·ča·p-ena·n-aki	'our (incl.) dolls (prox.)'
ke-ni·ča·p-ena·n-ani	'our (incl.) doll (obv.)'
ke-ni·ča·p-ena·n-ahi	'our (incl.) dolls (obv.)'
ke-ni·ča·p-wa·w-a	'your (pl.) doll (prox.)'
ke-ni·ča·p-wa·w-aki	'your (pl.) dolls (prox.)'
ke-ni·ča·p-wa·w-ani	'your (pl.) doll (obv.)'
ke-ni·ča·p-wa·w-ahi	'your (pl.) dolls (obv.)'
ne-ni·ča·p-ena·n-a	'our (excl.) doll (prox.)'
ne-ni·ča·p-ena·n-aki	'our (excl.) dolls (prox.)'
ne-ni·ča·p-ena·n-ani	'our (excl.) doll (obv.)'
ne-ni·ča·p-ena·n-ahi	'our (excl.) dolls (obv.)'
o-ni·ča·p-wa·w-ani	'their doll (obv.)'
o-ni·ča·p-wa·w-ahi	'their dolls (obv.)'
o-ni·ča·p-inaw-a	'one's doll (prox.)'[4]
o-ni·ča·p-inaw-aki	'one's dolls (prox.)'
o-ni·ča·p-inaw-ani	'one's doll (obv.)'
o-ni·ča·p-inaw-ahi	'one's dolls (obv.)'

ošehki·ta·kan-i	'clothing'
ošehki·ta·kan-ani	'garments'
ket-o·šehki·ta·kan-i	'your (sg.) clothing'
ket-o·šehki·ta·kan-ani	'your (sg.) garments'
net-o·šehki·ta·kan-i	'my clothing'
net-o·šehki·ta·kan-ani	'my garments'
ot-o·šehki·ta·kan-i	'his/her clothing'
ot-o·šehki·ta·kan-ani	'his/her garments'
ket-o·šehki·ta·kan-ena·n-i	'our (incl.) clothing'
ket-o·šehki·ta·kan-ena·n-ani	'our (incl.) garments'
ket-o·šehki·ta·kan-wa·w-i	'your (pl.) clothing'
ket-o·šehki·ta·kan-wa·w-ani	'your (pl.) garments'
net-o·šehki·ta·kan-ena·n-i	'our (excl.) clothing'
net-o·šehki·ta·kan-ena·n-ani	'our (excl.) garments'
ot-o·šehki·ta·kan-wa·w-i	'their clothing'
ot-o·šehki·ta·kan-wa·w-ani	'their garments'

ot-o·šehki·ta·kan-inaw-i	'one's clothing'
ot-o·šehki·ta·kan-inaw-ani	'one's garments'

Animate noun inflection does not distinguish obviatives from secondary obviatives, and inanimate noun inflection does not distinguish proximates from obviatives. Note that in 3 one of the three animate obviative nouns is coindexed with animate obviative verbal inflection, while the other two are coindexed with animate secondary obviative verbal inflection. In 4, the inanimate noun is coindexed with inanimate proximate verbal inflection. In 5, the inanimate noun is coindexed with an inanimate proximate participle and inanimate proximate verbal inflection. In 6, the inanimate noun is coindexed with an inanimate obviative participle.

(3)	o·s-ani	e·h=wi·kam-a·niči	owi·neno·-ni,	mahk-owi·neno·-ni.
	3father-obv.sg	aor=like.the.taste.of-3'>3".conj	fat-obv.sg	bear-fat-obv.sg

'His father was fond of eating fat, bear fat.'[5]

(4)	'kehkinawa·či	ke-tehkina·kan-i	mi·kesiwi-wi',
	as.an.indication	2-cradleboard-inan.sg	have.wampum.beads-0s.ind
	e·h=in-a·či.		
	aor=say{so}to-3s>3'.conj		

' "A sign you may know it by is that your cradleboard is decorated with wampum beads", she told him.'[6]

(5)	meše·nah=meko	šwa·šika	me·me·ša·-kini	ki·ke·nowi-ana·kan-ani
	perhaps=emph	eight	ic.ɪred.be.large-0.ppl(inan.pl)	clan.feast-bowl-inan.pl
	e·h=a·yahkwa·wise-ki.			
	aor=ɪred.be.brimful-0.conj			

'Eight large clan-feast bowls were more or less filled to the brim.'[7]

(6)	e·sa·wa·waki·-niki	ahk-i	e·h=we·ši·ho-či,
	ic.be.yellow.earth-0'.ppl(inan.sg)	earth-inan.sg	aor=paint.face-3s.conj
	e·h=a·htawa·ši-ki.		
	aor=lie.on.back-3s.conj		

'She painted her face with yellow clay and lay down on her back.'[8]

3. Meskwaki Verb Stem Types, Verb Inflection, and Verbal Arguments

Meskwaki verb stems pattern according to four basic types: intransitive taking an inanimate subject (henceforth, inanimate intransitive or II verb stems), intransitive taking an animate subject (animate intransitive or AI verb stems), transitive taking an inanimate object (transitive inanimate or TI verb stems), and transitive taking an animate object (transitive animate or TA verb stems). The variations on these basic types include ditransitives (TA+O verb stems), morphologically intransitive verbs which nonetheless take an object (AI+O verb stems), morphologically transitive yet objectless verbs (TI-O verb stems), and a few other, rarer argument configurations.

All Meskwaki verbs inflect for mood and for certain characteristics of the subject: person, often number, and, if third person, gender (animate or inanimate) and often proximacy (proximate, obviative, or secondary obviative). Transitive animate verbs (TAs and TA+Os) moreover inflect for certain characteristics of an object: person, often number, and, if third person, often proximacy (proximate, obviative, or secondary obviative).[9] A great many verbs, both transitive and intransitive, also obligatorily or optionally take an uninflected object, an object not referenced in any way by the verbal inflection. Uninflected objects of verbs are termed secondary objects. Examples 7–13 give sentences in which an animate intransitive verb stem contains the final element *-a·hkwe·* 'throw 2Obj', which obligatorily takes a secondary object. Examples 14–17 give instances of ditransitive verbs: in each of these sentences a transitive animate verb stem contains the final element *-amaw* 'do to 2Obj for Obj, do to 2Obj positively or adversely affecting Obj', which obligatorily takes a secondary object.

(7) e·h=te·pi-sakiwine·sah-a·či,
aor=succeed-grab.by.the.horns-3s>3'.conj
e·h=kwe·hta·na·hke·-či i·nini kehči-nenoso·-ni.
aor=throw.fearsomely-3s.conj that.obv.sg great-buffalo-obv.sg
'He succeeded in seizing it by the horns and threw that huge buffalo with fearsome force.'[10]

In 7, an ordinary transitive TA verb stem *sakiwine·sah-* 'grab Obj by the horns', modified by preverb *te·pi*, is inflected for an animate third-person proximate singular subject and an animate third-person obviative object. This verb is followed by a morphologically intransitive but semantically transitive AI+O verb stem *kwe·hta·na·hke·-* 'throw 2Obj fearsomely', which is inflected for an animate third-person proximate singular subject but also takes an animate third-person obviative singular object (a secondary object which happens in this instance to be animate third-person obviative singular).

(8) aškači·meki·hi onakeš-i e·h=pye·či-nowa·hke·-niči mečemo·k-ani.
a.little.later entrail-inan.sg aor=hither-fling.out-3'.conj old.woman-obv.sg
'A little later the old woman flung the guts out-of-doors hither.'
Or: 'A little later the guts came flying out the door, flung by the old woman.'[11]

The perspective in 8 is that of an animate proximate third person mentioned previously in the discourse. A morphologically intransitive but semantically transitive AI+O verb stem *nowa·hke·-* 'fling 2Obj outside', modified by preverb *pye·či*, is inflected for an animate third-person obviative subject but also takes an inanimate third -person singular secondary object.

(9) ki·ši-nes-eči, e·h=saka·nowe·n-eči,
ic.perf-kill-X>3.cc aor=seize.by.the.tail-X>3.conj
e·h=we·pa·hke·-ki ka·ka·wikaše·w-a, e·h=ki·ša·kotwe·we·ya·ke·poso-či.
aor=throw-X.conj grizzly.bear-prx.sg aor=whiz.tremendously.loudly-3s.conj
'After she was killed, the grizzly was grabbed by the tail and thrown, and she whizzed through the air with tremendous noise.'[12]

The first two verbs in 9 are transitive and are inflected for an indefinite subject acting on an animate third-person proximate object. The third verb is morphologically intransitive but semantically transitive, and is inflected for an indefinite subject but also takes an uninflected secondary object which the accompanying noun specifies as animate third-person proximate singular. The fourth verb is both morphologically and semantically intransitive (plain AI rather than AI+O), and is inflected for an animate third-person singular subject.

(10) ‘nahi´, ma·hani mawi-nowa·hke·-no’, e·h=in-a·či
well this.inan.pl go.and-fling.out-2s.imp aor=say{so}to-3s>3’.conj
o-mešo·h-ani, o-kye·-ni o·s-ani.
3-grandfather.dim-obv.sg 3-mother-obv.sg 3father-obv.sg
. . . anehkikan-ani e·h=nowa·hke·-či.
. . . Canada.goose.bone-inan.pl aor=fling.out-3s.conj
‘“Well, go and throw these out!” he (the grandson) told his grandfather, his mother’s father. ... And he (the grandfather) threw out the goose bones.’[13]

The AI+O stem *nowa·hke·-* ‘fling 2Obj outside’ occurs twice in 10, and each time, as the accompanying nominals indicate, it takes an inanimate third-person plural secondary object.

Note that the AI+O stem in *-a·hke·* in 7 takes an animate obviative singular object, while the AI+O stem in *-a·hke·* in 8 takes an inanimate singular object, the AI+O stem in *-a·hke·* in 9 takes an animate proximate singular object, and the two AI+O stems in *-a·hke·* in 10 each take an inanimate plural object. Because no information about the secondary object of an AI+O is indexed on the verb, such secondary objects can be animate or inanimate, singular or plural, and proximate or obviative, according to the context.

First and second persons in Meskwaki are referenced inflectionally, or else by means of freestanding emphatic pronouns, or else by means of vocative nouns or participles, or else by means of possessed nouns where the noun stem is *i·yaw-* ‘body, life, self’. An example of this last type, where the verb stem is an AI+O ending in *-a·hke·*, is given in 11.

(11) e·h=a·čimoh-a·či,
aor=inform-3s>3’.conj
‘i·ni =ya·pi wi·h=we·pa·hke·-ya·ni k-i·yaw-i’,
then =here’s.the.thing fut=throw-1s.conj 2-self-inan.sg

e·h=in-a·či.
aor=say{so}to-3s>3'.conj
'And he explained to her, telling her, "Listen up: I'm going to throw you now."'[14]

The second verb in 11 is morphologically intransitive but semantically transitive, with an inflected animate first-person singular subject acting on what is morphologically an inanimate third-person singular secondary object, but which semantically speaking is an animate second-person singular secondary object. Not only are the nouns *ki·yawi* 'you (singular)', *ki·ya·wa·wi* 'you (plural)', *ki·ya·na·ni* 'us (inclusive)', *ni·yawi* 'me', and *niya·na·ni* 'us (exclusive)' inanimate singular, but Meskwaki first- and second-person emphatic pronouns and Meskwaki first- and second-person participles agree as if they, too, are inanimate singular.

The secondary object of an AI+O verb sometimes has no overt expression at all, as is the case in 12 and 13.

(12) e·h=wi·šika·hke·-či, 'sah!' e·h=inwe·hw-a·či.
aor=throw.hard-3s.conj (noise) aor=sound{so}as.a.blow.by.a.tool-3s>3'.conj
'He threw (the rock) hard, and the blow he struck against (his uncle) went, "THUNK!"'[15]

The secondary object of *wi·šika·hke·-* 'throw 2Obj hard' exists semantically but has no overt expression in the sentence in 12, neither in the verbal inflection nor as a nominal accompanying the verb.

In 13, the unexpressed secondary object of *we·pa·hke·-* 'throw 2Obj' refers to the same animate third-person obviative object inflected on the preceding verb.

(13) ki·ši-ša·ša·kwikome·sah-a·či =’pi· =’ni e·h=we·pa·hke·-či.
ic.perf-quickly.smash.the.nose.of-3s>3'.cc =hrsy =then aor=throw-3s.conj
'After he crumpled its nose, he hurled it from him.'[16]

Meskwaki transitive inanimate verbs take secondary objects only in highly specialized circumstances which I will not discuss here. By contrast, transitive animate verbs taking an uninflected secondary object in addition to their inflected animate object (TA+Os) are plentiful in Meskwaki. Examples of morphologically transitive but semantically ditransitive verbs are given in 14–17. All four of the verb stems in question end in *-amaw* 'do to 2Obj for Obj, do to 2Obj positively or adversely affecting Obj'.

(14) nahi´, k-i·h=kawahamo·-nepwa =ča·hi
well 2-fut=chop.down.for-1s>2p.ind =so
peškipe·h= mo·se·wi-ki.
hickory.tree.inan.sg= ic.be.wormy-0.ppl(inan.sg)
'Well, so I will chop down a wormy hickory tree for you folks.'[17]

(15) e·h=nehtamaw-oči pene·w-ahi na·hka e·sepa·h-ahi. (wo: <|o>)
aor=kill.for/on-X>3.conj turkey-obv.pl again/and raccoon-obv.pl
'Turkeys and raccoons were killed for him.'[18]

(16) 'ne-taši·hkama·-kwa n-i·w-ani neno·te·w-a',
1-deal.with.there.for-3s>1s.ind 1-wife-obv.sg Indian-prx.sg
e·h=i-či mesihpike·w-a.
aor=say{so}-3s.conj Solid.Rib-prx.sg
'"The human has been messing with my wife on me," said Solid-Rib.'[19]

(17) i·ni ='pi =wi·na e·h=pemo·tamaw-a·či, e·h=ša·konamaw-a·či.
then =hrsy =but aor=carry.along.on.back-3s>3'.conj aor=break/crush.for-3s>3'.conj
'Then he carried them on his back for him (for his benefit), and broke them for him (to his detriment).'[20]

The verb in 14 takes an inflected animate first-person singular subject, an inflected animate second-person plural object, and an uninflected inanimate third-person proximate singular secondary object, with the particulars of the secondary object supplied by a noun and a participle. The verb in 15 takes an inflected indefinite subject, an inflected animate third-person proximate object, and an uninflected animate third-person obviative plural secondary object, with the particulars of the secondary object supplied by conjoined nouns. The first verb in 16 takes an inflected animate third-person proximate singular subject, an inflected animate first-person singular object, and an uninflected animate third-person obviative singular secondary object, with the particulars of the secondary object supplied by a noun. The two verbs in 17 each take an inflected animate third-person proximate singular subject, an inflected animate third-person obviative object, and an uninflected and unexpressed secondary object, which from the preceding sentence of the narrative we know to be an inanimate third-person plural, a set of dishes.

In addition to inflected subjects, inflected objects, and uninflected secondary objects, many Meskwaki verbs optionally take uninflected instrumental obliques, which function similarly to secondary objects. The sentence in 6, in which a woman paints her face with yellow clay, gives an instance of this. In 6, the AI verb stem *we·ši·ho-* 'paint one's own face' takes the inanimate noun phrase *e·sa·wa·waki·niki ahki* 'yellow earth' as an instrumental oblique: *e·sa·wa·waki·niki ahki e·h=we·ši·hoči* 'she painted her face with yellow clay'. Note that in English the semantics of this sentence requires a prepositional phrase.

Two more examples of instrumental obliques are given in 18 and 19. Note that the instrumental obliques in 6 and 18 are inanimate, while the instrumental oblique in 19 is animate. As with secondary objects, because no information about a given instrumental oblique is indexed on the verb, the instrumental oblique in question can be animate or inanimate, singular or plural, and proximate or obviative.

(18) o-pehkwa·hk-i =’p =a·pehe· =’ni
3-lacrosse.ball-inan.sg =hrsy =usually =then
e·h=ki·ki·watahw-a·či apeno·h-ahi.
aor=1red.go.around.striking-3s>3'.conj child-obv.pl
'Then, it's said, he would go around hitting the children with his lacrosse-ball, one after the other.'[21]

(19) na·hka· =’nini e·h=anohkaw-a·či mi·kon-ahi.
again/and =that.obv.sg aor=fletch.for-3s>3’.conj pinion.feather-obv.pl
‘Once again she fletched that (bow) for him with pinion feathers.’[22]

In 19, no fewer than three different animate obviatives appear in a single clause: the inflected object of TA+O *anohkaw-* (the narrative’s hero, here indicated solely by the verbal inflection), the uninflected but obligatorily semantically present secondary object of TA+O *anohkaw-* ‘fletch 2Obj for Obj’ (the bow the hero’s sister is making for him, here indicated by the obviative singular distal demonstrative *i·nini*), and an uninflected and only optionally semantically present instrumental oblique of TA+O *anohkaw-* (the thing used to fletch the bow, here indicated by the obviative plural noun *mi·konahi*).

4. Meskwaki Verbal Moods, Participial Moods, and Participial Inflection

Examples 3–19 contain instances of several different verb moods: aorist conjunct in 3–13 and 15–19, changed conjunct in 9 and 13, future conjunct in 11 (also in the second paragraph of this chapter), imperative in 10, independent indicative in 4 and 16, and future indicative in 14, as well participles in 5, 6, and 14. There are three orders of verb moods in Meskwaki, defined by distinct inflectional patterns: imperative, independent, and conjunct. The imperative order consists solely of the imperative mood.[23] The independent order consists of a handful of moods which occur chiefly in conversation and in quoted speech in narrative. The conjunct order consists of a bewildering variety of moods with a bewildering variety of functions. All Meskwaki moods that occur in subordinate clauses and all Meskwaki moods that occur in participles are conjunct; however, a few conjunct order moods do occur exclusively in main clauses.

Meskwaki participles consist at least of initial change (an operation which replaces the first vowel of a word with *(w)e·* if and only if that vowel is short), a verb stem, verbal inflection, and participial inflection. Meskwaki participles consist at most of initial change, an aorist or future proclitic, one or more preverbs, a verb stem, verbal inflection, and participial inflection. Participles can only take one of the following three conjunct order verbal inflections: basic conjunct inflection (with neutral semantics), interrogative inflection (with uncertain or non-firsthand-knowledge semantics), or past inflection (with pluperfect semantics). The past marker *-ehe* has the idiosyncratic trait that no other morpheme can follow it within the word. Just as initial change is masked but still semantically present when the initial vowel of the word is long, participial markers of gender, number, and proximacy are masked but still semantically present when the participle is a past or a future past participle.

It so happens that every inflection (every suffixed portmanteau of mood marking, subject marking, and, if relevant, object marking) for interrogative verbs ends in *-i*, and every inflection for aorist conjunct verbs, future conjunct verbs, and changed conjunct verbs ends in *-i* or *-e*. Except in the case of inanimate singular participles, basic-conjunct participles (henceforth, simply conjunct participles) and interrogative participles replace the final *-i* or *-e* of the verbal inflection with participial inflection. Participial inflection is a modified form of nominal inflection. Inanimate singular participial inflection has no effect on the verbal inflection; in most cases, this means that inanimate singular participles end in *-i*, identical to inanimate singular noun inflection, which is also *-i*. Otherwise, participles replace the final vowel of the participle's conjunct or interrogative verbal inflection with one of the following: inanimate plural *-ini* (versus nominal *-ani*), animate proximate singular *-a* (identical to nominal *-a*), animate proximate plural *-iki* (versus nominal *-aki*), animate obviative singular *-ini* (versus nominal *-ani*), or animate obviative plural *-ihi* (versus nominal *-ahi*). There are also vocative participles which replace a final *-i* of the participle's conjunct or interrogative verbal inflection with vocative singular *-e*.

Examples 20–25 give instances of participles consisting of masked or overt initial change, plus a verb stem, plus conjunct or interrogative or past verbal inflection, plus masked (for past participles) or overt (for conjunct or interrogative participles) participial inflection: ic + stem + verbal inflection + participial inflection. The verb stem is inanimate intransitive or II in 20, transitive inanimate or TI in 21, ditransitive or TA+O in 22 and 24, and animate intransitive or AI in 23 and 25. The head of the participle is the subject of the verb in 20, 22, 23, and 25, the object of the verb in 21, and the secondary object of the verb in 24.

(20) e·sa·wa·waki·-niki ahk-i
ic.be.yellow.earth-o'.ppl(inan.sg) earth-inan.sg
'yellow clay'[24]

Compare: e·h=asa·wa·waki·-niki ahk-i.
aor=be.yellow.earth-o'.conj earth-inan.sg
'The clay was yellow.'

(21) ma·mi·čit-aminičini
ic.1red.dung.on-3'>o'.ppl(inan.pl)
'the various things they had soiled'[25]

Compare: e·h=ma·mi·čit-aminiči.
aor=1red.dung.on-3'>o'.conj
'They soiled them (severally).'

(22) pye·taw-ikwe·na pene·w-ani
ic.bring.to-3s>1s.int.ppl(prx.sg) turkey-obv.sg
'whoever brings me a turkey'[26]

Compare: pye·taw-ikwe·ni pene·w-ani.
bring.to-3s>1s.int turkey-obv.sg
'S/he must have brought me a turkey.'

(23) wi·škeno·hehka·hi-čiki kwi·yese·h-aki
ic.hunt.birds.dim-3s.ppl(prx.pl) boy-prx.pl
'boys who were bird-hunting'[27]

Compare: e·h=wi·škeno·hehka·hi-wa·či kwi·yese·h-aki.
aor=hunt.birds.dim-3p.conj boy-prx.pl
'Some boys were bird-hunting.'

(24) pešekesiw-ani pye·taw-a·tehe =’yo·we ow-i·w-ahi
deer-obv.sg ic.bring.to-3s>3'.pst.ppl(obv.sg) =formerly 3-wife-obv.pl
'the deer that he had been bringing to his wives'[28]

Compare: pešekesiw-ani e·h=pye·taw-a·tehe =’yo·we ow-i·w-ahi.
deer-obv.sg aor=bring.to-3s>3'.pst =formerly 3-wife-obv.pl
'He had been bringing a deer to his wives.'

(25) ihkwe·w-ahi pe·ma·kwapi-ničihi
woman-obv.pl ic.sit.grouped.in.a.row-3'.ppl(obv.pl)
'women sitting ranged in a row'[29]

Compare: ihkwe·w-ahi e·h=pema·kwapi-niči.
woman-obv.pl aor=sit.grouped.in.a.row-3'.conj
'The women sat ranged in a row.'

Note that the participles in 20 and 25 show overt initial change (unchanged II *asa·wa·waki·-* vs. changed *e·sa·wa·waki·niki*, and unchanged AI *pema·kwapi-* vs. changed *pe·ma·kwapiničihi*), while the participles in 21–24 have masked initial change, as the first vowel in each of those participles is long. The past participle in 24, like all past participles, lacks overt participial inflection. The conjunct participle in 23 displays another peculiar wrinkle of Meskwaki grammar: namely, that for third-person animate participles, the verbal inflection corresponding to the head of the participle is third-person animate singular even if the participle itself is third-person animate plural.

Participles can modify nouns, as in 20 and 23–25, or they can stand alone, as in 21 and 22. Not only can the head of the participle be any argument of the verb (subject, object, or secondary object, in the earlier examples), but participles can themselves take subjects, objects, and secondary objects, just like regular verbs. In 22, for instance, the participle takes an animate obviative singular secondary object. In other words, not only do participles take both verbal inflection and (modified) noun inflection, but they function simultaneously as verbs and as nouns.

Examples 26–28 give instances of participles consisting of masked initial change, plus a future proclitic, plus a compound verb stem consisting of one or more preverbs modifying a verb stem, plus conjunct or interrogative or past verbal inflection, plus masked (for past participles) or overt (for conjunct or interrogative participles) participial inflection: ic + fut= + [preverb (+ preverbs) + stem] + verbal inflection + participial inflection.

(26) wi·h=kaški- otehten-a·kwe·na i·nini apeno·h-ani
ic.fut=able- obtain-3s>3'.int.ppl(prx.sg) that.obv.sg child-obv.sg
'whoever might be able to get that child'[30]

The vowel of the future proclitic *(w)i·h=* is a long vowel, and the future proclitic is the first element of any future participle; hence all future participles have masked initial change. In 26, TA *otehten-* 'obtain Obj' is modified by a preverb *kaški* 'able', yielding a compound TA verb stem *kaški-otehten-* 'be able to obtain Obj'. Compare the future interrogative participle in 26 with the corresponding future conjunct verb: *wi·h=kaški-otehtena·či i·nini apeno·hani* 'S/he will be able to get that child'. Compare also the corresponding interrogative verb: *kaški-otehtena·kwe·ni i·nini apeno·hani* 'S/he must have been able to get that child'.[31]

(27) wi·h=wi·šiki- =mekoho -nenehkot-ame·koha
ic.fut=firmly- =emph -mention-2p>o(').pst.ppl(inan.sg)
'what you folks were on the verge of mentioning resolutely'[32]

Another quirk of Meskwaki grammar is that inflectional *kwe* followed by the pluperfect marker *-ehe* yields *koha*. In 27, TI *nenehkot-* 'mention Obj' is modified by a preverb *wi·šiki* 'firmly', yielding a compound TI verb stem *wi·šiki-nenehkot-* 'mention Obj firmly'.

Compare the participle in 27 with the morphologically indistinguishable (on the surface) future past verb: *wi·h=wi·šiki-=mekoho -nenehkot-ame·koha* 'You folks were about to mention it resolutely'. The past rather than future past version of this verb would be *e·h=wi·šiki-=mekoho -nenehkot-ame·koha* 'You folks mentioned it resolutely'.

Meskwaki intonation marks a word boundary after every preverb, and after every preverb, material extraneous to the verb stem (enclitics, subjects or objects or secondary objects of the verb, instrumental or locative obliques of the verb, or entirely distinct sentence constituents) can be inserted into the middle of the compound verb stem. In 27, an emphatic enclitic is inserted after the preverb *wi·šiki*.

(28) wi·h=anemi- 'ši- a·ya·nehke·wi- =mekoho
ic.fut=continue- {so}- generation.after.generation- =emph
-wi·ke·či- pešikwi- anemi- a·čiha·čimoheti·-ye·kwe
-carefully- uprightly- continue- 2red.inform.each.other-2p.ppl(inan.sg)
'a way that you folks will keep on, generation after generation, carefully and truthfully telling each other about it'[33]

The participle in 28 contains a reciprocal AI or AI+O verb stem *a·čimoheti·-* (AI+O in this particular sentence) modified by no less than six preverbs, with preverb *anemi* repeating once: *anemi* 'continue off', *iši* '{so}, {thus}; {thither}', *a·ya·nehke·wi* 'one after the other, generation after generation', *wi·ke·či* 'carefully, thoroughly, completely, solidly', *pešikwi* 'uprightly, straight', and *anemi* 'continue off' again, bracketing the whole preverb chain. There is also one intrusion, of an emphatic enclitic inserted after preverb *a·ya·nehke·wi*. The whole compound AI+O verb stem is *anemi-'ši-a·ya·nehke·wi-wi·ke·či-pešikwi-anemi-a·čiha·čimoheti·-* 'continue {thus} generation after generation carefully and uprightly continuing to tell each other about 2Obj'.

Preverb *iši* is a relative root. Like other Meskwaki relative roots, it adds a valence to a verb stem, which then near-obligatorily has to find a complement elsewhere in the sentence. In 28, the complement of *iši* is the very nominal within which *iši* is embedded. Relative root *iši* acts as the head of the participle. Participles headed by relative roots are invariably inanimate, and are usually inanimate singular.

Compare the participle in 28 with the future conjunct clause *i·ni wi·h=anemi-'ši-a·ya·nehke·wi-=mekoho -wi·ke·či-pešikwi-anemi-a·čiha·čimoheti·ye·kwe* 'You folks will keep on, generation after generation, carefully and truthfully telling each other about it that way', with the inanimate singular distal demonstrative *i·ni* acting as a complement to *iši*. Compare also the same clause without *iši* and its complement: *wi·h=anemi-a·ya·nehke·wi-=mekoho -wi·ke·či-pešikwi-anemi-a·čiha·čimoheti·ye·kwe* 'You folks will keep on, generation after generation, carefully and truthfully telling each other about it'.

5. Meskwaki Relative Roots and Their Complements

I will briefly explain how relative roots work using the example of a single Meskwaki relative root, locative *taši*. The locative relative root occurs both as the initial element of many verb stems (in which case it takes the form *taš-* before *i(·)* and *tan-* before other vowels) and as the particle (preverb, prenoun, preparticle, or free particle) *taši*. It introduces a locative valence which must be satisfied by a locative complement which at least partly precedes it in the sentence.

Locative relative root *taši* has a homonym which is not a relative root at all, but an ordinary preverb or verb stem initial indicating a stretch of time during which the activity described is taking place. This second *taši* does not require a complement, but can optionally be accompanied by a temporal particle.

Examples 29–32 contain passages including two juxtaposed instances of *taši*: one instance apiece of the locative relative root *taši* and one instance apiece of the temporal particle *taši*.

(29) pene·w-a =ke·h wa·natohka paya·hkiči
turkey-prx.sg =moreover unconcernedly in.another.direction
e·h=ki·- taši- tanahkye·-či.
aor=around- {there}- feed.there-3s.conj

'Now, without a care in the world, the turkey was going about feeding in another direction.'[34]

In 29, the first *taši* is one of two preverbs modifying AI *tanahkye·-*. It is a locative relative root whose complement is the locative particle *paya·hkiči*. The second *taši* immediately follows the first: it is the initial element in the AI verb stem *tanahkye·-* 'feed there, busy oneself with feeding', and here *tan-* has a temporal rather than a locative reading.

In English, we have something similar to *e·h=tanahkye·či* 'he was feeding there' when we say 'he was sitting there' to mean 'he spent some time just sitting around'. And as in the English case, in Meskwaki the locative use of *taši* is more specific and more restricted than the temporal use, which is rather abstract and rather bleached.

(30) meše·='nah=meko i·nahi e·h=taši- kehči- nepa·-wa·či
perhaps=emph that.loc aor={there}- greatly- sleep-3p.conj
mehtek-oki ahpemeki. mani =ke·hi:
tree/wood/stick-loc up.aloft this.inan.sg =moreover
e·h=taši- kehči- kemiya·-niki.
aor=there- greatly- rain-o'.conj
'They were more or less sleeping soundly high up in that tree. And there was this: it was raining hard.'[35]

In 30, the first *taši* is one of two preverbs modifying AI *nepa·-*. It is a locative relative root whose complement is a three-part discontinuous locative phrase. The second *taši* is one of two preverbs modifying II *kemiya·-*. In this case, *taši* is a temporal preverb. Compound AI *taši-kehči-nepa·-* in this sentence means 'sleep soundly {there}', while compound AI *taši-kehči-kemiya·-* in this sentence means 'rain hard there, be a continuing heavy rain'.

(31) e·h=taši- owi·wi-či i·nini kohpičinenoswihkwe·w-ani
aor=there- have(as)a.wife-3s.conj that.obv.sg buffalo.woman-obv.sg
na·mahki·ki =tašihi.
deep.in.the.ground ={there}
'He stayed there married to that buffalo woman deep underground.' Or: 'He stayed there married to that buffalo woman of the deep underground.'[36]

In 31, the verb is an AI or AI+O (an AI+O, in this particular instance) taking an overt secondary object. The first *taši* is a temporal preverb, and the second *taši* (*tašihi* here, with an echo vowel which can optionally be inserted before a pause) is a postposed locative preverb or prenoun. There are two readings of this sentence, one in which *na·mahki·ki=tašihi* is modifying the verb *e·h=taši-owi·wiči* and one in which it is modifying the secondary object *i·nini kohpičinenoswihkwe·wani.* In either case, *tašihi* takes locative particle *na·mahki·ki* as its complement.

(32) ma·haki=wi·na šama·kaneš-aki, kenwe·ši=meko e·h=taši- koht-amowa·či
this.prx.pl=but soldier-prx.pl a.long.time=emph aor=there- fear-3p>o'.conj
i·tepi· ='h=a·-wa·či e·nemi- 'ši- nehki·-niči.
thither =fut=go{thither}-3p.conj ic.continue- {thither}- go.out.of.sight-3'.ppl(inan.sg)
waninawe =ke·h =meko e·h=taši- mama·twe·-wa·či,
in.all.directions =moreover =emph aor={there}- moan-3p.conj
e·h=kekesi-wa·či aša·ti·h-ani.
aor=have-3p.conj arrow-inan.pl

'Meanwhile, as for the soldiers, for a very long time they were afraid to go in the direction in which (the Meskwakis) had gone out of sight. What's more, on each and every side they were moaning, because they had arrows (stuck in them).'[37]

The first *taši* in 32 is a preverb modifying TI *koht-*. It is a temporal preverb, and it is accompanied by a temporal particle, *kenwe·ši*. The second *taši* is a locative relative root satisfied by the locative particle *waninawe*. Incidentally, note that verb stem initial *kek-* or preverb *keki* adds a valence for a secondary object to any verb stem it helps to form; in this case the secondary object is an overt inanimate plural noun *aša·ti·hani*.

Note that TI *koht-* takes a future conjunct clause as its object. AI *a·-* 'go {thither}' (a variant of AI *iha·-*, which originally more transparently had as its initial a variant of the relative root *iši* in the sense of '{thither}') contains an allative relative root whose complement in this sentence is the two-part discontinuous allative phrase *i·tepi e·nemi-'ši-nehki·niči* 'the direction in which obviative had gone out of sight'. The participle *e·nemi-'ši-nehki·niči* has the relative root *iši* as its head, in the sense of '{thither}'.

Just as in examples 28 and 32 the relative root *iši* acts as the head of a participle, with the participle itself satisfying the valence introduced by the embedded verb stem's relative root, the locative relative root *taši* can also act as a head of a participle. Examples 33–35 give instances of locative participles with *taši* as their head.

(33)	e·h=taših-a·či	=meko	e·h=taši-	nesa·hkohw-a·či.
	ic.aor=kill{there}-3s>3'.ppl(inan.sg)	=emph	aor={there}-	roast.on.spit-3s>3'.conj

'He roasted it on a spit right there where he'd killed it.'[38]

Like other participles headed by relative roots, locative participles are invariably inanimate. Locative participles also invariably occur with either an aorist or a future proclitic. Since the aorist and future proclitics each contain a single long vowel, and since they are the first element of any word in which they appear, all locative participles have masked initial change. Inanimate singular conjunct, future conjunct, past, and future past locative participles are morphologically indistinguishable (on the surface) from their corresponding aorist conjunct verbs, future conjunct verbs, past verbs, and future past verbs.

It is perhaps worth mentioning that the aorist proclitic occurs exclusively with aorist conjunct verbs, past verbs, all non-future locative participles, certain kinds of temporal participles, and two other types of participles (generic oblique and aorist-as-participle) which I will not discuss here.

In 33, the first instance of *taši* (*taš-*, in this case) is the initial element of the TA verb stem *taših-* 'kill Obj {there}'. It is the head of a locative participle meaning 'the place where proximate singular killed obviative'. The locative participle is itself the complement of a locative preverb *taši* modifying TA *nesa·hkohw-*.

(34) e·h=na·piša·m-a·či,
aor=urinate.on.the.same.spot.as-3s>3'.conj

e·h=taši-	šeki-nitehe	e·h=taši-	šeki-či.
ic.aor={there}-	urinate-3'.pst.ppl(inan.sg)	aor={there}-	urinate-3s.conj

'She peed in the selfsame spot he did; she peed where he had peed.'[39]

In 34, *taši* again appears twice, once as a locative preverb acting as the head of a past locative participle and again as a locative preverb taking that past locative participle as its complement.

(35)

či·kepye·ki	e·h=taši-	wanih-emeči
close.to.the.water	ic.aor={there}-	lose-X>3'.ppl(inan.sg)

e·h=ina·wanete·-ki.
aor=be.a.going{thither}.en.masse-0.conj

'The entire village headed for the place at the water's edge where (the baby) had been lost.'[40]

In 35, allative *iši* (verb stem initial *in-*, here) takes a two-part locative phrase as its complement. The locative phrase consists of locative particle *či·kepye·ki* and a conjunct locative participle with *taši* as its head. Note that 35 is one of the rare instances where an inanimate takes proximate status relative to an animate. The inanimate in this case is a stand-in for an entire village of Meskwakis.

Some Meskwaki verb stems carry an inherent locative valence which can take locative complements and act as the head of locative participles even in the absence of *taši*. Examples are given in 36 and 37.

(36)

waninawe	=meko	e·h=pemi-	po·ni·-wa·či
in.all.directions	=emph	aor=along-	camp({there})-3p.conj

wi·h=taši-	aškesike·-wa·čini.
ic.fut={there}-	make.maple.syrup-3p.ppl(inan.pl)

'One very side they ranged their camps in the places where they were going to make maple syrup.'[41]

In 36, the compound AI verb stem *pemi-po·ni·-* 'camp along in sequence ({there})' carries a covert and optional locative valence, which in this sentence takes a two-part discontinuous locative phrase as its complement. The locative phrase consists of the locative particle *waninawe* and a future plural locative participle with overt locative relative root *taši* as its head.

(37) e·h=we·pi- nana·tohtaw-a·wa·či e·h=awi-nikwe·ni neno·te·w-ahi.
aor=begin- ask-3p>3'.conj ic.aor=be{there}-3'.int.ppl(inan.sg) Indian-obv.pl
'They started asking them (the wolves) where humans might be.'[42]

In 37, the compound TA+O verb stem *we·pi-nana·tohtaw-* 'start to ask Obj about 2Obj' takes an interrogative singular locative participle as its secondary object. AI *awi-* 'be {there}' carries a covert but obligatory locative valence. In 37, the covert locative valence of AI *awi-* acts as the head of the participle.

Locative participles can act not only as the locative obliques of verbs, as in 33–36, and as the secondary objects of verbs, as in 37, but as the subjects and objects of verbs. An example of a locative participle as the subject of an II verb is given in 38. An example of a locative participle as the object of a TI verb is given in 39.

(38) 'i·ya·ma·h =ahte·-wi wi·h=owi·ki-yakwe',
over.there(visible) =be{there}-0s.ind ic.fut=dwell{there}-12.ppl(inan.sg)
e·h=in-a·či.
aor=say{so}to-3s>3'.conj
' "The house we'll live in is just over there", he told her.'[43]

In 38, II *ahte·-* 'be {there}' carries a covert but obligatory locative valence, which is satisfied by the locative demonstrative *i·ya·ma·hi*. The subject of *ahte·wi* is an inanimate singular future conjunct locative participle. The head of the participle is the covert and optional locative valence of AI or AI+O (AI in this instance) *owi·ki-* 'dwell {there}, dwell, have 2Obj as a house'.

(39) e·h=taši- pekeše·hi-niki e·h=mawinat-aki.
ic.aor={there}- be.smoke.dim-0'.ppl(inan.sg) aor=run.at/attack-3s>0'.conj
'He ran at the place where the wisp of smoke was.'[44]

In 39, TI *mawinat-* 'run at Obj, attack Obj' takes an inanimate singular aorist conjunct locative participle as its object. The head of the participle is the locative relative root *taši*.

6. Heads of Participles

The range of things that can act as heads of Meskwaki participles is dauntingly inclusive. As we have seen, the list includes the inflected subject of a verb (examples 5–6, 14, 20, 22–23, 25–26), the inflected object of a verb (examples 21 and 27), an uninflected secondary object of a verb (example 24), a relative root occurring in the verb (examples 28, 32–36, 39), and a covert locative valence carried by a verb (examples 37 and 38).

Another item in the list of possible heads of Meskwaki participles is *nehki*, a free particle meaning 'as long a time as'. Rather like relative roots, *nehki* requires a complement. In contrast to relative roots, *nehki* never occurs as a preverb or as the initial element of a verb stem. Also in contrast to relative roots, *nehki* typically precedes its complements rather than following them.

Nominals even more loosely implicated in the semantics of a verb than the verb's subject, object, or secondary object sometimes act as the heads of Meskwaki participles. These include such things as instrumental obliques of the verb, possessors of arguments of the verb, and even possessors of locative obliques of the verb.

Last but not least, the covert temporal valence that is part of every Meskwaki verb stem can act as the head of a participle.

The participles in 40–42 are headed by an inflected subject, inflected object, and uninflected secondary object, respectively. The participles in 43–44 are headed by *nehki*. Each of the participles in 45–47 is headed by an instrumental oblique of the verb. The participle in 48 is headed by a special category of instrumental oblique of the verb. Each of the participles in 49–50 is headed by a possessor of the verb's subject. The participle in 51 is headed by a possessor of the verb's object. The participle in 52 is headed by a possessor of the verb's locative oblique.

(40)

ma·wači-	menehta	=meko	ot-o·škote·-m-wa·w-i	mi·n-ekowa·čini
among.all-	first	=emph	3-fire-poss-pl-inan.sg	ic.give-3'>3p.ppl(obv.sg)

'the one who gave them their first fire'[45]

(41)

kohpičinenoso·-ni	mi·n-ekota	mi·nes-ani
buffalo-obv.sg	ic.give-3'>3s.ppl(prx.sg)	head.hair-inan.pl

'the one to whom a buffalo gave hair'
Or:'the one who was given hair by a buffalo'[46]

(42)

me·meškwi-	matete·h-ani	mahkw-ani	mi·n-ekočini
ɪred.red-	leggin-inan.pl	bear-obv.sg	ic.give-3'>3s.ppl(inan.pl)

'the red leggins which the bear had given him'[47]

Each of the participles in 40–42 contains the TA+O verb stem *mi·n-* 'give 2Obj to Obj' inflected for an animate obviative person acting on an animate proximate person. In each case the uninflected secondary object is inanimate. In 40, the obviative subject is the head of the participle; in 41, the proximate object is the head of the participle; and in 42, the inanimate secondary object is the head of the participle.

Each of the three participles in 43 and 44 has free particle *nehki* as its head.

(43)

nehki	=mani	me·htose·neniwi-ya·ni,	a·kwi	me·h-	ne·t-ama·nini.
as.long.a.time.as	=as.it.is.now	ic.live-ɪs.ppl(inan.sg)	not	yet-	see-ɪs>o(').neg

'In all my life, I've never seen them yet.'[48]

(44)

nehki	=meko	pe·mihta-nikwe·ni	si·po·w-ani,
as.long.a.time.as	=emph	ic.flow.along-o'.int.ppl(inan.sg)	river-inan.pl

nehki	=we·	=meko	pe·mi-	tako-nikwe·ni	nep-i,
as.long.a.time.as	=in.fact	=emph	ic.along-	exist-o'.int.ppl(inan.sg)	water-inan.sg

e·h=išim-eči.
aor=speak{so}to-X>3.conj

'For however long a time as rivers continue to flow, or in fact, for so long as water still exists, he was told.'[49]

Note that the conjunct inanimate singular participle in 43 and the two interrogative inanimate singular participles in 44 are all preceded by *nehki*. Free particle *nehki* is the head of each of these three participles. All three participles show overt initial change: the unchanged forms are AI *mehtose·neniwi-*, II *pemihtan-*, and compound AI or II (II in this case) *pemi-tako-*.

The three participles in 45–47 are headed by instrumental obliques of their embedded verb stems.

(45) i·nini =ke·h =meko· =’nini mese·h-ani
that.inan.pl =moreover =emph =that.inan.pl piece.of.firewood-inan.pl
pe·htawe·-čini nehkanipepo·nwe e·h=tanete·-niki.
ic.make.a.fire-3s.ppl(inan.pl) all.winter.long aor=be.burned.there-o’.conj
‘Those same pieces of firewood he used to make the fire went on burning all winter long.’[50]

In 45, the participle *pe·htawe·čini* ‘the things with which he made a fire’ is headed by an instrumental oblique of AI *pehtawe·-*. Compare the aorist conjunct verb *e·h=pe·htawe·či* ‘s/he made a fire’. Note that the doubled demonstrative in 45 means ‘those same’. Verb initial *tan-* (*taši*) is here used in its temporal sense and is accompanied by a temporal particle.

In 45, the inanimate plural participle *pe·htawe·čini* is the subject of II *tanete·-* ‘be burned there’; in 46, the inanimate plural participle *so·kiso·hiya·nini* is the secondary object of TA+O *papahkahamaw-* ‘severally cut stringlike 2Obj for Obj’.

(46) ‘nahi´, ne-mešo, papahkahamaw-ino
well 1-grandfather.voc.sg 1red.cut(stringlike.thing)by.tool.for-2s>1s.imp
ma·hani so·kiso·hi-ya·nini’, e·h=in-a·či.
this.inan.pl ic.be.bound.dim-1s.ppl(inan.pl) aor=say{so}to-3s>3’.conj
‘ “Well, grandfather, cut these bonds of mine for me!” she told him.’[51]

In 46, the participle *so·kiso·hiya·nini* ‘the things with which I’m bound (pitifully)’ is headed by an instrumental oblique of AI *so·kiso·hi-*. Compare the aorist conjunct verb *e·h=so·kiso·hiya·ni* ‘I am bound, tied up (pitifully)’.[52]

(47) e·h=natawi- paškwa·hkwičito·-či
aor=seek.to- get.rid.of.by.scraping.against.a.tree-3s>o'.conj
asapa·p-i se·kikwe·piso-či.
string/thread/cord-inan.sg ic.be.tied.by.the.neck-3s.ppl(inan.sg)
'He set about trying to get rid of the rope that was tied around his neck by scraping it against a tree.'[53]

In 47, the participle *se·kikwe·pisoči* 'the thing with which his neck was tied' is headed by an instrumental oblique of AI *sakikwe·piso-*. Compare the aorist conjunct verb *e·h=sakikwe·pisoči* 's/he is tied by the neck'. The inanimate singular participle *se·kikwe·pisoči* is the object of compound TI *natawi-paškwa·hkwičito·-* 'seek to get rid of Obj by scraping Obj against a tree'.

In 45, the instrument evoked by the familiar mechanics of making a fire is made even more salient by the mention of pieces of firewood, *mese·hani*. In 47, the instrument evoked by the verb final *-apiso* 'be tied' is made even more salient by the mention of the rope, *asapa·pi*. In 46, the participle *so·kiso·hiya·nini* 'my (piteous) bonds' has no accompanying noun: instrumental participles formed from AI *so·kiso-* 'be bound' are common enough to be instantly graspable without extra help from the context.

Striking and difficult-to-characterize but, as with *so·kiso·hiya·nini*, familiar and therefore instantly-graspable participles sometimes arise in the context of visions. In traditional Meskwaki narratives, visions of future blessings are bestowed in waking or sleeping dreams by manitous, who act in this plane of the world by the power of their will or wishes or thoughts. The head of the participle in 48 perhaps counts as an instrumental oblique of the verb *ine·neta·kosi-* 'be thought of {thus}, be blessed {thus}'.

(48) i·na =ča·h e·ne·neta·kosi-ya·na
that.prx.sg =so ic.be.thought.of{thus}-1s.ppl(prx.sg)
net-o·te·wen-i wi·h=wi·šikešk-aki.
1-village-inan.sg fut=make.secure.by.dwelling.in-3s>o'.conj
'So that is the one I was blessed with that way, so that it would make my village strong.'[54]

Compare the aorist conjunct verb phrase *i·ni e·h=ine·neta·kosi-ya·ni*, with the inanimate singular distal demonstrative *i·ni* acting as the complement of relative root *in-* (*iši*): 'I was thought of that way, blessed that way'.

In light of the fact that instrumental obliques of verbs can act as the heads of participles, as in 45–47 and probably 48, it seems clear that any entity evoked by a verb's semantics can be the head of a participle formed from the verb. But on top of this, entities not directly evoked by the verb but evoked by one of the verb's arguments can be the head of a participle formed from the verb. The examples of this which I have seen so far are either possessors of a direct argument of the verb (usually the subject of the verb) or else possessors of a locative oblique of the verb.

The two participles in 49 and 50 are each accompanied by an overt nominal subject of the participle's embedded verb stem; in each case, the possessor of the subject is the head of the participle.

(49)	'ke·htena	=meko	ke-te·pwe',	e·h=išiwe·-či
	truly	=emph	2-speak.the.truth.2s.ind	aor=declare{so}-3s.conj

	i·niya	se·sekeše·-nika	o-ne·mowen-i.
	that.previous.prx.sg	ic.shoot.sparks-o'.ppl(prx.sg)	3-breath-inan.sg

' "Indeed, what you say is true", declared that aforementioned one whose breath shot flames.'[55]

In 49, the participial phrase *se·sekeše·nika one·moweni* 'the one whose breath shot flames' is headed by the animate proximate singular possessor of the inanimate singular subject of II *sesekeše·-* 'shoot sparks'. Compare the aorist conjunct verb phrase *e·h=sesekeše·niki one·moweni* 'his/her breath shot flames'. Compare also the inanimate singular participle *se·sekeše·niki* 'that which shot flames', and the participial phrase *se·sekeše·niki one·moweni* 'his/her fiery breath'. The head of *se·sekeše·niki* is *one·moweni*, the inanimate singular subject of the embedded II verb stem *se·sekeše·-* 'shoot flames'. The head of *se·sekeše·nika* in 49 is the animate proximate singular possessor of *one·moweni*.

(50) ča·ki =meko iš- owi·ya·s-i e·h=ma·ne·hto·-wa·či
all =emph {thus}- meat-inan.sg aor=have.in.numbers-3p>o'.conj
ke·htwe·wesi-nita o-na·pe·m-ani.
ic.have.a.knack.at.getting.game-3'.ppl(prx.sg) 3-husband-obv.sg
'The one whose husband was proficient at getting game, along with (her family), had a great quantity of every kind of meat.'[56]

In 50, the participial phrase *ke·htwe·wesinita ona·pe·mani* 'the one whose husband was proficient at getting game' is headed by the animate proximate singular possessor of the animate obviative singular subject of AI *ke·htwe·wesi-* 'have a knack at getting game'. Compare the aorist conjunct verb phrase *e·h=kehtwe·wesiniči ona·pe·mani* 'her husband was proficient at getting game'. Compare also the obviative singular participle *ke·htwe·wesiničini* 'the one who was proficient at getting game', and the participial phrase *ke·htwe·wesiničini ona·pe·mani* 'her proficient-at-getting-game husband'. The head of *ke·htwe·wesiničini* is *ona·pe·mani*, the animate obviative singular subject of the embedded AI verb stem *kehtwe·wesi-* 'have a knack at getting game'. The head of *ke·htwe·wesinita* in 50 is the animate proximate singular possessor of *ona·pe·mani*.

Note that the object of the verb in 50 is a compound noun *iš-owi·ya·si* '{such} meat'. This compound noun contains a relative root as a prenoun. In 50, the free particle *ča·ki* is the complement of relative root *iši*.

The participle in 51 is accompanied by an overt nominal object of the participle's embedded verb stem. The possessor of that object is the head of the participle.

(51) we·pa·mo-wa ='pi· ='na ow-i·hka·n-ani ne·s-emeta.
flee-3s.ind =hrsy =that.prx.sg 3-friend-obv.sg ic.kill-X>3'.ppl(prx.sg)
'That one whose friend was killed fled, they say.'[57]

In 51, the participial phrase *owi·hka·nani ne·semeta* 'the one whose friend was killed' is headed by the animate proximate singular possessor of the animate obviative singular object of TA *nes-* 'kill Obj'.

Compare the aorist conjunct verb phrase *owi·hka·nani e·h=nesemeči* 'his friend was killed'. Compare also the obviative singular participle *ne·semečini* 'the one who was killed', and the participial phrase *owi·hka·nani ne·semečini* 'his friend who was killed'. The head of *ne·semečini* is *owi·hka·nani*, the animate obviative singular object of the embedded TA verb stem *nes-* 'kill Obj'. The head of *ne·semeta* in 51 is the animate proximate singular possessor of *owi·hka·nani*.

The participle in 52 is headed by a possessor of a locative oblique of the participle's embedded verb stem.

(52) we·tani·pi·me·h-a, o-hka·hk-eki ne·mate·-nika ani·p-i.
Has.an.Elm-prx.sg 3-chest-loc ic.stand({there})-o'.ppl(prx.sg) American.elm-inan.sg
'Has-an-Elm, the one with an elm tree growing from his chest'.[58]

The participial phrase in 52, *ohka·hkeki ne·mate·nika ani·pi*, literally means 'the one with an elm tree standing in his chest'. The II verb stem *nemate·-* 'stand upright ({there})' carries a covert and optional locative valence; in 52, *nemate·-* takes a third-person-possessed locative noun as a locative complement. Compare the aorist conjunct verb phrase *ohka·hkeki e·h=nemate·niki ani·pi* 'an elm tree stood in his/her chest'. Compare also the inanimate singular participle *ne·mate·niki* 'the thing standing', and the participial phrase *ohka·hkeki ne·mate·niki ani·pi* 'the elm tree standing in his/her chest'. The head of *ne·mate·niki* is *ani·pi*, the inanimate singular subject of the embedded II verb stem *nemate·-*. The head of *ne·mate·nika* is the possessor of a locative oblique of *ani·pi*: the owner of the human breast from which the elm tree is sprouting.[59]

One more surprising feature of Meskwaki participles is that some of them have two heads. The participle in 48 is an example of this. In a sense, *e·ne·neta·kosiya·na* is simultaneously two participles, one layered on top of the other, just as the participle itself is a nominal layered on top of a verb: detransitive AI *ine·neta·kosi-* means 'be thought of {thus}, be blessed {thus}'; the inanimate singular participle *e·ne·neta·kosiya·ni* means 'the way I was blessed'; the animate proximate singular participle *e·ne·neta·kosiya·na* means 'the one I was blessed with that way'. Animate proximate singular *e·ne·neta·ko-siya·na* has two heads, relative root *in-* '{thus}' and the instrument of the blessing, the animate proximate singular mystical white creature with which the dreamer will fortify his village.

The most common type of double-headed participle involves one relative-root-headed participle layered on top of another, and in fact, typically involves an *ot-* '{thence}' participle layered on top of an *in-* '{thus}' participle. Consider example 53, from a text about the traditional Meskwaki names of the months.

(53) o·ni papo·hkwi·h-a, ma·č-a,
and.then Papo·hkwi·h-prx.sg March-prx.sg
papo·hkwi· ='ni wi·h=naha·wi-ki.
ɪred.half =then fut=be.warm(weather)-0.conj
i·ni we·či- 'šitehka·so-či.
that.inan.sg ic.{thence-} be.named{thus}-3s.ppl(inan.sg)
'And then as for *Papo·hkwi·h*, March, half of it will be warm weather. That's the reason for what it's called.'[60]

As a side note, in the Meskwaki language months (like the moon itself) are animate, but weather is inanimate. This leads to a single proximate singular entity in 53 being treated as simultaneously animate and inanimate.

In 53, *papo·hkwi* is a particle meaning 'half and half (and half ...)' and *papo·hkwi·h-* is an animate noun stem formed from particle *papo·hkwi*. The participle *we·či-'šitehka·soči* has two relative roots as its heads, and functions as an *ot-* '{thence}' participle layered on top of an *in-* '{thus}' participle. The inanimate singular participle *e·šiteh-ka·soči* (with *e·š-* as the changed, palatalized form of initial *in-*) means 'what it's called'; the inanimate singular participle *we·či-'šitehka·soči* (with *we·či* as the changed form of preverb *oči*, which itself consists of the palatalized form of initial *ot-* combined with particle-forming *i*) means 'the reason for what it's called'. Participle *e·šitehka·soči* 'what it's called' is nested inside participle *we·či-'šitehka·soči* 'the reason for what it's called' just as in 48 participle *e·ne·neta·kosiya·ni* 'the way I was blessed' is nested inside participle *e·ne·neta·kosiya·na* 'the one I was blessed with that way'.

7. Participles: Summary

Morphologically speaking, a Meskwaki participle is a verb nested inside a nominal. But semantically speaking, a Meskwaki participle is not merely a verb nested inside a nominal, but a whole clause nested inside a nominal. Any salient entity evoked by the clause can function as the head of the participle. Such entities include the inflected subject of the verb that is the germ of the participle; an inflected object of a TA or TI verb; an uninflected secondary object of the verb (including secondary objects introduced by verb finals such as AI+O *-a·hke·* and TA+O *-amaw* and secondary objects introduced by verb initials such as *kek-* or preverbs such as *keki*); an instrumental oblique of the verb; a possessor of the verb's subject; a possessor of the verb's object; a possessor of a locative oblique of the verb; the free particle *nehki*; an overt relative root forming part of the verb stem; a covert locative valence carried by the verb stem; and the covert temporal valence carried by any verb stem.

8. Temporal Participles

Not every Meskwaki verb stem carries a covert locative valence.[61] But every Meskwaki verb stem carries a covert temporal valence for the time when the verbal action takes place. Hence any Meskwaki verb stem is potentially the basis of a temporal participle.

I first encountered an unmistakable temporal participle in 1995 while transcribing and editing Alfred Kiyana's epic manuscript describing the childhood of the Earth.[62] Up until that time, I believed that the Meskwaki aorist proclitic *e·h=* occurred exclusively with aorist conjunct verbs (all aorist conjunct verbs, not counting conjunct participles), past verbs (all past verbs, not counting past participles), and locative participles (the majority of locative participles: all those lacking a future proclitic). Accordingly, I believed that the aorist proclitic and interrogative verbal inflection co-occurred only if the interrogative verb in question was the germ of an interrogative locative participle.

However, scattered through the 1,200 pages of Kiyana's *masahkamikohkwe·wa* manuscript were ten instances of aorist proclitics marking interrogative verbs which did not seem to be locative participles.[63] Locative interpretations of these verbs seemed forced in some cases, and impossible in others. Each of the ten verbs was accompanied by the free particle *na·hina·hi*, which can mean '(at) the distance' but which most often means '(at) the time'. And in the English translation commissioned by Truman Michelson shortly after Kiyana wrote his *masahkamikohkwe·wa* text, Horace Poweshiek, a talented translator and a fluent speaker of both Meskwaki and English, translated all ten of the puzzling aorist-proclitic-marked *na·hina·hi*-modified interrogative verbs as temporal expressions. Consider example 54.

(54)	na·hina·h	=mekoho	e·h=po·ni-	ne·mo-kwe·ni,
	(at)the.time/distance	=emph	ic.aor=cease-	breathe-3s.int.ppl(inan.sg)
	i·ni mahkwa·či	wi·h=šekiši-ki.		
	then quietly	fut=lie-3s.conj		

'Whenever she ceases breathing, she will lie there still,' (HP)

'At the exact time when she ceases breathing, whenever that is, she will lie quietly.' (LT)

? 'At the exact distance where she ceases breathing, wherever that is, she will lie quietly.' (LT)[64]

Poweshiek translates *na·hina·h=mekoho e·h=po·ni-ne·mokwe·ni* as a temporal participle: 'whenever she ceases breathing'. The interrogative mood supplies the speaker's uncertain knowledge as to the exact time in question. It is difficult to see what *na·hina·h=mekoho* would contribute if this sentence had a locative meaning. Moreover, I have not yet seen any indication that either AI *ne·mo-* 'breathe' or preverb *po·ni* 'cease' carries a covert locative valence, optionally or obligatorily. In the absence of a covert locative valence, for *e·h=po·ni-ne·mokwe·ni* to have a locative reading, it would have to include the locative relative root *taši* and take the shape *e·h=taši-po·ni-ne·mokwe·ni*. Consider for instance the sentence in 55, from another of Kiyana's texts.

(55) ke·keya·h =meko e·h=šekiši-ki
finally =emph ic.aor=lie({there})-3s.ppl(inan.sg)
e·h=taši- po·ni- ne·mo-či.
aor={there}- cease- breathe-3s.conj
'Eventually he ceased breathing where he lay.'[65]

In 55, AI *šekišin-* carries a covert locative valence and does not need to combine with a preverb *taši* in order to form a locative participle. The compound verb stem AI *po·ni-ne·mo-*, by contrast, carries no covert locative valence and requires the addition of a preverb *taši* in order to take a locative complement.

The aorist proclitic combined with interrogative inflection indicates that *e·h=po·ni-ne·mokwe·ni* in 54 is a participle rather than a verb. The semantics of AI *po·ni-ne·mo-* indicate that *e·h=po·ni-ne·mokwe·ni* cannot be a locative participle accompanying locative *na·hina·h=mekoho* 'the exact distance'. Both the context of the sentence and Poweshiek's translation suggest that *e·h=po·ni-ne·mokwe·ni* in 54 is instead a temporal participle accompanying temporal *na·hina·h=mekoho* 'the exact time'.

Once I knew that Meskwaki temporal participles existed, I started finding instances of temporal participles that were not marked by the aorist proclitic. I also found instances of temporal participles that were not interrogative. I also found instances of temporal participles that were not accompanied by free particle *na·hina·hi* '(at) the time/distance' or by any other temporal particle. Examples 56 and 57 give instances of interrogative temporal participles with a future proclitic and with no proclitic, respectively. Examples 58 and 59 give instances of past temporal participles with a future proclitic and with no proclitic, respectively. Examples 60 and 61 give instances of conjunct temporal participles with a future proclitic and with no proclitic, respectively. Examples 62 and 63 give instances of temporal participles unaccompanied by temporal particles.

(56) mešeke·h, =ne-kwi·hi, ke·waki =meko ahte·-toke
(or)perhaps =1-son.dim.voc.sg still/as.yet =emph be.left-os.dub
na·hina·hi wi·h=wi·tamawe·weniwi-wane·ni.
(at)the.time/distance ic.fut=be.told-2s.int.ppl(inan.sg)

'And perhaps, my son, time has not come for you to be told.' (HP)

'Perhaps, my son, the time when you will be told is yet to come.' (LT)[66]

Both the independent-order dubitative mood and the conjunct-order interrogative mood in 56 convey the speaker's lack of direct or precise knowledge about the event described. In 56, the future interrogative temporal participle *wi·h=wi·tamawe·weniwiwane·ni* is the inanimate proximate singular subject of the dubitative verb. In this case, the temporal participle takes a future proclitic and is accompanied by the temporal particle *na·hina·hi*.

(57) na·hina·h =meko pye·ya·-kwe·ni
(at)the.time/distance =emph ic.come({there})-3s.int.ppl(inan.sg)
ayo·h= we·wi·ki-ta, ayo·h= pemi- pi·tike·-te,
here= ic.dwell{there}-3s.ppl(prx.sg) here= along- enter-3s.subj
a·ya·neši wi·h=pi·ša·kaninekwe·he·hi-wa.
instead fut=be.a.bat.dim-3s.ind

'Whenever the one who lives here comes back, when he walks in here, he will turn into a little bat instead.'[67]

In 57, the interrogative temporal participle *pye·ya·kwe·ni* is part of an elaborate temporal expression modifying a future indicative verb. In this case the temporal participle takes no proclitic. It is once again accompanied by the temporal particle *na·hina·hi*. Temporal participles without proclitics versus temporal participles with aorist proclitics behave a bit like changed conjunct verbs versus aorist conjunct verbs: changed conjunct verbs have perfective semantics and suggest a sharp temporal boundary between one event and the next, whereas aorist conjunct verbs have imperfective semantics and suggest a more open-ended stretch of time in which an event takes place. In 57, the arriving-at-home wholly precedes the turning-into-a-bat; in 55, the not-breathing coincides with the lying-still.

Note that the clause containing the temporal participle in 57 (*na·hina·h=meko pye·ya·kwe·ni ayo·h=we·wi·kita* 'whenever the one who lives here comes back') modifies the main verb in much the same way as the clause containing the subjunctive verb (*ayo·h=pemi-pi·-tike·te* 'when he walks in here'), even though one is a nominal time expression and the other is a purely verbal time expression.

(58) e·h=ki·ši- kwe·hkwe·weška·-niki
aor=perf- become.over-late-o'.conj
na·hina·hi wi·h=pya·-wa·tehe.
(at)the.time/distance ic.fut=come({there})-3p.pst.ppl(inan.sg)
'The time when they should have arrived is already past.'[68]

The future past temporal participle in 58 is the inanimate obviative subject of compound II *ki·ši-kwe·hkwe·weška·-* 'already be over-late'. In this case, the temporal participle takes a future proclitic. It is once again accompanied by the temporal particle *na·hina·hi*.

(59) me·mešihka =ča·h =mekoho i·nina·h =ye·toke
maybe =so =emph at.that.time =evid
pe·ma·waneti·-wa·tehe.
ic.go.past.en.masse-3p.pst.ppl(inan.sg)
'So perhaps it was at that time that the whole crowd of them went by.'[69]

The sentence in 59 is equational: temporal particle *i·nina·hi* is paired with past temporal participle *pe·ma·waneti·wa·tehe*. This temporal participle takes no proclitic; a crowd of enemies in canoes paddling past a Meskwaki village is treated as a single bounded event.

Here the temporal participle is accompanied by temporal particle *i·nina·hi* 'at that time' rather than temporal particle *na·hina·hi* 'at the time'.

(60) k-i·h=kehkah-a i·nina·h =meko
2-fut=designate-2s>o(').ind at.that.time =emph
i·ya·h= wi·h=pya·-yani.
there= ic.fut=come({there})-2s.ppl(inan.sg)
'You can name the exact time when you'll arrive over there.'[70]

In 60, the future conjunct temporal participle *wi·h=pya·yani* is the inanimate object of TI *kehkah-*. It takes a future proclitic and is accompanied by temporal particle *i·nina·hi.*

AI *pya·-* optionally carries a covert locative valence. Note that in 60 *pya·-* takes a locative complement, whereas in 58 it does not. In contrast to *pya·-*, AI *awi-* obligatorily takes a covert locative valence and requires a locative complement whenever it occurs, as in 37 and 61.

(61) ta·nina·h =ya·pi ayo·hi e·wi-ye·kwe.
when?/at.what.distance? =here's.the.thing here ic.be{there}-2p.ppl(inan.sg)
'So tell me, how long have you two been living here?'[71]

The sentence in 61, like the sentence in 59, is equational: in 61, the question-word temporal or locative particle *ta·nina·hi* is paired with conjunct temporal participle *e·wiye·kwe*. Literally, *ta·nina·hi ayo·hi e·wiye·kwe* means 'when were you two here?'. In Kiyana's text, the answer given to this question is *o·´, našawaye=meko* 'Well, quite long ago'.

The temporal participle in 61 takes no proclitic. It is accompanied by temporal particle *ta·nina·hi* 'when?' rather than temporal particle *na·hina·hi* 'at the time' or temporal particle *i·nina·hi* 'at that time'.

In Michelson's corpus of Meskwaki texts, unambiguous temporal participles (temporal participles that cannot be mistaken for verbs) are almost always accompanied by temporal particles. Examples 62 and 63 give instances of exceptions to this rule. Both sentences are equational.

(62) mani ni·na =mekoho wi·h=na·kwa·-ya·ni.
this.inan.sg 1s.emph =emph ic.fut=depart({thither})-1s.ppl(inan.sg)
'This is when I shall go.' (HP)
'For my part, this is when I'll set out.' (LT)[72]

Not only Poweshiek's translation but also the semantics of the inanimate singular demonstrative *mani* (which can only be a nominal) and AI *na·kwa·-* (which never takes a secondary object) require *wi·h=na·kwa·ya·ni* in 62 to be a nominal paired with *mani*. Hence, *wi·h=na·kwa·ya·ni* must be a participle. In this sentence, the only possible heads of the participle are the covert locative valence (in this case, an allative valence; allatives are treated as a subset of locatives in Meskwaki) which AI *na·kwa·-* optionally carries and the covert temporal valence which all verb stems carry. Proximal *mani* 'this right here' cannot refer to a separate destination. Paired with a temporal participle or a locative participle, *mani* must refer to the exact time of the utterance or the exact place of the utterance. Since AI *na·kwa·-*, when it takes a locative complement, only takes a destination as its complement, by a process of elimination *wi·h=na·kwa·ya·ni* in 62 must be a temporal participle.

(63) e·h=nešiwana·ča·-kwe·ni mani ahk-i
ic.aor=be.destroyed-0.int.ppl(inan.sg) this.inan.sg land-inan.sg
i·ni wi·h=ahkwi- kano·n-ena·ni.
that.inan.sg ic.fut={so.far}- speak.to-1s>2s.ppl(inan.sg)
'Up to the time when this earth is distructed [sic] is how far my instructions to you will go.' (HP)
'When this earth is destroyed, whenever that is, that will be the end of what I am telling you.' (LT)[73]

The sentence in 63 pairs *e·h=nešiwana·ča·kwe·ni mani ahki* with the inanimate singular demonstrative *i·ni* and with the inanimate singular future conjunct participle *wi·h=ahkwi-kano·nena·ni*. Preverb *ahkwi* is a relative root referring to the end of a bounded stretch of time or space. The participle *wi·h=ahkwi-kano·nena·ni* is double-headed: *kano·nena·ni* 'what I am telling you' is headed by the optional secondary object of TA or TA+O *kano·n-* 'speak to Obj; tell 2Obj to Obj'; the participle *kano·nena·ni* 'what I am telling you' is nested inside the participle *wi·h=ahkwi-kano·nena·ni* 'the future end of what I am telling you'.

As a word containing both interrogative inflection and an aorist proclitic, *e·h=nešiwana·ča·kwe·ni* must be a locative or temporal participle. In Michelson's corpus of texts, the end of the earth is a recurring trope referring to the time when the current earth ends rather than to the edge of the current earth in space. More than half of the unambiguous and unaccompanied-by-temporal-particles temporal participles I have seen refer to the end of the earth.

Unambiguous plural temporal participles are much rarer than plural locative participles, but they do exist. Consider examples 64 and 65.

(64) kotak-i e·na·towa·-ta
other-inan.sg ic.speak{such}language-3s.ppl(prx.sg)
na·hina·h =meko e·h=ne·woti·-čini
(at)the.time/distance =emph ic.aor=see.each.other-3s.ppl(inan.pl)
e·h=neseti·-či i·nina·hi.
aor=kill.each.other-3s.conj at.that.time
'The Indians of other languages killed each other every time they met in those days.'[74]

In 64, *kotaki e·na·towa·ta*, literally 'the one who spoke another language', is an instance of a morphologically singular nominal used for what is semantically a generic plural, 'those who spoke different languages' (with the inanimate singular noun *kotaki* acting as the complement of relative root *in-*). The conjunct temporal participle and aorist conjunct verb in 64 likewise take animate-proximate-singular-for-generic-plural inflection. The temporal participle in 64 is plural because it refers to a series of times rather than to a single time: the sentence in 64 literally means, 'As for the one who spoke another language, at the exact times when s/he saw one another, s/he killed one another at those times'.

Note that the particles *na·hina·hi* and *i·nina·hi* are not only ambiguous as to whether they refer to space or time but are also ambiguous as to whether they refer to singular or to plural places and times.

(65) ki·na·na =’yo =mani mešemeko ke-we·we·ne·nem-a·pena
12.emph =for =as.it.is.now freely 2-have.control.over-12>3.ind
na·hina·hi wi·h=nes-akwini.
(at)the.time/distance ic.fut=kill-12>3.ppl(inan.pl)
'For as things stand, we ourselves freely control the times when we want to kill them.'[75]

The sentence in 65 figures in a passage about hunting game animals. The future temporal participle in 65, *wi·h=nesakwini*, is the secondary object of TA or TA+O *we·we·ne·nem-*, with raising-to-object of the animate proximate third-person object of the lower clause over the inanimate lower clause itself. The raising-to-object yields *kewe·we·ne·nema·pena na·hina·h wi·h=nesakwini*, literally, 'we control animate proximate with regard to the times when we want to kill animate proximate' (with inanimate plural *na·hina·hi wi·h=nesakwini* as the uninflected secondary object of TA *we·we·ne·nem-*), in place of *kewe·we·ne·neta·pena na·hina·h wi·h=nesakwini* 'we control the times when we want to kill animate proximate' (with inanimate plural *na·hina·hi wi·h=nesakwini* as the inflected object of TI *we·we·ne·net-*).

As in 64, the temporal participle in 65 is plural because it refers to a series of times rather than to a single time.

For purposes of comparison, consider the aorist conjunct plural locative participle in example 66. See also the future conjunct plural locative participle in example 36.

(66) e·h=pemi- =mekoho -taši- ne·w-a·čini
ic.aor=along- =emph -{there}- see-3s>3'.ppl(inan.pl)
e·h=pemi- tana·čimoh-a·či.
aor=along- inform{there}-3s>3'.conj

'[W]here ever he saw them he told them.' (HP)
'In the places where he saw them he told them about it.' (LT)[76]

In 66, an aorist conjunct plural locative participle with relative root *tan-* (in preverb form, *taši*) as its head acts as the complement of the relative root *tan-* in compound verb stem TA *pemi-tana·čimoh-*. As with the distributed series of times marked by plural temporal participles in 64 and 65, *e·h=pemi-=mekoho -taši-ne·wa·čini* in 66 refers to a distributed series of places. Preverb *pemi*, in TA *pemi-taši-ne·w-* and TA *pemi-tana·čimoh-*, means 'in sequence'.

9. Aorist Conjunct Temporal Participles and Aorist Past Temporal Participles

Interrogatives that take aorist proclitics have to be participles. Specifically, they have to be locative or temporal participles. By contrast, aorist conjunct locative or temporal participles and aorist past locative or temporal participles are morphologically indistinguishable (on the surface) from aorist conjunct verbs on the one hand and past verbs on the other. As a result, unambiguous examples of aorist conjunct temporal participles and past temporal participles are rare. An example of a probable aorist conjunct temporal participle is given in 67.

(67) 'na·hina·h =meko e·h=po·ni- kesi·tepehki·-ki,
(at)the.time/distance =emph ic?.aor=cease- be.a.cold.night-0.ppl?(inan.sg)?
i·nina·hi wi·h=ahčike·-ye·kwe', e·h=in-a·či.
at.that.time/distance ic?.fut=plant-2p.ppl?(inan.sg)? aor=say.so.to-3s>3'.conj

'"At the time when the nights cease to be cold, that (*i·nina·hi*) is when you'll do the planting", he told them.'
Or: '"When the nights cease to be cold, you will do the planting then (*i·nina·hi*)", he told them.'[77]

The quoted sentence in 67 is almost certainly a temporal equation, with a complex temporal expression consisting of temporal particle *na·hina·hi* and an aorist conjunct temporal participle *e·h=po·ni-kesi·tepehki·ki* paired with another complex temporal expression consisting of the temporal particle *i·nina·hi* and a future conjunct temporal participle *wi·h=ahčike·ye·kwe*. A prevailing pattern of similar equational constructions in quoted speech in narratives in Michelson's corpus of Meskwaki texts suggests that the quoted sentence in 67 is such an equation. However, there is no overt morphological difference and almost no semantic difference if *e·h=po·ni-kesi·tepehki·ki* and *wi·h=ahčike·ye·kwe* in 67 are read as verbs rather than as temporal participles. If they are verbs, the meaning is 'When the nights cease to be cold, you will do the planting then'. If they are participles, the meaning is 'At the time when the nights cease to be cold, that's when you'll do the planting'. The difference in meaning is so subtle that this type of ambiguity presumably presents no difficulty (rather, likely enhances the aesthetics) for the language user, despite presenting endless difficulties for the language glosser.

I have seen exactly three examples to date of completely unambiguous non-interrogative aorist temporal participles. All three are aorist past temporal participles. In order to explain them, I first need to describe a Meskwaki idiom involving the question words 'who?' and 'what?'.

The Meskwaki animate noun stem *we·ne·h-* means 'who?' or 'who is it?' or 'what kind of animate person/creature/thing is it?' It occurs as animate proximate singular *we·ne·ha*, animate proximate plural *we·ne·haki*, animate obviative singular *we·ne·hani*, and animate obviative plural *we·ne·hahi*. The Meskwaki inanimate noun stem *we·kone·h-* means 'what?' or 'what is it?' or 'what kind of inanimate thing is it?' It occurs as inanimate singular *we·kone·hi* and inanimate plural *we·kone·hani*. Idiomatically, AN *we·ne·h-* can mean 'animate does not exist' or 'animate is gone'; IN *we·kone·h-*, similarly, can mean 'inanimate does not exist' or 'inanimate is gone'.

The unmarked use of AN *we·ne·h-* and IN *we·kone·h-* is illustrated by examples 68–71.

(68) 'nahi´, we·ne·h-a =ya·pi. kaši išiso-wa',
well who?-prx.sg =here's.the.thing what? have.name.be{so}-3s.ind
e·h=in-a·wa·či.
aor=say{so}to-3p>3'.conj
' "Well, who is he, and what is his name?" they asked her.' (HP)
' "Well, may I ask, who is he? What is his name?" they asked her.' (LT)[78]

The first quoted sentence in 68 is an equation of a type we have not yet seen: animate proximate singular *we·ne·ha* is paired with an unexpressed animate proximate singular pronoun. In 69, obviative singular *we·ne·hani* participates in an equational construction of the type we have already seen, and is paired with an obviative singular participle whose head is the secondary object of AI or AI+O (in this case AI+O) *ona·pe·mi-* 'have (2Obj as) a husband'.

(69) 'we·ne·h-ani =ča·h= we·na·pe·mi-čini', [e·h=]i-či.
who?-obv.sg =so= ic.have(as)a.husband-3s.ppl(obv.sg) [aor=]say{so}-3s.conj
' "Well,so who is it she married?" he asked.'[79]

(70) 'kaši´, a·šito·nika·ti·-yakwe', e·h=išiwe·-či šama·kaneš-a.
why! trade.to.each.other-12.subj aor=declare{so}-3s.conj soldier-prx.sg
'we·kone·h =ča·hi', e·h=i-či.
what?.inan.sg =so aor=say{so}-3s.conj
'ne-makohkway-i', e·h=i-či.
1-hat-inan.sg aor=say{so}-3s.conj
' "Say, let's trade (things) to each other", the soldier proposed.
"What kind of thing?" (our hero) said.
"My hat", (the soldier) said.'[80]

Examples 70 and 71, like examples 68 and 69, are equational. In the second quoted sentence in 70, inanimate proximate singular *we·kone·hi* is paired with an unexpressed inanimate singular pronoun referring to the obligatory secondary object of reciprocal AI+O *a·šito·nika·ti·-* 'trade 2Obj to each other'. In 71, inanimate plural *we·kone·hani* is paired with an inanimate plural participle modified by a subjunctive clause.

(71) we·kone·h-ani =’yo a·mi-ayo·-kini
what?-inan.pl =for ic.pot-use-X>o.ppl(inan.pl)
mi·ka·ti·-ke ow-i·či·škwe·h-inaw-aki.
fight.each.other-X.subj 3-enemy-indef-prx.pl
‘What could a person use when fighting an enemy?’ (HP)
‘What kinds of things might one use when fighting one’s enemies?’ (LT)[81]

In the marked, idiomatic uses of AN *we·ne·h-* and IN *we·kone·h-*, as in the unmarked uses, *we·ne·h-* and *we·kone·h-* are typically paired with nominals. The exceptions involve particle *tane·nemo*, as in 72 and 73.

(72) we·ne·h-ani tane·nemo wi·h=nešiwih-ekoči.
who?-obv.sg nothing.to.fear fut=overpower-3’>3s.conj
e·h=pwa·wi- =meko -nešiwih-ekoči owiye·h-ani.
aor=not- =emph -overpower-3’>3s.conj someone-obv.sg
‘There was nobody to fear that could defeat him. He was never defeated by anybody.’[82]

(73) i·na =ke·hi =’pi· =’ni =pe·hki, ‘we·kone·h-i· =’nah tane·nemo’,
that.prx.sg =moreover =hrsy =then =really what?-inan.sg =with.that nothing.to.fear
e·h=išite·he·-či =’pi.
aor=think{so}-3s.conj =hrsy
‘And they say that he, then, really thought to himself, “With that, there’s nothing standing in my way”.’[83]

In the absence of free particle *tane·nemo*, idiomatic AN *we·ne·h-* and IN *we·kone·h-* are paired with unexpressed pronouns (or what must originally have been unexpressed pronouns), as in 74; nouns, as in 75; or participles, as in 76–78.

(74) i·ya·h= pe·kama·ška·-či, we·ne·h-ahi =ke·h =wi·na.
over.there= arrive.rapidly({there})-3s.cc who?-obv.pl =moreover =but
‘When he arrived over there on the run, they were gone.’
Or: ‘When he arrived over there on the run, nobody was there.’[84]

(75) aškači ašaško·h-a e·h=pya·-či.
after.a.while muskrat-prx.sg aor=come({there})-3s.conj
we·ne·h-ahi =ke·hi o-ni·ča·nese·h-ahi.
who?-obv.p l =moreover 3-child.dim-obv.pl
še·ški e·h=aye·ši- ki·wihkawe·-niči.
just aor=still- have.tracks.go.around-3'.conj

'After a while Muskrat came back. But her children were gone. All that was left of them was their footprints.'[85]

(76) we·ne·h-ani =we· =ke·hi wi·h=ašam-eko·hičini.
who?-obv.sg =or.rather =moreover ic.fut=feed-dim.3'>3s.ppl(obv.sg)
a·kwi ='pi owiye·h-ani ašam-ekočini.
not =hrsy someone-obv.sg feed-3'>3s.neg

'What's more, there wasn't anyone who could feed poor him. He wasn't fed by anyone, they say.'[86]

(77) to·hki·-či, i·h=wi·seni-tehe. we·kone·h =ke·hi· ='niye
wake.up-3s.cc fut=eat-3s.pst what?.inan.sg =moreover =that.previous.inan.sg
pe·hkwapito·-či, e·h=ašeno-niki.
ic.tie.into.a.bundle-3s>o'.ppl(inan.sg) aor=be.absent-o'.conj

'When he woke up, he was about to have a meal. But that bundle he had tied was gone; it had disappeared.'[87]

(78) i·ya·h= pye·ya·-či,
over.there= come({there})-3s.cc
we·kone·h =ke·h =wi·na e·h=ahta·so-wa·tehe.
what?.inan.sg =moreover =but ic.aor=put.indef.away.for.self-3p.pst.ppl(inan.sg)

'When he arrived over there, the place where they had stashed their things was gone.'[88]

The animate/inanimate distinction can get blurred in these expressions, as in 79.

(79) o·ni metemo·he·h-a wa·pa-niki wi·h=ka·hkesw-a·tehe,
and.then old.woman.dim-prx.sg be.morning-o'.cc fut=dry.with.heat-3s>3'.pst
we·kone·h =ke·hi, e·h=akih-a·či.
what?.inan.sg =moreover aor=lose-3s>3'.conj

'The next day when the old woman was going to dry them, she found that she had lost them.' (HP)
'And then as for the little old lady, the next day, when she was going to dry them (the deer feet), there was nothing there; she had lost them.' (LT)[89]

In 79, *we·kone·h=ke·hi* ought to be an inanimate equation meaning 'what's more, it was gone', but in fact, here and elsewhere when idiomatic *we·kone·hi* is used after animate things such as deer feet have vanished, seems to mean something more like 'every trace (inanimate) of it/her/him/them (animate) had vanished'.

Example 80 has an animacy clash in the opposite direction. In 80, animate obviative *we·ne·hani* is paired with an inanimate singular past temporal participle. This sentence is author Charley H. Chuck's description of a beautiful young woman shedding the enchantment that made her appear as a crone.

(80) we·ne·h-ani· =’niye·na· =’nahi
who?-obv.sg =that.previous.obv.sg =with.that
e·h=metemo·he·hi-nitehe.
ic.aor=be.an.old.woman.dim-3'.pst.ppl(inan.sg)
'And with that, that (woman's) time for being a little old lady was gone.'[90]

Instead of writing *we·ne·hani·=’niye·na·=’nahi metemo·he·hani* 'with that, poof went that heretofore little old lady' or *we·kone·hi·=’niye=’nahi e·h=metemo·he·hinitehe* 'with that, poof went that bygone stretch of time when she was a little old lady', Chuck construed an animate with an inanimate, writing <we ne a ni ni ye na na i . e me te mo e i ni te e .> *we·ne·hani·=’niye·na·=’nahi e·h=metemo·he·hinitehe* 'with that, she went poof, that previous person, her stretch of time when she was a little old lady'. This sentence in 80 is strung together a little loosely. And yet *e·h=metemo·he·hinitehe* in 80 must be a temporal participle rather than a verb, not only because AN *we·ne·h-* and IN *we·kone·h-* never seem to be paired with verbs, but only with nominals and with one unusual particle, but also because in Chuck's story it is not the woman herself who vanishes, but rather the time she spent in the guise of an old woman which is now gone for good. 'She went poof, that previous person, having been a little old lady in the past' (with *e·h=metemo·he·hinitehe* interpreted as if it were a verb rather than a participle) does not make sense in the context of the story.

My other two examples of unambiguous non-interrogative aorist temporal participles are rendered in 81 and 82.

(81) we·kone·h-i· ='nahi· ='niye
what?-inan.sg =with.that =that.previous.inan.sg
e·h=menwi- to·tawe·weniwi-tehe.
aor=well- be.acted.upon.so-3s.pst.ppl(inan.sg)
'There was nothing left of that good treatment he was given.' (HP)
'With that, gone was the time when he was treated well.' (LT)[91]

(82) e·h=pi·ne·škesi-wa·či mena·škono·n-i aniwe·we.
aor=have.plenty-3p.conj fresh.meat-inan.sg contrarily
we·kone·h-i· ='nahi i·niye še·ški
what?-inan.sg =with.that that.previous.inan.sg just
e·h=mačimači- wi·seni-wa·tehe.
ic.aor=2red.bad- eat-3p.pst.ppl(inan.sg)
'In contrast to before, they had plenty of fresh meat. Gone now were the days when all they had to eat was poor food.'[92]

In 81 and 82, more prosaically than in 80, inanimate singular *we·kone·hi* is paired with an inanimate past temporal participle. In 81, *e·h=menwi-to·tawe·weniwi-tehe* must be a temporal participle rather than a verb because of the modifying demonstrative and because *we·kone·hi* elsewhere is always paired either with a nominal or with *tane·nemo*. In 82, similarly, *e·h=mačimači-wi·seniwa·tehe* must be a temporal participle rather than a verb, not only because of the modifying demonstrative and because *we·kone·hi* elsewhere is always paired either with a nominal or with *tane·nemo*, but because, as the first sentence in 82 makes clear, what is gone for good here is the time when the heroes of the story only had poor meals to eat.

10. Conclusion: Temporal Participles Summarized

Aorist past temporal participles certainly exist, then, and aorist conjunct temporal participles almost certainly exist. This means that there are twelve different types of temporal participles in Meskwaki, illustrated here with TA *ne·w-* 'see Obj ({there})' and with animate proximate plural acting on animate obviative inflection.

conj temporal ppl (sg)	*ne·w-a·wa·či*	'the time when they saw them'
aor conj temporal ppl (sg)	*e·h=ne·w-a·wa·či*	'the time when they saw them'
fut conj temporal ppl (sg)	*wi·h=ne·w-a·wa·či*	'the time when they will see them'
past temporal ppl (sg)	*ne·w-a·wa·tehe*	'the time when they saw them formerly'
aor past temporal ppl (sg)	*e·h=ne·w-a·wa·tehe*	'the time when they saw them formerly'
fut past temporal ppl (sg)	*wi·h=ne·w-a·wa·tehe*	'the time when they will be about to see them'
int temporal ppl (sg)	*ne·w-a·kwe·hiki*	'at whatever time they saw them'
aor int temporal ppl (sg)	*e·h=ne·w-a·kwe·hiki*	'at whatever time they saw them'
fut int temporal ppl (sg)	*wi·h=ne·w-a·kwe·hiki*	'at whatever time they will see them'
conj temporal ppl (pl)	*ne·w-a·wa·čini*	'the times when they saw them'
aor conj temporal ppl (pl)	*e·h=ne·w-a·wa·čini*	'the times when they saw them'
fut conj temporal ppl (pl)	*wi·h=ne·w-a·wa·čini*	'the times when they will see them'

In terms of surface morphology, the conjunct temporal participle *ne·wa·wa·či* 'the time when they saw them' could also be a changed conjunct verb meaning 'at the exact juncture when they saw them, . . .'

In terms of surface morphology, the aorist conjunct temporal participle *e·h=ne·wa·wa·či* 'the time when they saw them' could also be an aorist conjunct locative participle meaning 'the place where they saw them' or an aorist conjunct verb meaning '(when) they saw them'.

In terms of surface morphology, the future conjunct temporal participle *wi·h=ne·wa·wa·či* 'the time when they will see them' could also be a future conjunct locative participle meaning 'the place where they will see them' or a future conjunct verb meaning 'they will see them', 'they should see them', or 'they want to see them'.

In terms of surface morphology, the past temporal participle *ne·wa·wa·tehe* 'the time when they saw them formerly' could also be a changed past verb meaning 'as it turns out, they saw them formerly'.

In terms of surface morphology, the aorist past temporal participle *e·h=ne·wa·wa·tehe* 'the time when they saw them formerly' could also be an aorist past locative participle meaning 'the place where they saw them formerly' or a past verb meaning 'they saw them formerly'.

In terms of surface morphology, the future past temporal participle *wi·h=ne·wa·wa·tehe* 'the time when they will be about to see them' could also be a future past locative participle meaning 'the place where they will be about to see them' or a future past verb meaning 'they were about to see them'.

In terms of surface morphology, the interrogative temporal participle *ne·wa·kwe·hiki* 'at whatever time they saw them' could also be a changed interrogative verb meaning 'if they see them, ...'.

In terms of surface morphology, the aorist interrogative temporal participle *e·h=ne·wa·kwe·hiki* 'at whatever time they saw them' can only be a participle (temporal or locative, depending).

In terms of surface morphology, the future interrogative temporal participle *wi·h=ne·wa·kwe·hiki* 'at whatever time they will see them' could also be a future interrogative locative participle meaning 'wherever they will see them' or an interrogative verb with a future proclitic meaning 'they probably want to see them'.

In terms of surface morphology, the plural conjunct temporal participle *ne·wa·wa·čini* 'the times when they saw them' could also be an iterative verb meaning 'whenever they saw them, ...'

In terms of surface morphology, the plural aorist conjunct temporal participle *e·h=ne·wa·wa·čini* 'the times when they saw them' can only be a participle (temporal or locative or something called generic oblique, depending).

In terms of surface morphology, the plural future conjunct temporal participle *wi·h=ne·wa·wa·čini* 'the times when they will see them' could also be a future conjunct locative participle meaning 'the places where they will see them' or a future iterative verb meaning 'whenever they were about to see them, ...'

Note that the only plural temporal participles in the list described earlier are conjunct temporal participles. Plural past temporal participles and plural interrogative temporal participles might also exist. The fact that I have not yet identified any could merely be an accident resulting from the fact that in Michelson's corpus of Meskwaki texts unambiguous temporal participles are relatively rare, and unambiguous plural temporal participles are extremely rare. Recall, too, that the past ending *-ehe* obscures the singular/plural distinction.

Although there is a great deal of overlap in Meskwaki between locative demonstratives, particles, and participles on the one hand and temporal demonstratives, particles, and participles on the other, there are two key differences between locative participles and temporal participles in Meskwaki. The first is that locative participles must have at their core a verb which either contains the locative relative root or which carries an obligatory or optional covert locative valence. Temporal participles, by contrast, can be formed from any verb: all Meskwaki verbs seem to carry a covert temporal valence. The second is that locative participles must take either an aorist or a future proclitic, whereas temporal participles can take an aorist proclitic, a future proclitic, or no proclitic at all. The difference in meaning between temporal participles which have an aorist proclitic and almost-identical temporal participles which lack a proclitic is often quite subtle.

I have not yet discovered a way to prove that changed conjunct verbs and iterative verbs are definitely verbs rather than temporal participles. Changed conjunct verbs and iterative verbs occur exclusively in subordinate clauses, modifying other verbs. There is nothing about Meskwaki syntax that prevents a participle from appearing in a similar position. Consider examples 83 and 84.

(83)	o·ni	ača·hmeko	na·kwa·-wa·či	e·h=kekeni·hi-wa·či.
	and.then	only.then	depart({thither})-3p.cc	aor=go.fast.dim-3p.conj

'And only then, when they went back, did they go fast.'[93]

(84) o·ni =ʼpi e·h=na·kwa·-či, e·hpi·hči·-či =meko
and.then =hrsy aor=depart({thither})-3s.conj ic.go{so.far}-3s.ppl(inan.sg) =emph
e·h=kekeni·hi-či.
aor=go.fast.dim-3s.conj
'[H]e started out walking as fast as he could.' (HP)
'And then, they say, he set out, hurrying along as fast as he could go.' (LT)[94]

The participle *e·hpi·hči·či* in 84 stands in much the same position to the verb *e·h=kekeni·hiči* as the presumed-verb-but-possibly-a-temporal-participle *na·kwa·wa·či* in 83 stands to the verb *e·h=kekeni·hiwa·či*. And there is no loss of meaning if *na·kwa·wa·či* in 83 is interpreted as a temporal participle: 'And only then, at the time when they went back, did they go fast'. In fact, there is no loss of meaning if both verbs in 83 are interpreted as temporal participles: 'And only then, at the time when they went back, is when they went fast'.

Incidentally, note that the changed conjunct verb in 83, *na·kwa·wa·či*, means that at the exact time when they set out they began to go fast, implying a fairly sharp delineation between the two events, while the aorist conjunct version of the same verb in 84, *e·h=na·kwa·či*, means that as they went they went fast, with the two events overlapping in time.

There are eight remaining types of temporal participles that correspond to verbs. Setting aside the singular conjunct temporal participles corresponding morphologically to changed conjunct verbs and the plural conjunct temporal participles corresponding morphologically to iterative verbs, these are the singular aorist conjunct temporal participles, singular future conjunct temporal participles, past temporal participles, aorist past temporal participles, future past temporal participles, interrogative temporal participles, future interrogative temporal participles, and plural future conjunct temporal participles. (Recall that the aorist interrogative temporal participles and plural aorist conjunct temporal participles have morphological combinations exhibited only by participles.) Many of the verbs corresponding to these eight types of temporal participles can be demonstrated to be verbs rather than participles, in that interpreting them as temporal participles would unacceptably distort their sentences' meanings. Consider example 85.

(85) o·ni i·nini e·h=na·kan-a·či,
and.then that.obv.sg aor=follow-3s>3'.conj
e·h=mya·ne·net-aki o-mami·ši·h-em-ani e·h=nes-emeči.
aor=dislike-3s>o'.conj 3-ceremonial.attendant-poss-obv.sg aor=kill-X>3'.conj

'He then began trailing her, as he became angry because his servant had been slain.' (HP)

'And then he followed her, because he was angry about his servant's being slain.' (LT)[95]

Two of the three aorist conjunct verbs in 85 could be interpreted as temporal participles without a nonsensical perversion of the sentence's meaning, but the third cannot. You could read 85 as 'And then is when he followed her, because he was angry about the time when his servant was slain', but you cannot very easily read 85 as 'And then is when he followed her, the time when he was angry about the time when his servant was slain'. The first verb in 85, *e·h=na·kana·či*, could be a conjunct temporal participle paired with temporal particle *o·ni* in an equational construction without distorting the meaning of the sentence at all. The third verb in 85, *e·h=nesemeči*, could be temporal participle acting as the object of TI *mya·ne·net-* rather than part of a clause acting as the object of TI *mya·ne·net-*, yielding an only slightly more implausible reading of the sentence. But the third verb in 85, *e·h=mya·ne·netaki*, can only be an aorist conjunct verb in the 'because' use of a subordinate aorist conjunct verb. Setting everything else aside, if *e·h=mya·ne·netaki* were part of an extended temporal equation, it would require an *i·ni* 'then' to link it to the foregoing temporal equation. Poweshiek's translation confirms the 'because' reading of *e·h=mya·ne·netaki* in this context. And it is worth noting that Poweshiek, with his fine feeling for both Meskwaki and English, translated all three aorist conjuncts in 85 as aorist conjunct verbs rather than as aorist conjunct temporal participles.

It is probably not an accident that, as in 85, the types of Meskwaki verbs that are difficult to distinguish from temporal participles typically occur either in combination with temporal particles or as the objects or secondary objects of other verbs, or both.

The existence of Meskwaki temporal participles, their partial but not total correspondence to Meskwaki locative participles, and their partial but not total semantic overlap with certain types of Meskwaki verbs, highlight both the mind-boggling intricacy and the great beauty of the Meskwaki language. They also create a situation in which nearly every sentence involving a non-subjunctive, non-potential, non-prohibitive, non-plain-conjunct conjunct-order verb requires at least two alternate and very different glosses and at least two alternate and subtly different English translations.

Kete·pihi. (I am grateful to you [for wading through this].)

11. Abbreviations

{} = encloses the gloss of a relative root. 0 = third-person inanimate proximate. 0s = third-person inanimate proximate singular. 0p = third-person inanimate proximate plural. 0' = third-person inanimate obviative. 0's = third-person inanimate obviative singular. 0'p = third-person inanimate obviative plural. 1 = first person. 12 = first-person plural inclusive. 1red = one-syllable reduplication. 1s = first-person singular. 1p = first-person plural exclusive. 2 = second person. 2Obj = uninflected secondary object. 2red = two-syllable reduplication. 2s = second-person singular. 2p = second-person plural. 3 = third-person animate proximate. 3s = third-person animate proximate singular. 3p = third-person animate proximate plural. 3' = third-person animate obviative. 3's = third-person animate obviative singular. 3'p = third-person animate obviative plural. 3" = third-person animate secondary obviative. AI = animate intransitive verb stem or verb (a morphologically intransitive verb taking an animate subject). AI+O = animate intransitive verb stem or verb taking an object (a morphologically intransitive verb taking an animate subject and a secondary object). AN = animate. aor = aorist proclitic. BL = Bill Leaf. cc = changed conjunct mood. conj = aorist conjunct mood or future conjunct mood. dim = diminutive. dub = independent dubitative mood. .emph = emphatic pronoun. =emph = emphatic enclitic. evid = evidential enclitic ('it seems'). excl. = exclusive. fut = future proclitic. HP = Horace Poweshiek. hrsy = evidential enclitic ('it is said'). ic = initial change. IG = Ives Goddard. II = inanimate intransitive verb stem or verb (a morphologically intransitive verb taking an inanimate subject). imp = imperative mood. IN = inanimate. inan = inanimate. incl. = inclusive. ind = independent indicative mood or future indicative mood. indef = indefinite-person possessor ('X's', 'one's'). int = interrogative mood (conjunct dubitative mood). int.ppl = interrogative participle. loc = locative. LT = Lucy Thomason. NAA = National Anthropological Archives. n.d. = no date. neg = negative mood (a conjunct order mood). Obj = (inflected) object. obv. = obviative. obv = animate obviative. perf = perfective preverb ('completed, finished'). pl = plural. poss = marker of alienable possession. pot = potential preverb ('would/should/could'). ppl = (conjunct) participle. prox. = proximate. prx = animate proximate. pst = pluperfect mood or future past mood (two conjunct order moods). pst.ppl = past participle. red = reduplication. sg = singular. subj = subjunctive mood (a conjunct order mood). TA = transitive animate verb stem or verb (a morphologically transitive verb taking an animate object). TA+O = ditransitive verb stem or verb (a morphologically transitive verb taking an animate object and a secondary object). TB = Thomas Brown. TI = transitive inanimate verb stem or verb (a morphologically transitive verb taking an inanimate object). TI-O = objectless transitive inanimate verb stem or verb (a morphologically transitive verb taking no object). TM = Truman Michelson. voc = vocative. X = indefinite person.

12. Notes on the References

The unpublished Meskwaki manuscripts cited in this bibliography can be found among Truman Michelson's papers in the Smithsonian Institution's National Anthropological Archives. The manuscripts in this collection were written in the 1910s and 1920s. They were written in Great Lakes Algonquian Syllabary (also known as *papepipo*) by some fifty different authors who were native speakers of Meskwaki.

Some (but not all) of the NAA's Meskwaki manuscripts have contemporary English translations, also (except in one instance) in the NAA's Truman Michelson collection; some (but not all) of the English translations are faithful to the original. High-quality images of some of the NAA's Meskwaki manuscripts, and of some of the English translations, are available online, courtesy of the Arcadia Fund and one or two other benefactors.

A few of the NAA's manuscripts, with editions and translations, have been published by Truman Michelson, Ives Goddard, Amy Dahlstrom, and me. A few more have been posted online by Goddard and Thomason. The latter can be found here: https://repository.si.edu/handle/10088/17270. The former can be found in the Smithsonian's *Bureau of American Ethnology Annual Report* 40 (by Michelson), in various Bureau of American Ethnology Bulletins authored by Michelson, in an article by Dahlstrom in *Contemporary Linguistics* 2, in a chapter by Dahlstrom in *Algonquian and Iroquoian Memoir* 13, in an article by Dahlstrom in *Anthropological Linguistics* 45(1), in *Algonquian and Iroquoian Linguistics Memoirs* 18 and 19 (by Goddard), and in chapters by Dahlstrom, Goddard, and me in David Costa's *New Voices for Old Words: Algonquian Oral Literatures*.

Copies of my dissertation, *The Proximate and Obviative Contrast in Meskwaki*, and of a draft of my 2018 Algonquian Conference talk on Meskwaki locatives, 'They were taken a little ways off and thrown away next to a black oak on the north side where the sun did not strike', are available upon request from ThomasonL@si.edu.

Endnotes

* I am more grateful than I can express to my mother, Sally Thomason, for introducing me to phonetics, phonology, morphology, syntax, and historical linguistics at a very young age; also to my mother, and to Lucy Vanderburg and Clarence Woodcock, and afterward many other speakers of Bitterroot Salish and Pend d'Oreille, for introducing me to the mind-opening and heartwringing beauty of polysynthetic languages, starting at age twelve; also to my mother, for introducing me to Ives Goddard, who turned me loose on nearly 27,000 pages of Meskwaki writing by Meskwaki speakers, a respite from my struggles with my tin ear; to Ives Goddard, for mentoring my work in Algonquian linguistics for more than three decades; to Tony Woodbury, for most of the rest of my linguistic education; to Franz Boas, for converting Truman Michelson from a Sanskritologist to an Americanist; to Truman Michelson, for his work on Algonquian languages; to the Smithsonian's National Anthropological Archives, for conserving and storing Michelson's papers; and most of all, to the Meskwaki authors whose linguistic and literary virtuosity is cited in this chapter.

1. Almost all the examples in this paper are taken from Truman Michelson's early twentieth-century corpus of Meskwaki texts, which were written in Great Lakes Algonquian syllabary by some fifty native speakers of Meskwaki. The vowel lengths, *h*s, and (apart from certain word dividers) all punctuation appearing in these examples have been inserted not by the original authors but by the editors. It is all too probable that some of the editing inadvertently mistakes the author's intent.

2. Bill Leaf, NAA ms. #1875.9, p. 4 l.O. Edited by LT. English translation by LT. Meskwaki *i·ni* can be either a temporal particle meaning 'then' or a distal demonstrative meaning 'that (inanimate singular)'.

3. My discussion of Meskwaki grammar in this chapter draws heavily on observations originally made by Ives Goddard, and in some cases on

observations originally made by Goddard's predecessors in Algonquian linguistics, notably Leonard Bloomfield and Truman Michelson. The current framing of some of the more surprising complexities of Meskwaki participles, and the choice of examples used to illustrate them, are mine. Meskwaki temporal participles and the ease with which they can be confused with Meskwaki verbs are my own personal bugbears.

4. A strict rule of Meskwaki grammar is that possessed nouns are always less central or salient than their possessors. Nouns possessed by a non-third person can be proximate or obviative, but nouns possessed by third persons must be obviative. Note that the indefinite person (X) behaves like a non-third person in this regard. The Meskwaki person hierarchy has six divisions: inclusive person + second persons + first persons > indefinite persons > proximate third persons > animate obviative third persons > animate secondary obviative third persons > inanimate obviative third persons (12, 2, 2s, 2p, 1, 1s, 1p > X > 3, 3s, 3p, 0, 0s, 0p > 3' > 3" > 0'). Although technically speaking inanimate proximates rank higher than animate obviatives, in transitive verb inflection it is impossible and in usage it is near-impossible for any inanimate to be ranked higher than a simultaneously invoked animate.

5. Alfred Kiyana, NAA ms. #2671.1, p. 1, l.F. Edited by IG and LT. English translation by LT and IG. *mahk(wi)* in *mahk-owi·neno·-ni* is a prenoun.

6. Maggie Morgan, NAA ms. #2790, p. 24, l.B. Edited by LT. English translation by LT.

7. Alfred Kiyana, NAA ms. #2157, p. 32, l.E. Edited by IG. English translation by LT. In example 5, *ki·ke·nowi* is a prenoun.

8. Young Bear, NAA ms. #2741a.2, p. 4, ll.EF. Edited by LT. English translation by LT.

9. Secondary obviatives are overtly marked only on transitive verbs taking both an animate subject and an animate object, in cases where both inflected arguments of the verb are obviative: cases where a primary or common-garden-variety obviative acts on a secondary obviative, or where a secondary obviative acts on a primary or common-garden-variety obviative. Somewhat similarly, inanimate obviatives are overtly marked only on verbs and only when no non-inanimate is indexed on the verb: hence, in cases where the verb is intransitive and the subject is inanimate, or in cases where both arguments of a transitive verb are inanimate.

10. Alfred Kiyana, NAA ms. #2730.6, p. 11, ll.CD. Edited by IG. English translation by IG, modified slightly by LT. In example 7, *te·pi* is a preverb and *kehči* is a prenoun.

11. Ša·poči·wa, NAA ms. #2664.8, p. 24, l.H. Edited by LT. English translations by LT. In example 8, *pye·či* is a preverb.

12. Alfred Kiyana, NAA ms. #2688, p. 20, ll.HI. Edited by IG. English translation by IG. Published in Goddard (2007). In 9, *ki·ši* is a preverb.

13. Alfred Kiyana, NAA ms. #2957, p. 96, ll.Q,T. Edited by IG. English translation by LT. In 10, *mawi* is a preverb.

14. Alfred Kiyana, NAA ms. #2693, p. 150, ll.DE. Edited by IG. English translation by IG, modified slightly by LT.

15. Charley H. Chuck, NAA ms. #2737.2, p. 10, ll.PQ. Edited by IG. English translation by IG, modified slightly by LT. English translation published in Goddard (2005).

16. Sa·kihtanohkwe·ha, NAA ms. #1879.5, p. 34, l.K. Edited by LT. English translation by LT. In 13, *ki·ši* is a preverb.

17. Sa·kihtanohkwe·ha, NAA ms. #2671.7a, p. 14, part of l.F. Edited by LT. English translation by LT.

18. Young Bear, 2741a.2, p. 6, l.E. Edited by LT. English translation by LT.

19. Sam Peters, NAA ms. #2024B.1, p. 34, l.H. Edited by LT. English translation by LT.

20. Bill Leaf, NAA ms. #1875.9, p. 1, l.E. Edited by LT. English translation by LT.

21. Sam Peters, NAA ms. #2794.84a, p. 16, l.B. Edited by IG. English translation by LT. I have omitted a changed conjunct clause which in the manuscript precedes the clause in 18.

22. Charley H. Chuck, NAA ms. #2794.93, p. 14, l.D. Edited by LT and IG. English translation by LT and IG.

23. The imperative mood is a full inflectional paradigm. It has imperative semantics in cases where the subject is non-third person and optative semantics when the subject is third person. Compare, for example, *wa·pam-i k-i·hka·n-a* (look.at-2s-3.imp 2-friend-prx.sg) 'Look at your friend!' [Jim Peters, NAA ms. #2794.75a, p. 9, l.E] and *wa·pam-eneče k-i·hka·n-aki* (look.at-3-2s.imp 2-friend-prx.pl) 'Let your friends look at you!' [Alfred Kiyana, NAA ms. #2080, p. 28, part of l.E].

24. Young Bear, NAA ms. #2741a.2, p. 4, part of l.E. Edited by LT. English translation by LT.

25. Alfred Kiyana, NAA ms. #2958, p. 4, part of l.D. Edited by LT. English translation by LT.

26. Alfred Kiyana, NAA ms. #2764.4, p. 9, part of l.M. Edited by LT and IG. English translation by LT and IG.

27. Sa·kihtanohkwe·ha, NAA ms. #2700, p. 65, part of l.P. Edited by LT and IG. English translation by LT and IG.

28. Ša·poči·wa, NAA ms. #2671.3, p. 20, part of l.G. Edited by LT and IG. English translation by LT and IG.

29. Jack Bullard, NAA ms. #2082.3, p. 35, part of l.L. Edited by LT and IG. English translation by LT and IG.

30. Anonymous 6, NAA ms. #2794.13, p. 23, part of l.D. Edited by IG. English translation by LT.

31. The future proclitic rarely occurs with interrogative verbs that are not participles, and when it does occur with interrogative verbs that are not participles, it means 'want to' rather than 'in the future'.

32. Alfred Kiyana, NAA ms. #2959, p. 105, part of l.I. Edited by LT. English translation by LT.

33. Alfred Kiyana, NAA ms. #2957, p. 106, part of l.L. Edited by IG. English translation by LT. Here and elsewhere in this chapter, the glosses of relative roots are enclosed in brackets.

34. Sam Peters, NAA ms. #2794.84b, p. 26, l.C. Edited by IG. English translation by LT.

35. Alfred Kiyana, NAA ms. #2717, p. 6, ll.CD. Edited by IG. English translation by LT.

36. Jack Bullard, NAA ms. #2082.3, p. 30, l.N. Edited by LT and IG. English translation by LT and IG. See also note 46.

37. Jack Bullard, NAA ms. #2432.4, p. 15, l.I through p. 16, ll.AB. Edited by IG. English translation by LT. The manuscript has <|maaaki> for *ma·haki* and <mamate> for *mama·twe·*.

38. Alfred Kiyana, NAA ms. #3065, p. 25, l.C. Edited by LT and IG. English translation by LT and IG.

39. Sam Peters, NAA ms. #2794.45a, p. 11, ll.LM. Edited by IG. English translation by LT.

40. Pearl Leaf, NAA ms. #2024D.1, p. 5, l.J. Edited by LT. English translation by LT. Ms. <čikepyi|ki> for < čikepyeki>.

41. Young Bear, NAA ms. #2741a.4, p. 8, l.L. Edited by LT. English translation by LT.

42. Sam Peters, NAA ms. #2008.4, p. 32, l.8. Edited by LT. English translation by LT.

43. Ša·poči·wa, NAA ms. #2794.26, p. 13, l.B. Edited by LT. English translation by LT.

44. Sam Peters, NAA ms. #2005.5, p. 179, l.D. Edited by LT and IG. English translation by LT and IG.

45. Alfred Kiyana, NAA ms. #2664.5, p. 5, part of l.C. Edited by IG. English translation by IG.

46. Anonymous 5, NAA ms. #2794.21, p. 10, part of l.G. Edited by LT. English translation by LT. The compound animate noun stem *kohpiči-ne-nosw-* literally means 'upland buffalo or cow', but in practice is a means of distinguishing *nenosw-* meaning 'buffalo' from *nenosw-* meaning 'cow'.

47. Anonymous 5, NAA ms. #2985, p. 47, part of l.B. Edited by LT and IG. English translation by LT and IG.

48. Alfred Kiyana, NAA ms. #2957, p. 89, l.I. Edited by IG. English translation by LT.

49. Sam Peters, NAA ms. #2005.1, p. 2, l.I through p. 3, l.A. Edited by IG. English translation by LT.

50. Alfred Kiyana, NAA ms. #2157, p. 49, l.B. Edited by IG. English translation by LT.

51. Jim Peters, NAA ms. #2024C, p. 25, l.G. Edited by LT and IG. English translation by LT and IG.

52. The diminutive version of the verb (AI *so·kiso·hi-*, versus nondiminutive *so·kiso-*) mildly emphasizes the heroine's piteous plight.

53. Sam Peters, NAA ms. #2794.84b, p. 36, l.C. Edited by IG. English translation by LT.

54. Sa·kihtanohkwe·ha, NAA ms. #1861, p. 2, part of l.I. Edited by LT and IG. English translation by LT and IG.

55. Alfred Kiyana, NAA ms. #2958, p. 718, l.M. Edited by LT. English translation by LT.

56. Anonymous 6, NAA ms. #2794.37, p. 29, l.A. Edited by IG. English translation by LT.

57. Anonymous 13, NAA ms. #2024A.12, p. 75, l.D. Edited by LT. English translation by LT. The manuscript has <ma|> for *mo*.

58. Bill Leaf, NAA ms. #2794.79, p. 1, l.A. Edited by LT and IG. English translation by LT and IG. This sentence is a story title. The name *we·tani·pi·me·h-* 'Has-an-Elm' consists of initial change (*we·* rather than *e·*

in this case) plus an AI or AI+O verb stem *otani·pi·mi-* 'have (as) an elm tree' plus a nominalizer.

59. Ives Goddard first remarked the existence of such possessor-of-a-locative-oblique-headed Meskwaki participles, with regard to the title of Alfred Kiyana's version of this story, *ani·pi ohka·hkeki sa·kenika* 'the one who had an elm tree growing from his chest'. (Goddard, personal communication; Alfred Kiyana, NAA ms. #2720.6, p. 1, l.A.)

60. Alfred Kiyana, NAA ms. #1859, p. 16, ll.FGH. Edited by LT. Translated by LT. NAA ms. #1859 was originally translated by Horace Poweshiek, a younger contemporary of Kiyana and a bilingual speaker of Meskwaki and English, and was subsequently edited, translated, and published by Truman Michelson (Michelson 1937: 68–78). Poweshiek's English translation of the two sentences in 53 is 'Then March. Part of the time, warm weather. That is the reason it is called that way.' Michelson's edition of the two sentences in 53, probably not coincidentally, omits the manuscript's syllable <di> [ši]. His English translation is 'And Half and Half (Pāpō'kwī'a, March): It will be warm part of the time. That is why it is so called.' (Michelson 1937: 73.)

61. See Thomason (2018).

62. Alfred Kiyana, NAA ms. #2959. Contemporary English translation by HP. Edited by LT.

63. The animate noun stem *masahkamikohkwe·w-* or *mesahkamikohkwe·w-* (also *misahkamikohkwe·w-*, *mašahkamikohkwe·w-*) literally means 'Entire-Earth-Woman'. Less literally, *masahkamikohkwe·wa* is our Grandmother Earth. HP translates *masahkamikohkwe·wa* as 'Mother-of-all-the-Earth'.

64. Alfred Kiyana, NAA ms. #2959, p. 1077, l.N. Edited by LT. English translations by HP and (a century later) by LT.

65. Alfred Kiyana, NAA ms. #2076.1, p. 10, l.D. Edited by LT. English translation by LT.

66. Alfred Kiyana, NAA ms. #2655.11, p. 14, l.C. Edited by LT. English translations by HP and (a century later) by LT.

67. Alfred Kiyana, NAA ms. #1875.16, p. 92, l.K and part of p. 93, l.A. Edited by IG. English translation by IG.

68. Jim Mamasaw, NAA ms. #2794.65b, p. 19, part of l.G. Edited by IG. English translation by LT.

69. Alfred Kiyana, NAA ms. #1786, p. 46, part of l.B. Edited by IG. English translation by LT.

70. Alfred Kiyana, NAA ms. #2082.2, p. 18, l.I. Edited by LT and IG. English translation by LT and IG.

71. Alfred Kiyana, NAA ms. #2153.5, p. 10, part of l.P. Edited by IG. English translation by IG.

72. Alfred Kiyana, NAA ms. #2959, p. 1052, part of l.B. Edited by LT. English translations by HP and (a century later) by LT.

73. Alfred Kiyana, NAA ms. #2007, p. 171, l.C. Edited by LT. English translations by HP and (a century later) by LT.

74. Alfred Kiyana, NAA ms. #2680, p. 1, l.G. Edited by IG. English translation by IG.

75. Alfred Kiyana, NAA ms. #2794.66, p. 169, l.A. Edited by IG. English translation by LT.

76. Alfred Kiyana, NAA ms. #2957, p. 424, l.I. Edited by IG. English translations by HP and (a century later) by LT.

77. Alfred Kiyana, NAA ms. #1875.8, p. 9, ll.CD. Edited by IG. English translation by LT.

78. Alfred Kiyana, NAA ms. #2959, p. 919, ll.DE. Edited by LT. English translations by HP and (a century later) by LT.

79. Alfred Kiyana, NAA ms. #2777.14, p. 29, l.A. Edited by IG. English translation by LT. The manuscript omits *e·h=* of *e·h=iči*.

80. Sa·kihtanohkwe·ha, NAA ms. #2794.49, p. 42, ll.MNO. Edited by IG. English translation by LT.

81. Alfred Kiyana, NAA ms. #2957, p. 84, part of l.F. Edited by IG. English translations by HP and (a century later) by LT.

82. Anonymous 19, NAA ms. #2769.7, p. 1, ll.BC. Edited by LT. English translation by LT.

83. Sa·kihtanohkwe·ha, NAA ms. #2794.49, p. 44, l.P. Edited by IG. English translation by LT.

84. Jack Bullard, NAA ms. #1875.10, p. 29, ll.KL. Edited by IG. English translation by LT.

85. Alfred Kiyana, NAA ms. #2720.7, p. 2, ll.DEF. Edited by IG. English translation by LT.

86. Alfred Kiyana, NAA ms. #2959, p. 1096, ll.NO. Edited by LT. English translation by LT.

87. Sa·kihtanohkwe·ha, NAA ms. #2794.49, p. 30, ll.FGH. Edited by IG. English translation by LT.

88. Charley H. Chuck, NAA ms. #2794.46(b), p. 23, l.S. Edited by IG. English translation by LT.

89. Alfred Kiyana, NAA ms. #2959, p. 954, ll.OP. Edited by LT. English translations by HP and (a century later) by LT.

90. Charley H. Chuck, NAA ms. #2794.93, p. 44, l.O. Edited by LT and IG. English translation by LT and IG.

91. Alfred Kiyana, NAA ms. #2221, p. 11, l.F. Edited by IG. English translations by HP and (a century later) by LT.

92. Alfred Kiyana, NAA ms. #2777.15, p. 12, l.F. Edited by IG. English translation by IG.

93. Alfred Kiyana, NAA ms, #1879.9, p. 12, l.C. Edited by IG. English translation by IG and LT.

94. Alfred Kiyana, NAA ms. #2959, p. 137, l.F. Edited by LT. English translations by HP and (a century later) by LT.

95. Alfred Kiyana, NAA ms. #2959, p. 11, l.B. Edited by LT. English translations by HP and (a century later) by LT.

References

Anonymous 5. n.d. Untitled ('The one whose eye was a bear's eye, and who was given a cougar's eye, and who was given a buffalo's hair'). NAA ms. #2794.21. English translation by Lucy Thomason in Swann 2005, 404–10.

Anonymous 5. n.d. me me sgwi ma te te a te so ka ka na 'The winter story of Red-Leggins'. NAA ms. #2985. Contemporary English translation by Ida Poweshiek.

Anonymous 6. n.d. ma ni e na tti me tti ma na ne ko ti ne ni wa me ne to wi ta 'This is what is related about a certain man who was a manitou' ('Bareshins'). NAA ms. #2794.13.

Anonymous 6. n.d. we ke ta te wa me 'Has-an-Otterskin'. NAA ms. #2794.37.

Anonymous 13. n.d. Untitled ('War stories'). NAA ms. #2024A.12. Contemporary English translation by Horace Poweshiek.

Anonymous 19. n.d. Untitled ('A Sioux warrior who was a manitou'). NAA ms. #2769.7.

Bloomfield, Leonard. 1946. Algonquian. In Hoijer et al., 85–129.

Bullard, Jack. n.d. we be ga ki 'Ball-Player'. NAA ms. #1875.10. Contemporary English translation by Ida Poweshiek.

Bullard, Jack. n.d. o bi wa ya . a te so ka ka na 'The winter story of Downy-Feather'. NAA ms. #2082.3. Contemporary English translation by Horace Poweshiek.

Bullard, Jack. n.d. pe na ni ma ga 'Summer-Bear'. NAA ms. #2432.4. Contemporary English translation by Truman Michelson, in consultation with Harry Lincoln.

Chuck, Charley H. n.d. we to se ni me 'Has-a-Rock'. NAA ms. #2737.2. English translation by Ives Goddard in Swann 2005, 345–67.

Chuck, Charley H. n.d. mi ke se te be . a te so ka ka na 'The winter story of Wampumhead'. NAA ms. #2794.46(b).

Chuck, Charley H. n.d. o te ga ma na 'This is about Caribou'. NAA ms. #2794.93.

Costa, David. 2015. *New voices for old words: Algonquian oral literatures*. Lincoln: University of Nebraska Press.

Dahlstrom, Amy. 1996. Edition and translation of *esamegamata.menetowita. sakimewa* [Mosquito, who fasted too long and became a spirit]. *Contemporary Linguistics*, 2: 121–30.

Dahlstrom, Amy. 1996. Narrative structure of a Fox text. In J. D. Nichols and A. C. Ogg (Eds.), *nikotwâsik iskwâhtêm, pâkihtêpayih! Studies in Honour of H.C. Wolfart. Algonquian and Iroquoian Memoir* 13. Winnipeg: Algonquian and Iroquoian Linguistics, 113–62.

Dahlstrom, Amy. 2015. Highlighting rhetorical structure through syntactic analysis: An illustrated Meskwaki text by Alfred Kiyana. In David J. Costa (Ed.) *New voices for old words: Algonquian oral literatures*. Lincoln: University of Nebraska Press, 118–97.

Goddard, Ives. 1990. Primary and secondary stem derivation in Algonquian. *International Journal of American Linguistics*, 56: 449–83.

Goddard, Ives. 2005. Winter stories. In Swann, Brian (Ed.), 2005. *Algonquian spirit: Contemporary translations of the Algonquian literatures of North America*. Lincoln: University of Nebraska Press, 320–57.

Goddard, Ives. 2006. *The autobiography of a Meskwaki woman: A new edition and translation. Algonquian and Iroquoian Linguistics Memoir* 18. Winnipeg: Algonquian and Iroquoian Linguistics.

Goddard, Ives. 2007. *The Owl Sacred Pack: A new edition and translation of the Meskwaki manuscript of Alfred Kiyana. Algonquian and Iroquoian Linguistics Memoir* 19. Winnipeg: Algonquian and Iroquoian Linguistics.

Goddard, Ives, and Lucy Thomason. 2014. *A Meskwaki-English and English-Meskwaki dictionary, based on early twentieth-century writings by native speakers*. Petoskey, MI: Mundart Press.

Hoijer, Harry, et al. (Eds.) 1946. *Linguistic structures of native America. Viking Fund Publications in Anthropology* 6. New York: Wenner-Gren Foundation.

Kiyana, Alfred. n.d. me we wi so tti ki 'The Wolf Clan'. NAA ms. #1786. Contemporary English translation by Thomas Brown. Edition and translation in Michelson (1937: 18–67).

Kiyana, Alfred. n.d. ki de so ki . ke te mi na wa wa tti ni 'The one blessed by the months'. NAA ms. #1859. Contemporary English translation by Horace Poweshiek. Edition and translation in Michelson (1937: 68–78).

Kiyana, Alfred. n.d. e ta mi ni wi ta o ski na we a . a tti ba na ki tti we me ko . e di ki tti ki ne no te wa ki na da wa ye 'The youth who became corn, and the Indians of long ago that grew as all different kinds of things'. NAA ms. #1875.8. Contemporary English translation by Ida Poweshiek.

Kiyana, Alfred. n.d. a sko te ne si wa . ma ne to wa i . e a di e ko tti 'When the Spirit of Fire was made by the manitous'. NAA ms. #1875.16. Contemporary English translation by Ida Poweshiek.

Kiyana, Alfred. n.d. mi da mi . ki di to ta . ne ni wa 'The man who made a sacred pack'. NAA ms. #1879.9. Contemporary English translation by Ida Poweshiek.

Kiyana, Alfred. n.d. ke ta ki ne no swi mi da mi 'The Spotted Buffalo Sacred Pack'. NAA ms. #2007. Contemporary English translation by Horace Poweshiek.

Kiyana, Alfred. n.d. wa be ski . ko bi tti ne no swa . o ne ma tti ne ki . o tti ka te . mi da mi . e di te ka te ki 'The one called The White Buffalo's Left-Hoof Sacred Pack'. NAA ms. #2076.1. Edition and translation in Michelson (1918–1919: 208–27).

Kiyana, Alfred. n.d. Untitled ('Wooden Figure'). NAA ms. #2080. Contemporary translation by Horace Poweshiek courtesy of the Davenport Public Museum.

Kiyana, Alfred. n.d. o bi wa ya 'Downy-Feather'. NAA ms. #2082.2. Contemporary English translation by Horace Poweshiek.

Kiyana, Alfred. n.d. e se ba na . ma sa ka ga ni . e o wi ka ni tti 'When Raccoon was friends with Badger'. NAA ms. #2153.5. Contemporary English translation by Truman Michelson, in consultation with Bill Leaf, Austin Grant, and Leo Walker.

Kiyana, Alfred. n.d. ma we wi . mi da mi . ni mi we ni e da wi ki 'What is done for a Wolf Clan Sacred Pack Dance'. NAA ms. #2157. Contemporary English translation by Horace Poweshiek.

Kiyana, Alfred. n.d. me te gi . ma ne to wi ne no so e a 'The Wooden Manitou Buffalo'. NAA ms. #2221. Contemporary English translation by Horace Poweshiek.

Kiyana, Alfred. n.d. me ka te wi tti ki 'Two people who fasted' ('The Wi·sahke·h Dance'). NAA ms. #2655.11. Contemporary English translation by Horace Poweshiek.

Kiyana, Alfred. n.d. na da wa ye . me to se ne ni wa ki 'People of long ago'. NAA ms. #2664.5.

Kiyana, Alfred. n.d. a ba ya di a ki 'The Apaya·ši·hs'. NAA ms. #2671.1. Contemporary English translation by Truman Michelson, in consultation with person(s) unknown.

Kiyana, Alfred. n.d. me sga ki a ki . e a ski me ko tta ko ka wo tti 'The first time everyone ganged up on the Meskwakis'. NAA ms. #2680. Contemporary English translation by Truman Michelson, in consultation with person(s) unknown.

Kiyana, Alfred. n.d. ki ya mo we wa . e ne se ko tti . wi sa ke a ni 'When the cannibal giant was killed by Wi·sahke·h'. NAA ms. #2688. English translation by Ives Goddard in Swann (2004: 432–53).

Kiyana, Alfred. n.d. Untitled ('The Owl Sacred Pack'). NAA ms. #2693. Contemporary English translation by Truman Michelson, in consultation with person(s) unknown. Edition and translation in Goddard (2007).

Kiyana, Alfred. n.d. be ne sa . mi da mi ni mi we ni 'Pene·sa, the sacred pack dance'. NAA ms. #2717. Contemporary translation by Thomas Brown.

Kiyana, Alfred. n.d. a ni bi . o ka ke ki . sa ke ni ka 'The one who had an elm tree growing from his chest'. NAA ms. #2720.6. Contemporary English translation by Ida Poweshiek.

Kiyana, Alfred. n.d. ma we wa 'Wolf'. NAA ms. #2720.7. Contemporary English translation by Ida Poweshiek.

Kiyana, Alfred. n.d. ne no te wa ki . e a ta bi wa tti . na da wa ye 'When some Indians moved camp long ago'. NAA ms. #2730.6.

Kiyana, Alfred. n.d. me me sgi ma te te 'Red-Leggins'. NAA ms. #2764.4.

Kiyana, Alfred. n.d. ni do ge wa ta 'The man who had two wives'. NAA ms. #2777.14.

Kiyana, Alfred. n.d. gi ye se a ki o ki wa wa ni wi tti a tti ki 'The boys who lived with their mother'. NAA ms. #2777.15.

Kiyana, Alfred. n.d. ba ba ske si ke a . o ko me sa ni . o me do a ni na i 'Shooter, his grandmother, and his grandfather'. NAA ms. #2794.66.

Kiyana, Alfred. n.d. wa ko i so tti ki . e ke te mi na we si wa tti . e da wi wa tti 'What the Fox Clan did when they were blessed'. NAA ms. #2957. Contemporary English translation by Horace Poweshiek.

Kiyana, Alfred. n.d. wi sa ke a . o sa ni . o kye ni . o si me a ni . o ko me se a ni 'Wi·sahke·h, his father, his mother, his younger brother, and his grandmother'. NAA ms. #2958. Contemporary translation by Horace Poweshiek.

Kiyana, Alfred. n.d. ma sa ka mi ko ge wa . e i sge se e tti . e a ski me ko . a be no e i tti 'Masahkamikohkwe·wa, when she was a little girl, when she was a newborn baby'. NAA ms. #2959. Contemporary English translation by Horace Poweshiek.

Kiyana, Alfred. n.d. we be ne me a ne ni wa 'Turkey-Owner, a man'. NAA ms. #3065. Contemporary English translation by Ida Poweshiek.

Leaf, Bill. n.d. a da da nwi yo na . e i ni tti no ste a ni . do ni ya i ka ta ni tti ni . a te so ka ka na 'The winter story of when the rooster with silver feet said "a da da nwi yo na"'. NAA ms. #1875.9. Contemporary English translation by Ida Poweshiek.

Leaf, Bill. n.d. we ta ni bi me a . o ka ke ki . ne ma te ni ka . a ni bi 'Has-an-Elm, the one with an elm tree growing from his chest'. NAA ms. #2794.79.

Leaf, Pearl. n.d. a da wa ye . me sga ki a ki e da wi wa te e 'What befell some Meskwakis long ago' ('Golden-Hide') (Meskwaki title written by Sam Peters). NAA ms. #2024D.1. Contemporary English translation by Horace Poweshiek. English translation by Lucy Thomason in Swann (2005: 397–403).

Mamasaw, Jim. n.d. me sgwa ki a ki . ne to ba a ki . e na to ba ni wa tti . e na ta di i wa tti . e me ta di wa tti nya na nwi 'Meskwaki warriors who went on the warpath, several of them, fifteen of them'. NAA #2794.65b.

Michelson, Truman. 1918–1919. The sacred pack called the White Buffalo's Left-Hoof Sacred Pack. In Michelson (1925: 208–27).

Michelson, Truman. 1925. *Fortieth Annual Report of the Bureau of American Ethnology to the Secretary of the Smithsonian Institution*. Washington, DC: U.S. Government Printing Office.

Michelson, Truman. 1937. *Fox miscellany. Smithsonian Institution Bureau of American Ethnology Bulletin* 114. Washington, DC: U.S. Government Printing Office.

Morgan, Maggie. n.d. Untitled ('The one whose father was the sun'). NAA ms. #2790. English translation by Lucy Thomason in Swann (2005: 379–96).

Nichols, John D., and Arden C. Ogg (Eds.). 1996. *nikotwâsik iskwâhtêm, pâkihtêpayih! Studies in Honour of H.C. Wolfart. Algonquian and Iroquoian Memoir* 13. Winnipeg: Algonquian and Iroquoian Linguistics.

Peters, Jim. n.d. Untitled ('The Meskwaki and the Whiteman'). NAA ms. #2794.75a.

Peters, Jim and Sam Peters. n.d. a te so ka ka na me me cgwi ma te te 'The winter story of Red-Leggins' (Meskwaki title written by Jim Peters). NAA ms. #2024C. Contemporary English translation by Horace Poweshiek.

Peters, Sam. n.d. a ya tti mo ni . ne me si so tti ki 'The story of the Fish Clan'. NAA ms. #2005.1. Contemporary English translation by Horace Poweshiek.

Peters, Sam. n.d. a te so ka ka na . ma na 'This is a winter story' ('The council at Mesoswa's'). NAA ms. #2005.5. Contemporary English translation by Horace Poweshiek.

Peters, Sam. n.d. a te so ka ka na 'A winter story' ('A man blessed by a wolf'). NAA ms. #2008.4. Contemporary English translation by Horace Poweshiek.

Peters, Sam. n.d. Untitled ('Downy-Feather'). NAA ms. #2024B.1. Contemporary English translation by Horace Poweshiek.

Peters, Sam. n.d. tti ta we a 'Či·tawe·h'. NAA ms. #2794.45a.

Peters, Sam. n.d. a te so ka ka na mi ke sa te ba ta 'The winter story of Wampumhead'. NAA ms. #2794.84a.

Peters, Sam. n.d. a te so ka ka na ko ko da 'The winter story of the pig'. NAA ms. #2794.84b.

Sa·kihtanohkwe·ha. n.d. me me sgi ma te te a 'Red-Leggins'. NAA ms. #1861.

Sa·kihtanohkwe·ha. n.d. Untitled ('Wi·sahke·h, Part 2'). NAA ms. #1879.5. Contemporary English translation by Ida Poweshiek.

Sa·kihtanohkwe·ha. n.d. Untitled ('The Apaya·ši·hs'). NAA ms. #2671.7a. Contemporary English translation by Truman Michelson, in consultation with person(s) unknown.

Sa·kihtanohkwe·ha. n.d. a te so ka ka na . ne ko ti bi . e da wi tti 'Winter story of what they say a certain person did' ('Red-Leggins'). NAA ms. #2700.

Sa·kihtanohkwe·ha. n.d. Untitled ('The young man who sailed across the sea to gamble'). NAA ms. #2794.49.

Ša·poči·wa. n.d. we ta ni bi me 'Has-an-Elm'. NAA ms. #2664.8.

Ša·poči·wa. n.d. Untitled ('The Apaya·ši·hs'). NAA ms. #2671.3. Contemporary English translation by Truman Michelson, in consultation with person(s) unknown.

Ša·poči·wa. n.d. wi na ke wa 'Buzzard'. NAA ms. #2794.26.

Swann, Brian. (Ed.). 2004. *Voices from four directions: Contemporary translations of the native literatures of North America*. Lincoln: University of Nebraska Press.

Swann, Brian (Ed.). 2005. *Algonquian spirit: Contemporary translations of the Algonquian literatures of North America*. Lincoln: University of Nebraska Press.

Thomason, Lucy. 2003. *The proximate and obviative contrast in Meskwaki* (PhD dissertation).University of Texas, Austin.

Thomason, Lucy. 2018. They were taken a little ways off and thrown away next to a black oak on the north side where the sun did not strike (Meskwaki locatives). Talk presented at the 50th Algonquian Conference in Edmonton, Alberta, Canada.

Young Bear. n.d. ma na na ka . i ge wa . a da a ka ka nwi ka de wa ni 'This is about a Sioux woman and a grizzly bear'. NAA ms. #2741a.2.

Young Bear. n.d. me cga ki a ki . ma ga ni . pi ti ka wa tti ki 'Two Meskwakis who visited a bear in its den'. NAA ms. #2741a.4.

CHAPTER 9

Lexical Suffixes in Nivaclé and Their Implications

Lyle Campbell

1. Introduction

Sarah Thomason has written about lexical suffixes in several publications on Montana Salish and on Salishan languages (see, e.g., Pharris and Thomason 2005; Thomason 1996, 1997, 2015: 732, 2016; Thomason et al. 1994; Thomason and Everett 1993; Thomason and Thomason 2004). Lexical affixes are bound morphemes that, because of their unexpectedly concrete semantic content, would be expected to be coded, based on experience with more familiar languages, as independent lexical items, as members of major lexical classes (e.g., nouns, verbs, adjectives), and not as affixes. Most Salishan languages have about 100 lexical suffixes (Carlson 1990, Czaykowski 1982, Gerdts 2003:346, Gerdts and Hinkson 1996, Mithun 1999:48–56), and lexical affixes are also found in several other language families of the northwest of North America (found, in addition to Salishan, also in Wakashan, Chimakuan, Tsimshian, and to a lesser extent in Eskimo-Aleut), and they have been been considered an areal trait of the Northwest Coast Linguistic Area (NWCLA) (see, e.g., Campbell 1997: 332–33; Mithun 1999: 315, 2015; Thomason 2000).

The purposes of this paper are to describe and analyze the lexical suffixes of Nivaclé, to discuss their possible implications for lexical suffixes in general, and to explore their possible consequences for some claims about languages in general. I begin with a description of the Nivaclé lexical suffixes, then compare their character with that of the lexical suffixes in languages of the NWCLA, and conclude with an examination of their broader implications for understanding lexical suffixes and for some claims about language in general.[1] I show that the lexical suffixes of Nivaclé share many characteristics with the lexical affixes of languages of the NWCLA. I examine several generalizations that have been made regarding lexical affixes in general and I argue that the lexical suffixes of Nivaclé call several of these claims into question. I argue also that the Nivaclé lexical suffixes present obstacles to interpretations that assume grammaticalization is behind these lexical suffixes.

Nivaclé (ISO 639-3 code [cag]) is a Matacoan language spoken in Argentina and Paraguay by between 8,500 and 16,850 speakers (calculations of speaker numbers vary, see Campbell et al. 2020 for details). Nivaclé has some twenty-five lexical suffixes, a substantial number but fewer than in many languages of the NWCLA. I return later to general characteristics of these Nivaclé affixes, but for now to set the stage, suffice it to indicate that these are true affixes, not compounds. They are bound and cannot stand alone as separate words. Most of them are quite unsimilar in phonological shape to any lexical root with similar meaning. Some are rare and unproductive, but others are quite productive, very affix-like given their frequency and behavior similar to that of other affixes in the language. (For details, see Campbell et al. 2020.)[2]

2. Nivaclé Lexical Suffixes and Clitics

Many of Nivaclé's lexical affixes and clitics have allomorphs that are determined by aspects of their phonological environments.[3] For example, a considerable number of affixes differ by having alternations of *ch* with *k*, and *sh* with *j*—with the *ch* and *sh* forms basically when the last vowel of the stem before the attached morpheme is non-back (/i, e, a/), and allomorphs with *k* and *j* when the last vowel before them is back (/i, e, ô/).[4] Several of the suffixes follow *-ja* 'ligature', an empty morph attached to stems in order to avoid non-permitted phonological sequences when morphemes come together in a word. The presence or absence of a glottal stop (/7/) in several allomorphic variants is also determined by the phonological context (where an underlying glottal stop or certain consonant cluster in the stem to which the suffix or clitic is attached causes a glottal stop to appear in the attached bound morpheme, though with loss of the glottal stop from the stem in certain other phonotactic environments).[5] The lexical suffixes and clitics of Nivaclé follow.

2.1. Lexical Suffixes Typically Attached to Noun Stems That Derive Other Nouns

The following are lexical suffixes that attach to noun stems and derive other nouns.

(1) -chat / -kat *(*-ichat, -ikat*)*

'a stand, grove, group of trees or plants of the same species, or an abundance of trees or plants of the same species in a particular place'. Forms with this suffix are collective nouns.

ajôy**chat**	'stand of mistol trees' (mistolar) (cf. *ajôyuk* 'mistol tree' [*Ziziphus mistol*], *ajôyej* 'mistol fruit')
asaktse**chat**	'place of *bolas verde* trees' (cf. *asaktsej* '*bola verde* fruit', *asaktsuk* 'bola verde tree' [*Anisocapparis speciosa, Capparaceae*])
fhtsônja**chat**	'stand of *sunchos*' (cf. *fhtsônaj* 'suncho') [*Baccharis dracunculifolia*]
klôtsik**ichat**	'stand of willows' (cf. *klôtsikiyuk* 'willow tree')
ôfhkatin**chat**	'stand of small willows' (cf. *ôfhkatinuk* '*duraznillo* tree/plant', *ôfhkatiniwa* '*duraznillo* fruit')
ôtjaye**chat**	'stand of *molles*' (*ôtjayej* 'molle fruit', *ôtjayuk* 'molle tree') [*Schinus molle*]
paktse**chat**	'stand of *doca*' (*Morrenia adorata*) (cf. *paktsej* '*doca* fruit', *paktseyuk* '*doca* plant')

t'apôy**chat**	'bunch of *ancoches*' (cf. *t'apôyuk* '*ancoche* bush') [*Vallesia glabra*]
ts'aklan**chat**	'of brea trees' (cf. *ts'aklanuk* 'brea / palo verde tree') [*Parkinsonia praecox*]
wôkjôkl**ichat**	'cotton patch' (cf. *wôkjôkli* 'cotton')
jok**kat**	'*palo santo* grove' (cf. *jo7ok* '*palo santo* tree') [*Bulnesia sarmientoi*]
jukôj**kat**	'*palo bobo* grove' (cf. *jukô7ôj* '*palo bobo* tree') [*Tessaria integrifolia*]
kijku**kat**	'*palo blanco* grove' (cf. *kiju7uk* '*palo blanco* tree') [*Calycophyllum multiflorum*]
kumôklu**kat**	'stand of *chañar* trees' (cf. *kumôklu* '*chañar* fruit') [*Geoffroea decorticans*]
shinta7ôw**kat**	'*palo rosado* grove' [*Aspidosperma polyneuron*]
sints'itsu**kat**	'mulberry stand' (cf. *sints'itsu7uk* 'mulberry') [*Chlorophora tinctoria*]
tisju**kat**	'quebracho grove' (cf. *tisu7uj* 'red quebracho') [*Schinopsis balansae*]
tnasku**kat**	'grove of *guayacán* trees' (cf. *tnasuk* '*guayacán* tree') [*Caesalpinia paraguariensis*]
tsanku**kat**	'stand of *duraznillos*' (cf. *tsanu7uk* '*duraznillo* tree') [*Ruprechtia triflora*]
tsjuju**kat**	'grove of trees (species)' (cf. *tsjujuk* 'a tree species') [*Capparis tweediana*]
wônô**kat**	'stand of *palo matacos*' (cf. *wônô7ôk* '*palo mataco* tree') [*Prosopis kuntzei*]
yi7klôj**kat**	'quebracho blanco grove' (cf. *yi7klô7ôj* 'quebracho blanco') [*Aspidosperma quebracho-blanco*]
yiktsu**kat**	'*yuchán* grove (silk-floss tree grove)' (cf. *yitsu7uk* '*yuchán* tree') [*Chorisia insignis* (*Ceiba insignis*)]

(2) -ej, *'kind of fruit, edible plant'*

This suffix occurs on several nouns but it is not especially frequent.

ajôy**ej**	'mistol fruit' (cf. *ajôy-uk* 'mistol tree')
asakts**ej**	'*bola verde* fruit' (cf. *asakts-uk* '*bola verde* tree') [*Anisocapparis speciosa*]

koyt**ej**	'*chagua*' (agave plant species)
ôkts**ej**	'*chagua*' (agave plant species)
ônjay**ej**	'wild bean' (cf. *ônjay-uk* 'wild bean plant')
ôp'ets**ej**	'fruit of the cardón cactus' (cf. *ôp'ets-uk* 'cardón cactus')
ôtjay**ej**	'*molle* fruit' (cf. *ôtjay-uk* '*molle* tree')
pakts**ej**	'a kind of fruit (of cactus, of yuchán trees)' (doca) (cf. *pakt-se-chat* 'place where ther are a lot of *doca* fruits', *paktse-yuk* stand of plants with *doca* fruit)
sklets**ej**	*cipoy* plant [*Jacaratia hassleriana*]
wayts**ej**	'algarrobo negro fruit' (fruta del algarrobo negro)
yite7**ej**	'grass, pasture' (pasto) (cf. *yita7* 'weeds, uncleared land, forest').

(3) -fha (-ja-fha) *'companion'*

ach'ak**fha**	'your spouse'
achi**fha**	'your relative, your compatriot'
kôw**fha**	'enemy, opponent'
lhk'uts**fha**	'his/her friend, boss, patron'
yey**fha**	'my namesake', 'person with the same name as mine' (cf. *y-ey* 'my name'). See also *yey**fha** che* 'my female namesake', 'woman with the same name as mine'
yik'o7owte**fha**	'my neighbor, husband of my [a male's] sister-in-law, wife of my [a female's] brother-in-law') (cf. *yi-k'o7wat* 'my place, my house')
yikumja**fha**	'my co-worker, my work companion' (cf. *ja-y-kum=7in* 'I work'). See also *yikumja**fha** che* 'my female co-worker, my female work companion'
yôjk'enja**fha**	'my boyfriend.' See also *yôjk'enja***fha** *che* 'my girlfriend' (cf. *-en* 'to love'?)

(4) -mat, -ma7at, -7mat, -i7mat

'defective in, suffering from, damaged in, bad because of, have something undesirable'

This suffix means that there is something defective, bad, damaged or suffering, or negative about the thing indicated by the stem to which it is attached.

ako7**mat**	'lame, crippled, limping' (cf. *ako* 'your hip')
akk'apo7**mat**	'stomach ache' (cf. *t'-akk'apo7* 'his upper abdomen, stomach')
asinô7**mat**	'speech impediment, dirty-mouthed, obscene, inappropriate of speech' (cf. *asinô* 'word, speech')
etsje7**mat**	'bad drunk' (cf. *y-etsej* 'he/she is drunk')
eyi7**mat**	'bad name' (cf. *ey* 'your name'; *eyimatan* 'to curse, swear')
fho7**mat**	'damaged foot, wound on foot' (cf. *yi-fho7* 'my foot')
kleshja**mat**	'difficult to wash' (cf. *ja-kle7esh* 'I will wash it')
klutsshe7**mat**	'poorly made firearm', 'bad weapon' (cf. *klutesh* 'weapon, firearm, rifle, shotgun')
nôyshi7**mat**	'bad trip, bad journey' (cf. *nôyish* 'road, path')
oti7**mat**	'suffering from tuberculosis' (cf. *otiwo* 'your tuberculosis')
ôtjô7**mat**	'badly formed skull' (cf. *ôtôj* 'your skull, craneum')
wakche7**mat**	'lame' (cf. *wakcheniyash* 'manner of walking')
yalh**imat**	'breathing with difficulty' (cf. *yalh* 'breath, breathing')
yinsha**ma7at**	'bad nose, deformed nose' (cf. *yi-na7ash* 'my nose', *yi-nsha7* 'my nostril')
yiwju7**ma7at**	'defective foot' (cf. *yi-wju7* 'my knot (in wood)')
yôja7**mat**	'bad drunk, defective drinking' (cf. *yi-yô7* 'he drinks')

(5) -matsej (-ematsej)

'good in, good because of, well-functioning in'

It means that there is something good or positive with regard to the stem to which this suffix is attached.

asinô**matsej**	'good speech, good speaking' (cf. *asinô* 'word, speech')
etsje**matsej**	'good drinking, good drinker' (cf. *etsej* 'drunk')
fho**matsej**	good foot, well-formed foot, healthy foot' (cf. *fho7* 'foot')
klutsshe**matsej**	'good weapon, well-made weapon' (cf. *klutsesh* 'weapon, firearm')
nôyshi**matsej**	'good trip, good road' (cf. *nôyish* 'road, path')
ôtjô**matsej**	'good skull, well-formed skull' (cf. *ôtôj* 'your skull')
tô**matsej**	'good eyesight, good eyes' (cf. perhaps *a-tôsej* 'your eye')
wakche**matsej**	'good walking, walking well' (cf. *yi-7wakcheniyash* 'my maner of walking'; *yi-wakcheyan* 'he/she/it makes him/her/it walk')

yalhi**matsej**	'good breathing' (cf. *yalh* 'breath, breathing')
yinsha**matsej**	'good nose' (*yi-nsha7* 'my nostril', cf. *na7ash* 'nose')
yôjô**matsej**	'good drinker, good drunk' (cf. *yi-yô7* 'he drinks')

(6) -mech, -me7ech

'expert, person who has power over something, has special knowledge of something, belongs to a profession concerning something, is a ritual specialist in something.'

itô**mech**	'person who knows much about fires, shaman who knows how to remove the ember that a patient is believed to have in his flesh' (cf. *itôj* 'fire')
ute**mech**	'shaman who know how to put the stone in the fire and then use it to put in the body of a dead person', 'someone who knows stones well' (cf. *utej* 'stone')
wotso**mech**	'person who know how to find *lechiguana* bees' nests (for honey)' (cf. *wotso* 'lechiguana' [bee species])
k'utsja**me7ech**	'person who likes old people, who treats old people well' (cf. *k'utsa7aj* 'old')
nafhju**me7ech**	'person who wields the stick for stirring the fire's coals' (cf. *nafhju7uj* 'stick for fire coals, stick with which to stir the fire')
tôyje**me7ech**	'person who pursues shamans/witches, person who kills witches' (cf. *tôye7ej* 'shaman, witch')
yiyjô**me7ech**	'man or dog who knows how to find jaguars, how to fight them, shaman who has the secret of jaguars' (cf. *yiyô7ôj* 'jaguar')

(7) -nôj *(and* -nôj-ô*)*

'eater of, hunter of, one fond of'

The *-nôj* suffix is masculine; *-nôjô* is feminine, composed of *-nôj* plus *-ô* 'feminine' [FEM].

ajô7klô**nôj**	'bird hunter (e.g., cat, falcon)' (cf. *ajô7klô* 'bird')
fhiyô**nôj**	'frog-eating snake' (cf. *fhiyô* 'frog')

kumjô**nôj** 'a drunk, person who likes drinking' (cf. *kumjô* 'chicha')
môjôktsi**nôj** 'hawk species that likes tuco-tucos, person or animal that likes tuco-tucos' (cf. *môjôktsi* 'tuco-tuco' [gopher-like rodent])
sheyô**nôj** 'falcon species (that likes to chase and eat bats)' (cf. *sheyô* 'bat')
yiye**nôj** 'bird species that likes to eat *chagua* fruit' (pájaro pepitero de collar) (cf. *yiye7* 'chagua species')
kumjô**nôjô** 'female drunk, drunk woman' (cf. *kumjônôj* 'a drunk, person who likes drinks'; cf. *kumjô* 'chicha')
môjôktsi**nôjô** 'female hawk that likes moles' (cf. *môjôktsinôj* 'male hawk that likes tuco-tucos [gopher-like rodent]'; cf. *môjôktsi* 'tuco-tuco')
tôlhjate**nôjô** 'bird species (*Asthenes sp.*)' (espinero) (cf. *tôlhjate* 'prickly pear flower' [flor de tuna])
waytse**nôjô** 'blue-capped tanager (bird) (*Thraupis bonariensis*)' (cf. *waytsej* 'fruit of the algarrobo negro' [*Prosopis nigra*, black carob tree])

(8) -nôk

'kind of fermented drink, kind of consumable liquid'[6]

Most of the words with this suffix mean a kind of fermented drink, made from the substance indicated by the meaning of the root to which the suffix is attached; a few involve other consumable liquids.

ajôye**nôk** 'mistol chicha' (cf. *ajôyej* 'mistol fruit' (*Ziziphus mistol*)
fha7ay**inôk** 'algarrobo blanco chicha' (carob tree) (cf. *fha7ay* 'algarrobo fruit')
fhtsuk**inôk** 'palm chicha' (cf. *fhtsu7uk* 'palm')
junshata**nôk** 'chicha from *tusca*' (an acacia species) (cf. *junshataj* '*tusca* fruit')
kumôklu**nôk** 'chicha from *chañar*' (*Geoffroea decorticans*) (cf. *kumôklu* '*chañar* fruit')
lhape**nôk** 'his/her/its grease (liquid form)' (cf. *lhape7* 'his/her/its grease, oil')
ôtjaye**nôk** 'chicha from *molle*' (*Schinus molle*) (cf. *ôtjayej* '*molle* fruit')
ôtjayeta**nôk** 'grape chicha, wine' (cf. *ôtjaye-taj* 'grape' [*molle*-SIM])

shinwo**nôk** 'chicha from dark honey' (cf. *shinwo7* 'dark honey')

shnakuwjata**nôk** 'chicha from *extranjera* bee honey' (cf. *shnakujataj* '*extranjera* bee')

waytse**nôk** 'chicha from algarrobo negro' (*Prosopis nigra*, black carob tree) (cf. *waytsej* 'algarrobo negro fruit')

wotso**nôk** 'chicha from *chiguana* bee honey' (cf. *wotso* '*chiguana* bee')

Possibly related to this *-nôk* morpheme are the following forms, though they have nothing to do with 'chicha' or etible liquids:

na7ap'ku**nôk** 'salty spicy plant' (cf. *na7p'uk* 'salty, anything salty')

fhi**nôk** 'tobacco, cigarrette' (cf. *ja-fhin* 'I suck, I smoke')

(9) -nuk, -inuk, -nu7uk

'ethnonym suffix (ethnic group suffix)' (*gentilicio*)

towôk**inuk** 'riverbank person' (along the Pilcomayo River) (cf. *towôk* 'river') (cf. *towôkinjus* 'riverbank people' [pl])

ekle7**nuk** 'Chorote' (cf. *eklenjuy* 'Chorotes')

ma7n**u7uk** 'Chorote Montaraz' (cf. *manjuy* 'Chorotes Montaraces' [pl])

Apossibly related example is the following:

lhum7ôkji**nuk** 'east, east wind' (cf. *lhum7ashi* 'tomorrow, morning', *7ôkji* 'below, under' [under]).

(10) -nuk, -inuk

'about the neck or mouth' (imprecise meaning)

This suffix shares its shape with an ethnonym suffix (in 9) that designates different ethnic groups. The examples of this *-nuk* (*-inuk*) are from Seelwische (2016) and in Fabre (2016: 138–39).[7]

<vatcôish**inuc**> 'necklace', <côish**inuc**> 'necklace'

<lhavo'**nuc**> 'his/her' scarf', <vo'**nuc**> 'scarf, shawl, tie' (cf. *yi-7wo7* 'my neck')

<lhashi**nju**s>	'its/his/her bridles/bits' (< //lh-ashi-**nuk**-Vs// [3POS-mouth-*nuk*-PL]), <ashi**nuc**> 'bridle' (cf. *y-ashi* 'my mouth')
<vatca'vo**nuc**>	'yoke' (cf. *wat-7wo7* 'neck' [NPOS-neck])

(11) -ôp, -up, (-o7op, -u7up, -ô7ôp)

'season' suffix

Nivaclé appears to have a lexical suffix for seasons of the year, though there are naturally few things that it attaches to. Nivaclé has five seasons and they take this suffix:

ônjay**up**	'summer' (February-March) (cf. *ônjay-uk* 'wild bean')[8]
tisj**u7up**	'summer' (April) (cf. *tisju7uj* 'red quebracho', [*Schinopsis balansae*])[9]
kl**o7op**	'winter' (May-July)
shnôw**ôp**	'Spring' (August-October)[10]
yink**ô7ôp**	'autumn, Fall', 'year' (otoño, año) (algarrobo ripening season) (November–January)

It appears that the words for seasons are composed (at least historically) of a root that has something to do with what is typically harvested during that season of the year plus a now frozen lexical affix -(*V*)*p* with some back vowel (*u*, *o*, or *ô*) (maybe something like *-up* where the *u* changes to match an *o* or *ô* of the vowel of the root that it is attached to).

(12) -shiy / -jiy

'concave, container'

The meaning of this suffix is abstract; it is attached to nouns meaning 'containers, concave things, enclosed or concave containers.'

kape**shiy**	'small jug, vase, glass (for grease)' (cf. *lh-k-ape* 'his/her/its grease, oil')
shtôkle**shiy**	'garbage dump' (cf. *shtôkley* [pl] 'garbage')
tin-ka7at**shiy**	'gourd spoon, small gourd with handle'
wat-paschi**shiy**	'ring (unpossessed)' (cf. *lh-pasche* 'his/her finger')[11]

wat-woy**shiy**	'boil, carbuncle (unpossessed)' (cf. *wo7oy* 'blood')
woye**shiy**	'oven' (cf. *woye* 'bread')
yakut**shiy**	'gourd dish, gourd with handle' (archaic) (cf. *yakut* 'black')
yi-tôsje**shiy**	is 'my eye-glasses' (cf. *yi-tôsj-ey* [1POS-eye-PL] 'my eyes')
yi-yalh**shiy**	is 'my lungs' (cf. *yalh* 'breath, respiration')
yukuwe**shiy**	'oven' (cf. *yukuwe* 'bread')
lhayomo**jiy**	'cow's second stomach [of four compartments] (omasum), cud'
ôtjô**jiy**	'your hat, cap' (< [*ôtôj-jiy*]) (cf. *ôtôj* 'your skull, craneum')
peso**jiy**	'bank' (cf. *peso* 'money')
samku**jiy**	'latrine, toilet' (cf. *samuk* 'excrement')
yulhu**jiy**	'my bladder' (cf. *y-ulhu* 'my urine')

A number of words have *-jat-shiy*, composed of the *-jat* 'instrumental nominalization' plus *-shiy*:

awku**jatshiy**	'your hammock' (cf. *waku7* 'to be in a hammock')
ôw**jatshiy**	'bus, vehicle'; 'your bus, vehicle'
uy**jatshiy**	'shirt, dress, clothes, clothing' (cf. *uy* 'enter!')
watsakkun**jatshiy**	'plate (someone's plate)' (plato) (< *wat-tsakkun-jat-shiy*) (cf. *ja-y-tsakkun* [1ACT-VBLZ-eat] 'I eat')
yiyô**jatshiy**	'jar, mug' (cf. *yi-yô7* 'he/she/it drinks')
yôs**jatshiy**	'my trousers, pants' (cf. *ja-7yôs* 'I step, kick', *ja-yôs=ch'e* 'I put on my shoes')

(13) -ta=7a, -ita=7a

'of no value, worthless' [DEPR]

is-**ta=7a**	'not important' (cf. *is* 'good')
niwakle-**ta=7a**	'lazy man, man who doesn't work, who does nothing' (cf. *niwakle* 'man, Nivacle')
ta7ôwkla-**ta=7a**	'lazy child, useless child, malnourished' (cf. *ta7ôwklaj* 'child')
ni7ch'ayech-**ita=7a**	'lazy young man' (cf. *ni7ch'ayech* 'young man')
ya7klish-**ita=7a**	'bad word, false word, lie' (cf. *ya7klish* 'language, word, message')

llhklish-**ita=7a** 'bad word' cf. (*lh-kli7ish* 'his/her word, language')

(14) -tach, -itach

'tree, plant suffix'

There is a suffix *-tach* that is attached in a few cases to terms for trees (and other plants). It may be related in some way to *-chat / -kat* (*-ichat, -ikat*) 'a stand, grove, group of trees or plants' (see earlier in the text).

jok**itach** '*lapacho* tree' (*Tabebuia lapacho*) (cf. *jo7ok* 'lignum vitae', palo santo')
junsha**tach** '*tusca* acacia plant' (cf. *junshataj* '*tusca* fruit')
jusch'anja**tach** '*tala* (tree)' (*Celtis tala*) (cf. *jusch'anjatayuk* '*tala* [whole tree]')
Perhapsalso in:

klo**tach** 'tree (species)'
sop'a**tach** '*socomorro*' (tree species)
su**tach** '*palanpalan* bush' (*Nicotiana glauca* ?) (cf. *sutayuk* '*palanpalan* bush [whole plant]')

(15) -taj, -itaj

'similar to, analogous to' (simulative) [SIM]

This is a very frequent and productive suffix. As in the typical pattern, the *-taj* allomorph appears after vowels, the *-itaj* variant after consonants. Also as with most other forms that end in *j*, the *j* is dropped when some other morpheme is attached after it, so, for example, the 'plural' is *-ta-s*, *-ita-s*.[12]

asakts**itaj** 'orange' (cf. *asaktsej* '*bola verde* fruit') (cf. *asakts-ita-s* 'oranges')
itô**taj** 'match' (cf. *itôj* 'fire') (cf. *itôtas* 'matches')
katis**itaj** 'flashlight, lightbulb, light' (cf. *kati7is* 'star') (cf. *katis-ita-s* 'flashlights')
klesa**taj** 'machete' (cf. *klesa* 'knife') (cf. *klesa-ta-s* 'machetes')
kôtse**taj** 'small armadillo (species)' (tatu, gualacate pequeño) (cf. *kôtsej* 'mouse-like rodent') (cf. *kôtse-ta-s* 'small armadillos [species]')

kôtseta**taj**	'large armadillo' (species) (tatu, gualacate) (cf. *kôtsetaj* 'small armadillo')
kuwayu**taj**	'burro, donkey' (cf. *kuwayu* 'horse') (cf. *kuwayu-ta-s* 'burros'; cf. *kuwayu-ta-che* 'female burro, donkey')
môjôktsi**taj**	'vizcacha' (large rodent) (cf. *môjôktsi* 'tuco-tuco [gopher-like rodent]')
oyinche**taj**	'large type of chilli, chilli pepper' (ají) (cf. *oyinche* 'chilli')
sheyô**taj**	'vampire bat' (cf. *sheyô* 'bat')
watsje**taj**	'large hole or cave' (cf. *watsej* 'animal's hole, den, cave') (cf. *watsje-ta-s* 'large holes or caves')

(16) -uk, -yuk, -u7uk

'plant suffix' [PLANT] (specifying individual trees or plants, individual stocks/stems of the plant identified in the word's root).

This suffix attaches to names of trees and other plants. It is very frequent. The allomorph *-uk* is attached to stems that end in a consonant, *-yuk* to those ending in a vowel.

ajôy**uk**	'*mistol* tree' (*Ziziphus mistol*) (cf. *ajôy-ej* '*mistol* fruit'; cf. *ajôy-k-uy* 'mistol trees')
asakts**uk**	'*bola verde* tree' (*Capparis salicifolia*) (cf. *asakts-ej* '*bola* verde fruit')
fha7ay**uk**	'algarrobo' (*Prosopis alba*) (cf. *fha7ay* 'algarrobo fruit'; cf. *fha7ay-k-uy* 'algarrobo trees')
kjat**uk**	'cactus species' (tall, like cardón) (cf. *kjat* 'fruit of this cactus species'; cf. *kjat-k-uy* 'cactus plants' [species])
nin**uk**	'*sachasandía*' (a bush species)
ôtjay**uk**	'*molle* tree' (*Schinus molle*) (cf. *ôtjay-ej* '*molle* fruit'; cf. *ôtjaye-chat* '*molle* grove')
ôfhkatin**uk**	'*duraznillo / saucillo* tree' (willow species) (*Acanthosyris falcata*) (cf. *ôfhkatin-aj* '*duraznillo / saucillo* fruit'; cf. *ôfhkatin-k-uy* '*duraznillo / saucillo* trees')
ôp'ets**uk**	'cardon cactus (species)' (cf. *ôp'et-sej* 'cardon cactus fruit [species]')
jokita**yuk**	'*lapacho* tree' (*Tabebuia lapacho*) (cf. *jokita-k-uy* '*lapacho* trees')

klôtsiki**yuk** 'willow tree' (cf. *klôtsiki-chat* 'stand of *lapachos*'; cf. *klôtsi-ki-k-uy* 'willow trees')
saniyô**yuk** 'watermelon plant' (cf. *saniyô* 'watermellon') (loan from Spanish *sandía* 'watermelon')
sôt'ô**yuk** 'cactus plant species' (cf. *sôt'ô* 'fruit of this cactus species'; cf. *sôt'ô-k-uy* 'cactus plants of this species')
waykla**yuk** 'a tall cactus species' (cf. *waykla7* 'fruit of this cactus species')
fhts**u7uk** 'palm tree' (cf. *fhis-chat* 'palm grove')
kij**u7uk** '*palo blanco*' (*Calycophyllum multiflorum*) (cf. *ki-jk-uy* '*palo blanco* trees', *kijku-kat* 'stand of *palo blanco* trees')
sints'its**u7uk** 'mulberry tree' (mora) (*Chlorophora tinctoria*) (cf. *sints'it-su-k-uy* 'mulberry trees')
tnas**u7uk** '*guayacán* tree' (*Caesalpinia paraguariensis*) (cf. *tnas-k-uy* '*guayacán* trees')
yikts**u7uk** '*yuchán* tree' (*Chorisia insignis* [*Ceiba insignis*]) (cf. *yiktsu-kat* 'stand of *yuchán* trees'; *yiktsi-k-uy* '*yuchán* trees')

(17) -wash, -Vwash, -wa7ash

'kind of wound, injury', 'print, track, impression', caused by or associated with the thing mentioned in the root.

fho**wash** 'footprint, track' (cf. *fho7* 'foot')
jokita**wash** 'shovel wound' (cf. *jokitaj* 'shovel')
klesa**wash** 'knife wound, axe wound' (cf. *klesa* 'knife')
klutsshe**wash** 'gunshot wound, wound from a weapon' (cf. *klutsesh* 'weapon, gun')
k'utjan**iwash** 'wound from a thorn' (cf. *k'utja7an* 'thorn')
lhpônôke**wash** 'his/her/its claw wound' (cf. *pônôke* 'claw, fingernail')
lhp'ô**wash** 'his/her/its arrow notch, notch in wood' (cf. *yi-7p'ôw-ja-yan* [3act-notch-LIG-VBLZ] 'he makes a notch')
lht'ijôjke**wash** 'his/her/its wound from fist beating' (cf. *ja-t'ijôj* 'I hit, beat (with fists)')
lhtsa**wash** 'his/her/its deep wound'
namch**awash** 'axe wound, cut from an axe' (cf. *namach* 'axe')

tink'u**wa7ash**	'club wound, wound from a stick or club' (cf. *tink'u7* 'club, mace')
wojolha-nsha-**wa7ash**	[peccary 3POS-nose-wound] 'track left by a peccary's nose' (cf. *na7ash* 'nose')
wônja**wash**	'piranha-bite wound' (cf. *wônaj* 'piranha')
yi7klô**wash**	'wound from wood, stick' (cf. *yi7klô7* 'wood, tree, stick')

(18) -yinjat *[MASC]*, -yinjate *[FEM]*

'mourning kinship morpheme'

chikla**yinjat**	'late elder brother' (finado hermano) (cf. *chikla7* 'elder brother')
tata**yinjat**	'late father' (finado padre) (cf. *tata* 'father')
yich'inshi**yinjat**	'my late younger brother' (mi finado hermano menor) (*lh-ch'inish* 'his/her younnger brother')
chita**yinjate**	'late elder sister' (finada hermana mayor) (cf. *chita7* 'elder sister')
mimi**yinjate**	'late mother' (finada madre) (cf. *mimi* 'mother')
yich'injô**yinjate**	'late younger sister' (finada hermana menor) (cf. *lh-ch'injô* 'his/her younger sister')

2.2. Affixes and Clitics That Attach Mostly to Verbs, Sometimes to Adjectives

(19) =kla7a

'a little', 'in the manner of a child'

jafhi7ich=**kla7a**	'I hide something small'
wakle7ech=**kla7a**	'he/she is beginning to walk (a baby)' (cf. *ja7-wa7klech* 'I walk')
waku7=**kla7a**	'he/she (a small child) is lying/swinging in a hammock' (cf. *waku7* 'he/she is lying/swinging in the hammock')
yitô7yesh=**kla7a**	'small child that knows how (to do something), is able'
jufhtsej=**kla7a**	'a little angry'
kaklek=**kla7a**	'small but heavy' (cf. *kaklek* 'heavy')
t'un=7in=**kla7a**	'strong child' (cf. *t'un=7in* 'strong')

(20) -lha, -elha

'verbalization: removal, extraction, separation' [EXTRAC]

This suffix attaches to noun stems to produce derived verbs whose meaning involves in some way removing, taking out, extracting what the noun stem refers to. The *-lha* variant comes after vowels, *-elha* after consonants. It appears in most of its occurrences together with the directional prefix *n-* hither.

ja-7n-i-**lha**	'I sqeeze out water, juice' [IACT-hither-liquid-EXTRAC] (cf. *t'-i7* 'its liquid, juice')
ja-n-fha-**lha**	'I defeather, take off the feathers' (cf. *lh-afh* 'its feather, wing')
ja-ni-jpekl-**elha**	'I take photos' (cf. *yi-jpek* 'my photo, my shadow')
ja-n-tôsj-**elha**	'I shell, take off/out the seeds, kernels' (yo desgrano) (cf. *lh-tôsej* 'its seed'
ja-n-ts'o7ts-**elha**	'I milk it' (cf. *ts'o7os* 'milk')

(21) -pjalh

'verbalization of action involving binding'

The meaning of this suffix is not precise, but it appears to involve, loosely, a sense of 'binding.' Also, most of the roots to which it is attached are not known in a form independent of this suffix.

jaklô**pjalh**-esh	'I roll it up with, wrap it up' (< *j-aklô-pjalh-esh* [IACT-much-binding-VAL ?])
j-ako**pjalh**	'I embrace him/her/it with my legs around' (cf. *y-ako* 'my hip')
ja-tap**jalh**	'I hobble (the horse)'
ja-tse**pjalh**=ch'e	'I sew'
j-eche**pjalh**	'I hug, embrace (with arms around)'

(22) -walh

'verbalization' [VBLZ]: 'to have large X'

This suffix attaches to noun stems and derives a stative verb with the meaning that the subject of the verb has a large one or large ones of the thing that is the referent of the noun stem. These verbs take the stative series of prefixes for their pronominal subject agreement markers.

tsi-kfhe-**walh**	'I have big ears' (cf. *yi-kfhe7* 'my ear')
na-kfhe-**walh**	'you have big ears'
nikfhe-**walh**	'he/she/it as large ears'
tsi-fho-**walh**	'I have big feet' (cf. *-fho7* 'foot')
na-fho-**walh**	'you have big feet'
tsi-nsha-**wa7alh**	'I have a big nose' (cf. *na7ash* 'nose')
tsi-pôse-**walh**	'I have a big beard' (cf. *-pôse* 'beard')
tsi-shatche-**walh**	'I have a big head', 'I am big-headed' (cf. *shatech* 'head')
tsi-tôsje-**walh**	'I have big eyes' (cf. *tôsej* 'eye, seed')
tsi-pasche-**walh**	'I have a big finger' (cf. *-pasche* 'finger')

Negatives of verbs derived with *-walh* can work as many negative adjectives do, where their meaning is that of the antonym, for example:

ni-n-ts'i7i-kfhe-**walh** 'I have small ears' (literally 'I don't have big ears') (*ni-* 'negative')

(23) =wa7ne

'together' ('united, joined') [JOINED]

This clitic seems to mean 'joined together.' This morpheme is probably related in some way to the relational noun *-w7ne* 'over, above.'

ja-nachaj=**wa7ne** [IACT-return=together] 'I fold it, package it, put it together, make it smaller, stack it' (cf. *ja-n-chaj* 'I return it')

ja-pôklen=**wa7ne** [IACT-not.keep.promise=together] 'I don't keep my word/my promise, I lie' (cf. *ja-pôklen* 'I lie, don't keep my promise')

ja-y-ay-elh=**wa7ne** [IACT-VBLZ-withdraw-PL.EXCL=together] 'we EXCL meet, meet together' (cf. *jay=7e* 'I leave, withdraw')

j-ôm-elh=**wa7ne** [IACT-arrive-PL.EXCL=together] 'we have sex, we copulate, we unite, we are together'

yi7=**wa7ne** [3ACT.be=together] 'it sticks, sticks together (e.g. clay, dough)'

ya-tk'a7=**wa7ne** 'I am joined, united with' ('I meet with, I join')

chi7-nachaj=**wa7ne** wat-pôkôt
NPERS-bring=together NPOS-fist
'oneforms a fist / clenches one's fists / grabs in one's hand'

(24) =watsham

'together, collective, in a group' [COL]

janachaj=**watsham** 'I fold it, roll it up' (cf. *janachaj* 'I return it' [lo devuelvo])
nayakchet=**watsham**=7in 'they are in a hurry' (cf. *nayakchet=7in* [nay-akchet'in] 'he/she is in a hurry, comes fast')
nika7aysiyu=**watsham**=7in 'they laugh, are agreeable together'
sht'aku7um=**watsham**=7in 'we are working (together)' (cf. *sht'aku7-um=7in* 'we work, we are working')
tklô7ôy=**watsham**=7in 'they play (together)' (cf. *tklô7ôy* 'he/she plays, dances')
tsi7sha7=**watsham**=7in 'they are naked' (cf. *kas-tsi7sha=sha7ne* 'we are naked')
yit'ôyin=**watsham**=7in 'they cry in mourning in a group, together' (cf. *yi-t'ôyin* 'he/she cries in mourning')
y-ô7ôlhjôn=**watsham**=7in na-pi7 tukus [3ACT-lie=COL=EMPH VIZ-PL.HUM soldier] 'the soldiers are lying'

Some examples with =*watsham* attached to adjectives are the following:

kas-7a7ôwt-es=**watsham**=7in 'we are sick' (cf. *kas-7a7ôwt-es* 'we suffer, we hurt, we are sick')
kas-suy=**watsham**=7in 'we are bad, angry/ aggressive' (cf. *kas-suy* 'we are bad, angry')
nijoway=**watsham**=7in 'they are afraid' (cf. *nijoway* 'fear' [miedo])

(25) -klôy

'appostional, suffer, abide'

Fabre (2016: 327) gives a suffix <-clôi> 'to suffer, withstand, endure.' It appears to be derived from or related to the verb 'to suffer', for example, *ja-klôy-it* [IACT-suffer-CAUS] ('I make him/her/it suffer, I punish him/her/it'). It takes the 'ligature' (*-ja-*) when attached to stems ending in a consonant, and no ligature following vowels. The examples here are from Seelwische (2016) and our own database.[13] From the glosses, its meaning appears not related so much to 'suffer, abide', as it conveys an opposite sense of the meaning of the root to which it is attached, that is, an 'appositional.' Examples are the following:

ts'apeklôy 'I am a glutton' (*ts'-ape-klôy* [IACT-be.full-*klôy*])
(cf. *ts'-ape7* 'I am full, satisfied') (cf. also Seelwische 2016: 11)

Other examples from Seelwische (2016) are the following:

<tsicachiĉlôi>'I have no compassion, I do not miss/long for' (cf. *-kachi7* 'belly, stomach')
<tsic'ôôvteĉlôi> 'I am gentle' (cf. *k'a7ôwte* 'trap'; <c'ôôvte> 'trap' in Seelwische 2016: 37).
<ts'etsjaĉlôi> 'I am able to drink a lot, I am a resistant drinker' (cf. *ts'-etsej* 'I am drunk')
<yimaĉĵaĉlôi>'it burns well, it is combustible' (cf. *yi-mak* 'it goes out, extinguishes [itself]')
<tsinutsjaĉlôi > 'I am peaceful, I have control over myself' (cf. *ja-nut* 'I am angry')
<tsivapenjaĉlôi> 'I am not ashamed, embarrassed' (cf. *ja-wapen* 'I am ashamed, embarrassed')
<tsiyalheĉlôi>'I can last a long time without breathing' (cf. *yalh* 'breath, air')

3. General Nature of Lexical Suffixes and of Nivaclé Suffixes

Here I turn to the general properties of Nivaclé lexical suffixes viewed from the perspective of the nature and behavior of lexical suffixes in the languages of the NWCLA.

3.1. Closed Class

The lexical suffixes constitute a closed class in both the NWCLA languages and in Nivaclé. The class is quite large in several NWCLA languages, with about 100 lexical suffixes in most Salishan languages, some with over 300; the class is smaller in Nivaclé, with twenty-five members, yet still with more members than most other closed classes in this language.

3.2. Functional Difference between Lexical Suffixes and Corresponding Roots

It is suggested that the NWCLA languages have independent root or stem that are counterparts in meaning to most of the lexical affixes, though in fact functions of these affixes can differ significantly from those of corresponding roots (Mithun 1999: 49). One difference is that the roots can stand alone as words, but lexical suffixes cannot—'the affixes are clearly distinct from roots . . . never constituting the bases of words alone' (Mithun 1997: 369). This is confirmed in Nivaclé, where almost none of the lexical suffixes or clitics presented here can ever stand alone as a word or lexical root.

3.3. Formal Difference between Lexical Suffixes and Corresponding Roots

Lexical suffixes typically differ in form (phonological shape) from corresponding independent words with which they share meaning. Gerdts (2003: 345) asserts that 'lexical suffixes usually bear little or no phonological similarity to freestanding nouns of similar meaning.' The following comparisons between the lexical suffixes and lexical roots with shared meanings confirm that Nivaclé is like the languages of the NWCLA in having lexical suffixes that differ in phonological form from corresponding independent words with which they share meaning.

-chat / -kat (*-ichat, -ikat*) 'a stand, grove, group of trees or plants of the same species, or an abundance of trees or plants of the same species in a particular place.'

Compare: *yi7klô7* 'tree, wood', *yita7* 'woods, forest'

-uk , **-yuk**, **-u7uk** 'plant suffix' [plant] (specifying individual trees or plants, individual stocks/stems of the plant identified in the word's root).

Compare: *tats-uk* 'stem, trunk', *tats-janja* 'trunk, log', *lha-w-nu* 'stem, stock' ([3POS-POSB-bone], literally 'its bone')

-ej, 'kind of fruit, edible plant'

Compare: *-a7* 'fruit' (*lh-a7* 'its fruit').

-fha(*-ja-fha)* 'companion'

Compare: *-kô7ya* 'companion, associate', *-ts'a* 'companion' (cf. *lha-ts'a-wot* [3POS-companion-PL] 'his/her companions')

-mat , **-ma7at** **-7mat** , **-i7mat** 'defective in, suffering from, damaged in, bad because of, have something undesirable'

Compare: *sas* 'bad, dirty, impossible', *-klôyit* 'suffer, make hurt', *pa7* 'deficient'

-matsej (*-ematsej*) 'good in, good because of, well-functioning in'

Compare: *is* 'good', *lhapa7* 'efficient', *-chen* 'function'

-mech, -me7ech 'expert, person who has power over something, has special knowledge of something, belongs to a profession concerning something, is a ritual specialist in something'

Compare: *nitôfha7kl-esh* 'he/she/it knows, knows how.' There are several terms for kinds of shamans, none similar in form to this suffix, however.

-nôk 'kind of fermented drink, kind of chicha, kind of consumable liquid'

Compare: *kumjô* 'chicha' (generic word), *-ô7ôt* 'drink' (cf. *lh-ô7ôt* 'his/her drink'), *-i7* 'liquid, juice, drink' (cf. *t'-i7* 'his/her/its liquid/juice/drink')

-shiy / **-jiy** 'concave, container'

Compare: *lhashiy* 'box, chest, coral' (possibly *lh-ashiy* 'its container'?)

-yinjat [masc], **-yinjate** [FEM] 'mourning kinship morpheme'

Compare: *t'ôyin* 'he/she/it mourns, cries for a deceased person'

-lha, -elha 'verbalization: removal, extraction, separation' [EXTRAC]

Compare: *-wenchat* 'to separate, divide', *-nklan* 'to remove, take out, take off'

-nuk , **-inuk** 'about the neck or mouth'

Compare: *-ashi* 'mouth', *-7wo7* 'neck', *-kôyish* 'throat, neck'

-pjalh 'verbalization of action involving binding'

Compare: *-kfha7* 'to tie, bind', *niyôk* 'string, rope, thread'

-taj, **-itaj** 'similar to, analogous to'

Compare: *-jo7* 'similar to, go ahead of, sleep inside', *-junash* 'similar to, equal to, like', *yi-7ya7ash* 'is similar to, resembles'

-walh 'verbalization [VBLZ]: 'to have large X'

Compare: *uj* 'big', *kaju7uj* 'of large size', *ma7yô* 'large, large-sized'

=kla7a'a little', 'in the manner of a child'

Compare: *tik'in* 'small, small child', *tuk'a* 'small (of stature)'

Since these forms do not match in any significant way any lexical roots (or other morphemes) in the language, it is not possible to derive them historically via grammaticalization from other known forms.

In a very few cases, there is formal similarity between what appears to be a lexical suffix or clitic and an identifiable lexical root. The cases are the following:

-klôy 'oppositional' (possibly also 'suffer, abide')

A precise meaning of this affix is difficult to determine. There are extremely few cases of it. My database (of 7,800 entries) contains only one example of it, Fabre (2016: 327) presents four possible examples, and Seelwische (2016) has seven possible examples. Fabre believes the suffix's meaning is 'to suffer, withstand, endure'; however, from the glosses of the potential examples its meaning appears not to relate to 'suffer, abide', but rather it appears to convey an opposite sense of the meaning of the root to which it is attached, that is, an 'oppositional.' It may possibly be derived from a verb root meaning 'to suffer'; see, for example, *ja-klôy-it* [1ACT-suffer-CAUS] 'I make him/her/it suffer, I punish him/her/it.'[14]

-shiy / -jiy 'concave, container'

Compare: *lhashiy* 'box, chest, coral' (possibly *lh-ashiy* 'its container')

=wa7ne 'together' ('united, joined') [joined]

This clitic seems to mean 'joined together.' This morpheme is probably related in some way to the relational noun *-w7ne* 'over, above.'

-wash, -Vwash , -wa7ash 'kind of wound, injury', 'print, track, impression', caused by or associated with the thing mentioned in the root.

Compare: *-wa7ash* 'print, track, trail, den/hole'

3.4. Meanings

While the lexical affixes can have fairly concrete meanings in languages of the NWCLA, they are nevertheless typically more general, abstract, and diffuse in their meaning than roots are (Mithun 1999: 54). The Salishan lexical suffixes can denote such things as 'body parts (hand, foot, heart, nose), basic physical/environmental concepts (earth, fire, water, wind, tree, rock), cultural items (canoe, net, house, clothing), and human/relational terms (people, spouse, child)' (Gerdts 2003: 346). Lexical suffixes with similar meanings are found also in numerous other NWCLA languages (Mithun 2015: 46–50).

The lexical suffixes of Nivaclé, though their semantic content is typically like that of full lexical items, are also in some cases quite abstract and diffuse in their meaning, making it difficult to pin down their meaning with precision. Still, in considering similarities between Nivaclé's lexical suffixes and those of NWCLA languages, we find several in Nivaclé whose meanings are similar to lexical suffixes found in languages of the NWCLA. For example, among the 100 or so lexical suffixes in Spokane, we find cases with the following meaning that are similar to meanings of several Nivaclé lexical suffixes: 'tree', 'fruit', 'plant', 'winter' (compared to Nivalcé's suffix for 'season'), 'nape' (also 'throat'), and 'child' (see the Nivaclé list earlier in the text). In Lushootseed, another Salishan language, we see lexical suffixes with the followings meanings that are similar to meanings of some of the Nivaclé lexical suffixes: 'enclosed area', 'people of', 'tree', 'odor', 'neck, throat', 'baby, child', 'nose', 'container', 'throat' (cf. Mithun 2015: 48–49).

With respect to the clitics that are like lexical suffixes, their meanings tend to be somewhat less abstract, less diffuse, and closer in meaning to what we expect of independent lexical items. Also, some of the clitics appear to be more recognizably similar in form to freestanding lexical items to which they correspond in meaning. For these cases, it is easier to speculate about a possible origin via grammaticalization from the matching independent lexical roots. (See the examples earlier in the text.)

3.5. Distribution of Lexical Suffixes

In several NWCLA languages, the lexical suffixes can attach to both noun stems and verb stems. Also, 'the suffixes themselves are not strictly categorical, sometimes adding more noun-like meaning, sometimes more verb-like meaning. The construction does not specify their semantic relationship to the root: sometimes they indicate a general kind of patient/goal/theme, often a location' (Mithun 2015: 48). This is also true in Nivaclé. Most of the Nivaclé lexical suffixes derive new nouns, but some produce new verbs (as seen in the examples presented earlier).

3.6. Meaning of Forms Bearing Lexical Suffixes

In Czaykowski's (1982: 1) description, 'lexical suffixes, although they are derivational affixes, do not affect the syntactic category of the root or stem to which they are attached; they function, instead, to change or augment its meaning' (Czaykowski 1982: 1). As she indicated for Columbian Salish (Moses), the meaning of a lexical item that bears a lexical suffix can be, mainly, '(1) merely the sum of the meanings of its component morphemes; (2) a semantic extension beyond the meaning of the component morphemes; and (3) a word with idiosyncratic meaning of its own not necessarily derived from the meaning of the conjunct elements' (Czaykowski 1982: 1). Nivaclé words with lexical suffixes exhibit the same range of meanings. Nivaclé has cases that illustrate each of these meaning relationships:

(1) Nivaclé has cases whose meaning is the sum of the meanings of its component morphemes, for example, *klesa-wash* 'knife wound', composed of *klesa* 'knife' and *-wash* 'kind of wound'.

(2) In some other cases, the meaning is the combination of the meaning of one component morpheme with semantic extension of another component morpheme, for example, *uti-y***uk** 'mountain' (cf. *utej* 'stone' + *-(y)uk* 'plant suffix, stock/stem of individual plants' (mostly trees), where *-(y)uk* appears to be extended in meaning beyond that of its principal meaning of 'plants, plant stocks.' Another example is *na7apk-unôk* 'salty spicy plant', based on *na7p'uk* 'salty, anything salty', and *-nôk* 'kind of fermented drink'; the meaning of this word appears to extend beyond the basic meaning of *-nôk* 'kind of fermented drink.'[15]

(3) In still other cases the meaning is idiosyncratic, not necessarily derived from the meaning of the conjunct elements, for example, *lhum7ôkji-nuk* 'east, east wind' appears to be composed of *lhum-* 'morning' (in combined forms, cf. *lhum7ashi* 'tomorrow, morning') + *7ôkji* 'below, under' + *-nuk* 'ethnonym suffix (ethnic group suffix)', with a meaning that does not reflect the meaning of these parts. Another example may be *fhinôk* 'tobacco, cigarrette',

apparently based on *fhin* 'to suck, to smoke' and *-nôk* 'kind of fermented drink.'

3.7. New Vocabulary Creation

Mithun (1999: 50) reports that lexical suffixes can serve as devices for building new vocabulary. This is true also in Nivaclé. For example, the very productive suffix *-taj* (*-itaj*) 'similar to, analogous to' is used very frequently in creating new vocabulary, especially items of acculturation, for example, *katis**itaj*** 'lantern, flashlight', from *kati7is* 'star' + *-itaj* 'similar to' (see Campbell and Grondona 2012; Campbell et al. 2020 for details).

3.8. Discourse Function of Lexical Suffixes

Mithun (1999: 51) reports that the lexical suffixes can also be used for discourse functions, serving to background established or incidental information. However, the lexical suffixes of Nivaclé do not fulfill discourse functions of this sort. They derive new words only. The lexical suffixes are not capable of standing in for specific arguments in the discourse, and no syntactic operation takes them into account in any way. For example, *tsi-fho-**walh*** 'I have big feet', composed of *tsi-* 'first person active' + *-fho* 'foot' + *-walh* 'to have big', never serves to background or track *fho* 'foot' in discourse; no syntactic operation takes the *fho* of this word as its target. Similarly, for example, *alhu**taj*** 'cayman, alligator', derived from *alhu* 'iguana' + *-taj* 'similar to' can never serve in any discourse function to background or track *alhu* 'iguana' since 'cayman/alligator' and 'iguana' are totally separate lexical items with distinct real-world referents, and *-taj* cannot stand on its own.

4. Nivaclé Lexical Suffixes in General Perspective

4.1. Compounding versus Lexical Suffixes

It is generally held that the combinations of root + lexical suffix show properties of compounds (Mithun 1999: 54). The boundary between compounding (conjoined lexical roots in compound words) and affixing may not always be clear in some languages. Therefore, the question could arise about whether some of the forms analyzed here as lexical suffixes in Nivaclé might not be more like the compounding and the word-formation processes that can give languages such as English such quasi-productive compounding elements as *auto-* (as in *auto-focus*, *autopilot*, *autodidactic*), *eco-* (as in *ecofriendly*, *ecotourism*, *eco-pirate*, *ecosphere*), *self-* (in *self-starting*, *self-cleaning*, *self-focusing*), and the like, which would not be considered grammatical affixes of the lexical affix sort, but rather as part of the word-formation processes available to English through compounding. Compounding is also observed in modern Salishan languages, in addition to their lexical affixes, though the degree of productivity of the compounding varies across the languages.

Nivaclé, too, has compounding, only mildly productive, in addition to these lexical affixes. However, Nivaclé's words with lexical suffixes are quite distinct from its compounds. The lexical suffixes usually do not match any lexical root in form (see earlier in the text), while the conjunct elements in the compounds are equivalent to independent lexical roots. The lexical suffixes cannot stand alone, but are known only in bound form; the conjunct elements of lexical compounds typically can stand alone as independent lexical items or roots. A few of the elements in Nivaclé analyzed here as lexical suffixes might have a certain compound-like feel to them if it were not for the fact that there is no clear lexical source from which to derive the lexical suffixes though there is for the conjuncts in the true compounds. The conjuncts in the compounds are scarcely found to recur in other combinations to form other words, while the lexical suffixes and clitics recur, attached to various roots/stems, some quite productive.

Nivaclé has compounds of several sorts, but they are unlike the cases with lexical suffixes or clitics. A few illustrative examples follow.

watwô7ôk lhawo7 'warrior' (cf. *wat-wô7ôk* 'war', *lhawo7* 'person')
k'utsjaklaya lhawank'ekleshjanja7wat 'Pleiades' (literally 'old woman's place for cleaning by sitting in the dirt and wiggling around

after defecating'; *k'uts-ja-klay-a* [old-LIG-AUG-FEM], *lha-wank'e-klesh-janja-7wat* [3POS-INTRSV-clean-FEMALE.AGENT-PLACE.OF])[16]

kati7is lhamimi 'morning star, venus' (cf. *kati7is* 'star', *lha-mimi* 'his/her/its mother') (literally 'mother's star')

klesa lhkô7klôy 'scissors' (cf. *klesa* 'knife', *lh-kô7klô-y* 'its shins, lower legs' [3POS-shin-PL]) (literally 'knife's legs')

kotsja7at lhawts'e7 'mushroom' (cf. *kotsja7at* 'earth, land, ground', *lha-w-ts'e7* 'its belly') (literally 'ground's belly')

kuwayu lhakô7ôs 'guitar' (cf. *kawayu* 'horse', *lha-kô7ôs* 'its tail') (literally 'horse's tail')

mákina lhôse 'pickup truck, van' (cf. *mákina* 'bus, truck', *lh-ôse* 'his/her/its daughter') (literally 'truck's daughter / bus' daughter')

t'un=t'ôj 'cockroach, animal with hard skin' (cf. *t'un* 'hard', *t'-ôj* 'its skin, hide, shell')

klesanilh kojiyaj 'gold' (cf. *klesanilh* 'metal', *kojiyaj* 'yellow')

ampa ka7 ni-tô7ye7esh 'computer' (literally 'there is nothing it doesn't know') (cf. *am=pa ka7 ni-tô7ye-7esh* [no.exist=REP IRR.CONJ 3NEG-know-VAL])

yifhin=ey=shi shtôkley 'vacuum cleaner' (literally 'it sucks rubbish'; cf. *yi-fhin=ey=shi shtôkley* [3ACT-suck=away=NSPEC.LOC rubbish])

yimpuntesh lhkli7ish 'bilingual' (cf. *yi-npunt-esh lh-kli7ish* [3ACT-two-VAL 3POS-language]; cf. *napu* 'two') (literally 'two are its language')

tsatakotsja7at 'I fall on the ground' (cf. *ts-at+kotsja7at* [1STAT-fall+ground]) (literally 'I ground-fall')

4.2. Lexical Suffixes versus Noun Incorporation

Gerdts (1998: 97), citing Carlson (1990), asserts that there is support for the notion that 'lexical suffixes can be regarded as incorporated nouns that have lost their status as freestanding nominals' (cited by Wojdak et al. 2003: 275). Noun-like lexical suffixes can share a number of properties with incorporated nouns (Gerdts 2003; Mithun 1999): they bear no distinctions of number, definiteness, or case; they do not represent grammatical arguments of the clause (Gerdts 2003: 345; Mithun 1999: 54–55), though opinion varies about to what extent lexical suffixes can alter argument structure (Gerdts 2003; Mithun 1999; Wojdak 2004).

Nevertheless, the lexical suffixes of Nivaclé seem much less like noun incorporation. Nivaclé has no morphosyntactic construction of noun incorporation, and even compounding, though it exists, is very rare. The lexical suffixes very rarely coincide in form or meaning directly with external nouns that could be said to be incorporated in verbs; lexical suffixes attached to verb roots (where noun incorporation might be suspected) are rare compared to the lexical suffixes attached to noun roots that function as nouns (where real noun incorporation cannot be suspected). There are extremely few compounds in which a noun is one of the conjuncts joined together with a verb root in a single word. The clearest examples are the following:

jemjaklesh 'I clean the cactus thorns off it' (< *j-emja-klesh* [IACT-fine.cactus.thorn-clean] (cf. *-emaj* 'fine cactus thorn' + *ja-kle7esh* 'I clean it'). Note that *-emja* is an expected allomorph of *-emaj* 'fine cactus thorn' in this environment; cf. *t-emj-as* [NPOS-fine.cactus.thorn-PL] 'thorns.' This is an isolated compound; *-emja* does is not compounded with any other verb (nor does any allomorph of *-emaj* occur in other compounds).

tsatakotsja7at 'I fall on the ground' (< *ts-at+kotsja7at* [ISTAT-fall+ground]).

tsiyalhp'o=7in 'I drown' (< *tsi-yalh-p'o=7in* [ISTAT-breath-cover/close=EMPH]; cf. *ja-p'o=7e* 'I cover it, bury it'; *-yalh* 'breath, air, respiration').

These examples are so few and idiosyncratic, and different in their formation, that it is not possible to think of a grammatical process of noun incorporation for Nivaclé.

Fleck (2006: 93) reaches the same result with respect to the lexical prefixes of Matses, that they are not cases of noun incorporation or compounding. He says,

> The point of arguing that these prefixes are not instances of synchronic noun incorporation or compounding is not just to indulge in squabbling over linguistic labels. Recognizing Matses prefixation as something different from noun incorporation allows us to study

more precisely what it can tell us about diachronic processes and grammaticalization.

4.3. Lexical Suffixes and Grammaticalization

So, what about grammaticalization? Grammaticalization is frequently invoked in discussions of lexical affixes. For example, Mithun (1999:55) says, 'The lexical affixes differ crucially from roots in showing exactly the effects of grammaticalization that we have come to expect of affixes: the generalizations and abstraction of meaning, and the erosion of form.' She explains,

> As we know from earlier attested forms in European languages as well as from comparative reconstruction of others, many modern grammatical morphemes underwent substantial grammaticization while still independent words, evolving slowly from roots designating concrete entities or actions, to grammatical particles, before ultimately fusing phonologically with their hosts to become affixes. The precursors of the Salishan lexical prefixes and suffixes, by contrast, appear to have followed a different path, first bonding phonologically with their hosts in compounds, at a time when they still retained their status as roots. Some functional changes would have occurred at that point, such as the loss of specific referentiality and case role. Others, however, such as the abstraction and extension of meaning, would have occurred only afterward, many over a considerable period of time. The origin in noun incorporation constructions explains well the vastness of the class of suffixes. Instead of each descending from a distinct grammatical pattern, the lexical suffixes would have evolved from a single general compounding pattern that originally involved a potentially large number of roots, an open class.
>
> (Mithun 1997: 369–70).[17]

So, could some of the 'lexical suffixes' in Nivaclé have originated in compounding of independent roots? That does not seem an obvious possibility to suspect here. Since for most of these lexical affixes there appears to be no identifiable lexical root that corresponds to the affix, there are no clear lexical sources that might have become compounded and then ultimately grammaticalized to result in these lexical suffixes, even allowing for later abstraction of meaning and the erosion of form.

However, if we were to assume grammaticalization is behind lexical suffixes, as many do—even though no source lexical items for the lexical suffixes can be identified—then lexical suffixes would have implications for views about grammaticalization in general, particularly for the explanatory value of grammaticalization.

It has been claimed that grammaticalization allows us to 'predict' and therefore to explain. It has been said that there are constraints on what can and cannot grammaticalize: not just any lexical item can grammaticalize with any grammatical meaning/function, and there are not as many grammatical meanings/functions available cross-linguistically as there are semantic meanings of lexical items, which could be drawn from for grammaticalizations if there were no constraints. For example, Heine (1993: 124) says of grammaticalization studies that they are 'not only a means of relating present language states to past situations, rather by proposing generalizations on past development they also allow us to **predict** future developments' [emphasis added, LC]. (See Campbell [2001] for discussion of other claims about the predictability and explanatory value of grammaticalization.) However, grammaticalizations that might give us lexical suffixes call this claim into question.

The emphasis placed on the recurrent grammaticalization channels as an approach to prediction and hence to explanation would seem overly optimistic and seems to fail to take into account the great number of very unusual and uncommon grammatical markers that arise through grammaticalizations and the many unusual and unexpected lexical sources that end up as grammatical affixes via grammaticalization that are encountered in languages from all around the world. It becomes a matter of where to place the emphasis: should we stress the recurrent cases at the expense of the many unexpected and unusual ones, or should we stress the unusual and unexpected cases, allowing this to divert attention away from the cases that recur frequently in languages in grammaticalizations? Perhaps the only acceptable answer is that we cannot afford to miss either the common or the unusual.

The main points are: (1) The existence of the 'exotic' grammaticalizations, such as those assumed to be behind some lexical affixes, calls into question any claims about strong predictability (and hence explanation) based essentially only on the 'common', recurrent cases. (2) The explanation for the 'constraints' on what lexical sources grammaticalize and what grammatical meanings/functions can be the outcomes of particular lexical sources will not be explained by looking merely inside grammaticalization theory alone, but will certainly require recourse to understanding of semantic change and grammatical typology in general. Thus, even if we can identify frequent pathways and targets of grammaticalization (and speak of them as involving constraints), they still provide no reliable predictability, nothing of the sort that would be needed to deal with many lexical suffixes as assumed products of grammaticalizations.

An important related question is, is it legitimate to speak of grammaticalization in the context of lexical affixes where there is no evidence that grammaticalization ever took place, where it is impossible to identify any plausible lexical sources that may have undergone grammaticalization to result in these lexical affixes? Sheer assumption that grammaticalization must be behind lexical affixes is neither evidence nor sufficient justification.

We must ask, why can a single lexical source develop in multiple directions, giving various different grammatical 'targets' as their outcomes, and at the same time, why can a single grammatical target (an outcome of grammaticalization) come about in different languages from various different lexical sources? As Heine et al. (1991: 38) say, 'It is by now well established . . . that one source concept can give rise to more than one grammatical category and that, conversely, a given grammatical category may be historically derived from more than one source concept or structure.' In short, since we have multiple lexical sources converging on a single grammatical target and a single lexical source giving multiple grammatical targets (results), claims for the predictive/explanatory power of grammaticalization are clearly exaggerated (see Campbell 2001). Greater understanding of lexical suffixes across languages will no doubt contribute to greater understanding of the potentials and limitations of grammaticalization.

Endnotes

1. The NWCLA languages share numerous similarities with respect to their lexical suffixes (see, e.g., in Mithun 2015), although some differences are also sometimes asserted. For example, it is said that Salishan lexical suffixes can sometimes be more concrete than those in the other languages typically are, more like incorporated nouns that have lost their status as free-standing nominals (cf. Gerdts 2003: 346; Wojdak et al. 2003: 275), whereas they may be less concrete in other languages. Wojdak (2003 and elsewhere), for example, analyzes the lexical suffixes of Nuu-cha-nulth (Nootka, a Wakashan language) as morphologically bound transitive predicates that incorporate their objects.

2. Specific examples for this paper are taken from the Nivaclé grammar by Campbell et al. (2020). Examples in this grammar are taken mostly from recorded texts but some from direct elicitation, and in some cases also from other published sources (as indicated here). The grammar and the data cited in this paper come from a large language documentation project (2003–2016) in Misión La Paz, Salta Province, Argentina. It involved many hours of audio and video recordings from more than twenty speakers, transcribed and translated by a team of trained native speakers with Lyle Campbell's help. In addition to the recordings, the project's results include the extensive grammar (Campbell et al. 2020) and a large lexical database (over 7,700 items), as well as booklets, recordings, and other materials for language conservation and education in the community. Part of this research was supported by a grant from the Endangered Languages Documentation Programme (Rausing Charitable Fund), (co-principal investigators Lyle Campbell, Verónica Grondona, and Filomena Sandalo), 'Description of Chorote,

Nivaclé and Kadiwéu: Three of least known and most endangered languages of the Chaco.'

3. Affixes and clitics play similar roles in Nivaclé grammar, distinct from lexical roots, and several clitics have the same kinds of content and behavior as the lexical suffixes do; therefore, the lexical suffixes and these clitics are considered together here. Lexical suffixes in some Salishan languages also appear in varied forms phonologically. The Nivaclé clitics differ from bound affixes in that the clitics can bear stress while at the same time the final syllable of the stems to which the clitics are attached also retains stress, not so with the bound suffixes, whose words bear only one primary stress. Some phonological processes take place across suffix boundaries but not across clitic boundaries; and many clitics can be attached to more than one grammatical category while affixes typically are restricted, being affixed to only one particular word class (part of speech).

4. Examples in this paper are cited in the practical orthography. Most of the orthographic symbols corresponds directly with the IPA symbols for the sounds, with the following exception:

ch	/tʃ/ or /č/	Voiceless alveopalatal (palato-alveolar) affricate
ch'	/tʃʼ/ or /čʼ/	Voiceless glottalized (ejective) alveopalatal (palato-alveolar) affricate
7	/ʔ/	Glottal stop
fh	/ɸ/	Voiceless bilabial fricative
sh	/ʃ/ or /š/	Voiceless alveopalatal (palato-alveolar) fricative
j	/x/	Voiceless velar fricative
kl	/k͡l/	Voiceless velar stop-voiced lateral approximant (no true IPA symbol exists for this segment)
lh	/l̥/	Voiceless lateral approximant
y	/j/	Voiced palatal glide
e	/ɛ/	Mid open front unrounded vowel
a	/a/	Low central unrounded vowel
ô	/ɑ/	Low back unrounded vowel

Note that <a> /a/ is not back but central, and it patterns with the non-back vowels in Nivaclé phonology, contrasting with back <ô> /ɑ/.

An affix boundary is signaled by a hyphen ('-'), a clitic boundary by an equal sign ('='). A morpheme-initial hyphen ('-') means that the morpheme must occur with some other morpheme before it, usually pronominal affixes before roots, or a root before suffixes.

The abbreviations used in this paper and what they stand for are the following:

3	third person
ABSTR	abstract, alienable
ACT	active
AUG	augmentative
CAUS	causative
COL	collective
CONJ	conjunction
EMPH	emphatic
EXCL	exclusive (first-person plural exclusive)
EXTRAC	extraction, removal, separation from
FEM	feminine, female
HUM	human
INTRSV	intransitivizer
IRR	irrealis
LIG	ligature, empty morph
NPOS	unpossessed, unspecified possessor
NSPEC	nonspecific (e.g., =*shi* NSPEC.LOC nonspecific locative, 'in', usually abbreviated LOC)
NWCLA	Northwest Coast Linguistic Area
PL	plural
POS	possessive
REP	reported, not known from firsthand experience but from what is reported or generally said to be
SIM	simulative, similar to
STAT	stative
VAL	valency-increasing
VBLZ	verbalizer, verbalization

6. These fermented drinks are called *aloja* in Spanish of this region, elsewhere called *chicha*.

7. Fabre (2016: 138) says it means 'atadura' (tie, binding), 'derivación con el significado de algo que se ata' (derivation with the meaning of something that is tied). From the examples, it might be imagined that perhaps several involve 'tying' in some way; however, 'tying' does not appear to be a necessary component of their meaning, where something to do with neck or mouth appears to be more central to the meaning.

8. There is apparently variation across dialects in the final vowel; Seelwische (2016: 103) has *ônjayep* 'época de floración del poroto del monte, verano' (season of the flowering of the wild bean, summer), and Gutiérrez (2015) has <ɑnxaji-p> (ônjayip) 'season when the scrubland bean blossoms (summer),' while Nivaclé in Misión La Paz it is *ônjayup*.

9. Seelwische (2016: 136) has <tisjuup> (*tisju7up* in our orthography), which is 'autumn, flowering of the coronillo/quebracho colorado'.

10. Seelwische (2016: 122) gives <shnôvôp> 'primavera, julio-septiembre' (Spring, July–September).

11. Seelwische (2016: 185) has <vat-pascheshi> 'ring' (in our orthography, *wat-pasche-shi*(*y*)).

12. We might speculate that *-taj* may originally have involved also the meaning of 'augmentative,' as the apparently cognate suffix *-taj* in Wichí does now, deriving augmentative forms but also used to derive new words (cf. Nercesian 2014: 196–98). However, there are numerous words in Nivaclé with *-taj* (*-itaj*) [SIM] that definitely do not have an 'augmentative' relationship to the stems they are attached to.

13. Again it does not appear that this form involves any detectable grammaticalization; it would be sheer speculation based on the barest reasoning to imagine that this *-walh* could somehow involve grammaticalization of *uj* 'big' (*u-* when attached in some forms) plus some suspected *-alh* ending, assumed perhaps to be exhibited also in the *-pjalh* 'binding' suffix, where again, there is no indication of what *pj-* could possibly come from, or what *-alh* might mean or be derived from.

14. The examples are the following. Their glosses illustrate how difficult it is to assign a specific meaning to this morpheme.

ts'apeklôy 'I am a glutton' (*ts'-ape-klôy* [IACT-be.full-*klôy*])
(cf. *ts'-ape7* 'I am full, satisfied') (from my database)

<tsicachiĉlôi> 'I have no compassion, I do not miss/long for' (cf. *-kachi7* 'belly, stomach')

<tsic'ôôvteĉlôi> 'I am gentle' (cf. *k'a7ôwte* 'trap'; <c'ôôvte> 'trap' in Seelwische 2016: 37).

<ts'etsjaĉlôi> 'I am able to drink a lot, I am a resistant drinker' (cf. *ts'-etsej* 'I am drunk')

<yimaĉĵaĉlôi> 'it burns well, it is combustible' (cf. *yi-mak* 'it goes out, extinguishes [itself]')

<tsinutsjaĉlôi> 'I am peaceful, I have control over myself' (cf. *ja-nut* 'I am angry')

<tsivapenjaĉlôi> 'I am not ashamed, embarrassed' (cf. *ja-wapen* 'I am ashamed, embarrassed')

<tsiyalheĉlôi> 'I can last a long time without breathing' (cf. *yalh* 'breath, air')

15. The form *na7apku-nôk* 'salty spicy plant' is underlyingly *//na7p'uk-Vnôk//*, which undergoes several phonological rules (processes) to reach its surface form, vowel epenthesis, vowel deletion, vowel assimilation, and deglottalization (see Campbell et al. 2020 for details).

16. This refers to the track/mark left in the dirt where after defecating, one sits in the dirt and wiggles to clean oneself. Cf. Seelwische (2016: 173)

17 Mithun's talk of grammaticization while the lexical affixes were still independent words, evolving from roots with concrete meanings to affixes attached to hosts, could lead us to wonder to what extent this might be interpreted to imply that the concrete 'lexical' meaning of these suffixes is because lexical roots were grammaticalized with much of their meaning intact. Mithun does not seem to be suggesting this directly. Fleck (2006: 94) argues explicitly against this:

> One might wonder if it is not possible for a free root to become a bound morpheme without changing meaning and function. Matses and Bella Coola suggest that this is not the case, but that there are fundamental differences between roots and affixes, and that these differences begin to appear as roots start to grammaticalize into affixes.

The lexical suffixes of Nivaclé are similar in that their meanings and functions are quite different from that of lexical roots.

References

Campbell, Lyle. 1997. *American Indian languages: The historical linguistics of Native America*. Oxford: Oxford University Press.

Campbell, Lyle. 2001. What's wrong with grammaticalization? In Lyle Campbell (Ed.), *Grammaticalization: A critical assessment*, Special issue of *Language Sciences*, 23: 113–61.

Campbell, Lyle, Luis Díaz, and Fernando Ángel. 2020. *Nivaclé grammar*. Salt Lake City: University of Utah Press

Campbell, Lyle, and Verónica Grondona. 2012. Linguistic acculturation in Nivaclé (Chulupí) and Chorote. *International Journal of American Linguistics*, 78: 335–67.

Carlson, Barry F. 1990. Compounding and lexical affixation in Spokane. *Anthropological Linguistics*, 32: 69–82.

Czaykowski, Ewa. 1982. An investigation of the lexical suffix in Columbian Salish. *Working Papers for the 17th International Conference on Salish and Neighboring Languages*. Portland, OR: Portland State University.

Fabre, Alain. 2016. *Gramática de la lengua nivacle*. Munich: LINCOM.

Fleck, David W. 2006. Body-part prefixes in Matses: Derivation or noun incorporation? *International Journal of American Linguistics*, 72: 59–96.

Gerdts, Donna B. 1998. *Incorporation*. Oxford: Blackwell.

Gerdts, Donna B. 2003. The morphosyntax of Halkomelem lexical suffixes. *International Journal of American Linguistics*, 69: 345–56.

Gerdts, Donna B., and Mercedes Hinkson. 1996. Salish lexical suffixes: A case of decategorialization. In Adele E. Goldberg (Ed.), *Conceptual structure, discourse, and language*, 163–76. Stanford, CA: CSLI.

Gutiérrez, Analía. 2015. *Segmental and prosodic complexity in Nivaĉle: laryngeals, laterals, and metathesis*. PhD dissertation, University of British Columbia.

Heine, Bernd. 1993. *Auxiliaries: Cognitive forces and grammaticalization*. Oxford: Oxford University Press.

Heine, Bernd, Ulrike Claudi, and Friederike Hünnemeyer. 1991. From cognition to grammar: Evidence from African languages. In Elizabeth Closs Traugott and Bernd Heine (Eds.), *Approaches to grammaticalization, vol. 1: Theoretical and methodological issues*, 149–88. Amsterdam: John Benjamins.

Mithun, Marianne. 1997. Lexical affixes and morphological typology. In Joan Bybee, John Haiman, and Sandra Thompson (Eds.), *Essays on language function and language type*, 357–71. Amsterdam: John Benjamins.

Mithun, Marianne. 1999. *The languages of native North America*. Cambridge: Cambridge University Press.

Mithun, Marianne. 2015. Morphological complexity and language contact in languages indigenous to North America. *Linguistic Discovery*, 13: 37–59.

Nercesian, Verónica. 2014. *Wichi Lhomtes: studio de la gramática y la interacción fonología-morfología-sintaxis-semántica*. Munich: LINCOM.

Pharris, Nicholas, and Sarah G. Thomason. 2005. Lexical transfer between Southern Interior Salish and Molalla-Sahaptian. *International Conference on Salish and Neighboring Languages*, 40: 184–209.

Seelwische, José. 2016. *Diccionario nivaclé: nivaclé-castellano* (3rd edition) (Biblioteca Paraguaya de Antropología, 94.) Asunción: Centro de Estudios Antropológicos de la Universidad Católica. (Comisión Lingüística Pueblo Nivaĉle (Napi T'acu'meshva'ne ca Nivaĉle Lhcliish). 2016. *Nuevo diccionario Nivaĉle-castellano José Seelwische O.M.I.* (3rd edition, revised and shortened). Online: http://www.nivacle-lhcliish.org/uploads/1/4/1/5/14157415/diccionario_nivacle_abreviado1.pdf.)

Thomason, Sarah G. 1996. Irregular velar developments in Montana Salish. *International Conference on Salish and Neighbouring Languages*, 31: 311–19.

Thomason, Sarah G. 1997. Plurals and transitivity in Montana Salish. *International Conference on Salish and Neighboring Languages*, 32: 352–62.

Thomason, Sarah G. 2000. Linguistic areas and language history. In Dicky Gilbers, John Nerbonne, and Jos Schaeken (Eds.), *Languages in Contact*, 311–27. Amsterdam: Rodopi.

Thomason, Sarah G. 2015. The Pacific Northwest linguistic area: Historical perspectives. In Claire Bowern and Bethwyn Evans (Eds.), *The Routledge handbook of historical linguistics*, , 726–36. Abingdon: Routledge.

Thomason, Sarah G. 2016. Irregular dorsal developments in Montana Salish. In Scott DeLancey and Mark W. Post (Eds.), *Language and culture in Northeast India and beyond: In honor of Robbins Burling*, 225–47. Canberra: Asia-Pacific Linguistics.

Thomason, Sarah G., Dorothy Berney, Gail Coelho, Jeffrey Micher, and Daniel Everett. 1994. Montana Salish root classes: Evidence from the 19th-century Jesuit dictionary. *International Conference on Salish and Neighboring Languages*, 29: 288–312.

Thomason, Sarah, and Daniel Everett. 1993. Transitivity in flathead. *International Conference on Salish and Neighboring Languages*, 28: 317–44.

Thomason, Lucy, and Sarah Thomason. 2004. Truncation in Montana Salish. In Marvin Dale Kinkade, Donna B. Gerdts, and Lisa Matthewson (Eds.), *Studies in Salish linguistics in honor of M. Dale Kinkade*, 354–376 (Occasional Papers in Linguistics, 17). Missoula: University of Montana.

Wojdak, Rachel. 2004. On the classification of Wakashan lexical suffixes. *Berkeley Linguistics Society*, 30: 139–50.

Wojdak, Rachel, J. C. Brown, and Michele Kalmar. 2003. Predicative lexical suffixes in Nuu-chah-nulth. *University of British Columbia Working Papers in Linguistics*, 11: 275–89.

CHAPTER 10

An Impersonal Construction in Jarawara?

Alan Vogel

1. Introduction

I welcome this opportunity to contribute to a volume honoring Sally Thomason. My main contact with Sally was while pursuing a PhD in linguistics at the University of Pittsburgh. I probably took more classes from her than from any other professor, and she was one of the heads of my dissertation committee, along with Alan Juffs. One of the qualities that I appreciated in Sally was her interest in the work of her students, including my own.

As Dixon (2004: 509ff.) discusses in his grammar of Jarawara,[1] the word *ihi/ehene*[2] has a dual function. In some contexts, it can be analyzed as an inalienably possessed noun like others in this class. But in other contexts, it marks a phrase as being an adjunct in the clause. The following two examples[3] from Dixon (2004: 509) show this contrast.[4] In example (1), which illustrates the first use, *ihi* can be glossed as 'result of'.

(1)	[me	ka	kanawaa	ifi	ihi]$_S$
	me	ka	kanawaa	ifi	ihi
	3PL	POSS	canoe.F	edge+F	result of+F

[watineke]$_V$	haaro
wata-ne-ke	haaro

be located-CONT+F-DECL+F that one+F
'There is the mark of the edge of their canoe [as it was dragged along the path, and it scraped against a tree].'

In contrast, in example (2), which illustrates the second use, the gloss 'because of' is more appropriate for *ehene*.

(2)	[okobi	ati	ehene]ADJU
	o-ka-abi	ati	ehene
	1SG.POSS-POSS-father.M	voice	because of+M

[fatara]O	[bore	ona]V
fatara	bore	o-na+F
garden.F	clear	1SG.S-AUX

'Because my father told me to, I cut down the forest for a new garden.'

In this paper, I discuss the analysis of examples like (3) below.

(3)	[[Isaki	ehene]?	[habo	nareka]V]$_{MC}$
	Isaki	ehene	habo	na-hare-ka
	Izac.M	because of (?)+M	bark	AUX-IP.E+M-DECL+M

'The dogs were barking because of Izac/there was barking because of Izac.'

At first glance, it looks like *ehene* in (3) should be glossed as 'because of', and that it should be analyzed as marking an adjunct. In this case, the verb would have some kind of impersonal meaning such as 'there was barking'.

As I show later, though, the phrase containing *ehene* in this example should be analyzed as the subject of the clause, and not as an adjunct, so there is no need for assigning a special impersonal meaning to the verb or postulating any kind of special syntax.

In section 2, this example is discussed in detail, along with other similar examples. First, though, in the following three sections, I give necessary introductory information on three topics of Jarawara syntax, narrowing the focus successively. In section 1.1, I give general information on word classes in Jarawara. In section 1.2, I focus on inalienably possessed nouns, and in section 1.3, I zero in on the subclass of just three words that *ihi/ehene* is a member of, which have two syntactic functions.

1.1. Jarawara Word Classes

Verbs are the most important word class in Jarawara; in fact, many sentences consist of just a verb, since there is agreement with the subject within the verb, and often with the object as well. There are transitive, intransitive, ditransitive, and copular verbs. Transitive and intransitive verbs are divided into two morphological classes, called inflecting and non-inflecting. Whereas inflecting verbs take prefixes and suffixes directly on the verb stem, for non-inflecting verbs these are located instead on an auxiliary, either *na* or *ha*, which occurs following the verb root.

The other major class is nouns, which may have masculine or feminine inherent gender. Inherent gender is not marked on the noun itself, but is detectable by agreement in the verb and within an NP.

There is a rather small subclass of nouns that are inalienably possessed. These do not have inherent gender, and many are marked with the gender of the possessor, either masculine or feminine.

In addition to verbs and nouns, there is also a very small class of adjectives. There are also conjunctions, pronominals, and several particles.

1.2. Inalienably Possessed Nouns

As the name suggests, most inalienably possessed nouns (hereafter PNs) refer to body parts or parts of objects. Whereas a relationship of possession between two inherent gender nouns is indicated by the particle *ka*, as in (4)–(6), this particle is not normally used when the possessed item is a PN, as in (7)–(9).[5]

(4)

[Botenawa	ka	kanawaa]$_{NP}$
Botenawa	ka	kanawaa
(man's name).M	POSS	canoe.F

'Botenawa's canoe'

(5)

[oko	yifo]$_{NP}$
o-ka	yifo
1SG.POSS-POSS	hammock.M

'my hammock'

(6)

[tee	ka	yobe]$_{NP}$
tee	ka	yobe
2PL	POSS	house.M

'your (PL) house'

(7)

[Maira	noki]$_{NP}$
Maira	noki
(woman's name).F	face+F

'Maira's face'

(8) [tiyehe]$_{NP}$
ti-yehe
2SG.POSS-hand
'your hand'

(9)

[otaa	ati]$_{NP}$
otaa	ati
1EX.POSS	voice

'our language'

As mentioned earlier, the form of a PN often shows agreement with the possessor. This is the case with *noki* in (7), which is feminine to agree with the possessor, who is a woman. If the possessor were a man, the form would be *noko*. In contrast, the PNs in the other two examples, *yehe* 'hand' and *ati* 'voice', do not have separate feminine and masculine forms. This can be seen, for example, in the fact that one would say *Botenawa ati* and *Maira ati* with the same form, *ati*, used for both a masculine and a feminine possessor. Whenever a PN has both a feminine and a masculine form, the two forms will be included with a slash between them, with the feminine form being followed by the masculine form. In this way, the word for 'face' will be referred to as *noki/noko*, whereas the word for 'voice' will be referred to as just *ati*, since it does not have separate feminine and masculine forms.

The PN *ati* 'voice', which can also mean 'language' or 'speech', is one of a number of PNs that do not refer to either a body part or a part of an object. Others include *tafe/tefe* 'food' and *tase/tesene* 'companion'. Some, such as *tamine* 'news about', can be quite abstract. In the next section, we consider three of the most abstract PNs, which also have an additional syntactic use that is not available to other PNs.

1.3. Three PNs That Are Also Postpositions

The PN that is the focus of this study, *ihi/ehene* 'result of', can also be used as a postposition, but it is not the only PN with this dual syntactic function. When *ihi/ehene* is used as a PN, one variation of the idea of 'result of' is 'wound', as in (10).

(10)	[[wati	eene]O	[kihematamonaka]V	nafi,	nafi]MC
	wati	ehene	kiha-himata-mona-ka	nafi	nafi
	arrow.M	result of+M	have-FP.N+M-REP+M-DECL+M	all	all

'He had arrow wounds all over him.'

Another variant of the meaning 'result of' is 'deed', as in (11).

(11)	[wakari	ehenemonaka]MC
	wakari	ehene-mona-ka
	Paumari.M	deed+M-REP+M-DECL+M

'They said it was a Paumari who did it.'

A third meaning variation is 'victim', as in (12).

(12) [[Bakoki]VOC [yama ihini]CC
Bakoki yama ihi-ni
(man's name).M monster.F victim of+F-1P.N+F

[ama tike]V]$_{MC}$
ama ti-ke
be 2SG.S-DECL+F

'Bakoki, you are the victim of a monster.'

In all these examples, *ihi/ehene* is a PN and is the head of an NP in each case. In (10), the NP *wati ene* is the O of the sentence. The sentence in (11) consists of an NP, with no verb. In (12), the NP *yama ihini* is the copular complement of the sentence.

But in other contexts, the phrase containing *ihi/ehene* is not an argument such as a subject or object, but is an adjunct. This is the case, for example, in (13) and (14).

(13) [[tiwakaraba ama tini,]V
ti-akara-haba ama ti-ni
2SG.S-be satiated-FUT+F SEC 2SG.S-BKG+F

[aba ehene]ADJU]$_{MC}$
aba ehene
fish.M because of+M

'You will be full because of the fish.'

(14) [[me ati ihi]ADJU
me ati ihi
3PL.POSS voice because of+F

[okomine oke]V]$_{MC}$
o-ka-ma-ne o-ke
1SG.S-go/come-back-CONT+F 1SG.S-DECL+F

'I have come because of what they said [i.e. they told me to come].'

Both of these sentences are intransitive, and the phrase containing *ihi/ehene* is not the subject, it is an adjunct with adverbial meaning, and *ihi/ehene* in contexts like these means 'because of'. Even though *ihi/ehene* has lexical meaning, it is also this word that marks the phrase as an adjunct, and this is the reason I have proposed that in this syntactic context, *ihi/ehene* is a postposition rather than a PN. Evidence for this analysis comes from other kinds of adjuncts that are marked with particles, especially *ya*, as in (15) and (16).[6]

(15)	[[maka]O	[owara	oke,]V	[hawi	yaa]ADJU]$_{\text{MC}}$
	maka	o-awa-hara	o-ke	hawi	yaa
	snake.F	1SG.S-see-IP.E+F	1SG.A-DECL+F	trail.F	ADJU

'I saw a snake on the trail.'

(16)	[[tomiko	ya]$_{\text{ADJU}}$	[onakakehabanake]V]$_{\text{MC}}$
	tomiko	ya	o-na-ka-kI-habana-ke
	Sunday.F	ADJU	1SG.A-CAUS-go/come-coming-FUT+F-DECL+F

'I will come to get it [the merchandise] on Sunday.'[7]

The idea is that just as *ya* marks the adjuncts in (15) and (16), *ihi/ehene* marks the adjuncts in (13) and (14).

It should be noted that, even though there is thus a different syntactic relation between the phrase with *ihi/ehene* and the rest of the clause, when *ihi/ehene* is a PN as opposed to a postposition, the argument associated with *ihi/ehene* in its immediate phrase is formally a possessor in both syntactic contexts. That is, in the phrase *aba ehene* in (13) above, *aba* is still the possessor of *ehene* just as *wati* is the possessor of *ehene* in (10), even though *aba ehene* in (14) is an adjunct, whereas *wati ene* in (10) is the O of the clause. This is in contrast with adjuncts that are marked with particles such as *ya*, in which there is no relation of possession involved. This is clear, for example, from the fact that for first and second person singular, the prefixes *o-* and *ti-* (without *ka*) are used with the postposition *ihi/ehene* just as they are with PNs in general. Compare, for example, the PN *tiyehe* in (8) with the adjunct *tiwehene* in (17).

(17)

[[tiwehene]ADJU	[maa	ohi
ti-ehene	maa	o-to-ha
2SG.POSS-because of	be tired	1SG.S-CH-AUX

onofara	oke]v]$_{MC}$
o-nofa-hara	o-ke
1SG.S-recently-IP.E+F	1SG.S-DECL+F

'I am always tired out because of you.'

In contrast, particles like *ya* attach to the forms *owa* and *tiwa* for first and second person, respectively, and these are not possessors, as in, for example, the adjunct *tiwa ni ya* in (18).

(18)

[[yama	hiyara]s	[kakeaboneke]v
yama	hiya-ra+F	ka-kI-habone-ke
thing.F	be bad-NEG	go/come-coming-INT+F-DECL+F

[tiwa	ni	yaa]ADJU]$_{MC}$
tiwa	ni	yaa
2SG	to	ADJU

'Bad things will come to you.'

The second PN that has this dual syntax is *tabiyo*, which means 'lack of' when used as a PN, as in (19).

(19)

[[Yasito	me	tabiyo]o
Yasito	me	tabiyo
(man's name).M	3PL.POSS	lack of

[owara	oke]v]$_{MC}$
o-awa-hara	o-ke
1SG.A-feel-IP.E+F	1SG.S-DECL+F

'I was wishing Yasito and the others were here with me [lit., I was feeling the lack of Yasito and the others].'

In this sentence, *tabiyo* is the head of the NP *Yasito me tabiyo*, which is the O.

But *tabiyo*, like *ihi/ehene*, can also be used to mark adjuncts, as is the case in (20). In this context, the meaning of *tabiyo* is something like 'wanting'.

(20) [[banee tabiyo]ADJU
banehe tabiyo
giant anteater.F wanting

[okamatibe]V]$_{MC}$
o-to-ka-mata-be
1SG.S-away-go/come-short time-IMMED+F
'I'm going out [hunting] for giant anteater.'

In this sentence, the verb is intransitive, and the phrase of which *tabiyo* is the head, that is, *banee tabiyo*, is not the subject, it is an adjunct.

The third word in this class is *namoni*, which means something like 'bringing a report of', as in (21).

(21) [[hiyama me namoni]ADJU [ee
hiyama me namoni ee
white-lipped peccary.M 3PL.POSS report 1IN.S

tokomaraba eke]V]$_{MC}$
to-ka-ma-ra-haba ee-ke
away-go/come-back-NEG-FUT+F 1IN.S-DECL+F
'Let's not go back to tell [the others] about the white-lipped peccaries.'

The phrase *hiyama me namoni* in this sentence is an adjunct, so *namoni* is a postposition and not a PN. In fact, there is no attested use of *namoni* as a PN. There are three reasons I have placed *namoni* in the same class as *ihi/ehene* and *tabiyo*. First, *namoni* has lexical meaning, unlike particles such as *ya* mentioned earlier. Second, the argument with which *namoni* is associated in its immediate phrase is its possessor, as is the always the case with *ihi/ehene* and *tabiyo*, but never with particles such as *ya*.

Third, like *tabiyo*, *namoni* participates in a construction that I described in Vogel (2015). In this construction, even though the phrase with *namoni* or *tabiyo* is structurally an adjunct, and the verb is intransitive, the verb agrees[8] with the adjunct as if it were the O of a transitive verb. The following examples illustrate this construction.

(22) [[namoni]ADJU [okomebanaka]v]$_{MC}$
namoni o-to-ka-ma-hibana-ka
report 1SG.S-away-go/come-back-FUT+M-DECL+M
'I'm going to take the report about it [the strange animal] back.'

(23) [[yomee tabiyo]ADJU
yomee tabiyo
wildcat.M lack of
[otaa yawebanoho]v]$_{PFC}$
otaa yawa-hiba-no-ho
1EX.S be upset-FUT+M-IP.N+M-DUP
'We were upset because of the wildcat.'[9]

In the text that (22) is from, the narrator had encountered an unknown creature in the forest, and he was saying he was going back to the village and would tell the others about it. The verb is intransitive with a first person singular subject, as indicated by the prefix *o*-, but the gender agreement in the verb is masculine, whereas agreement with a first person subject is always feminine. The verb is agreeing in gender with the (null) possessor of *namoni*, that is, the creature.

In the text that (23) is from, the narrator had found a young wildcat in the forest, and was keeping it as a pet. But the wildcat caught a cold and died, so the sentence expressed the fact that the narrator and his family were upset because the wildcat died. The phrase *yome tabiyo* is an adjunct, and the verb is intransitive. Again, gender agreement with a first person subject is always feminine, so the masculine agreement in the verb is agreement with the adjunct, which has a masculine possessor.

As I state in Vogel (2015), this construction is so far unattested with *ihi/ehene*, but if an example with *ihi/ehene* were found it would not be surprising. In any case, the construction provides evidence of *namoni* being in the same class with *tabiyo*.

To summarize, there are two PNs in Jarawara, *ihi/ehene* and *tabiyo*, that are also used to mark adjuncts, and in this use I analyze them as postpositions. There is also one other postposition, *namoni*.[10] There are other Jarawara morphemes that mark adjuncts, such as *ya*, but unlike the three postpositions, they do not have lexical content, and for this reason I analyze them as particles.[11] This situation seems similar to the situation of prepositions in English. Prepositions have puzzled syntacticians because they have characteristics of both lexical and functional heads. Furthermore, some linguists have proposed that a small minority of prepositions are exclusively functional, with no lexical content, most especially the preposition *of*, but also for some linguists, *to* (Littlefield 2005: 4). The big difference between Jarawara and English in this respect is that *ihi/ehene* and *tabiyo* can be used as PNs with only lexical and no functional meaning, as in (10)–(12), whereas English prepositions always have functional meaning.[12]

This classification of these three words differs in some respects from that of Dixon, who dedicates a chapter of his grammar (2004: ch. 22) to *ihi/ehene*. Noting the dual function of *ihi/ehene*, he for this reason calls it a "relational noun," following a use of this term in Meso-American linguistics (Dixon 2004: 509). He observes that "an NP whose final element is *ihi/ehene* can function as a core argument in a main clause"—as in examples (10)–(12) above—and that *ihi/ehene* can also "mark a type of peripheral NP"—as in (13)–(14) above. Noting that in the first use *ihi/ehene* behaves "just like a PN," he does however not analyze it as a PN, only conceding that this is probably its diachronic origin. Nor does he use the label postposition that I have used, instead regarding *ihi/ehene* as uniquely a relational noun in its dual function.[13]

Dixon (2004: 502ff.) does in fact call *tabiyo* and *namoni* postpositions. But he also uses this label for morphemes such as *ya*, which I have called particles. As discussed earlier, even though it is true that like the postpositions, *ya* (and other particles) do mark adjuncts, the same as the postpositions do, there are significant morphological and syntactic differences between the postpositions and particles like *ya*. The most obvious of these differences is that, as discussed earlier, in the case of the postpositions, the argument most immediately associated with the postposition within its phrase is its possessor, whereas this is not the case with particles such as *ya*.

All of Dixon's examples with *tabiyo* and *namoni* except for one are similar to (20) and (21) above. The exception is one of his examples (21.30) for *tabiyo*, that is, (24), which has a use of *tabiyo* like that in (19).

(24)	[Rosira]VOC	[titabiyo]O	[Tieko]A	[awaka]V]$_{MC}$
	Rosira	ti-tabiyo	Tieko	awa-ka
	Lucilia.F	2SG.POSS-absence	Diego.M	feel-DECL+M
	'Lucilia, Diego wants you [lit., feels your absence].'			

While noting (2004: 504) that *tabiyo* "is here behaving rather like a PN," he does not however classify *tabiyo* as a "relational noun" like *ihi/ehene*.

There is one other way besides those that have been mentioned, in which the postpositions are like PNs and unlike particles: adjuncts with postpositions can occur with a null category rather than an NP, whereas this is not the case with particles. The first word in (25), *ehene*, is an adjunct, and the postposition has a null possessor, that is, the dog.

(25)	[[ehene]ADJU	[Boroko]S	[ohi	nemari	ama]V]$_{MC}$
	ehene	Boroko	ohi	na-himari	ama
	because of+M	(man's name).M	cry	AUX-FP.E+M	SEC
	'Boroko cried because of it [the dog that died].'				

Similarly, the PN *ehene* in (26), which is the O of the clause, has a null possessor, that is, the hunter.

(26) [[ehene]o [tee kabamataho]v]$_{\text{MC}}$
ehene tee kaba-mata-ho
victim of+M 2PL.S eat-short time-IMP+M
'Eat what he killed.'

In contrast, particles like *ya* cannot occur by themselves. In (16) above, for example, the adjunct *tomiko ya* 'on Sunday' cannot be substituted by just *ya*. So even though both postpositions and particles mark adjuncts, only postpositions can occur with a null category, and in this they are like PNs.

Kulina, another language of the Arawá family, has a word that is cognate with Jarawara *ihi/ehene*, that is, *hini*, which has a phonological alternate *hine*. In his recent grammar of Kulina, Dienst (2014) uses the postposition label for *hini*. In Kulina, while there are uses of *hini* parallel to those in (13) and (14) above, there apparently are not uses like those in (10)–(12). So Dienst is undoubtedly justified in not calling *hini* an inalienably possessed noun, although like Jarawara, Kulina does have a class of these.

In the next section, I introduce the data, which is the main focus of this study.

2. Data and Analysis

After many years of researching Jarawara, I noticed that there seemed to be something strange about the syntax and semantics of some sentences with *ihi/ehene*, like (27), the example cited earlier in the introduction.

(27) [[Isaki ehene]? [habo nareka]v]$_{\text{MC}}$
Isaki ehene habo na-hare-ka
Izac.M because of (?)+M bark AUX-IP.E+M-DECL+M
'The dogs were barking because of Izac/there was barking because of Izac.'

In the story that (27) is from, the narrator heard the dogs barking when Izac arrived in the village. The phrase *Isaki ehene* appears to be an adjunct meaning 'because of Izac," but in that case the syntax of the verb is puzzling. The verb has masculine gender agreement, indicating that it has a third person singular masculine subject. But there is no dog mentioned in the text at all, and in any case, it was not a single dog that barked. I hypothesized that possibly the sentence meant "there was barking because of Izac," and that the verb had some special impersonal syntax.

However, by comparison with other similar examples, it became apparent that the phrase *Isaki ehene* in (27) is not an adjunct, it is the subject of the sentence. This is why there is masculine agreement in the verb, and it is why there is no pluralizer *me* in the clause, which would have been expected if the subject were a group of dogs.

Another example that provides some insight is (28).

(28)	[[hinaka	toni	me	ihi]?	[ee
	hinaka	toni	me	ihi	ee
	3SG.POSS	familiar spirit.M	3PL.POSS	because of (?)+F	yell

kanemetemoneke]v]$_{MC}$
ka-na-hemete-mone-ke
COMIT-AUX-FP.N+F-REP+F-DECL+F

'There was crying out because of his familiar spirits.'

For a long time I thought that this sentence meant that a woman was crying out, and this understanding is in fact reflected both in the free translation in Dixon's (2004: 512) grammar, and in the online version of the text (Vogel 2012) that I published on the internet in 2012.[14] But it was not a woman who was crying out. The story is about two men, Aba Tosi and Mano Boni. Aba Tosi sent his familiar spirits after Mano Boni, and they encountered him in the forest. At that point Mano Boni cried out, and came back to his village. His wife, who was at their home, asks him why he was yelling. This doesn't make sense if she was the one yelling. Also, he answers, "Something scared me, and that's why I've come home." So his wife wasn't even with him in the forest. The sentence refers to Mano Boni crying out, but the gender agreement in the verb is not masculine, it is feminine. This is because the subject of the sentence is *hinaka toni me ihi*, which is a feminine NP. The word *toni* itself is masculine, but the pluralizer *me* makes the NP feminine, as is seen by the fact that *ihi* is feminine.

A couple more examples will make the phenomenon clearer.

(29)

[[[yomee	ehene]s	[kayawa
yomee	ehene	ka-yawa
jaguar.M	because of (?)+M	COMIT-be excited

nakani]v]$_{\text{INDQ}}$	[ona]v]$_{\text{MED}}$
na+M-kani	ati o-na+F
AUX-CNTRFACT	say 1SG.A-AUX

'The monkeys were excited and I thought it was because of a jaguar.'

(30)

[tokome]MED	[[eene]s	[hora	ne]$_{\text{V}}$]$_{\text{MED}}$
to-ka-ma+M	ehene	hora	na+M
away-go/come-back	because of (?)+M	exclaim	AUX

'He went home. The people were exclaiming because of him.'

There are two clauses in (29), the second clause being the matrix clause meaning 'I think', and the first clause being formally an indirect quote stating what the narrator thought. The verb of the subordinate clause, which is intransitive, has masculine gender agreement, to agree with the subject, that is, *yome ehene*. But the verb refers to the monkeys being excited, and the monkeys are nowhere in the sentence, structurally speaking.

Subordination is not involved in (30), which consists of two medial clauses, which are followed by a main clause in the text which is not in the example. Both verbs, and also *eene*, are masculine to agree with the man in the story, who was arriving back to the village with game. *Eene* is the subject of the second clause. But the ones who were exclaiming were the people in the village, not the man. The sentence means there was exclaiming because of the man who was arriving back.

In the following example, the status of the phrase with *ihi/ehene* as subject is especially clear.

(31)	[[me	ihi]s	[banabani	mati]v]$_{PFC}$
	me	ihi	bana-haba-ni	mati
	3PL.POSS	because of (?)+F	move away-FUT+F-1P.N+F	3PL.POSS

'The people moved away because of them.'

The situation referred to in this clause is that two men of the village saw signs of other Indians in the forest, and when they came back to the village and told the others, the people of the village were afraid and decided to move away. The clause is a postposed finite clause, with the main clause it is attached to in the original text not included in the example. The *mati* at the end is a kind of agreement, which I call possessor agreement (Vogel 2009).[15] In this kind of agreement, the pronominal can agree with the possessor of a subject or an object, but not the possessor in an adjunct.[16] So *me ihi*, which is what *mati* is agreeing with, cannot be an adjunct. As in the previous examples, the phrase with *ihi/ehene*, in this case *me ihi*, is the subject of the intransitive verb. But the verb is singular, as seen by the fact that there is no *me* immediately preceding it, whereas it actually refers to a group of people. The verb is singular because the subject, *me ihi*, is singular. The reason *me ihi* is singular in spite of the possessor being plural is that the head of the NP is *ihi*, and structurally an NP with a PN as its head is always singular. In any case, both *me* and *mati* syntactically reference the two men, not the group that moved, whereas the clause as a whole refers in the story to the group that moved.

At first glance, these examples might suggest an impersonal construction analysis. That is, the construction would be used to communicate "there was verb-ing because of x," with the identity of who was verb-ing left unspecified. This formula certainly fits all the examples given so far. The free translation I gave for (28), in fact, follows this formula exactly.

2.1. Impersonal?

In the examples we have seen so far, the phrase with *ihi/ehene* has always been the subject of an intransitive verb. This is usually the case, but it is not necessary. In (32), for example, the phrase with *ihi/ehene*, that is, *oko hawa ii*, is the O of the transitive verb *fora ona.*

(32)

[[[oko	hawa	ii]$_{O}$	[fora
o-ka	hawa	ihi	fora
1SG.POSS-POSS	palm. sp.F	result of+F	shoot with blowgun

ona]v]$_{O(RC)}$	[kaa	kane	awa?]v]$_{MC}$
o-na+F	kaa	ka-na+M	awa
1SG.A-AUX	chop	COMIT-AUX	seem+M

'Did he cut down the *hawa* palm where I shoot toucans?'

Let's unpack the syntax of this sentence. The main clause verb is *ka kane awa*, and the rest of the sentence preceding it, that is, *oko hawa ii fora ona*, is an internally headed relative clause that is the O of the main clause verb. The relative clause also is transitive, and as already mentioned, the phrase *oko hawa ii* is the O of the relative clause. This phrase actually refers to toucans, even though toucans are not mentioned. It was toucans that the *hawa* palm's fruit was attracting, and which the man was hunting. This mismatch between the syntax and the reference is what makes this example similar to the intransitive examples listed earlier. It is in fact the same phenomenon. The meaning 'because of' is in the situation in that the toucans were there because of the *hawa* palm fruits, but it is difficult to put 'because of' in the translation. I have used the gloss 'result of' because the NP *oko hawa ii* can be taken to mean 'the one or ones affected by my *hawa* palm', referring to the toucans. They were affected by the *hawa* palm because they were attracted by its fruits. The meaning 'the one(s) affected by x', where x is the possessor of *ihi/ehene*, is very close to the meaning 'victim of' illustrated in (12) above, which is one of the variants of the 'result of' meaning of *ihi/ehene.*

With this idea in mind, we can go back to the intransitive examples. For (27), instead of saying "there was barking because of Izac," we can use the interpretation, "the one or ones affected by Izac was/were barking." They were affected because his presence made them bark. In this case, the gloss 'result of' can be used for this sentence instead of 'because of', the idea being that 'one or ones affected by' is a variation of 'result of'. This is a satisfactory result, because as noted in section 1.2, the gloss 'result of' is used when *ihi/ehene* is a PN, while the gloss 'because of' is normally reserved for when *ihi/ehene* is a postposition.

When this change in point of view on *ihi/ehene* is considered, it no longer seems necessary to analyze this as an impersonal construction. It is not necessary to view the verbs in the intransitive clauses in (27)–(31) as communicating 'there was verb-ing', because the subject in each case can be seen as 'the one or ones affected by x', where x is the possessor of *ihi/ehene*. To the extent that the identity of the referent of the phrase 'the one or ones affected by x' is not grammatically present, including whether it is singular or plural, the construction may be considered impersonal, but it is not the verb that is impersonal, but the phrase with *ihi/ehene*. But this is just part of the semantics of *ihi/ehene*, and it is not restricted to just these kinds of examples.

However, it does not appear that it is the speakers' intention to hide the identity of the referent of the phrase with *ihi/ehene*, because in the communication context the hearers seem to know the identity of the referent of this phrase in each case. The hearers know that it was dogs that were barking in (27); they know that it was Mano Boni that cried out in (28); they know that it was monkeys that were excited in (29); they know that it was the people in the village who were exclaiming about the man who arrived back from hunting in (30); and they know that it was the people of the village that moved away in (31). It appears that this is partly due to the predictability of the nature of the subject in at least some cases, since, for example, it is dogs that bark and monkeys that get excited. And for the transitive context in (32), the Jarawaras know that the ones that they shoot with blowguns at *hawa* palms are toucans.

At the same time, it must be admitted that there is a lot about the identity of the referent of the phrase with *ihi/ehene* that is unspecified. In each case, the phrase could refer to a single person or animal, or a group; and if an individual, either male or female. Probably one of the reasons that it took me so long to figure out that (28) was about Mano Boni, even though I went over the text a number of times with Jarawara speakers, is that it refers to a single person, whereas apparently it is more common for these kinds of phrases with *ihi/ehene* to refer to groups of people or animals.

In the next section, I present a couple additional syntactic contexts in which these kinds of phrases with *ihi/ehene* occur.

2.2. Additional Data

In the examples we have seen so far, *ihi/ehene* has always been the head of the NP it is located in. But there are other cases in which the same phenomenon with *ihi/ehene* occurs, but without *ihi/ehene* being the final head of the NP. In (33), for example, the subject NP of the main verb *kama* is a complement clause with a non-finite verb as its head, that is, *ehene ohi ni*. *Ehene* in turn is the subject of the non-finite verb.

(33)	[[[ehene]s	[ohi	ni]v]s	[kama]v]MC
	ehene	ohi	na.NFIN	ka-ma.CONT+M
	result of+M	cry	AUX	go/come-back

'They are coming crying because of him.'

In the text that (33) is from, one man had put a spell on another man, which had killed him in the forest, and the brothers of the man who had died were coming back to the village carrying their dead brother. The sentence expresses the fact that they were crying because of their dead brother as they were coming back to the village. The matrix verb *kama* is masculine to agree with *ehene*, but it actually refers to a group of men, which normally (i.e., if *ihi/ehene* were not present) would produce feminine agreement because the subject would contain *me*. That is, it would be *me ohi ni kamine* 'they are coming crying'.

Example (34) is similar. In the text that it is from, a group of women headed off a herd of white-lipped peccaries so that they turned around and came back toward the waiting hunters. The sentence expresses the fact that the women were successful, that is, because of them the peccaries came toward the hunters as intended.

(34)	[[[me	fanawi	ihi]s	[kana	ni]$_{V}$]$_{S}$
	me	fanawi	ihi	kana	na.NFIN
	3PL	woman.F	result of+F	run	AUX

[taminemetemone	amake]v]$_{MC}$
tamina-hemete-mone	ama-ke
be good-FP.N+F-REP+F	SEC-DECL+F

'They came running just right because of the women.'

Again, if the sentence expressed the meaning in the normal way without the phrase containing *ihi*, it would be *me kana ni taminemetemone amake* 'they came running just right', where *me* references the peccaries. The *me* in (34) does not express the plurality of peccaries, but the plurality of the women.

An example was given in the previous section of a phrase with *ihi* as the O of a clause. This can also occur when the phrase is a complement clause with a non-finite verb as head, as in (35).

(35)	[me	kamakira]MED	[[[me	ihi]s
	me	ka-makI-ra+F	me	ihi
	3PL.S	go/come-following-NEG	3PL.POSS	result of+F

[afo	ni]$_{V}$]$_{O}$	[otaa	nofamaramaro
afo	na.NFIN	otaa	nofa-ma-ra-hamaro
blow snuff into	AUX	IEX.A	want-back-NEG-FP.E+F

otake]V	fahi	waha]MC
otaa-ke	fahi	waha
IEX.S-DECL+F	then	now

'Because they didn't come, we didn't want to be trained by them as shamans anymore.'

In the context of the story, the boys of the village were going to be initiated as shamans, and the people of the village called an old shaman from another village to come and do the initiating. But the old shaman (and the others with him) did not come. So then the boys didn't want to be initiated as shamans anymore. The sentence literally means 'we didn't want people to be initiated as shamans', but in the context it actually means they didn't want themselves to be initiated. The phrase *me ihi afo ni* is the O of the main clause verb, and the clause *me kamakira* 'they didn't come' preceding it is a medial clause giving the setting for the main clause. The non-finite verb *afo ni* is from a transitive verb meaning literally 'blow snuff into', which is a part of what is involved in training shamans, but in this context the transitive verb has been detransitivized, and so means 'have snuff blown into'.

Instead of a non-finite verb, it is also possible to have another PN as the head of the subject NP, as in (36). The situation expressed in the text that (36) is from is much the same as that in (33) above: a group of people were crying as they came to the village carrying a dead person.

(36)	[[ehene	ati]S	[kama]$_V$]$_{MC}$
	ehene	ati	ka-ma.CONT+M
	result of+M	voice	go/come-back

'The ones who are coming because of him are crying.'

The subject of the intransitive verb is *ehene ati*, and *ati*, the head of the subject, is a PN. The PN functions much like the non-finite verbs in (33)–(34) above. The PN literally is 'voice', but it refers to crying. Again, whereas *kama* is masculine because of *ehene*, the verb actually refers not to a singular man but to a group of people, and so without *ehene* the normal way of expressing the meaning would be *me ati kamine* 'they are coming crying'.

In a final section, I consider whether an expression that means 'kill' which is formed by the combination of *ihi/ehene* with a verb that has the form *iti*, might be considered to be a further example of the phenomenon I have been describing.

2.3. *Ihi/ehene* with *iti*

There is an intransitive expression for 'kill' in Jarawara, which, since it cannot have a syntactic object, really means 'kill someone or something'. The following examples show that it can refer to killing people (37) or killing animals (38).

(37)	[faya	[me	ihi]s	[itiemetemone
	faya	me	ihi	iti-hemete-mone
	SO	3PL.POSS	victim of+F	?-FP.N+F-REP+F

	amake]v	fahi]MC
	ama-ke	fahi
	SEC-DECL+F	then

'Then they killed people.'

(38)	[[tee	ka	yibote	me	ihi]s	[itihara]v]MC
	tee	ka	yibote	me	ihi	iti-hara
	2PL	POSS	husband.M	3PL.POSS	victim of+F	?-IP.E+F

'Your husbands have gotten fish.'

The expression itself does not specify what is killed, nor does it specify the number of what is killed.[17] In these two examples, the number of victims in the situations referred to in the texts was plural, but the following example (39) refers to a situation in which just one person had been killed. In the story, a boy that had turned into an eagle had killed a man.

(39) [[eene]s [iti amane]v]$_{MC}$
ehene iti+M ama-ne
victim of+M ? SEC-BKG+M
'It killed someone.'

It is just a coincidence that one person was killed in (39) and the agreement is singular, while there were a plural number of victims in (37) and (38) and the phrase with *ihi/ehene* contains the pluralizer *me*. In each case, the number in the phrase containing *ihi/ehene* refers to the number of killers, not the number of victims. This becomes clear when (39) is compared to the next example (40). The sentence to focus on is the second sentence, but the preceding sentence in the text is included for context.

(40) [[me aabemetemoneke]v [ehene,]ADJU yati.]MC
me ahaba-hemete-mone-ke ehene yati
3PL.S die-FP.N+F-REP+F-DECL+F because of+M Apurinã.M

[[ehene iti]s(RC) [winarematamonaka]v]$_{MC}$
ehene iti+M wina-ra-himata-mona-ka
victim of+M ? live-NEG-FP.N+M-REP+M-DECL+M
'The people died because of him, the Apurinã. He had killed people, so he didn't live there anymore.'

The second sentence says that the man had killed people, but the sentence has singular agreement throughout. In the first sentence, we learn that it was a plural number of people that died.

We can thus see first of all that the expression is impersonal in the same sense as the phrases discussed in the preceding sections, since the number of victims is not syntactically specified. Also, although in the present expression the meaning of *ihi/ehene* is always specifically 'victim', this is a variant of the 'result of' meaning discussed earlier when *ihi/ehene* is a PN. The 'victim' meaning of *ihi/ehene* can occur in contexts in which the verb *iti* is not present, as discussed earlier in conjunction with example (12), and as is also shown in (41).

(41)

[[me	ihi]O	[ee	kabi	nofara]V]$_{MED}$
me	ihi	ee	kaba	nofa-ra+F
3PL.POSS	victim of+F	1IN.A	eat	recently-NEG

'They don't kill anything for us to eat [lit., we don't eat what they kill].'

Dixon (2004: 515) calls the expression with *ihi/ehene* and *iti* an idiom, and he says that *iti* is an intransitive verb that apparently is only used in this idiom. There are a number of verbs in Jarawara of the form *iti*, but it does seem that *iti* when it is used with *ihi/ehene* in this way cannot be identified with any of these other verbs.

However, I don't think it is correct to give the gloss 'killing' to *iti* and 'due to' for *ihi/ehene* in these kinds of contexts, as Dixon (2004: 515) does. I believe I have shown in the preceding discussion that the 'killing' meaning in these contexts is derived entirely from the fact that *ihi/ehene* means 'victim', and that the verb *iti* just means something like 'exist'.

Besides the examples of *ihi/ehene iti* already given, there are other syntactic contexts for this expression that exactly parallel the contexts given in the other sections earlier. The following example consists of two clauses, the first being juxtaposed to the second, which is the main clause, and that is the reason for 'but' in the free translation.

(42)

[[[abi	ehene]S	[iti]V]$_S$	[tamateno]V]$_{JUXT}$
abi	ehene	iti.NFIN	tama-tee-hino
2SG.POSS.father.M	victim of+M	exist	be many-HAB-IP.N+M

[[abi]O	[otaa	nakomekare]V]$_{MC}$
abi	otaa	na-komeha-ka-re
2SG.POSS.father.M	1EX.A	CAUS-be fearsome-DECL-NEG+F

'It may be that many people were killed by your father, but we aren't afraid of your father.'

The juxtaposed clause, that is, *abi ehene iti tamateno*, in turn, consists of the complement clause *abi ehene iti* followed by its matrix verb, *tamateno*, of which the complement clause is the subject. Focusing on just the juxtaposed complex clause, this parallels very closely the examples with complement clauses given earlier, that is, (33) and (34). The matrix verb *tamateno* is masculine and singular to agree with *abi* 'your father', but in the context of the story it refers to many people being killed, which if represented grammatically would be feminine and would require the pronominal *me*.

The O of the following sentence consists of a relative clause containing *ihi/ehene iti*, similarly to (32) above. There is one syntactic difference between this example and (32), and that is that the relative clause here is intransitive, while the relative clause in (32) is transitive. Otherwise the sentences are similar.

(43)	[[[banee	ii]$_S$	[itiha]v]$_{RC}$	[me	naabowa
	banehe	ihi	iti+F	me	na-aboha.LIST
	giant anteater.F	victim of+F	exist	3PL.A	CAUS-die

nemetemoneni]v]$_{MC}$
na-hemete-mone-ni
AUX-FPN.+F-REP+F-BKG+F

'They also killed the giant anteater which had killed someone.'

Just as the toucans are referenced by *ihi* in (32), the person or persons that were killed by the anteater are referenced by *ihi* in (43). In both sentences, it is the possessor of *ihi* which is the O of the main clause verb.

My conclusion regarding *ihi/ehene iti* is that there is no need to consider it an idiom, since it can be seen as having the same syntax and semantics of other phrases with *ihi/ehene*.

2.4. Summary

Starting with the idea that *ihi/ehene* can be used as an inalienably possessed noun or as a postposition, I have examined examples in which it may appear that *ihi/ehene* is used as a postposition, marking adjuncts, suggesting some kind of impersonal analysis. But when *ihi/ehene* is analyzed instead as a possessed noun in these examples, the impersonal nature of the subject or object is a natural semantic consequence, requiring no special syntax. I have also applied this analysis to the expression *ihi/ehene iti* 'kill', the meaning of which can be seen as flowing naturally from the syntax.

Endnotes

1. Jarawara is a dialect of what has been called Madi (along with Jamamadi and Banawá), a language of the Arawá family of southwestern Amazonia. I want to express my gratitude for suggestions by R. M. W. Dixon, Stefan Dienst, Robert Dooley, David Eberhard, and Mark Sicoli, without implying their agreement with any specific analysis presented.

2. The form *ihi* shows feminine agreement, and the form *ehene* shows masculine agreement.

3. In the interlinear examples, the first line is orthographic (except that long vowels are represented by double vowels, whereas in the orthography they are not distinguished from monomoraic vowels), the second line has underlying forms, the third line has glosses, and the fourth line is a free translation. (The labels for grammatical categories that are realized by vowel alternations on verb stems are on the second rather than the third line, i.e., NFIN, NOM, LIST, and the marking of feminine and masculine agreement on verb stems.) Most of the examples are from my own fieldwork (from recorded texts or spontaneous sentences heard in conversations and written down), but some are from R. M. W. Dixon's fieldwork, which he graciously has given permission to use. In this paper, all of the examples are unelicited.

By using brackets and labels, I have tried to give the reader an idea of the syntactic structure of the examples. I follow Dixon (2004) in labeling transitive subject as A and intransitive subject as S.

Abbreviations used are the following: 1 = first person, 2 = second person, 3 = third person, A = transitive subject, ADJU = adjunct, AUX = auxiliary, BKG = backgrounding mood morpheme, CAUS = causative, CC = copular complement, CH = change of state, CNTRFACT = counterfactual, COMIT = comitative, CONT = continuative, DECL = declarative, DUP = reduplication, E = eyewitness, EX = exclusive, F = feminine inherent gender, +F = feminine agreement, FP = far past, FUT = future, HAB = habitual, IMMED = immediate, IMP = imperative, IN = inclusive, INDQ = indirect quote, INT = intentive, IP = immediate past, JUXT = juxtaposed clause, LIST = list construction, M = masculine inherent gender, +M = masculine agreement, MC = main clause, MED = medial clause, N = non-eyewitness, NEG = negative, NFIN = non-finite, NOM = nominalized clause, NP = noun phrase, O = object, OC = O-construction marker, PFC = postposed finite clause, PL = plural, POSS = possessor/possessor marker, RC = relative clause, REP = reported, RP = recent past, S = intransitive subject, SEC = secondary verb, SG = singular, SP = species, V = verb, VOC = vocative.

4. The examples correspond to Dixon's (22.3) and (22.1), respectively. I use my own notation, glosses, and analyses when citing Dixon's examples.

5. There are a few PNs that use *oko* and *tika* for first and second person singular possessors rather than just the prefixes *o-* and *ti-*, for example, *oko nafi* 'all of me' rather than **onafi*. Also, kinship possession has characteristics of both alienable and inalienable possession (cf. Dixon 2004).

6. The particle *ya* has a lengthened form *yaa* when it occurs in a phrase that follows a clause rather than preceding it. The phrase with *ya(a)* follows the clause that it relates to in (15), but precedes the clause in (16).

Stimulated by a question by Mark Sicoli, I looked at the distribution of the full and reduced forms of *ihi/ehene* (the reduced forms being *ii* and *eene*), and it turns out that the reduced forms are used much less frequently when the phrase containing *ihi/ehene* follows the clause that it relates to. In the examples in this paper, the full form is always used when the phrase containing *ihi/ehene* follows the clause it relates to (as in (13)); whereas when the phrase containing *ihi/ehene* precedes the clause that it relates to, either the full form or the reduced form can occur. In the whole corpus of Jarawara data, there are just a few occurrences of the reduced masculine form *eene* when the phrase containing it follows the clause it relates to, and no occurrences of the reduced feminine form *ii* in this position. This corresponds to the distribution of the longer and shorter forms of *ya(a)*, although with less regularity.

7. The *I* in the suffix *-kI* represents a morphophoneme that can be realized on the surface as either *i* or (as in this example) *e*, depending

on whether the preceding number of moras in the word is even or odd (cf. Dixon 2004: 40ff.).

8. In (22) and (23), the agreement is only gender agreement, but when the subject is third person, the person prefix *hi-* is also used, whereas this prefix otherwise is only used to reference the third person subject and object of a transitive (O-construction) clause (cf. Vogel 2015: 46f.). For an example of this construction with *hi-*, see (i) in footnote 16.

There is not space here to discuss in detail the more common use of the O-construction and its counterpart, the A-construction, in transitive clauses; the reader is referred to Dixon (2004: ch. 16). Very briefly, these constructions are used to track the main discourse topic in Jarawara, the A-construction for when the topic is the subject, and the O-construction for when the topic is the object. In the following sentence, the first clause, which is a medial clause, is an A-construction, and the second clause, which is the main clause, is an O-construction.

(i)	[owa	me	fiya	tonama	me,] MED
	owa	me	fiya	to-na-ma+F	me
	1SG.O	3PL.A	pass	away-AUX-back	3PL.A

	[yome	me	me	waka	hinarani] MC
	yomee	me	me	waka	hi-na-hara-ni
	jaguar.M	3PL.O	3PL.A	kill	OC-AUX-IP.E+F-BKG+F

'They [i.e. the girls] passed by me, and the jaguars killed them.'

The effect of the successive use of these constructions is to track the argument referencing the girls in both clauses, because it is the main discourse topic. This argument is the subject in the first clause, and the object in the second clause. There are many clues that show whether a clause is an A-construction or an O-construction in various contexts, but in this particular sentence it is clear that the medial clause is an A-construction because of the repetition of *me* after the verb stem, and the main clause is clearly an O-construction because of the presence of *hi-*. Example (10) above is clearly an A-construction because it does not have *hi-*. One can tell that (15) above is an A-construction by the fact that the subject agreement prefix *o-* is repeated after the verb stem. Similarly, one can tell that (16) above is an O-construction by the fact that *o-* is not repeated after the verb stem.

9. Whereas up to this point the examples have been complete sentences or at least main clauses of sentences, this clause is marked as a kind of subordinate clause that Dixon (2004) calls a "postposed dependent clause," and which I (Vogel In preparation) am now calling a postposed finite clause.

10. In an e-mail, Robert Dooley notes that in English adjuncts are often of the category NP, as in **this very day** *I saw the man*. According to this idea, there would be no need to have a dual classification for *ihi/ehene*, *tabiyo*, and *namoni*; they would be just PNs. But I believe that the case of *ihi/ehene*, *tabiyo*, and *namoni* in Jarawara is different than the case of adjuncts like *this very day* in English. First of all, this is a phenomenon that is limited to just these words in Jarawara (for Dixon only to *ihi/ehene*), whereas the phenomenon in English is not lexically limited. Also, with many adjuncts of this type in English, it is possible to add a preposition without changing the meaning, for example, **on** *this very day*. But it is not possible to add *ya* to phrases with these three words in Jarawara, when they are used as in (13), (14), etc.. These words and *ya* are mutually exclusive, because they have the same function, that is, to mark a phrase as an adjunct.

11. The other particles in the same class as *ya* are *ni ya* (a syntactic variant of *ya*, cf., e.g., (18) above), *karo/kari* 'which (and various other meanings)', and *nima* ~ *tima* 'similar to', Cf. Dixon (2004: chs. 20, 21) and Vogel (2003: 82ff.; 2015: 81ff.).

12. It might appear that if one were to apply the analysis presented here to English, we would classify *of* and *to* not as prepositions but as particles. However, there is a significant morphological difference between the three postpositions as opposed to particles such as *ya* in Jarawara, in that the argument associated with the postposition in its immediate phrase is a possessor, as noted above, whereas this is not true with *ya*. That is, postpositions are morphologically like PNs. In English, there is no corresponding morphological difference between *of* and *to* as opposed to other prepositions.

13. Dixon also lists what he considers to be a third use of *ihi/ehene*, which is to mark a clause as a peripheral constituent. One of the examples he (2004: 513) gives is (i), which is his example (22.19).

(i)

[me	[yawemetemoneke]o	[[Airowa]s
me	yawa-hemete-mone-ke	Airowa
3PL.S	be upset-FP.N+F-REP+F-DECL+F	(man's name).M

[sone]v	ehene]ADJU]MC
sona+M	ehene
fall	because of+M

'They grieved because Airowa had died.'

As I see it, though, there is no reason to consider this a separate syntactic context. In this example, if the clause *Airowa sone* is analyzed as a relative clause, then the adjunct can be seen as having the same structure as any adjunct like the ones in (13) and (14) above, that is, consisting of an NP plus the postposition *ihi/ehene*. In his discussion of relative clauses, Dixon (2004: 528) gives examples of relative clauses followed by the particle *ya*, for example, (ii), which is his example (24.10).

(ii)

[[[[Manoware] A	[hawi]o	[tii	hinehete]$_V$]$_{RC}$	ya]ADJU
Manoware	hawi	tii	hi-na-hete	ya
(man's name).M	trail.F	cut through	OC-AUX-RP.N+F	ADJU

[tasi	onama]$_V$]$_{MED}$
tasi	o-na-ma+F
emerge	1SG.S-AUX-back

'I came out onto the trail that Manoware had cut.'

In proposing to call *ihi/ehene* in this use a postposition as I have above, I have drawn attention to its similarity to the use of particles such as *ya*. So, the occurrence of relative clauses with *ihi/ehene* is not at all surprising, since they also occur with *ya*.

14. The text, by Yowao Jarawara, is called "Aba Tosi," and the sentence in question is number 14 in the text.

15. Dixon (2004) calls this phenomenon "possessor copying."

16. The exception to this generalization is that possessor agreement with the possessor of an adjunct is possible in the construction mentioned in the previous section in conjunction with examples (22) and (23). In (i), for example, both the possessor of the adjunct and the subject of the verb are plural and are referenced by *me*, but the *me* at the end of the verb references the possessor of the adjunct, and not the subject.

(i)	[[me	namoni]ADJU	[me	hikama	me]V]MED
	me	namoni	me	hi-ka-ma+F	me
	3PL.POSS	report	3PL.S	go/come-back	

'They came and told us about them.'

But example (31) cannot be an example of this construction, because if it were it would have *hi-*, since both the possessor of the adjunct and the subject are third person, as in (i).

17. Jarawara also has several transitive verbs that have the meaning 'kill', that is, *naabowa*, *nahabi*, and *waka na*. For examples of use, cf. Vogel (2016).

References

Dienst, Stefan. 2014. *A grammar of Kulina*. Berlin: De Gruyter Mouton.

Dixon, R. M. W. 2004. The Jarawara language of southern Amazonia. Oxford: Oxford University Press.

Littlefield, Heather. 2005. Lexical and functional prepositions in acquisition: Evidence for a hybrid category. In Alejna Brugos, Manuella R. Clark-Cotton, and Seungwan Ha (Eds.), *BUCLD Online proceedings supplements*, 29: 1–10. Boston, MA: Boston University Conference on Language Development.

Vogel, Alan. 2003. *Jarawara verb classes* (PhD dissertation). University of Pittsburgh, Pittsburgh, PA.

Vogel, Alan. 2009. Covert tense in Jarawara. *Linguistic Discovery*, 7: 43–105.

Vogel, Alan. 2012. Jarawara interlinear texts vol. 1. http://www.silbrazil.org/resources/jarawara_interlinear_texts_vol_1, date of access: November 1, 2019.

Vogel, Alan. 2015. Jarawara complement clauses: Some new perspectives. *SIL Electronic Working Papers* 2015. Dallas, TX: SIL International.

Vogel, Alan. 2016. Jarawara-English dictionary. http://www.silbrasil.org.br/resources/archives/72031.

Vogel, Alan. In preparation. A typology of finite subordinate clauses in Jarawara.

CHAPTER 11

On Zapotecan Glottal Stop, and Where (Not) to Reconstruct It[1]

Eric W. Campbell

> The rules governing these changes are so varied in the different [Zapotec] dialects that there are few cognate sets in which the dialectal forms all have a glottal stop in the same position.
>
> (Swadesh 1947: 225)

1. Introduction

Sally Thomason (1997: 153) reminds us that the "foundation on which all of historical-comparative linguistics rests is the comparative method," and in turn, the foundation on which the comparative method rests is the regularity of internally motivated sound change. She also notes that while the method is based on false assumptions about how languages diverge—for example, the assumed lack of variation in protolanguages and the oversimplified notion of clean splits between diverging speech varieties—it usually provides very reliable results, and what the "false assumptions leave us with, in the typical case, is not a total mess, but a nice systematic set of regular correspondences with some residue" (Thomason 1997: 154). While the residue that she refers to is often due to the effects of language contact, the aim of the present paper is to explore another type of apparent residue: a residue that remains due to some long-standing gaps in our understanding of sound change.

The comparative method and knowledge about sound change has so far rested largely on patterns of segmental change, while knowledge about the diachrony of suprasegmental phonological features, such as tone and other laryngeal articulations, lags far behind (for tone, see Campbell, in press; Janda and Joseph 2003: 173).[2] The lack of a detailed diachronic suprasegmental typology to draw from makes reconstructing suprasegmental features challenging, and it may leave the results tentative or incomplete. The Zapotecan language group (a branch of the Otomanguean family), which consists of the Zapotec and Chatino languages of southern Mexico, illustrates.

Recent advances in Chatino reconstruction and subgrouping (Campbell 2013, 2018; Sullivant 2016) have confirmed the accuracy of Kaufman's (2016) proto-Zapotec segmental reconstructions to the point that very little in the way of segmental correspondences between the two groups remains unexplained. Where the challenging residue lies in Zapotecan reconstruction is in the correspondences involving tone and laryngealized syllable nuclei or glottal stop, which are diachronically (and in some varieties synchronically) interrelated. While preliminary—though unfortunately still unpublished—tonal reconstructions exist for Zapotec (Benton 2001) and Chatino (Campbell and Woodbury 2010), there has been no attempt to reconstruct proto-Zapotecan tone. Likewise, no study has yet accounted for some recalcitrant Zapotec and Chatino sound correspondences that involve laryngealized nuclei and/or glottal stop, which are the focus of the present study.

Some proto-Zapotec (pZp) and proto-Chatino (pCh) cognates display straightforward laryngeal correspondences. For example, pZp so-called "broken syllables" <*VʔV> (Kaufman 2016: 8), also referred to as "rearticulated vowel nuclei" (Suárez 1973: 237), which in Zapotec varieties are often realized as laryngealized vowels or a vowel with a soft glottal interruption followed by a short rearticulation of the vowel, most often correspond to pCh intervocalic glottal stop in disyllabic words (Campbell 2013: 400), as in the word 'fence' (table 11.1). The "checked syllables" of pZp <*Vʔ>, which in

Table 11.1 Regular pZp and pCh Glottal Correspondences

Gloss	*pZp*	*pCh*
'fence'	*loʔo	*lòʔó
'pot'	*kessoʔ	*ketǫʔ
'lightning'	*ko=seʔju	*k^{w}i-tìʔjú

Table 11.2 Opposite Laryngeal Correspondences

Gloss	*pZp*	*pCh*
'sleeping mat'	*ta:ʔa	*hààʔ
'see'	*-naʔ	*-nàʔà

Zapotec varieties tend to be produced as a vowel with a stronger glottalization and no following rearticulated vowel, most often correspond to pCh glottal stop elsewhere, either word-finally as in 'pot' or word-medially before a sonorant, as in 'lightning'.[3]

However, there are exceptions to the fairly regular sound correspondences presented in table 11.1. For example, the broken vowel in pZp 'sleeping mat' corresponds to word-final, and not the expected intervocalic, glottal stop in pCh (table 11.2). The checked vowel in pZp monosyllabic 'see' corresponds to a disyllabic form in pCh with intervocalic (not the expected word-final) glottal stop.

Other cognate sets involve no laryngealization in pZp where there is a glottal stop in pCh, either word-finally ('fire') or intervocalically ('go around, walk'), as shown in table 11.3, and still other cognate sets involve pZp checked vowels in word-final syllables ('broom'), penultimate syllables ('work'), or even both syllables ('cry') where there is no corresponding pCh glottal stop in either position (also shown in table 11.3).

Since laryngeal nuclei are ubiquitous and glottal stop is rare in Zapotec varieties, while glottal stop is ubiquitous and laryngealized nuclei are never contrastive in Chatino varieties, one might imagine that proto-Zapotecan had both laryngeal nuclei and a glottal stop, with the former being lost or merged in pCh and the latter being lost or merged in pZp. However, the laryngeal correspondences between the two proto-languages appear to be too regular and too numerous to support such

Table 11.3 Laryngeals in One but Not the Other Protolanguage

Gloss	*pZp*	*pCh*
'fire'	*kii	*kiiʔ
'go around, walk'	*-są	*-taʔą
'broom'	*k-okʷaʔ	*k-ùkʷá
'work'	*tʲi:ʔna	*tìną́
'cry'	*-o:ʔnaʔ	*-ùná

a scenario of complementary large-scale losses or mergers. Meanwhile, about 27 percent of the cognate sets that involve some type of laryngealization do not fit into the "regular" laryngeal correspondences, which leaves an uncomfortable amount of residue, especially when compared to the quite modest amount of segmental residue between the two protolanguages. Tone, unsurprisingly, must be a significant player.

The aims of this paper are to lay out and examine the Zapotecan laryngeal residue, present some initial hypotheses about where (not) to reconstruct proto-Zapotecan glottal stop, outline some next steps for clearing up the remaining uncertainties, and pave some of the path toward a greater understanding of laryngeal diachrony. To get there, previous work on Zapotecan historical segmental phonology §2 and suprasegmental phonology §3 are first summarized. Some methodological notes for the present study are discussed in §4, before moving on to detailed presentations of the regular (§5) and irregular (§6) laryngeal correspondences, which are discussed along with the conclusions in §7.

2. Zapotecan Subgrouping and Comparative Segmental Phonology

Zapotecan is one of the major subgroups of the diverse Otomanguean language family of Mesoamerica (Campbell 2017a; Kaufman 1988; Rensch 1976). It consists of the Zapotec languages, which are spoken mostly and widely in central and southern Oaxaca state, Mexico, and the Chatino languages of southwestern Oaxaca. Varieties of both language groups are also spoken in diaspora communities in other parts of Mexico and the United States. Zapotec proper consists of many languages and varieties that are spoken by an estimated 450,000 people (INEGI 2010). Chatino, which is spoken by an estimated 45,000 people, is a less-diversified cluster of about twenty speech varieties that make up at least three distinct modern languages: Zenzontepec, Tataltepec, and the Eastern Chatino group (Ezéquiel Vásquez, in Boas 1913; Campbell 2013).

A typical Zapotecan language displays head-initial syntax with VS and VAO basic constituent orders, juxtapositional syntactic structures, accusative alignment, pied-piping with inversion in interrogatives (Smith Stark 2002a), synthetic head-marking morphology that ranges from agglutinating to fusional, obligatory verbal aspect/mood inflection with no morphological tense, relational nouns more prominent than prepositions, alienable versus inalienable noun possession, limited plural marking on nouns, inclusive versus exclusive pronouns, prolific lexical compounding, elaborate base 20 numeral systems, lexical and grammatical tone, and other laryngeal articulations that may interact with tone (see Campbell and Broadwell, in press, for a synthesis of Zapotecan linguistic structure).

Figure 11.1 presents the state-of-the-art Zapotecan language classification (Campbell 2017b). While the Chatino subgrouping is

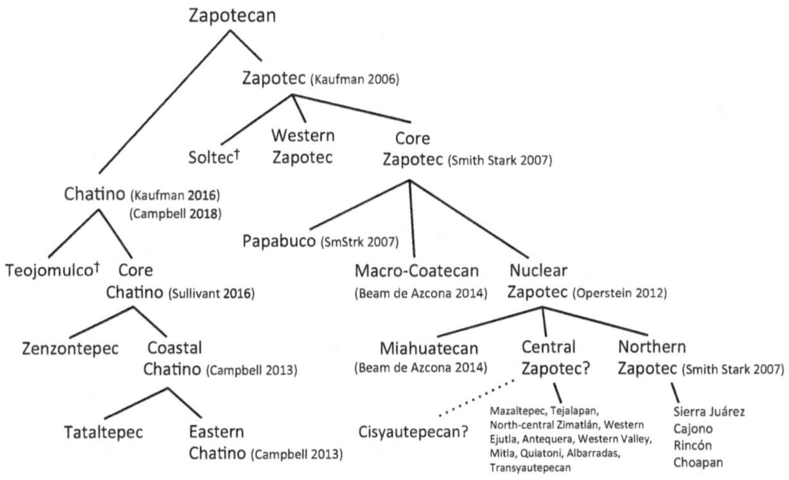

Figure 11.1 Zapotecan Language Classification

Source: Adapted from Campbell (2017b: 12)

firmly established (Campbell 2013; Sullivant 2016), many nodes on the Zapotec side remain tentative (Campbell 2017b; Campbell and Broadwell, in press).

Kaufman (2016) reconstructs roughly 850 proto-Zapotec forms, incorporating and expanding earlier works (Benton 1988; Fernández de Miranda 1995; Suárez 1973; Swadesh 1947). Chatino reconstructions are less numerous, consisting of about 200 recent proto-Chatino reconstructions (Campbell 2013, 2018; Campbell and Cruz 2010) that overlap with and refine Upson and Longacre's (1965) roughly 250 reconstructions.[4] The most divergent Chatino language is the now reportedly dormant and sparsely attested Teojomulco Chatino. Although the available information about that variety from Belmar (1902) is limited and inconsistent, the data are nevertheless sufficient to confirm parts of the segmental inventory that Kaufman (2016) proposes for proto-Zapotec and proto-Zapotecan (Campbell 2018: 21–22; Sullivant 2016). However, the Teojomulco Chatino data are not otherwise sufficient to contribute substantively to the reconstruction of proto-Chatino.

Following Swadesh (1947), Kaufman (2016) reconstructs a contrast between single and geminate consonants for Zapotec(an), excluding the glides **y* and **w* (always single) and the borrowed and rare **mm* (always geminate).[5] By the time of proto-Chatino, the geminate series had unconditionally merged with the single series, leaving no known trace of the single-geminate contrast in Chatino. Basic pZp and pCh consonantal correspondences and the proto-Zapotecan (pZn) consonants that they reflect are presented in table 11.4.[6]

Based on the correspondences presented in table 11.4, and aside from the merger of geminates with single consonants, Kaufman (2016) identifies the unconditioned changes involving consonants from pZn to pCh shown in (1).

(1) Unconditioned changes from pZn to pCh

a. *(t)t > *h
b. *(s)s > *t
c. *(t)tʲ > *t
d. *(ʃ)ʃ > *s

Table 11.4 Basic Consonantal Sound Correspondences between pZp and pCh

Gloss	*pZp*	*pCh*	*pZp*	*pCh*	*pZn*
'skin'	*ki**t**i	*ki**h**į	*t	*h	*t
'tortilla'	*ke**tt**a	*kʲa**h**a	*tt		*tt
'pine torch'	*ke**tʲ**e	*ki**t**è	*tʲ	*t	*tʲ
'vine'	*lu**ttʲ**i	*lù**t**í	*ttʲ		*ttʲ
'fat, lard'	***s**aa	***t**àą̀	*s		*s
'black'	*ka**ss**ak	*n-kà**t**á	*ss		*ss
'village'	*kee**ts**e	*ki**ts**ę	*ts	*ts	*ts
'rabbit'	*kʷ=i**tts**i	*kʷi**ts**ì	*tts		*tts
'cornfield'	***k**ela	***k**ela	*k	*k	*k
'be possible'	*-a**kk**a	*-a**k**à	*kk		*kk
'noise'	***kʷ**e	***kʷ**èę̀	*kʷ	*kʷ	*kʷ
'four'	*k-ta**kkʷ**a	*ha**kʷ**a	*kkʷ		*kkʷ
'wide'	***ʃ**e	***s**èę̀	*ʃ	*s	*ʃ
'net'	*ke**ʃʃ**ok	*ke**s**u	*ʃʃ		*ʃʃ
'smoke'	*tse**n**i	*tsi**n**i	*n	*n	*n
'three'	*ttso**nn**a	*tsú**n**a	*nn		*nn
'beard'	***l**uʃu	***l**usu	*l	*l	*l
'fish'	*kʷ=e**ll**a	*kʷe**l**a	*ll		*ll
'tree'	***j**aka	***j**aka	*j	*j	*j
'two days after'	***w**itsak	***w**itsa	*w	*w	*w
'basket'	*tsu**mm**i	—	*mm	—	?

The changes in (1) occurred in counterfeeding orders: (a) preceded both (b) and (c), and (b) preceded (d). The changes in (a), (b), and (d) were a chain shift: **t* > **h*; **s* > **t*; **ʃ* > **s*. Several conditioned changes involving consonants also occurred in proto-Chatino (Campbell 2018), a few of which are shown in (2–4).

(2) Nasalization of **l* before *V̨*

$*\text{l} > *\text{n} \,/\, \_\_\, \text{V}_{[+\text{nasal}]}$

(3) Harmonic glide insertion

Ø > *w / u h __ $V_{[+front]}$
Ø > *j / i h __ $V_{[-front]}$

(4) Glide deletion

*w > Ø / __ o
*j > Ø / e __ e, o

In the discussion so far, where pZp and pCh disagree, Chatino was the innovator. However, all Zapotec varieties reflect two unconditioned innovations that did not occur in Chatino: (i) the loss of contrastive vowel nasality and (ii) a shift in prominence from root-final syllables to penultimate syllables (Kaufman 2006: 122). While most Zapotec varieties display develarization of the pZn labiovelars (*kk^w > *p*; *k^w > b), Smith Stark (1999) shows that these changes reflect a develarization cline across Zapotec varieties and were thus probably only incipient at the time of proto-Zapotec. Some vowel correspondences within Zapotec that had been problematic are recently explained by Beam de Azcona et al. (2018), and aside from some unresolved correspondences involving front vowels (Campbell 2018: 24)—which do not impact the current study—Zapotecan historical segmental phonology is well understood.

3. Zapotecan Comparative Suprasegmental Phonology

In his preliminary proto-Zapotec reconstruction, Swadesh (1947) reconstructed tone based on two varieties: Isthmus (Central) and Ixtlán (Northern). Since these two varieties belong to close sister subgroups, Swadesh's tonal reconstructions cannot simply be extended back to proto-Zapotec. Benton (2001) offers a more detailed, but still preliminary and unpublished, reconstruction of proto-Zapotec tone, including two Northern varieties, two Central varieties, and two "Southern" varieties,[7] one of which is now considered part of the Miahuatecan group and the other the Macro-Coatecan group (Beam de Azcona 2014). This at best gives us a partial view of proto-Core-Zapotec tone. Benton reconstructs *High, *Mid, *Low, *Rising, and *Falling tones, as well as a contrast between "high-intensity" and "low-intensity" syllables (something like ballistic vs. controlled syllables as reported for Amuzgo by Bauernschmidt [1965]), and only one type of laryngealization. Little or no subsequent work has attempted to validate, adopt, or adapt Benton's tonal reconstruction. Suárez (1973), Fernández de Miranda (1995), and Kaufman (2016) do not include tone in their proto-Zapotec reconstructions.

Upson and Longacre (1965) did not include tone in their Chatino reconstruction either, but later works (Campbell 2013, 2018; Campbell and Cruz 2010) adopt Campbell and Woodbury's (2010) preliminary proto-Chatino tone reconstruction, which includes six basic tonal melody contrasts: ØØ, *ØH, *ØL, *LH, *HØ, and *LL. At least three of these melodies in some cases occurred with an initial floating high tone: $*^{H}$ØØ, $*^{H}$ØL, and $*^{H}$LH. However, many irregular and less-frequent Chatino tone correspondences remain unexplained (Campbell, in press).

As for other laryngeal features, Chatino is straightforward. There is no voicing contrast in Chatino varieties, except perhaps where such a contrast has recently been innovated due to monosyllabification (see, e.g., McIntosh 2015: 43). All Chatino languages have glottal stop /ʔ/ and glottal fricative /h/ (< pZn *tt, *t*) consonants, but no contrastive laryngealized syllables or phonation types (Campbell 2014: 76–82; Cruz 2011; McIntosh 2015; Pride 2004; Sullivant 2015; Villard 2015). Glottal stop correspondences are nearly exceptionless across Chatino varieties, and the reconstruction of glottal stop in pCh is not at all problematic.

Nontonal laryngeal features are more varied across Zapotec varieties.[8] As Nelson (2004: 8) summarizes for San Juan Mixtepec

(Cisyautepecan) Zapotec, most Zapotec varieties display contrastive laryngealization of syllable nuclei (or phonation type) but no glottal stop consonant (see also Antonio Ramos 2015; Arellanes Arellanes 2009; Beam de Azcona 2004; Black 1995; Chávez Peón 2010; Gutiérrez Lorenzo 2014; Hernández Luna 2019; Jones and Knudson 1977; López Nicolás 2016; Pérez Báez and Kaufman 2016; Smith Stark 2002b; Sonnenschein 2004, inter alia), while other Zapotec varieties are analyzed as having both laryngealized nuclei and glottal stop (Avelino Becerra 2004) or only glottal stop (Foreman 2006). Reconstructions for pZp differ as well (table 11.5): Swadesh (1947) reconstructs only glotal stop (no laryngealization), and Benton (2001) reconstructs no glottal stop and only one type of laryngealization (*Vʔ). Fernández de Miranda (1995) and Kaufman (2016)—as already mentioned—reconstruct no glottal stop but two types of laryngealized syllables: checked syllables <Vʔ> and broken syllables <VʔV>. The significant variation across these reconstructions reflects the difficulty of comparing and reconstructing laryngeals (and other suprasegmental-like features).

In the following discussion, Kaufman's (2016) proto-Zapotec reconstructions involving laryngeals are compared with proto-Chatino reconstructions in order to shed light on the status of laryngealization in proto-Zapotecan. But first, some methodological notes are in order.

Table 11.5 Reconstruction of pZp Laryngeals

	*Glottal Stop *ʔ*	*Checked Syllables *Vʔ*	*Broken Syllables *VʔV*
Swadesh (1947)	✓	—	—
Benton (1988, 2001)	—	✓	—
Fernández de Miranda (1995)	—	✓	✓
Kaufman (2016)	—	✓	✓

4. Methodological Notes and Assumptions

While Kaufman's (2016) proto-Zapotec reconstruction unfortunately does not include primary data, it is nevertheless the most extensive and reliable of the various pZp reconstructions (Campbell 2013, 2018; Sullivant 2016). It is also the only one that is significantly informed with reference to Chatino. Kaufman's reconstructions, laryngeal and otherwise, are assumed to be correct here, and henceforth the comparisons will be between Kaufman's (2016) proto-Zapotec and proto-Chatino (following Campbell 2013, 2018).[9] Reference to individual Zapotec or Chatino varieties will be made only when pertinent.

Unfortunately, as discussed earlier, there is no reliable reconstruction of proto-Zapotec tone that can be incorporated here, but proto-Chatino tone, based on Campbell and Woodbury (2010), will help shed some light on some of the laryngeal correspondences. Where the tone of pCh forms still cannot be reconstructed with confidence, due to irregular or unexpected tone correspondences (Campbell, in press), these forms are presented in parentheses: for example, pCh (**laʔwe*) 'black zapote.'

In a working database of about 400 proto-Chatino reconstructions, about 320 of them have cognates among Kaufman's (2016) proto-Zapotec reconstructions. Some 160 of the 320 cognate sets display some kind of glottal stop or laryngeal syllable in either pCh or pZp, and these are the cognate sets that are considered in the subsequent discussion.

5. Where pZn *ʔ Is Easy to Reconstruct

Of the 160 cognate sets that have some type of laryngealization or glottal stop in either pZp or pCh, a total of 18 (11.25 percent) have a pZp broken vowel <*VʔV> that corresponds to a pCh intervocalic glottal stop (table 11.6).[10] None of these forms in either protolanguage have any other laryngealization or glottal stop in them. For

Table 11.6 **V?V* in Both pZp and pCh

Gloss	*pZp*	*pCh*
'split (trn.)'	*-k=laʔa	*-u-laʔa
'woman'	*ko=naʔ(a)	*ku-naʔą́
'witch'	*kʷe=tseʔa	*(kʷi-tsaʔą)
'huaje' (*Leucaena leucocephala*)	*laʔa	*ntaʔa
'blow'	*-laʔa	*-làʔá
'lick'	*-lleʔe	(*-leʔe)
'fence'	*loʔo	*loʔó
'mother'	*naʔa	*(kʷi-)naʔą́
'house'	*niʔi	*niʔą
'toast (trn.)'	*-ok=keʔi	(*-u-kiʔi)
'sell'	*-ottiʔ	*-uhwìʔ
'fresh ear of corn'	*seʔA	*n-taʔą
'heavy'	*siʔi	*tiʔį
'poor'	*siʔi	*ᴴtiʔi
'relative,' 'companion'	*ssaʔa	(*taʔa)
'festival'	*ssaʔa	*taʔa
'(water) jug'	*tʲeʔe	*tèʔę̀
'raw,' 'unripe'	*jeʔa	(*jaʔá)

proto-Zapotecan, these forms can thus be confidently reconstructed with the shape *(...)CVʔV. However, the question remains of what the phonological nature of the *VʔV sequence would have been in pZn. Was it a laryngealized, or broken, vowel as in pZp? An intervocalic glottal stop that was the onset of a final syllable, as it was in pCh? Or was it something else?

In another primary correspondence, a total of 55 of the 160 cognate sets have a pZp word-final checked vowel <*Vʔ> that corresponds to a pCh word-final glottal stop. Of these 55 sets, 38 of them (38/160 = 23.75 percent of all of the sets) have no other laryngealization or glottal stop elsewhere in the cognates in either protolanguage (table 11.7). It is therefore unproblematic to reconstruct word-final *Vʔ in these

Table 11.7 Word Final **Vʔ* in pZp and pCh

Gloss	*pZp*	*pCh*
'drip (v.)'	*-ak^{w}aʔ	*-àk^{w}àʔ
'nurse (v.)'	*-at^{j}iʔ	*-atiʔ
'water gourd'	*k=ekaʔ	*kekaʔ
'mamey', 'soursop'	*kellaʔ	*kelaʔ
'pot'	*kessoʔ	*ketǫʔ
'thorn'	*kettseʔ	*kitseʔ
'wax'	*kinaʔ	*kinaʔ
'hair'	*kittsa(ʔ)	*kìtsą̀ʔ
'urine'	*k-iʃʃeʔ	*seʔ
'dew'	*k-okk^{w}aʔ	*kuk^{w}aʔ
'charcoal'	*k^{w}awoʔ	*kooʔ
'mouse'	*k^{w}e=sinaʔ	*k^{w}itinaʔ
'frog'	*k^{w}=et^{j}iʔ	*k^{w}itìʔ
'ant'	*k^{w}e=t^{j}eʔ	*k^{w}i-tèèʔ
'deer'	*k^{w}e=tsinaʔ	*k^{w}inął́ʔ
'honey'	*(k^{w}e=)tsinaʔ	*k^{w}ì-ną̀ʔ
'raccoon'	*k^{w}e=ʃeʔ	*k^{w}i-sèèʔ
'measure (n.)'	*k^{w}ejaʔ	*k^{w}èjáʔ
'spider'	*k^{w}=ejuʔ	*k^{w}ijuʔ
'crab'	*(k^{w}=ettsuʔ)]k^{w}-e:ʔ	*k^{w}eeʔ
'eight'	*k-ʃonuʔ	*sunǫʔ
'leaf'	*llakaʔ	*lakaʔ
'bitter'	*(na=)]llaʔ	*ti-]lààʔ
ɪsg	*na(ʔ)	(*naaʔ)
'sour'	*na=j-i:ʔ	*tì-jèʔ
'hand'	*naʔ ~ jaʔ	*jaàʔ
'cook (trn.)'	*-o(=)ki(ʔ)	*-ù-kéʔ
'untie (trn.)'	*-ok=sAt^{j}iʔ	*-u-s-atiʔ
'douse (trn.)'	*-ok=s-uwiʔ	(*-u-sowiʔ)

(*Continued*)

Table 11.7 (Continued)

Gloss	*pZp*	*pCh*
'salt'	*seteʔ	*teheʔ
'far'	*sittuʔ	*tihjuʔ
'lizard,' 'iguana'	*(ko=)wattsiʔ	*kʷàtsíʔ
'gourd'	*ʃikaʔ	*sìkàʔ
'breast, udder'	*ʃitʲiʔ	*sitiʔ
'pineapple'	*ʃ]itsuʔ	(*kʷi-t]itsuʔ)
'shelled corn'	*ʃ-okʷaʔ	*n-sukʷàʔ
'cheek'	*ʃʃakaʔ	*sàkàʔ
'get doused'	*-j-uwiʔ	(*-j-uwiʔ)

forms in proto-Zapotecan, but again, the question remains about whether this was phonologically a sequence of a vowel followed by glottal stop consonant or a laryngealized nucleus consisting of a vowel with some laryngeal articulation.

In proto-Zapotec, checked vowels *Vʔ could occur in penultimate syllables, regardless of what the initial consonant of the following syllable was. In pCh, however, word-medial glottal stop only preceded vowels or sonorant consonants: that is, it did not precede obstruents. In the data used for this study, there are thirty-five cognate sets (35/160 = 21.88 percent) in which pZp checked vowels in penultimate syllables preceded obstruents (table 11.8).[11] To account for this correspondence, a single change in which glottal stop elided before obstruents is posited for proto-Chatino (Campbell 2018): *ʔ > Ø / __ $C_{[\text{-son}]}$.

Proto-Zapotec checked vowels in penultimate syllables that preceded sonorant consonants (**n*, **y*, or **w*) regularly correspond to proto-Chatino word-medial glottal stop preceding the same sonorants. Of the 160 cognates sets that have some type of laryngealization or glottal stop in either pZp or pCh, 17 of them (10.63 percent) involve word-medial *Vʔ followed by **n*, **j*, or **w* (table 11.9) in both

Table 11.8 pCh *ʔ > Ø / _ $C_{[\text{-son}]}$

Gloss	*pZp*	*pCh*
'get cooked'	*-Aʔkiʔ	*-àkéʔ
'plant (v.)'	*-a:ʔsa	*-ata
'chew'	*-aʔssaʔ	*-àtáʔ
'lie down'	*-aʔttaʔ	*-àháʔ
'river'	*ke:ʔku	*kekú
'flour'	*ke:ʔsak	*ketà
'hole'	*ke:ʔtʲu	*ketú
'tobacco'	*keʔsa	*keta
'pimple'	*keʔtsuʔ	*kètsúʔ
'metal'	*ki:ʔkʷa	*kìkʷą
'quern'	*ki:ʔttsi	*kitsi
'paper'	*kiʔttʲi	*kitì
'herb,' 'brush'	*kiʔʃʃiʔ	*kisį̀ʔ
'pus'	*ku:ʔtseʔ	*kùtséʔ
'louse'	*kʷ=e:ʔttʲeʔ	*kʷitįʔ
'large wild feline'	*kʷ=e:ʔtsi(k)	*kʷìtsí
'skunk'	*kʷ=eʔtti(k)	*kʷìjí
'bag,' '8,000'	*kʷe=(s)su:ʔti	*kʷìjį̀
'squirrel'	*kʷe=tʲi:ʔ(s)sa	*titá
'coati'	*kʷe=ʃi:ʔtsuʔ	*kʷ/t-ìtsúʔ
'leaf-cutter ant'	*kʷe=joʔkʷaʔ	*kʲukʷàʔ
'six'	*k-ʃo:ʔkkʷa	*súkʷa
'flat, level'	*l-aʔkkʷa	*ti-lakʷa
'flat land'	*laʔttʲiʔ	*natęʔ
'boil (itrn.)'	*-lla:ʔkʷi	*-lakʷí
'get swept'	*-l-o:ʔkʷa	*-lùkʷá
'tongue'	*lu:ʔtseʔ	*lutseʔ
'corn gruel'	*nissa] ja:ʔkʷa	*jàkʷá
'hide'	*-o(k)=ka:ʔttsiʔ	(*-u-katsiʔ)
'dry (up)'	*-ok=]kʷi:ʔtʲi	*-ʃi-]wití

(*Continued*)

Table 11.8 (Continued)

Gloss	*pZp*	*pCh*
'sweep'	*-ok=l-o:ʔkʷa	*-u-lùkʷá
'pass'	*-teʔti	*-tihį̀
'word,' 'language,' 'advice'	*ti:ʔtsaʔ	*hìtsáʔ
'kill'	*-u:ʔtti	*-ù-hwì
'swim'	*ʃ-o:ʔkʷa	*-sùkʷá

Table 11.9 Word-Medial **Vʔ* Preceding **n*, **y*, and **w* in Both pZp and pCh

Gloss	*pZp*	*pCh*
'plate'	*keʔna	*keʔnà
'mountain'	*keʔja	*keʔjà
'bed'	*kiʔna	*kìʔną̀
'guilt'	*kiʔja	*kiʔja
'lightning'	*ko=seʔju	*kʷi-tìʔjú
'fifteen'	*k-tʲi:ʔ+nuʔ	*tíʔnų
'forty'	*k-tʲoʔwa	*túʔwa
'caiman'	*kʷ=eʔnak	*kʷeʔna
'macaw'	*kʷ=eʔwa	*ᴴkoʔma
'flea'	*kʷ=eʔju	*kʷ-iʔjù
'man'	*kʷe=kiʔju	*kiʔjú
'(black) zapote'	*(kʷe=)laʔwe	(*laʔwé)
'hawk'	*kʷe=ssiʔja	*kʷeʔja
Parmentiera aculeata (> 'banana')	*kʷe=toʔwa	(*haʔwa)
'tooth'	*(l)leʔja	*leʔja
'mouth'	*tʲoʔwa	*tuʔwa
'lime (stone)'	*keʔjo	*kʲoʔo

protolanguages. The pCh word-medial glide in 'lime (stone)' was elided due to its adjacency to mid vowels, as mentioned in (4).

A couple of cognate sets (2/160 = 1.25 percent) display a pattern in which the pZp forms contain checked vowels in both syllables, while the pCh cognates contain only one glottal stop, in word-final position (table 11.10). The loss of the glottal stop in the initial syllables of the pCh forms is likely due to a restriction of maximally one glottal stop per phonological word in pCh—referred to here as culminative *ʔ—which is reflected in modern Chatino varieties (see, e.g., Campbell 2014: 175 for Zenzontepec Chatino).

Proto-Zapotec checked vowels preceded the other (presumably) sonorant consonant *l, but in pCh the glottal stop did not occur there. Thus, either *l was not a sonorant in pCh or another change occurred: pCh *ʔ > Ø / _ l. The loss of glottal stop before pCh *l must have preceded the pCh sound change mentioned in (2): *l > n / _ $V_{[+nas]}$. The evidence for this relative chronology is observable in the last three lines of table 11.11. If the order of changes were reversed, then glottal stop would remain in the Chatino forms since pCh *ʔ was generally retained preceding *n (as shown in table 11.9). A total of seven of the cognate sets considered in this

Table 11.10 Two Instances of pZp *Vʔ and only Word-Final pCh *Vʔ

Gloss	*pZp*	*pCh*
'chili'	*ki:ʔnaʔ	*kìnáʔ
'moon,' 'month'	*kʷ=eʔjoʔ	(*kooʔ)

Table 11.11 pZp *Vʔ before *(l)l with No Corresponding pCh *ʔ

Gloss	*pZp*	*pCh*
'deep (water),' 'depth'	*keʔla	*kelà
'sleepiness'	*kʷa=ka:ʔlla	*kàlá
'make music'	*-o:ʔlla	*-ùlá
'night'	*tʲ-e:ʔla	*ᴴtelà
'clay griddle'	*tʲiʔla	*ntiną
'flesh,' 'meat'	*kʷe:ʔlaʔ	*kʷeną́ʔ
'snake'	*kʷ=e:ʔlla	*kʷeną́

study (4.38 percent) display word-medial pZp **Vʔl* corresponding to pCh word-medial **Vl* or **Vn*.

The cognate sets and sound correspondences presented in this section represent a majority 117 of the 160 cognate sets considered in this study (73 percent). All of these sets involve quite regular correspondences of laryngeal nuclei in pZp corresponding to glottal stop in the same position of the pCh cognate—or otherwise no glottal stop in pCh due to its regular elision preceding obstruents or **l*. Therefore, laryngealization or glottal stop is straightforwardly reconstructable in these positions in the proto-Zapotecan forms that these cognate sets reflect, even though the precise phonological nature of the reconstructed elements is not straightforward. These 117 sets are thus considered the "regular" laryngeal/glottal correspondences: where pZn laryngeals/glottals are "easy" to reconstruct. The remaining forty-three cognate sets—a smaller but significant percentage (43/160 = 27 percent)—do not lend themselves to straightforward reconstruction given the current state of our knowledge about proto-Zapotec, proto-Chatino, and, by extension, their shared ancestor proto-Zapotecan.

6. Where pZn **ʔ* Is *Not* Easy to Reconstruct

In 10 of the 160 cognate sets (6.25 percent), proto-Zapotec forms display a word-final checked vowel **Vʔ* where there is no corresponding word-final glottal stop in proto-Chatino; these are presented in table 11.12. In one case, pCh **kàʔjú* 'five,' the lack of a word-final glottal stop could be due to glottal stop culminativity (as shown in table 11.10).

Similarly, 4 of the 160 cognate sets (2.5 percent) display a pattern in which the pZp form contains a word-medial checked vowel preceding a sonorant consonant where there is no corresponding pCh word-medial glottal stop (table 11.13). As shown in the sets in table 11.9, pZp and pCh usually display corresponding word-medial

Table 11.12 Word-Final **Vʔ* in pZp but No Word-Final Glottal Stop in pCh

Gloss	*pZp*	*pCh*
'five'	*ka:ʔjuʔ	*kàʔjú
'copal'	*ja:ʔlaʔ	*janá̜
'nine'	*kAʔ	*kàá
'broom'	*k-okʷaʔ	*(k/l)-ùkʷá
'ten'	*k-tʲi:ʔ	*tíi
'thread,' 'rope'	*to(ʔ)	*huú̜
'bean'	*(kʷe=)sa:ʔ	(*n-taa) *ØH or *LH
'give'	*-saʔ	(*-taa) *ØH or *LH
'bee'	*kʷ=esoʔ	*kʷetǫ
'sky'	*ke=kʷaʔ	*kʷaą̀

Table 11.13 Cognate Sets with pZp *Vʔ Preceding a Sonorant but no pCh Glottal

Gloss	*pZp*	*pCh*
'flower'	*keʔjek	*keè
'leave (trn.)'	*ok=s-a:ʔnna	*-u-t-anó
'work'	*tʲi:ʔna	*tìná̜
'corn cob'	*ja:ʔna	*jàná̜

laryngeal nuclei and glottal stop, respectively, where a sonorant consonant follows. In the case of 'flower' the lack of the glide **j* is due to the glide deletion change shown in (4), but the lack of glottal stop still remains unexplained.

How do we explain the lack of word-final (table 11.12) or word-medial (table 11.13) glottal stop in pCh forms whose pZp cognates would lead us to expect pCh glottal stop, based on the regular correspondences? One observation is that most of the pCh forms in these cognate sets (eleven out of fourteen) reflect one of the pCh basic tone melodies that involve H tone: *ØH, *LH, or *HØ. It is possible that the loss of some pZn laryngeal articulation has left a H tone in pCh in these forms. Loss of glottal stop has been shown to result in H tone in Athabaskan languages (Kingston 2005, 2011) and Mixtec languages (Dürr 1987; Pankratz and Pike 1967), but in those same language groups, the same loss of a laryngeal articulation may result in L tone in some varieties. Furthermore, cognate sets such as pZp **kʷejaʔ* and pCh **kʷèjáʔ* 'measure (n.)' (see table 11.7) show word-final checked vowel or glottal stop in both protolanguages and the *LH tone melody in pCh. Therefore, if the H tones in pCh in tables 11.12 and 11.13 have in fact resulted from the loss of some pZn laryngeal articulation, then we are looking at the results of some type of merger.

A small but similar and intriguing group of cognate sets (3/160 = 1.88 percent) involves proto-Zapotec forms with checked vowels in both the final and penultimate syllable, where there is no glottal stop in either syllable in proto-Chatino (table 11.14). The pCh forms all bear the *LH tone melody, which is reminiscent of Matisoff's (1970) account of the genesis of the high-rising tone of Lahu (Tibeto-Burman), which he argues resulted from the loss of two laryngeal articulations, or "glottal incidents," in a single syllable (but see Thurgood 1977 for an alternative account).

Another substantial set of cognates (12/160 = 7.5 percent) presents a pattern somewhat the reverse, in which pCh forms display a word-final glottal stop where there is no reconstructed word-final checked vowel in pZp (table 11.15). Only a few of these pCh forms contain *H,

Table 11.14 Two Instances of pZp **Vʔ* and No pCh Glottal Stop

Gloss	*pZp*	*pCh*
'cry'	*-o:ʔnaʔ	*-ùná
'run'	*-o=ʃo:ʔ(n)naʔk	*-sùná
'tump-line'	*toʔ=kʷa:ʔnaʔ	(*huų) kʷàná

Table 11.15 Word-Final *ʔ in pCh with No Corresponding pZp Laryngealization

Gloss	*pZp*	*pCh*
'get dressed'	*-akku	*-akùʔ
'speak'	*-akʷi	*-akwiʔ
'get wet'	*-atsa(k)	*-àtzàʔ
'fire'	*ki:	*kiiʔ
'peccary'	*kʷ=ewe	*kùwèʔ
'armadillo'	*kʷe=kukkʷe	*kùkʷę̀ʔ
'deity,' 'respect'	*ne	*=neʔ
'short in height'	*ʃa(t)ta	*sàtàʔ
'shell, degrain corn'	*-ʃ-o:ʔkʷa	*-u-sukʷáʔ
'spindle'	*kʷe=kussi	*kùtę́ʔ
'get closed, covered'	*-j-Aʔku	*-j-àkǫ́ʔ
'cover, close (trn.)'	*-ok=s-Aʔku	*-u-t-àkǫ́ʔ

while most of them display pCh tone melodies that likely would have involved phonetically low pitch: *ØØ, *LL, or *ØL. However, not much can be confidently determined here without further pZp tone reconstruction or without reexamining primary Zapotec data. The last two forms are a pair of derivationally related verbs whose final glottal stop in pCh is reconstructed based on its presence in Zenzontepec Chatino *-j-àkǫ́ʔ*, *-u-t-àkǫ́ʔ*, and Tataltepec Chatino *-t-akǫ́ʔ* (Sullivant 2015: 328), but the Zacatepec (Eastern) Chatino form lacks the glottal: *-j-akǫ̌*, *-o-t-akǫ̌*.[12] Since Zenzontepec together with Tataltepec represent the two primary subgroups of pCh, reconstructing the glottal here for pCh is advised, but the Zacatepec and Zapotec forms suggest possible variation in proto-Zapotecan, or else some other change that is not yet identified.

A similar correspondence shared by 2 of the 160 cognate sets (1.25 percent) involves no laryngealization in pZp forms where the cognate pCh forms have an intervocalic glottal stop (table 11.16). Note that pCh had a minimality preference for bimoraic phonological

Table 11.16 pZp *V Corresponding to pCh *VʔV

Gloss	*pZp*	*pCh*
'green'	*(na=)ka	*n-kàʔà
'go around, walk'	*sA	*-taʔą

words (Campbell 2013: 400), which could explain why the pCh forms are bimoraic while the pZp forms contain monomoraic roots.[13]

The basic correspondences discussed earlier in table 11.6 (*VʔV : *VʔV) and table 11.7 (*Vʔ# : *Vʔ#) are common and fairly regular. However, other cognate sets that involve proto-Zapotec laryngeal nuclei and proto-Chatino glottal stop differ from the regular correspondences by showing a mix of the two correspondences. For example, the five cognate sets (5/160 = 3.13 percent) shown in table 11.17 contain a word-final pZp checked syllable corresponding to a pCh intervocalic glottal stop (*Vʔ : *VʔV), and the three cognate sets (3/160 = 1.88 percent) shown in table 11.18 display pZp broken syllables corresponding to pCh word-final glottal stop (*VʔV : *Vʔ). In both groups of cognates, the pCh forms bear the low-pitch tone melodies *ØØ, *ØL, *LL.

A final minority group of cognate sets (4/160 = 2.5 percent) displays another pattern, in which the pZp forms contain a checked vowel in the initial syllable while the pCh forms display a word-final glottal stop (table 11.19), suggesting that an otherwise corresponding laryngeal articulation has moved in one or other of the proto-languages. The pCh forms display a range of tone melodies, and no explanation for this pattern has yet been found.

The discussion in this section has presented relatively small groups of cognate sets that display minority sound correspondences that involve laryngeal nuclei in proto-Zapotec and/or glottal stop in proto-Chatino. These cognate sets display laryngeal correspondences that diverge from the more common sound correspondences presented in §5, or they involve the same correspondences but in different positions within the cognate forms. So, where does this

Table 11.17 Word-Final pZp **Vʔ* Corresponding to pCh **VʔV*

Gloss	*pZp*	*pCh*
'scorpion'	*ko]=neʔ	*ʃu]-neʔę
'air,' 'wind'	*k^{w}=e:ʔ	*k^{w}iʔį
'image of a god'	*k^{w}e=tawoʔ	*hoʔò
'see it'	*-naʔ	*-nàʔą̀
'get full'	*-tsAʔ	*-t͡saʔą

Table 11.18 pZp **VʔV* Corresponding to pCh **Vʔ*

Gloss	*pZp*	*pCh*
'soap'	*(k^{w}e=)jaʔa	(*k^{w}ijaʔ)
'sleeping mat'	*ta:ʔa	*hààʔ
'offspring'	*ʃiʔinne	*sinęʔ

Table 11.19 pZp Word-Medial **Vʔ* and pCh Word-Final **Vʔ*

Gloss	*pZp*	*pCh*
'trunk,' 'box'	*kiʔna	*kìnàʔ
'mushroom'	*k^{w}=eʔja	*k^{w}ejaʔ
'foot'	*k-iʔja	*kijaʔ
'very young'	*k^{w}-eʔne	*k^{w}enéʔ

laryngeal residue leave us in progressing toward a more complete reconstruction of laryngeal features in proto-Zapotecan? Where do the remaining issues lie? And how can we move forward?

7. Discussion and Conclusions

While the non-laryngeal segmental phonology of proto-Zapotecan is now well understood, this is not the case for the suprasegmental phonology. No reconstruction of proto-Zapotecan tone has yet been put forth, and the present study has demonstrated that although laryngeal nuclei and glottal stop are relatively confidently reconstructed for pZp and pCh, respectively, a significant number of laryngeal correspondences between the two protolanguages remain unexplained. Surprisingly, almost all possible laryngeal-glottal correspondences are attested in the data, excluding pZp *VʔV : pCh *V. A total of 117 of the 160 cognate sets (about 73 percent) display laryngeal-glottal sound correspondences that fit into the "regular" correspondences presented in §5, while the other 43 cognate sets (about 27 percent) display the "irregular" or less frequent sound correspondences presented in §6. The laryngeal-glottal sound correspondences, their frequencies in the data set, and some observations with respect to pCh tone are summarized in table 11.20, with the "regular" correspondences presented in the top portion of the table, and the "irregular" ones in the bottom portion.

Some tendencies emerge from the examination of the irregular correspondences in the bottom half of table 11.20:

1. Correspondences that involve laryngealization in proto-Zapotec but no glottal stop in proto-Chatino correlate with pCh tonal melodies that include *H tone.
2. The three pCh forms that have no glottal stop at all that are cognate with pZp forms that contain two checked syllables all bear the pCh tonal melody *LH.
3. In the sets that display the other irregular correspondences, including those in which pZp lacks laryngealization where pCh displays glottal stop, most of the pCh forms bear the low-pitch tonal melodies, *ØL, *LL, or *ØØ.

These tendencies suggest that there has been some diachronic interplay between tone and laryngealization and/or glottal stop in Zapotecan languages. This is not at all surprising given that similar patterns are displayed in modern Zapotec languages (Nelson 2004) and other groups of tone languages, such as Tibeto-Burman

Table 11.20 Summary of pZp and pCh Laryngeal/Glottal Correspondences

pZp	*pCh*	*Changes, notes*	*Qty.*	*%*	*Table #*
*VʔV#	*VʔV#	Primary correspondence	18	11.3%	T. 11.6
*Vʔ#	*Vʔ#	Primary correspondence	38	23.8%	T. 11.7
*VʔC$_{[-son]}$	*VC$_{[-son]}$	pCh *ʔ > Ø / __ C$_{[-son]}$	35	21.9%	T. 11.8
*VʔC$_{[+son]}$	*VʔC$_{[+son]}$	Primary correspondence	17	10.6%	T. 11.9
*VʔC$_{[+son]}$Vʔ	*V(C$_{[+son]}$)Vʔ	pCh *ʔ > Ø (culminativity?)	2	1.3%	T. 11.10
*Vʔl	*Vl/n	pCh *ʔ > Ø /__l	7	4.4%	T. 11.11
		Subtotal	**117**	**~73%**	
*Vʔ	*V	pCh tone melodies involving *H	10	6.3%	T. 11.12
*VʔC$_{[+son]}$	*VC$_{[+son]}$	pCh tone melodies involving *H	4	2.5%	T. 11.13
*VʔnVʔ	*VnV	pCh *LH	3	1.9%	T. 11.14
*V	*Vʔ	Mostly pCh low-pitch melodies	12	7.5%	T. 11.15
*V	*VʔV	pCh low-pitch melodies	2	1.3%	T. 11.16
*Vʔ	*VʔV	pCh low-pitch melodies	5	3.1%	T. 11.17
*VʔV	*Vʔ	pCh low-pitch melodies	3	1.9%	T. 11.18
*VʔC$_{[+son]}$V	*VC$_{[+son]}$Vʔ	No notable pattern	4	2.5%	T. 11.19
		Subtotal	**43**	**~27%**	
			160	100%	

(see, e.g., Matisoff 1970), Danish (Ejskjær 1990), and Mixtec (Dürr 1987), and loss or changes in laryngeal features are the main known mechanisms for tonogenesis (Haudricourt 1954; Hombert et al. 1979; Kingston 2011, Matisoff 1973; Mei 1970). However, the specific details of any such interplay between tone and laryngealization or glottal stop in Zapotecan unfortunately cannot yet be determined. With the information that is currently available, the irregular laryngeal correspondences cannot be shown to be in complementary distribution since the pCh tone tendencies observed in particular irregular correspondences are also found in other irregular correspondences, as well as throughout the regular correspondences, and we still have no reliable pZp tone reconstruction. It is possible that language contact between earlier forms of Chatino and Zapotec languages has further obscured some of the correspondences.

It is also possible that morpho-phonological processes have created some of the irregular laryngeal correspondences that we find between proto-Zapotec and proto-Chatino. Laryngeal alternations can be observed in inflectional paradigms in many modern Zapotec varieties, as displayed in the Juchitán (Central) Zapotec verb *-uni* 'to do' (Pérez Báez and Kaufman 2016: 245) in table 11.21, which is compared with its Zenzontepec Chatino cognate. While the Chatino verb has a glottal stop preceding the word-medial sonorant in all inflected forms, the Zapotec verb has a checked vowel only in the perfective form of the verb and no laryngealization in the other forms.

Similar laryngeal alternations can be observed in derivational morphology. For example, some Lachixío Zapotec verb pairs display no laryngealization in less active verbs but checked vowels in their derived more active counterparts, as shown in table 11.22 (Sicoli 2015). The checked vowel in the more active verb of one pair occurs in the final syllable, and in the other pair it occurs in the initial syllable. The Zenzontepec Chatino cognate verbs display no glottal stop in any of the forms—which we expect for the second pair since the glottal preceded an obstruent—and the more active verbs are derived

Table 11.21 Laryngeal Alternation in Zapotec TAM Inflection

Gloss	*Juchitán Zapotec*	*Zenzontepec Chatino*
'do'	-uni (< pZp *-uni)	-ʔne (< *-ùʔnì)
POT	g=ŭni	ʔne
HAB	r=uni	ʔne
PFV	be=uʔni [biʔni]	nka-ʔne

Table 11.22 Laryngeal Alternation in Zapotec Derivation

Gloss	*Lachixío Zapotec*	*Zenzontepec Chatino*
'pass (by)'	-dete (< *-teʔti)	-tehę̄ (< *-tihį̀)
'pass it (to someone)'	-deteʔ	-u-tēhę́
'get punctured'	-ato	-j-áhā
'puncture (tr.)'	-aʔto (< *-k-i:]ʔtok)	-u-t-áhā

with the causative prefix *u*-. In the case of 'pass it (to someone)' the pCh causativization is also marked by tone change, reflecting the pCh *LH tone melody found in forms whose pZp cognates have a checked vowel corresponding to no glottal stop in pCh.

The synchronic laryngealization alternations that occur in inflectional and derivational morphology in Zapotec languages likely offer important clues to either refining pZp laryngeal reconstructions or understanding some of the sound changes that have led to the irregular laryngeal correspondences between pZp and pCh. However, as pCh tone patterns appear to be relevant in the irregular laryngeal correspondences, in order to better understand Zapotecan laryngeal diachrony and clean up the laryngeal residue laid out in this study, an updated and more complete reconstruction of proto-Zapotec tone is badly needed, and it would be useful to recheck the pZp laryngeal reconstructions by incorporating more Zapotec varieties into the reconstruction. As Sally Thomason (1994) notes, "Reliable historical linguistic hypothesis testing requires applying the comparative method with the highest level of methodological rigor." If we hope to clear up the proto-Zapotecan laryngeal residue to better understand suprasegmental diachrony in general, such rigor must first be applied to proto-Zapotec tone reconstruction and an expanded proto-Chatino tone reconstruction.

Endnotes

1. I am grateful for the input of the many people who have made this chapter possible and/or helped improve it significantly: Chatino Language Documentation Project colleagues Emiliana Cruz, Hilaria Cruz, Justin McIntosh, Ryan Sullivant, Stéphanie Villard, and Tony Woodbury for sharing data and insights; Terrence Kaufman for sharing knowledge of Zapotecan languages; audiences at the 2014 *Fifteenth Spring Workshop on Theory and Method in Linguistic Reconstruction* at the University of Michigan and the 2020 LSA Winter Meeting in New Orleans for valuable comments and questions; Zenzontepec Chatino collaborator Tranquilino Cavero Ramírez; and the editors of the present volume, Anna Babel and Mark Sicoli. Finally, I express my sincerest thanks to Sally Thomason, to whom this paper is dedicated, for the early foundational mentorship and invaluable and rigorous historical linguistic training.

2. This brings to mind the proto-Indo-European elements that de Saussure (1879) indirectly reconstructed based on their effects on neighboring vowels, which are often regarded to have been laryngeal consonants.

3. All pZp forms are from Kaufman (2016) and all pCh forms are from Campbell (2013, 2018) or are new reconstructions. The orthography used here differs from the IPA as follows: <ts> = [t͡s], <V̨> = nasal vowel; <V́> = high tone; <V̀> = low tone; pCh <V_1V_1> and pZp <V:> = [Vː]. Geminates in pZp are represented as <CC>: for example, <kk>, <kk^w>, <tts>.

4. Upson and Longacre (1965) mistakenly included Elotepec Papabuco (Zapotec) in their Chatino reconstruction.

5. According to Kaufman (2016), proto-Zapotec(an) borrowed forms with **mm* from early forms of Zoquean and Matlatzinca.

6. Kaufman (2016: 50) recognizes the pZp form with **mm* as a borrowing from Matlatzinca(n) **tsɨmi*. A possible Chatino cognate is Zenzontepec Chatino *ki* **chuwī** 'large (woven) basket'.

7. According to Beam de Azcona (2014), no shared innovations have yet been identified that support what de Angulo and Freeland (1935) referred to as "Southern" Zapotec (see also Smith Stark 2007).

8. The reflexes of the pZp geminate-single contrast, often analyzed as a fortis-lenis contrast in Zapotec varieties (see, e.g., Avelino Becerra 2001; Jaeger 1983, inter alia), are not pertinent to the discussion here.

9. If a pZp reconstruction has at least one Chatino cognate (and borrowing does not provide a likely explanation), then that form is taken to be reconstructable for pCh and pZn.

10. The quality of the vowel represented as <A> in pZp 'fresh ear of corn' is undetermined (Beam de Azcona et al. 2018: 50).

11. In some cases, the pZp forms also have checked vowels in final syllables corresponding to pCh word-final glottal stop.

12. This is one of very few forms for which modern Chatino varieties vary in the presence or absence of glottal stop.

13. Sets such as pZp *na(ʔ) : pCh (*naaʔ) 1sg and pZp *naʔ ~ jaʔ : pCh *jaàʔ 'hand' also had short vowels in pZp but do not display intervocalic glottal stop in pCh. This issue is not yet resolved, but it's possible these forms had long vowels in pZn.

References

Antonio Ramos, Pafnuncio. 2015. La fonología y morfología del zapoteco de San Pedro Mixtepec (PhD dissertation). Centro de Investigaciones y Estudios Superiores en Antropología Social, D.F.

Arellanes Arellanes, Francisco. 2009. El sistema fonológico y las propiedades fonéticas del zapoteco de San Pablo Güilá. Descripción y análisis formal. Tesis de PhD, El Colegio de México.

Avelino Becerra, Heriberto. 2001. The phonetic correlates of fortis-lenis in Yalálag Zapotec consonants. MA thesis, University of California, Los Angeles.

Avelino Becerra, Heriberto. 2004. Topics in Yalálag Zapotec, with particular reference to its phonetic structures (PhD dissertation). University of California, Los Angeles.

Bauernschmidt, Amy. 1965. Amuzgo syllable dynamics. *Language*, 41: 471–83.

Beam de Azcona, Rosemary. 2004. A Coatlán-Loxicha Zapotec grammar (PhD dissertation). University of California, Berkeley.

Beam de Azcona, Rosemary. 2014. Algunas isoglosas de la Sierra Sur. Paper presented at the Seminario de Lenguas Indígenas, IIFL, UNAM.

Beam de Azcona, Rosemary, Francisco Arellanes Arellanes, Mario E. Chávez Peón, Mario Hernández Luna, Sofía Gabriela Morales Camacho, and Carlos de Jesús Wagner. 2018. *Umlaut* y otros procesos de los sistemas vocálicos de las lenguas zapotecas. In Elsa Cristina Buenrostro Díaz, Lucero Meléndez Guadarrama, and Marcela San Giacomo Trinidad (Eds.), *Lingüística histórica de lenguas indomexicanas: hallazgos y discusiones recientes*, 39–83. México: Universidad Nacional Autónoma de México, Instituto de Investigaciones Antropológicas.

Belmar, Francisco.1902. *Investigaciones sobre la lengua chatina*. Oaxaca: Imprenta del Comercio.

Benton, Joe. 1988. Proto-Zapotec phonology. Ms.

Benton, Joe. 2001. A reconstruction of the tone system of Proto Zapotec. Ms.

Black, Cheryl A. 1995. Laryngeal licensing and syllable well-formedness in Quiegolani Zapotec. *Workpapers of the Summer Institute of Linguistics*, 39: 11–32.

Boas, Franz. 1913. Notes on the Chatino language of Mexico. *American Anthropologist, New Series*, 15: 78–86.

Campbell, Eric. 2013. The internal diversification and subgrouping of Chatino. *International Journal of American Linguistics*, 79: 395–420.

Campbell, Eric W. 2014. Aspects of the phonology and morphology of Zenzontepec Chatino, a Zapotecan language of Oaxaca, Mexico (PhD dissertation). University of Texas at Austin.

Campbell, Eric W. 2017a. Otomanguean historical linguistics: Past, present and prospects for the future. *Language & Linguistics Compass*, 11: e12240.

Campbell, Eric W. 2017b. Otomanguean historical linguistics: Exploring the subgroups. *Language & Linguistics Compass*, 11: e12244.

Campbell, Eric W. 2018. Una mirada al desarrollo fonológico del protochatino. In Elsa Cristina Buenrostro Díaz, Lucero Meléndez Guadarrama, and Marcela San Giacomo Trinidad (Eds.), *Lingüística histórica de lenguas indomexicanas: hallazgos y discusiones recientes*, 15–37. México: Universidad Nacional Autónoma de México, Instituto de Investigaciones Antropológicas.

Campbell, Eric W. In press. Why is tone change still poorly understood, and how might documentation of less-studied tone languages help? In Patience L. Epps, Na'ama Pat-El and Danny Law (Eds.), *Historical linguistics and endangered languages: Exploring diversity in language change*. New York: Routledge.

Campbell, Eric W., and Anthony C. Woodbury. 2010. The comparative tonology of Chatino: A prolegomenon. Paper presented at the Society for the Study of the Indigenous Languages of the Americas, Annual Meeting, Baltimore, MD.

Campbell, Eric W., and Emiliana Cruz. 2010. El sistema numérico del proto-chatino. In *Proceedings of the Conference on Indigenous Languages of Latin America-IV*. Austin, TX: AILLA.

Campbell, Eric W., and George Aaron Broadwell. In press. The Zapotecan languages. In Sören Wichmann (Ed.), *The languages and linguistics of Middle America: A comprehensive guide*. Berlin: De Gruyter Mouton.

Chávez Peón, Mario E. 2010. The interaction of metrical structure, tone, and phonation types in Quiaviní Zapotec (PhD dissertation). University of British Columbia.

Cruz, Emiliana. 2011. Phonology, tone and the functions of tone in San Juan Quiahije Chatino (PhD dissertation). University of Texas at Austin.

de Angulo, Jaime, and L. S. Freeland. 1935. The Zapotekan linguistic group: A comparative study of Chinanteco, Chocho, Mazateco, Cuicateco, Mixteco, Chatino, and especially of Zapoteco proper and its dialects. *International Journal of American Linguistics*, 8: 1–38.

de Saussure, Ferdinand. 1879. *Memoire sur le systeme primitif des voyelles dans les langues indo-europeennes*. Leipzig: Vieweg

Dürr, Michael. 1987. A preliminary reconstruction of the proto-Mixtec tonal system. *Indiana*, 11: 19–61.

Ejskjær, Inger. 1990. Stød and pitch accents in the Danish dialects. *Acta Linguistica Hafniensia*, 22: 49–75.

Fernández de Miranda, María Teresa. 1995. *El protozapoteco*. México, DF: El Colegio de México and Instituto Nacional de Antropología e Historia.

Foreman, John Olen. 2006. The morphosyntax of subjects in Macuiltianguis Zapotec (PhD dissertation). University of California, Los Angeles.

Gutiérrez Lorenzo, Ambrocio. 2014. Construcciones de verbos seriales en el zapoteco de Teotitlán del Valle. MA thesis, Centro de Investigaciones y Estudios Superiores en Antropología Social, DF.

Haudricourt, André-Georges. 1954. De l'origine des tons du vietnamien. *Journal Asiatique*, 242: 69–82.

Hernández Luna, Mario Ulises. 2019. Fonología del miahuateco. Sincronía, diacronía y clasificación (PhD dissertation). El Colegio del México.

Hombert, Jean-Marie, John J. Ohala, and William G. Ewan. 1979. Phonetic explanations for the development of tones. *Language*, 55: 37–58.

INEGI. 2010. Censo de Población y Vivienda 2010. https://www.inegi.org.mx/default.html, date of access: August 7, 2018.

Jaeger, Jeri J. 1983. The fortis/lenis question: Evidence from Zapotec and Jawon. *Journal of Phonetics*, 11: 177–89.

Janda, Richard D., and Brian D. Joseph. 2003. On language, change, and language change—or, of history, linguistics, and historical linguistics. In Brian D. Joseph and Richard D. Janda (Eds.), *The Handbook of historical linguistics* 3–180. Oxford: Blackwell.

Jones, Ted E., and Lyle M. Knudson. 1977. Guelavía Zapotec phonemes. In William R. Merrifield (Eds.), *Studies in Otomanguean phonology*, 163–80. Dallas, TX: Summer Institute of Linguistics.

Kaufman, Terrence. 1988. Otomanguean tense/aspect/mood, voice, and nominalization markers. Unpublished monograph.

Kaufman, Terrence. 2006. Oto-Mangean languages. In Keith Brown (Ed.), *Encyclopedia of Language and Linguistics*, 2nd ed., vol. 9, 118–24. Oxford: Elsevier.

Kaufman, Terrence. 2016. Proto-Sapotek(an) reconstructions. Institute for Mesoamerican Studies, University at Albany, State University of New York.

Kingston, John. 2005. The phonetics of Athabaskan tonogenesis. In Sharon Hargus and Keren Rice (Eds.), *Athabaskan prosody*, 137–84. Amsterdam: John Benjamins.

Kingston, John. 2011. Tonogenesis. In M. van Oostendorp, C. J. Ewan, E. Hume, and K. Rice (Eds.), *Blackwell Companion to Phonology*, vol. 4, Ch. 97. Oxford: Blackwell.

López Nicolás, Oscar. 2016. Estudios de la fonología y gramática del zapoteco de Zoochina (PhD dissertation). Centro de Investigaciones y Estudios Superiores en Antropología Social, DF.

Matisoff, James A. 1970. Glottal dissimilation and the Lahu high-rising tone: A tonogenetic case-study. *Journal of the American Oriental Society*, 90: 13–44.

Matisoff, James A. 1973. Tonogenesis in Southeast Asia. In Larry M. Hyman (Ed.), *Consonant types and tone*, 71–95. Los Angeles: University of Southern California.

McIntosh, Justin D. 2015. Aspects of phonology and morphology of Teotepec Eastern Chatino (PhD dissertation). University of Texas at Austin.

Mei, Tsu-lin. 1970. Tones and prosody in Middle Chinese and the origin of the rising tone. *Harvard Journal of Asiatic Studies*, 30: 86–110.

Nelson, Julia Louise. 2004. Tone and glottalization on nominals in San Juan Mixtepec Zapotec. MA thesis, University of Texas at Arlington.

Pankratz, Leo, and Eunice V. Pike. 1967. Phonology and morphotonemics of Ayutla Mixtec. *International Journal of American Linguistics*, 33: 287–99.

Pérez Báez, Gabriela, and Terrence Kaufman. 2016. Verb classes in Juchitán Zapotec. *Anthropological Linguistics*, 58: 217–57.

Pride, Kitty. 2004. Gramática chatina de la zona alta. In Kitty Pride and Leslie Pride (Eds.), *Diccionario chatino de la zona alta*, 341–426. México, DF: Instituto Lingüístico de Verano.

Rensch, Calvin R. 1976. *Comparative Otomanguean phonology*. Bloomington: Indiana University.

Sicoli, Mark A. 2015. Agency and verb valence in Lachixío Zapotec. In Natalie Operstein and Aaron Huey Sonnenschein (Eds.), *Valence changes in Zapotec*, 191–212. Amsterdam: John Benjamins.

Smith Stark, Thomas C. 1999. El solteco y el zapoteco occidental: un aprecio a partir de los vocabularios de Peñafiel. Paper presented at the V Congreso Nacional de Lingüística, Monterrey, México.

Smith Stark, Thomas C. 2002a. Pied-piping with inversion in information questions. Ms, prepared for the Festschrift for Terrence Kaufman.

Smith Stark, Thomas C. 2002b. Las clases verbales del zapoteco de Chichicapan. In *Proceedings of the VI Encuentro Internacional de Lingüística en el Noroeste*, 165–212. Hermosillo: Editorial UniSon.

Smith Stark, Thomas C. 2007. Algunas isoglosas zapotecas. In Cristina Buenrostro et al. (Eds.), *Memorias del III Coloquio Internacional de Lingüística Mauricio Swadesh*, 69–133. México, DF: Universidad Nacional Autónoma de México and Instituto Nacional de Lenguas Indígenas.

Sonnenschein, Aaron Huey. 2004. A descriptive grammar of San Bartolomé Zoogoho Zapotec (PhD dissertation). University of Southern California.

Suárez, Jorge A. 1973. On proto-Zapotec phonology. *International Journal of American Linguistics*, 39: 236–49.

Sullivant, J. Ryan. 2015. The phonology and inflectional morphology of *Cháʔknyá*, Tataltepec de Valdés Chatino, a Zapotecan language (PhD dissertation). University of Texas at Austin.

Sullivant, J. Ryan. 2016. Reintroducing Teojomulco Chatino. *International Journal of American Linguistics*, 82: 393–423.

Swadesh, Morris. 1947. The phonemic structure of proto-Zapotec. *International Journal of American Linguistics*, 13: 220–30.

Thomason, Sarah G. 1994. Hypothesis generation vs. hypothesis testing: A comparison between Greenberg's classifications in Africa and in the Americas. Ms, University of Pittsburgh.

Thomason, Sarah G. 1997. On reconstructing past contact situations. In Jane H. Hill, P. J. Mistry, and Lyle Campbell (Eds.), *The life of language: Papers in linguistics in honor of William Bright*, 153–68. Berlin: Mouton de Gruyter.

Thurgood, Graham. 1977. Lisu and proto-Lolo-Burmese. *Acta Orientalia*, 38:147–207.

Upson, B. W., and Robert E. Longacre. 1965. Proto-Chatino phonology. *International Journal of American Linguistics*, 31: 312–22.

Villard, Stéphanie. 2015. The phonology and morphology of Zacatepec Eastern Chatino (PhD dissertation). University of Texas at Austin.

CHAPTER 12

The Early Stages of Ecuadorian Quechua

Pieter Muysken

1. Introduction

This paper is about the early history of Ecuadorian Quechua.[1] This variety of Quechua is of interest because the Quechuan languages are not native to Ecuador, so it must have come about through shift. Quechua[2] spread there in the fifteenth century with the expansion of the Inca Empire northward roughly to what is now the Colombian border. However, the spread of Quechua to Ecuador cannot be credited exclusively to the Incas: when the Spanish invasion took place after 1530, Quechua was by no means established yet as the vernacular language. Thus, the emergence of Ecuadorian Quechua also became part of the Spanish colonial project, ironically enough (Hartmann 1979; Muysken 1977). This is in itself already remarkable.

As Quechua spread from Peru to Ecuador, it underwent many changes, in part due to progressive restructuring and substrate influence of the languages (mostly Barbacoan and Chicham or Jivaroan) originally spoken in the Ecuadorian highlands. I will not discuss the issue of substrate here; it is discussed in Muysken (2019). However, I will try to answer the question of the speed with which the changes took place, trying to find evidence in the written sources; these need to be treated with caution, however, because the missionary materials may deliberately present a somewhat antiquated version of the language, in some cases. The reason for this is twofold: first of all, religious ceremonies would require a 'high' register, often associated with more traditional language. Second, the written models at the missionaries' disposal often reflected earlier stages of the language.

After briefly surveying some of the relevant sources, I discuss the external history of the Quechuan languages in section 2, and in section 3 I zoom in on some linguistic variables that underwent changes in Ecuador, in light of the overall discussion. In section 4, I summarize and draw some conclusions.

2. External History and the Historical Antecedents of Ecuadorian Quechua

2.1. The Quechuan Language Family

The Quechuan language family is a comparable in time depth and internal diversity to the Romance language family. The Quechuan languages are an important language family in South America. It is a large family, with varieties spoken (from north to south) in Colombia, Ecuador, Peru, possibly Brazil, Bolivia, Chile, and Argentina. Undoubtedly, the heartland of the family is Peru (Cerrón Palomino 1987; Adelaar with Muysken 2004). Here we find most variation between varieties, and the largest number of speakers. Speaker numbers are notoriously difficult to establish, with rapid language shift to Spanish in most areas, but an estimate could be somewhere around 8 million speakers (Adelaar & Muysken 2004: 168), to give a first indication. It is mostly spoken in the Andean highlands, but there are increasing numbers of speakers in the Andean foothills on the Amazonian fringe as well (Muysken 2000). Historically, it is a fairly shallow family, with the Central Peruvian Andes as the most likely place of origin, datable around 200 CE perhaps. In many respects, the Quechuan languages are similar in major components of their morpho-syntax. Table 12.1 gives a schematic account of the family northward (see also Van de Kerke and Muysken 2014). There was also spread into Bolivia, Argentina, and Chile, but that is not relevant here.

Table 12.1 Part of the History of Quechuan Languages Relevant to the Emergence of Ecuadorian Quechua

Date	*Event*
2–500 CE	Quechua present in the highlands of Central Peru (roughly the area east of Lima), with a subsequent split into two branches: QI (Central Peru), QII (South and North Peru, other countries) (Torero 1970)
800	Consolidation of QII varieties in the Ayacucho area, where the language became part of important supra-regional polities
1000	Varieties of Quechua II were taken to northern Peru as part of the Huari Empire, where they underwent some influence from neighboring Quechua I varieties (the early northern expansion). Varieties were diffused from Cajamarca and the neighboring regions into the lowlands, San Martin, as late as the colonial period
1200	Spread of QII further south into Aymara territory, such as the Cuzco era and adoption by Inca rulers, who founded an empire centered around Cuzco
1500	Spread into Ecuador of 'northern' Quechua
1540	Spread into Colombia and from northern Peru into San Martin and Lamas, the Peruvian lowlands
1600	Spread into upper Amazon from the Ecuadorian highlands, including territory that is now northern Peru

2.2. The Varieties Involved

In this paper, four related varieties are discussed, which together form Northern Quechua: Highland Ecuadorian Kichwa (HiKi), with most speakers (around 600,000); Amazonian Ecuadorian Kichwa (AmKi), with possibly 50,000 speakers; Inga, spoken in Colombia by 30,000 people; and Southern Pastaza Quechua (SPast), spoken in Peru by a few thousand people. All varieties have been reasonably well documented. Inga has been studied by Stephen Levinsohn from the Summer Institute of Linguistics (SIL) together with a number of Inga speakers (Levinsohn 1974, 1976; Levinsohn and Mongui 1974). SPast has been documented by Peter Landerman (1973) and subsequently by Tödter, Waters, and Zahn (2002), also from the SIL. The four varieties differ at a time depth of 400 years, and therefore share many similarities, but different language contact effects and lack of communication between at least the Peruvian, Colombian, and Ecuadorian varieties have caused also quite a few changes leading to divergence. I do not know whether there would be mutual comprehension, although for basic utterances this must be so, certainly after some exposure.

2.3. What Was the Quechua That Was Brought to Ecuador?

Logically speaking, Quechua varieties must have spread into Ecuador from northern Peru, but Ecuadorian Quechua is not really like the varieties spoken there currently. Different types of Quechua must have arrived in Ecuador. We can imagine various varieties, which in part may overlap, as in table 12.2.

It is obvious that members of the Inca elite came to the country, supposedly speaking Cuzco varieties. In addition, there was an Inca army, recruited from zones with much population in Peru, possibly including southern sectors of the country such as Ayacucho. Once an area was conquered, the Incas brought in people from elsewhere

Table 12.2 Actors and Varieties Involved in the Spread of Quechua to Ecuador

Actors	*Varieties Involved*
Inca elite	Cuzco Quechua
Inca army	Lingua franca based on Quechua varieties especially from the south of Peru, such as the Ayacucho area
Mitimaes (forced resettlement from elsewhere in the empire)	Quechua and Aymara varieties spoken in different zones of Peru and even Bolivia
Mindalaes (local traders already predating the Inca period)	Varieties from the north of Peru, spoken by the trading partners of the *mindalaes*

to help colonize the area and assure the loyalty of the local populations, the *mitimaes*. Hartmann (1985) has underlined the potential importance of these groups of *mitimaes* in the process of quechuization, and they are documented to have come from all parts of the empire. Finally, Salomon (2007) shows that there were networks of merchants, the so-called *mindalaes*, which had a special status and may have contributed to the diffusion of Quechua slightly preceding and independently of the actual spread of Inca power. These *mindalaes* probably had connections mostly in northern Peru.

Thus, all kinds of Quechua may have been present in the country, and in effect they must have blended as part of a koiné. The conception of Ecuadorian Quechua as a koiné gains credibility in the light of this manifold importation of varieties and it is precisely in this historical context, a series of commercial settlements in the fourteenth and fifteenth centuries, followed by an invasion in the late fifteenth century, that the basis for the form of Quechua that we find today can have been formed. Native elites of these northern regions could have learned the language of the commercial minority for functionally restricted purposes and incompletely. The reductions encountered (analyzed in section 3) are explicable from the perspective of a theory of incomplete L2 learning.

As regards Cuzco influence, which is manifested, among other things, in the series of aspirated stops, I wish to argue that this is a case of superstrate influence. When the Incas conquered Ecuador in the fifteenth century, it is quite possible that varieties of Cuzco Quechua were mixed in an incomplete way with the local koiné, producing the described effects.

As regards the relation of Ecuadorian Quechua with northern Peruvian varieties such as the Quechua of Cajamarca, much remains to study both linguistically and historically. It is possible that the commercial ties between Cajamarca and Ecuador in the Inca Empire and in the Colonial period have led to the diffusion of regional areal features such as voicing in post-nasal contexts and the palatalization of the /s/. Nonetheless, this requires more comprehensive

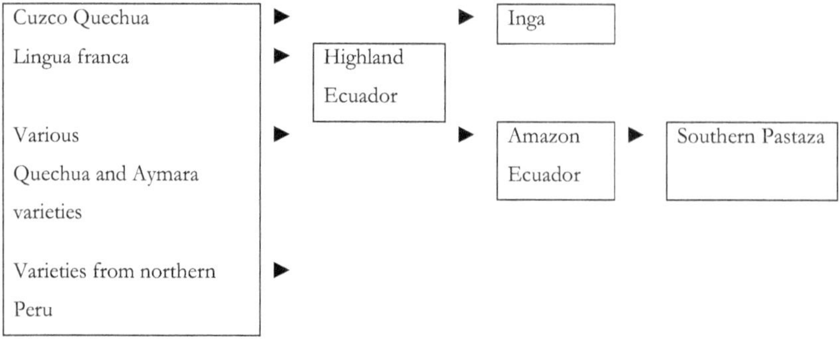

Figure 12.1 Relation between the Varieties Involved

comparative study of all the varieties of Amazon Quechua, including the Peruvian varieties such as Lamas and San Martin.

Once again, the historical relations between the varieties involved would be roughly as in figure 12.1.

2.3. The Consolidation of Kichwa in Ecuador

While the Inca expansion was responsible for the spread of Quechua to Ecuador, it is the Spanish colonization that led to its consolidation as the language of the *runa* caste. Several factors must have been involved in the process of consolidation, and were responsible for the emergence of Kichwa as the new language.

First of all, population decline weakened the existing ethnic communities and their languages, which led to ethnic restructuring. Consider table 12.3.

There was also considerable movement of workforce to serve the needs of the new colonial economy.

Kichwa provided a welcome channel of communication within this new economy, as is sketched in figure 12.2, which sketches the power relations in the early colony as well as giving an indication of speaker numbers.

The Spanish communication specialists were the clergy, primarily. They were educating the children of the local elite and started parishes with indigenous converts.

Table 12.3 The Population of Ecuador before the Spanish Invasion and at the End of the Sixteenth Century (from Newson 1995: 341, 350), in Thousands of People

	Pre-Conquest	*End of the Sixteenth Century*	*% of Loss*
Sierra	838.6	164.5	80.4
Costa	546–572	26.5	95.3
Amazonía Selva Alta	98	26.2	73.3
Amazonía Selva Baja	132–152	36.1–44.5*	71.7

*Data from the end of the seventeenth century

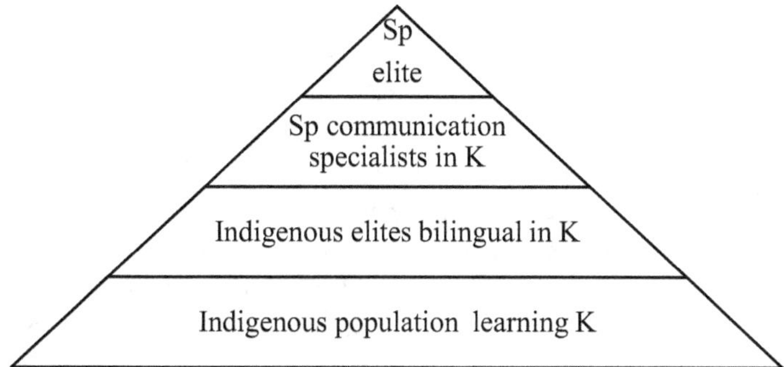

Figure 12.2 Kichwa as a Channel of Communication in the Early Colony (Sp = Spanish, K = Kichwa)

Cieza de León underlines the value of Kichwa as a communicative language for the Spanish, writing around 1550 (Cieza Señorío XXIV; 1553, no date):

Y con tanto, digo que fue mucho beneficio para los españoles haber esta lengua, pues podían andar por todas partes, en algunas de las cuales ya se va perdiendo. . . .	. . . and with this, I say there was much benefit for the Spanish having this language, because they could travel through all parts, and in some of them it is already getting lost.

Y entendido por ellos cuán gran trabajo sería caminar por tierra tan larga y a donde a cada legua y a cada paso había nueva lengua, y que sería gran dificultad el entender a todos por intérpretes, escogiendo lo más seguro ordenaron y mandaron, so graves penas que pusieron, que todos los naturales de su imperio entendiezen y supesen la lengua del Cuzco generalmente, así ellos como sus mujeres de tal manera que aún la criatura no hobiese dejado el pecho de su madre cuando lo comenzasen a mostrar la lengua que había de saber . . .	And it being understood by them how much work it would be to walk through such a large area and at every step there was a new language, and it would be a great difficulty to understand through all the interpreters, and choosing the most secure one they ordered and commanded, under serious punishments that they put out, that all the inhabitants of their empire understood and knew the language of Cuzco generally, thus they like their wives so that the child would not have left his mother's breast when they started showing them the language that they had to know ...
. . . y tan de veras se entendió en ello que en el tiempo de pocos años se sabía y se usaba una lengua en más de mil doscientas leguas; y aunque esta lengua se usaba todos hablaban las suyas, que eran tantas que aunque lo escribiese no lo creerían.	. . . and it stretched out over it so definitively that in the span of a few years a language was known and used in more than a twelve hundred leagues; and although this language was used also everyone spoke their own (languages), of which there were so many that even if one writes it down one would not be believed.

Cieza de León at the same time was well aware of the distinct ethnic groups, their languages, and their mutual relations, as is evident from various quotes (Cieza Crónica, p. 392).

Estos [los Panzaleos de Machachi] . . .. todos los deste reino en más de mil y doscientas leguas hablaban la lengua general de los ingas, que es la que se usaba en Cuzco. Y hablábase esta lengua generalmente	These [the Panzaleos of Machachi] ... all the people of this kingdom in more twelve hundred leagues spoke the general language of the Incas, which is the one used in Cuzco. And this language is spoken generally ...
Mas, no embargante que hablaban la lengua del Cuzco (como digo), todos se tenían sus lenguas, los que usaron sus antepasados	But even though they spoke this language of Cuzco (as I said), all has their languages, those that their ancestors used.

Y así, estos de Panzaleo tienen otra lengua que los de Carangue y Otabalo.	And thus, those of Panzaleo have another language than those of Caranqui and Otavalo.

The words from Kichwa cited by Cieza de León (Cieza 1553 Señ XXIV) suggest a close affinity with present-day Highland Kichwa; most of the terms used are the same or very similar. For the kinship terms probably the Spanish were not aware that the term for 'brother' and 'sister' depends on the gender of the speaker as well.

2.4. Colonial Society in the Eighteenth Century

If Cieza de Leon writing around 1550 described a situation with spots of Quechua being spoken in the cities as an elite language, the situation had changed dramatically two centuries later. The Spanish travelers Jorge Juan and Antonio de Ulloa (1826, II, p. 377) visited Ecuador in 1742 at the request of the Spanish king, to inform the Metropolis in Madrid about the state of the continent. They come with alarming news: everybody in the Ecuadorian highlands speaks Kichwa, in their experience. *Criollos* or Creoles are people of Spanish descent born in the colony.

Table 12.4 Kichwa Words in Cieza de León (Cieza 1553 Señ XXIV)

	Cieza	*current*		*Cieza*	*current*
man	*luna*	*runa*	night	*tota*	*tuta*
woman	*guarare*	*warmi*	head	*oma*	*uma*
father	*yaya*	*yaya/tayta*	ears	*lile*	*rinri*
brother	*guayqui*	*wawki* [m]/*turi* [f]	eyes	*naui*	*ñawi*
sister	*nana*	*ñaña* [f]/*pani* [m]	noses	*sunga*	*singa*
moon	*quilla*	*killa*	teeth	*queros*	*kiru*
year	*guata*	*wata*	arms	*maqui*	*maki*
day	*pinche*	*puncha*	feet	*chaqui*	*chaki*

. . . Inga: particularmente los Criollos hacen tanto uso de esta última, como de la primera; y por lo general en una, y otra hay reciprocamente mezcla de muchos términos.	. . . Inga [Kichwa, pm]: especially the Creoles make as much use of the latter as of the former [Spanish, pm]; and generally in one and the other there is a reciprocal mixing of many terms.
La primera que pronuncian las Criaturas pequeñas, es la del Inga; porque siendo las Amas de leche, que los crian, Indias, ademas de serles esta natural, por lo común ni hablan, ni entienden la Castellana: assi cuando empiezan a percebir las primeras sylabas de la pronunciación, siendo de este idioma, quedan tan impresionados en èl, que suelen algunos no hablar el Español, hasta tener cinco, ò seis años;	The first one that the little children utter is the Inga language; because the nurse maids, who raise them, Indians, and in addition to being indigenous generally they neither speak nor comprehend the Castilian language: so when they start perceiving the first syllables of the pronunciation, being in that language, they are so impressed by it that some do not speak Spanish until they are five or six years old.
. . . y siempre se mantienen viciados de modo, que en una misma conversación mezclan indiferentemente las oraciones de una, y otra.	... and they always remain contaminated so that in the same conversation they mix without distinction utterances of one and the other.

The Criollos speak a lot of Kichwa and engage in frequent code-switching. The indigenous population also speaks mostly Kichwa (Juan and Ulloa 1826, II, p. 551):

Por lo general los Indios fuera de los que se han criado en las Ciudades, ò Poblaciones grandes no hablan otra lengua, que la suya propia nombrada Quechua; la qual fue establecida, ò divulgada por los ingas en lo que estentendia su Imperio, para que assi todos se entendiessen y tratassen; de donde nació llamarla la Lengua del Inga.	Generally the Indians apart from those that have been raised in the cities or larger towns do not speak another one that their own called Kichwa; which was established or spread by the Incas as they spread their Empire, so that thus all could understand each other and interact; from which was born calling it the Language of the Inca.
Hay no obstante algunos, que entienden la Castellana, y la hablan; pero rara vez se reducen à responder en ella, aun quando conocen, que la persona con quien comunican, no les puede entender en la Quechua.	There are nonetheless some who understand Spanish, and speak it; but rarely do they lower themselves in responding in that language, even when they are aware that the person with whom they communicate cannot understand them in Kichwa.

Assi es en vano cansarse en persuadirles, que se expliquen en Castellano, porque no es facil con ellos el conseguirlo.	Thus one tires oneself in vain convincing them that they explain themselves in Spanish, because it is not easy with them to make this happen.
Los Indios criados en las Poblaciones grandes no incurren a esta tenaz idea; y antes bien quando se les habla en su lengua suelen respondre en la nuestra.	The Indians raised in the big towns do not have this tenacious idea; and rather when you address them in their language they are wont to answer in our language.

The rural indigenous population only responds in Spanish hesitatingly. This may be because of linguistic insecurity, a factor Juan and Ulloa did not consider. However, in the cities the bilingual indigenous population does answer in Spanish when addressed in that language.

2.5. Sources

Before going on, a brief note about the sources. In this paper both historical sources were used, published materials on different Northern Quechua varieties and my own fieldwork data.

Most historical sources are ecclesiastical in nature. This means they tend to represent a more formal register of the language. Also, the authors of the texts often based their work in part on earlier text. This makes the interpretation of the material difficult. Finally, sometimes they wrote a text that was meant to be used in quite large area (like the whole *Reino de Quito* 'Kingdom of Quito', much larger than the current Republic of Ecuador), an area which at the time covered several distinct Kichwa- or Quechua-speaking varieties. Nonetheless, comparing the data from the different regions and taking the concern for variation in language varieties of the audience they were addressing seriously makes it possible to interpret and evaluate the different sources. Muysken (2008) presents an overview of the different sources over time.

A decade ago the Italian linguist Luca Ciucci discovered what is probably the earliest manuscript grammar of Kichwa in the Vatican archives (Ciucci and Muysken 2011). It can be dated around 1680, perhaps. The author, the Jesuit Hernando de Alcocer became a priest in 1657 and died in 1688. He was from Riobamba in central Ecuador but spent his working life in Quito, as far as we know. There is much evidence for early Kichwa features in the manuscript, and in this paper I will limit myself primarily to the material presented by Alcocer. It is the earliest source, and Alcocer clearly presents Ecuadorian Kichwa, a language he probably learned early in life since he grew up far from the capital.

I will also refer to a document dating from around 1750 (Alexander-Bakkerus 2010), discovered in the British Library, with a grammar and dictionary for the Lengua de Maynas. This label is a broad term for the entire mission region administered from Quito, including parts of northern Peru where a different variety of Quechua was spoken. It mostly reflects Kichwa (and is partly based on and elaborated from Alcocer), but extends to the broader missionary area.

3. Changes

Kichwa in Ecuador differs from its Peruvian antecedent varieties in many ways. I will discuss a few of these here and in each case try to answer three questions.

- What are the changes found?
- What do the early offshoots from Ecuadorian Quechua in Colombia and Lowland Peru tell us?
- Is there information about the changes in the early sources?

These questions are interrelated. If we can show that a particular change has occurred in all Northern Quechua varieties, it must antedate the split off of Inca and SPastazaQ.

3.1. The Collapse of Genitive and Benefactive

A first example is the collapse of the genitive and benefactive cases in all Northern Quechua varieties, PeQ *-pa* [GEN] and *–paq* [BEN], merge into a single form *-pa(k)* [GEN, BEN] in Kichwa.

(1)	Inga	HiKi	AmKi	SPast	ProtoNQ	Ayacucho
GEN	*pa*	*pak*	*pa(k)*	*pa*	***pak***	*pa*
BEN	*pa*	*pak*	*(pa)k*	*pa*	***pak***	*paq*

I argue in Muysken (2017) that there have been many secondary developments in which individual varieties have tried to compensate for this initial loss through some secondary strategy, but the basic fact remains that all northern varieties have collapsed the two Peruvian suffixes. This must have been part of the original early Northern Quechua variety.

Alcocer sometimes distinguished between the genitive (*-pax*) and the benefactive (*-pac*) in the paradigms given (Ciucci and Muysken 2011: 377). This may mean that both suffixes ended in a velar consonant in early Northern Quechua but one is given as a stop [k] and the other one as a fricative [x]. However, in the examples given through the text Alcocer is far from consistent in making the distinction, and in current Kichwa word final /k/ is often pronounced [x]. It could be that the distinction suggested is simply an attempt to formally distinguish genitive from benefactive, which may still have variably been present at the time.

The Lengua de Maynas manuscript simply gives *–pac* for both cases.

3.2. The Suffixes *-ku* and *-ri*

In EcQ two highly frequent verbal particles productively have a different meanings than in PeQ. This is one of the important diagnostic features of Northern Quechua. PeQ *-ku* = 'reflexive' has become Kichw *-ku* 'progressive', while PeQ *-ri* 'inchoative' has become Kichwa *-ri* 'reflexive'.

PeQ *-sh(k)a* 'progressive' has been lost. Kichwa *-gri* 'inchoative' is an innovation, modeled on *V-k ri-* [V-AG GO-].

The following examples illustrate the changes involved:

(2)	PeQ			Ecuador	
a.	*riku-ku-ni* see-REF-1SG	Cusihuamán (1976: 212)	b.	*riku-ri-ni* see-REF-1SG	reflexive
		'I see myself.'			
c.	*puri-sha-ni* walk-PR-1SG	Cusihuamán (1976: 183)	d.	*puri-ku-ni* walk-PR-1SG	progressive
		'I am walking.'			
e.	*puri-ri-ni* walk-INC-1SG	Cusihuamán (1976: 210)		*puri-gri-ni* walk-INC-1SG	inchoative
		'I am about to walk.'			

However, in northern varieties there are lexical retentions of reflexive *–ku-* and diminutive / inchoative *–ri-* (Muysken 1977), often with specialized meanings. Thus, the change was by no means across the board and complete process.

The full array is as in (3):

(3)	**Inga**	**HiKi**	**AmKi**	**SPast**	**ProtoNQ**	**Ayacucho**
DIM		*ri*		*stu*	***?ri***	*ri*
INC	*ri*	*gri*	*gri*		***ri***	*ri*
REF	*ri*	*ri/(ku)*	*ri*	*ri/(ku)*	***ri***	*ku*
PR	*ku*	*ku/xu*	*u/xu*	*xu*	***ku***	*shka*

The suffix *–ri-* is sometimes diminutive in Northern Quechua. In SPast, we also find *–stu*:

(4) *aycha-ya-stu-hu-n*

meat-VRB-DIM-PR-3

'it is bit by bit gaining some meat' SPast (Tödter et al. 2002: 48)

The form *-stu* is used as a verbal suffix in (4), but it is based on the nominal diminutive *-itu/-ita*; however, the behavior of *-stu* is like *-lla* in other Northern Quechua varieties, which can be both nominal and verbal as well.

Alcocer has *-cu* 'progressive' (Ciucci and Muysken 2011: 385), while the suffix *-ri* is not mentioned, but the Lengua de Maynas dictionary has many examples of verbs to which *-cu* and *-ri* are attached with different resulting meaning changes.

Thus, this set of changes had an early productive dimension, particularly with respect to the reinterpretation of *-ku*, but for *-ri* the situation probably was more complex and the change gradual. Even with *-ku* we find lexicalized combinations where it has kept its meaning.

3.3. Verbal Person Marking

Parts of the person reference system have been affected by the transformations in Northern Quechua. In (5) and (6), the unmarked (present) and the future paradigm are presented. The forms marked with an asterisk are affected by changes.

(5)	**Inga**	**HiKi**	**AmKi**	**SPast**	**ProtoNQ**	**Ayacucho**
1SG	*ni*	*ni*	*ni*	*ni*	*ni*	*ni*
2SG	*ngi*	*ngi*	*ngi*	*ngi*	*ngi*	*nki*
3SG	*n*	*n*	*n*	*n*	*n*	*n*
*1PL.IN	*nchi*	*nchi(k)*	*nchi*	*nchi*	*nchik*	*nchis/*
*1PL.EX						*iku*
2PL	*ngichi*	*ngichi*	*ngichi*	*ngichi*	*ngichi*	*nkichis*
		N nakun		*nakun*		
*3PL	*nakun*	*S -nguna*	*nakun*	*nkuna*	*n*	*nku*
1.OB	*wa*	*(wa)*	*wa*	*wa*	*wa*	*wa*
*1>2	*iki* 1>2,3	*Ø*[3]	*Ø*	*iki*	*iki*	*iki*
*3>2	*Ø*	*Ø*	*Ø*	*Ø*	*Ø*	*-su-nki*
*3>4	*Ø*	*Ø*	*Ø*	*Ø*	*Ø*	*-wa-nchis*

An important change shared by all varieties is the loss of the clusivity distinction (Crevels and Muysken 2005), that is, the split between first-person plural inclusive and exclusive, characteristic of Peruvian varieties of Quechua.

For future marking, we find the following paradigms:

(6)	**Inga**	**HiKi**	**AmKi**	**SPast**	**ProtoNQ**	**Ayacucho**
1SG.FUT	*sa*	*sha*	*sha*	*sha*	*sa*	*saq*
*2SG.FUT	*nka*	*ngi*	*ngi*	*ngi*	*ngi*	*nki*
3SG.FUT	*nga*	*nga*	*nga*	*nga*	*nga*	*nqa*
1PL.FUT	*sunchi*	*shun/chi*	*nchi*	*shu/nchi*	*sun/chi*	*sun/chis*
2PL.FUT	*ngichi*	*ngichi*	*ngichi*	*ngichi*	*ngichi*	*nkichis*
3PL.FUT	*nkangichi*	*ngakuna*	*nakunga*	*ngakuna*	*nga*	*nqaku*
1>2.FUT	*sa-yki/chi*	Ø	Ø	*shka-yki/chi*	*sa-yki/chi*	*sqa-yki/chis*

The changes can be summarized as in (7) for subject marking, and in (8) for subject-object marking, where → means conservation of a category, ↕ a collapse of distinctions, and ↘ loss of a category.

(7)	**Transition to Highland Kichwa**			
→	*riku-ni*	see-1		'I see'
→	*riku-nki*	see-2		'you see'
→	*riku-n*	see-3		's/he sees'
↕	*riku-nchik*	see-4	'we IN see'	
↘	*riku-y-ku*	see-1-PL	'we EX see'	> 'we see'
→	*riku-ngi-chis*	see-2-PL	'you PL see'	
↘	*riku-n-ku*	see-3-PL	'they see'	

Altogether, the simpler forms have survived, the more complex forms have been affected.

(8)	Transition to Highland Kichwa			
→	*riku-wa-n*	see-1OB-3	's/he sees me'	
→	*riku-wa-ni*	see-1OB-2	'you see me'	
↘	*riku-wa-nchik*	see-4OB/3SU	's/he sees us'	early
....↘	*riku-yki*	see-1SU/2OB	'I see you'	later
↘	*riku-su-nki*	see-3SU/2OB	's/he sees you'	early

The resulting person marking forms correspond to the following template in (9), which may be interpreted as the matrix used in the learning strategy of Kichwa by speakers of other languages.

(9) V—([object])—([tense)—([subject])

All the forms that have survived conform to this template. One will also have to assume that it was used independently of the L1 of the learners. One of the major substrate language groups, the Barbacoan languages, do not have object markers, as far as I can establish.

3.4 The Loss of Nominal Person Marking

There was a decisive grammatical change in several of the Northern Quechua varieties involving the loss of nominal person marking. In its most radical form this loss was total, as in modern highland varieties, illustrated in (10):

(10)	Peru		Ecuador	
	mama-yki	[mother-2SG]	*kan-pak mama*	2SG.PRO-GEN mother
	'your mother'			
	riku-sqa-yki	[see-NMLZ-2sg]	*(kan) riku-shka*	(2SG.PRO) see-nmlz
	'that you have seen'			
	riku-pti-yki	[see-SUDI-2SG]	*(kan) riku-kpi*	(2SG.PRO) see-sudi
	'if you see'			

However, this nominal deflection was not categorical, nor was it a rapid process, as can be seen when we consider the second-person form with *-yki* in (11):

(11) Peru			Ecuador	
mama-yki	mother-2SG	'your mother'	*kan-bak mama*	2SG.PRO-GEN mother
Present in SPastaza (Peru)				
Variably present in religious texts from eighteenth century				
Variably present in HiKi texts of the late-nineteenth-century lay texts of Luis Cordero and Juan Leon Mera				
Absent in Inga, HiKi, and AmKi at present				

While Alcocer simply gives the full paradigm for nominal person marking, the Lengua de Maynas (ca. 1750) (Alexander-Bakkerius 2010: 56) shows that at least in the eighteenth century there was considerable variation. For the first-person possessive three forms are mentioned, including the contemporary form (12c):

(12)			
	a.	*yayai* *yaya-y* father-1SG	'my father'
	b.	*ñucapac yaya* *ñuka-pak yaya* 1SG.PRO-GEN father	Suelen tambien, y con mucha frecuencia, en lugar de estas partículas usar de los primitivos en genitivo . . . 'They are wont to use, and with great frequency, instead of the possessive particles the full pronouns in the genitive. ...'
	c.	*ñuca yaia* *ñuka yaya* 1SG.PRO father	Adviertase àcerca del primitivo ñuca, ue usan con mucha frecuencia los indios, poner en nominativo, asi singular como plural, en lugar de poner en genitivo, ... 'Notice that with respect to the pronoun ñuca, which the Indians use a lot, to put it in the nominative, both in the singular and in the plural, rather than in the genitive.'

3.5. Switch Reference

The Quechua languages show switch reference marking. In Cuzco and Ayacucho Quechua, the relevant distinction is as in (13):

(13) a. *mikhu-***spa** *hamu-saq* subject identical
eat-SUID come-1SG.FUT
'I will come when I have eaten.'

b. *mikhu-***qti** *-n hamu-saq* subject different
eat-SUDI-3 come-1SG.FUT
'I will come when s/he has eaten.'

In Kichwa, the form *–spa* has been maintained, but the form *–qti* has disappeared and has been replaced by *–kpi* (which probably results from the combination *–k-pi* 'agentive-locative'. This corresponds to the general pattern for subordination marking without person marking, as in [V—subordinator]. While in the different varieties identical subject marking *–spa* has been maintained, for different subject marking several options have emerged.

(14)	Inga	HiKi	AmKi	SPast	ProtoNQ	Ayacucho
Subject identical	*spa*	*shpa*	*sha*	*shpa*	***spa***	*spa*[(-ps)]
			-kpi			
Subject different	*k-pi*	*kpi*	*-shka-pi*	*shpa*[ps]	Ø	*pti*

Strikingly, in SPast, -*shpa* can be used with nominal person marking to indicate different subject, as in (15):

(15) a. *waka-shpa-yki-pas mana ku-yki-chu*
cry-SUB-2SG-IND not give-1>2-NEG
'Eventhough you cry, I won't give it.'

b. *maska-shpa-pas mana tari-shka-ni-chu*
look.for-SUB-IND not find-PST2-1SG-NEG
'Even though I was looking for it, I didn't find it.' SPast (Landerman 1973: 111)

In Alcocer, the form *–spa* is given (Ciucci and Muysken 2011: 390) but not *–pti*. The *sujuntivo propio* 'proper subjunctive' is reported (Alexander-Bakkerius 2010: 58) for the varieties in that grammar as in (16).

(16)	a.	*ñuca cacpi* *ñuka ka-kpi* 1SG.PRO COP-SUDI	*propio presente no se usa por estas partes* *'the present is not used in these parts'*
	b.	*captini* *ka-pti-ni* COP-SUDI-1SG	Adviertase lo segundo, que en Maynas en lugar de cacpi usan captini 'Notice that in Maynas they use captini in stead of cacpi'

3.6. The Suffixes *-pa* and *-pu*

In Ecuadorian Kichwa, *-pu* 'benefactive' has completely disappeared and *–pa* is used as a courtesy or endearment marker, as in (17c).

(17) a. *llank'a-pu-ni*
work-BEN-1SG
'I work for someone.' (Q)

b. *llank'a-pu-wa-n*
work-BEN-OB-3
's/he works for me' (Q)

c. *shamu-pa-y*
venir-AFF-IM
`just come please' (HiKi)

The origin of *-pa* as a contracted form from *-pu-wa* [ben-1ob] is confirmed by the data from Inga and SPast, where *–pu* occurs next to *–pu-wa/-pu-a*.

(18)	Inga	HiKi	AmKi	SPast	ProtoNQ	Ayacucho
benefactive	*-pu*	-	-	*-pu*	*-pu*	*-pu*
benefactive first person	*-pua*	*-pa*	*-pa*	*-pa*	*-pu-wa*	*-pu-wa*

The suffix *-pu* is not mentioned by Hernan de Alcocer, and neither is it found in *Lengua de Maynas*. It does occur in some of the religious texts included in the manuscript, the *Doctrina Cristiana* (Alexander-Bakkerus 2010: 155).

3.7. The Comparative

An interesting innovation in some Highland Kichwa varieties involved the serial verb *yalli* 'surpass' used in comparative constructions (Muysken 1977). The basic construction is as in (19):

(19) *Manil-da* **yalli** *puri-ni.*
Manuel-AC surpass walk-1SG
'I walk faster than Manuel.'

The verb *yalli* is the only verb that I know of in the Quechuan languages that can occur in bare form. The reason to call it a verb is that it assigns accusative case *-ta*. It may also occur by itself, I assume reanalyzed as an adverb. There is no clear substrate construction identified yet for this highly unusual change. It covers only part of the Highlands, from Imbabura in the north to Chimborazo in the center, and is not present in southern Ecuador, nor in the lowlands, Colombia, or Peru. Links to serial constructions in other languages in the area still need to be established.

Alternatives elsewhere in Northern Quechua involve the verb 'surpass' with an adverbial subordination marker, as in (20a), an ablative with the adverb *aswan* 'more' or *yalli* used adverbially, coupled with an ablative *-manta* 'from' (20b). Occasionally, we find *yalli-* used as a main verb with the quality compared in locative form (20c).

(20) a. *Manil Juan-da ati-sh(pa)/yalli-sh(pa)/pasa-sh(pa) puri-n*
Manuel Juan-AC succeed-SUID/surpass-SUID/pass-SUID walk-3
b. *Manil Juan-manda aswan/yalli puri-n.*
Manuel Juan-ABL more/exceed walk-3
c. *Manil Juan-da puri-y-pi yalli-n*
Manuel Juan-AC walk-INF-LOC exceed-3
'Manuel walks faster than Juan.'

The colonial document *Lengua de Maynas* (Alexander-Bakkerius 2010: 67) provides three options:

(21)	a.	*Pedro Juanmanta ashuan yachan* *Pedro Juan-<u>manta aswan</u> yacha-n* Pedro Juan-ABL more know-3	Pedro sabe más que Juan. 'Pedro knows more than Juan.'
	b.	*Pedro Juanta iachaipi yallin* *Pedro Juan-ta <u>yacha-y-pi yalli-n</u>* Pedro Juan-AC know-INF-LOC surpass-3	
	c.	*Pedro Juanta ialli iachan* *Pedro Juan-<u>ta</u> <u>yalli</u> yacha-n* Pedro Juan-AC surpass know-3	el verbo yallini convertido en partícula simple 'the verb *yallini* converted in a simple particle'

Alcocer presents variants of (21a) and (21b), while the bare form *yalli* is mentioned, but not in combination with an object of comparison marked accusative. I think we can conclude that the innovative accusative + *yalli* construction is an innovation from the late seventeenth century in central Ecuador, and not part of Northern Quechua as such.

4. Summary and Conclusions

This brief overview sketches and contextualizes some of the changes that have affected Northern Quechua varieties.

How gradual was the linguistic development of EcQ away from PeQ models in the colonial period? Did it involve many intermediate stages, and for which features? There is converging evidence from older sources and the current distribution for a differentiation in the speed with which the changes took place in early Northern Quechua.

With a few exceptions, the information gathered from the different sources points in the same direction. The morphological collapse of benefactive and genitive, the replacement of *-shka* by *-ku*, and the loss of the third-person plural *-nku*, the marking of third-person

Table 12.5 Summary of the Features Discussed in this Chapter

§	*Change*	*Present in All Varieties*	*Categorical in Early Sources*	*Northern Quechua*
3.1	Collapse *-pak* [BEN]/*-pa* [GEN]	+	+	+
3.2	*-shka* → *-ku* progressive	+	+	+
3.3	*-nku* [3PL] → Ø	+	+	+
3.3	3>2 → Ø	+	+	+
3.3	3>4 → Ø	+	+	+
3.5	*-pti* [SUDI] → Ø	+	+	+
3.3	Loss of clusivity distinction	+	Optional	+
3.2	*-ri* reflexive or lexicalized; *-ku* progressive or lexicalized	+	Variable in early sources	?
3.4	Nominal person marking → Ø	-	Optional	-
3.5	Emergence of *-kpi* [SUDI]	-	-	-
3.6	*-pu* benefactive → Ø	-	-	-
3.7	*-ta yalli* serial comparative	-	Optional	-

subject-second-person object, third-person subject-first-person inclusive object, and of the *-pti* switch reference marker were rapid and complete. The loss of the inclusive/exclusive distinction occurred in all varieties and some early sources mention the distinction. Probably the reanalysis of *-ku* and *-ri* was gradual and lexical, but occurred everywhere. Finally, the loss of nominal person marking was local and gradual, different subject *-kpi* did not emerge everywhere, *-pu-* was not lost categorically, and the serial comparative was local and gradual.

Combining a comparison of the four relevant modern varieties with the study of the early sources thus yields good insight into the history of this new form of Quechua that arose at the northern border of the Inca Empire and consolidated in the period of Spanish colonial occupation.

Abbreviations in Glosses

1>2	first-person subject, second-person object	LOC	locative
3>4	third-person subject, first-person inclusive object	M	masculine
ABL	ablative	NEG	negation
AC	accusative	NMLZ	nominalizer
AFF	affective	OB	object
AG	agentive	PL	plural
BEN	benefactive	PR	progressive
COP	copula	PRO	pronominal
DIM	diminutive	PS	person marking
F	feminine	REF	reflexive
FUT	future	SG	singular
GEN	genitive	SUB	subordinator
IM	imperative	SUDI	different subject
IND	indefinite	SUID	identical subject
INF	infinitive		

1. The paper is respectfully dedicated to Sarah Thomason. We first met in New Haven when I took my first linguistics course as an undergrad and she taught her first (I think) linguistics course as a graduate student around 1970 at Yale. The next time we met was at a large Pidgin and Creole conference in Hawai'i in 1975 where she presented a paper that became the foundation for her groundbreaking book on language contact with Terry Kaufman (1988). I presented my first conference paper there, on the history of Ecuadorian Quechua, to which the present paper is a sequel.

2. I will use 'Quechua' as a generic term here, otherwise giving it a regional label, such as 'Cuzco'. For Ecuadorian varieties I use the term 'Kichwa'.

3. Absent at present but it probably went extinct around 1900.

References

Adelaar, Willem F.H, in collaboration with Pieter Muysken. 2004. *The languages of the Andes*. Cambridge: Cambridge University Press.

Alexander-Bakkerus, Astrid. 2010. *Lengua de Maynas. Ms. Egerton 2881 de la British Library*. München: Lincom.

Cerrón Palomino, Rodolfo. 1987. *Lingüística Quechua*. Cuzco: Centro Bartolomé de las Casas.

Ciucci, Luca, and Pieter Muysken. 2011. Hernando de Alcocer y la Breve declaración del Arte y Bocabulario de la lengua del Ynga conforme al estilo y vso de la provincia de Quito. El más antiguo manuscrito de quichua del Ecuador. *Indiana*, 28: 359–94.

Cieza de León, Pedro. 1553 [1967]. *La Crónica del Perú. Primera Parte*. Lima: Instituto de Estudios Peruanos.

Cieza de León, Pedro. No date. [1880]. Segunda parte de la crónica del Perú, que trata del señorío de los incas yupanquis y de sus grandes hechos y gobernación. In M. Jiménez de la Espada (Ed.), *Biblioteca de Autores Españoles, Historiadores primitivos de Indias*, [1906] Vol. II. Madrid: Don Enrique de Vedia.

Crevels, Mily, and Pieter Muysken. 2005. Inclusive/exclusive distinctions in the languages of south-western South America. In E. Filomónova (Ed.), *Clusivity*, 311–38. Amsterdam: Benjamins.

Cusihuamán, Antonio G. 1976. *Gramática Quechua Cuzco-Collao*. Lima: Instituto de Estudios Peruanos.

Hartmann, Rosewith. 1979. "Quechuismo preincaico" en el Ecuador? *Ibero-Amerikanisches Archiv*, 5(3): 267–99.

Hartmann, Rosewith. 1985. El papel de los mitimaes en el proceso de quichuización: el caso del Ecuador y la problemática de las fuentes. *América Indígena*, 4: 61–98.

Juan, Jorge, and Antonio de Ulloa. 1826. [1747]. *Noticias secretas de América sobre el estado naval, militar, y político de los reinos de Perú y provincias de Quito, costas de Nueva Granada y Chile. Gobierno y régimen particular de los pueblos de indios. Cruel opresión y extorsión de sus corregidores y curas: abusos escandalosos introducidos entre estos habitantes por los misioneros. Causas de su origen y motivos de su continuación por espacio de tres siglos*. 2 volumes. London: R. Taylor.

Landerman, Peter. 1973. *Vocabulario Quechua del Pastaza*. Lima: Instituto Lingüístico de Verano.

Levinsohn, Stephen H., and Raúl Mongui. 1974. *Una gramática pedagógica del inga. Primera parte*. Bogotá: Instituto Lingüístico de Verano.

Levinsohn, Stephen H. 1974. Sufijos despectivos en inga. *Revista Colombiana de Antropología*, 16: 357–61.

Levinsohn, Stephen. H. 1976. *The Inga language*. The Hague: Mouton.

Muysken, Pieter .1977. *Syntactic developments in the verb phrase of Ecuadorian Quechua*. Lisse: Peter de Ridder Press/Dordrecht, Netherlands: Foris/Berlin: De Gruyter Mouton.

Muysken, Pieter. 2008. The gradual development of Ecuadorian Quechua. In Margot van den Berg, Hugo Cardoso, and Rachel Steinbach (Eds.), *Gradualism in creole studies: In honour of Jacques Arends*, 77–100. Amsterdam: Benjamins.

Muysken, Pieter. 2000. Semantic transparency in Lowland Ecuadorian Quechua morphosyntax. *Linguistics*, 38: 973–88.

Muysken, Pieter. 2017. Collapse of genitive and benefactive case in Ecuadorian Quechua? *Stellenbosch Papers in Linguistics*, 48: 255–60. doi:10.5774/48-0-295.

Muysken, Pieter. 2019. *El kichwa ecuatoriano: orígenes, riqueza, contactos*. Quito: Abya-Yala.

Newson, Linda A. 1995. *Life and death in early colonial Ecuador*. Norman: University of Oklahoma Press.

Salomon, Frank. 2007. *Native lords of Quito in the age of the Incas: The political economy of North-Andean chiefdoms*. Cambridge: Cambridge University Press.

Tödter, Christina, William Waters, and Charlotte Zahn (Eds.). 2002. *Shimikunata Asirtachik Killka. Inka-Kastellanu. Diccionario Inga-Castellano (Quechua del Pastaza)*. Lima: Instituto Lingüístico de Verano.

Torero, Alfredo. 1970. Lingüística e historia de la sociedad andina. Congreso Internacional de Americanistas. *Anales Científicos de la Universidad Nacional Agraria*, VIII: 3–4.

Van de Kerke, Simon, and Pieter Muysken. 2014. The Andean matrix. In Loretta O'Connor and Pieter Muysken (Eds.), *The native languages of South America: Origins, development, typology*, 126–51. Cambridge: Cambridge University Press.

www.ingramcontent.com/pod-product-compliance
Lightning Source LLC
Chambersburg PA
CBHW070306230426
43664CB00015B/2650

* 9 7 8 1 6 0 7 8 5 6 0 7 8 *